Mobile Mapping

# Mobile Mapping

*Space, Cartography and the Digital*

*Clancy Wilmott*

Routledge
Taylor & Francis Group
LONDON AND NEW YORK

The publication of this book is made possible by a grant from the European Research Council (ERC) under the European Community's 7th Framework program (FP7/2007-2013)/ ERC Grant Number: 283464

First published in 2020 by Amsterdam University Press Ltd.

Published 2025 by Routledge
4 Park Square, Milton Park, Abingdon, Oxon OX14 4RN
605 Third Avenue, New York, NY 10158

*Routledge is an imprint of the Taylor & Francis Group, an informa business*



ISBN: 9789462984530 (hbk)
ISBN: 9781041182955 (pbk)
ISBN: 9781003699880 (ebk)
NUR 670

Cover illustration: Clancy Wilmott

Cover design: Suzan Beijer

DOI: 10.5117/9789462984530

# Table of Contents

## Part 4 – Digital/Hong Kong



## Part 5 – Mobile Mapping

# Acknowledgements

This book is a collective effort.

I would like first and foremost to thank those who participated in this research: Marianna, Kyja, Tanija, Sarah, Nick, Shaun, Cliff, Ben, Cassie, Daren, Ellen, Ravi, Vicki, Taylor, Camille, Magdalena and Mohammed. This project grew out a desire to include a plurality of voices into ongoing debates about space, cartography and code – and your generosity, openness and willingness to let me walk with you for a while forms the foundations – heart and soul – of this book.

This research was supported by an ERC grant, *Charting the Digital* (grant agreement no. 283464), led by Sybille Lammes at the Centre for Interdisciplinary Methodologies at the University of Warwick. Special thanks go to Chris Perkins and Sybille Lammes, who read and commented on early draft versions of this book and were extremely supportive in the process of finding suitable publishers. More than this, my colleagues on that project, Sam Hind, Alex Gekker and Nanna Verhoeff, read, critiqued, commented and strengthened many of ideas in this project.

The field research was financially supported by the Department of Geography and the School of Environment, Education and Development at the University of Manchester through a series of travel grants, conference scholarships and awards. My specific thanks goes to Monique Brown for her diligence, patience and flexibility. As part of the research for this project, I held two visiting scholarships – one with the Transforming Cultures research centre at the University of Technology, Sydney, and another with the Department of Cultural Studies at Lingnan University. I would like to express my sincere thanks to Ilaria Vanni and Rolien Hyong for their support in setting these up. I would also like to thank the archivists at the Mitchell Library at the State Library of New South Wales, the curators of the *Mapping This World* exhibition at the National Library of Australia, the Hong Kong Maritime Museum, the map librarians at the Central Library in Hong Kong, and the archivists at the City of Sydney. I would also like to thank Donna Sherman, the map librarian at the University of Manchester, for her support in obtaining digital resources.

A number of colleagues and mentors have read and commented on ideas, writing or presentations of the topics of this book: Helen Wilson, Jeremy Crampton, Stephanie de Smale, Larissa Hjorth, Mike Duggan, Agnieszka Leszczynski, Jonathan Burrows, Shannon Mattern, Gillian Rose, James

Ash, Sarah Marie Hall, Pat Noxolo, Jim Thatcher, Craig Dalton, Franck Billé, Heather Zwicker, Heidi-Rae Cooley, Mo Engels, Kate McLean, Dan Evans, Amy Mulvenna, Samir Harb and Joe Blakey. The final stages of editing were undertaken at a writing retreat hosted by the Cities, Politics and Economies research group at the University of Manchester. Special thanks go to Jamie Doucette, who organised it, and Cristina Temenos, who gave excellent advice on Chapter 5. Finally, late stage conversations with researchers at the Digital Ethnography Research Centre at RMIT University helped hone the final ideas: Megan Kelleher, Rowan Wilken, Ellie Rennie, Yee Man Louie and Kelly Chan.

The Amsterdam University Press (AUP) has been extremely supportive and patient throughout this entire process. I'd like to express my gratitude to Maryse Eliot, Chantal Nicolaes, Jeroen Sondervan, the editors of the MediaMatters series and my reviewers for their incisive and extremely helpful comments on pulling this amorphous project together into a coherent book, and finding value in sections when I faltered.

And finally, my warmest and most personal thanks go to Lee, who ran around Sydney with a camera when I was not able to, and Luke, who was always willing to talk to me about maths, and helped my understanding of the quadrature of the circle. And of course, Emma, without whom there would not have been a book at all.

# Part 1

## Maps, Mappers, Mapping

# 1. Introduction: Mapping beyond the map

> We do not feel the disruptions of space, the coming upon difference. On the road map you won't drive off the edge of your known world. In space, as I want to imagine it, you just might.
>
> – Massey, *For Space* (2005: 111)

How can we understand mobile mapping in its amorphous liquidity? Boundless, mutable, personal, digital, what does mapping mean in an age of mobile digital media? Or, more precisely, who are the mappers and what is the map? What does it mean to see, read, capture, catalogue, comprehend, calculate and represent the vast networks of spatial relations that assemble on a day-to-day basis? 'Mapping' is a complex term – not least because of its ambiguity. It is based in action rather than in the distinction between subject (mapper) and object (map). It is a practice of drawing relations together in and through movement, of moderating our everyday lives between what Doreen Massey (2005) describes as the fixity of representation and the openness of space. Maps have historically and geographically borne this intermediary role: mappings may be carvings in rock walls, pliable sticks strung together, songs or stories describing a landscape, naval charts, urban plans, or digital applications on mobile phones. 'Mobile mapping' is specifically an embodied practice: it requires movement (Carter, 2009) (even though many maps only express stillness), the sensation of going through, around, along, above or under space and then the re-presentation of the information collected through lines, or contours or sounds. However, maps, we have learned since J.B. Harley's (1992) seminal text, *Deconstructing the Map,* are more than simple spatial representations – they are political *objets*, performative practices, always in becoming and always out of date. Maps are imbued with ideologies and discourses, filled with empty silences and vast absences, cultural remnants of the enunciators who shape the world (Black, 1997). Cartography is one such example, filled with desires to capture and preserve the world in image – cartographic images (Farinelli, 1992) and cartographical reason

Wilmott, C., *Mobile Mapping. Space, Cartography and the Digital.*
Taylor & Francis Group, 2020
DOI 10.5117/9789462984530_CH01

(Farinelli, 1998), cartographic impulses (Said, 1990), cartographic strategies (Mitchell, 2008), geographical imaginations (Gregory, 1994), resonant images (Cosgrove and Daniels, 1988), or fixed representations, an imposed stillness against the transformative potential of space, which is always open and filled with possibility (Massey, 2005).

Today, we barely recognise the maps that we use on our mobile devices (Chen, 2017). As digital media like smartphones and tablets usher in new forms of mobile mapping through geographic applications (digital maps) on mobile devices, we are once again left to stare in wonderment at the new complexity of old tools. Digital maps (geographic applications), as they appear on mobile phones, hide algorithmic workings and smooth scrolling surfaces that give the illusion of a representational flatness while hiding integral architectures of binary logic, digital codes and coordinates, and lines of commands (Thielmann, 2010). The digital map is a fluid map, a mutable map that updates into another as you read it, a Möbius strip without sides or edges that can be scrolled ad infinitum: a map that is not fixed but is always becoming. The digital map becomes as software interacts with device and screens bleed into code. However, these workings are not immune to the discourses in cartographic forms so critiqued by digital and cartographic theorists (Schuurman, 2009; Schuurman, 2000). Every day across the world millions of applications are opened on millions of phones, by millions of people located in millions of places. Where mappings were once precious informational resources they are now deployed throughout the world, in what Warf and Sui (2010) argue is an increasing democratisation of geographic data. Much of this data is gathered and aggregated in cartographic terms through coordinate locations embedded in geocode, a specific kind of code that deals with geographic information. The process of mapping and finding where you are is dissolved into sets of algorithms, built from lines of code drawn from servers all over the world. These data networks are combined to display a cumulative representation that constantly updates, using new information fed at a continuous rate as algorithms track the speed of hundreds of thousands of individuals to tell you if the traffic is heavy or light. Sometimes we appear on these maps – as blue dots or red markers – a unique relationship between our screens and global positioning systems (GPS), which accounts for how your mobile phone reads where you are. Much has been made of this digital transition from coordinates to code (cf. Pickles, 2004; Pickles, 2000), from cartography to geographic information systems (GIS), and now, from navigation to global positioning systems (GPS) or, location-based-services (LBS) (Spinney, 2003).

Whether digital maps manifest as check-in apps like Foursquare or Facebook, micro-chat services like Twitter or Weibo, or mapping applications like Open Street Map, Google Maps, Apple Maps or Baidu Maps, there seems to be a consensus that something new within cartography, technology and media is happening – that it is now performative, participatory and political (Crampton, 2009). Automation, algorithms, interfaces, code spaces, big data, computability are the buzzwords of the digital transition (Crampton, 2011a; Crampton, 2011b) – not least of all for the new age of digital cartography and geographic information systems. What is mapping is in the digital age? What does it mean when networks of geocoding and satellite transmissions, coordinate systems and binary languages are free from the representational fixities described by Massey (2005) and the cartographic impulses described by Said (1990)? How can such a map fix the world, when its design is to be situated and mutable, to be *un*fixed?

*Mobile Mapping* considers how the fixity of the digital map extends beyond the representational and the interfacial – beyond media and map; beyond digital map – into a vast field of discursive statements found embedded in landscapes and spaces, and are constantly encountered and brought forth by people in the course of their everyday lives. It tells the stories of how discourses, imaginations and impulses can bring together spaces, cartographies and codes to sit side by side in everyday life. Through seventeen walks with seventeen people in two cities – Sydney and Hong Kong – it points towards how people navigate between the discourses imposed upon them and the 'ghosts' (Gordon, 2008) of postcolonial landscapes. It discusses how cousins in cartographic order might have different representational appearances but similar rules, and how, against the powerful discourses that govern representations, space can still be open, heterogeneous and filled with possibilities (Massey, 2005) – especially in postcolonial contexts. Sydney and Hong Kong, two cities that are undergoing a transition from outposts on the edges of the British Empire that centred on Europe to global cities that are gateways to the vastly productive Asia-Pacific region, offered specific insight into the global impact of cartographic thinking, digital transitions and this archaeology of mobile mapping. At once centre and periphery, the mobile mapping practices engaged by each of the people in each of the stories in each city say something fundamental about the way in which the digital, the cartographic, and the otherwise and haunted come into contact. In an ongoing conversation about representation and space, this contact occurs – even at the most local, banal and every day of scales.

Historically, cartographic forms have a complex relationship with the notion of 'truth', representation and transcendence, born out of the scientific methods of the Enlightenment (Harley, 1988a; Harley, 1988b), what Farinelli (1992) calls the 'modern age' (*età moderna*),[1] and Foucault (2002b) the 'Age of Reason'. The maps that we find on our mobile phones in are the descendants of the hydrographs of the coast of the South China Sea by Alexander Dalrymple, and the charts that Lt James Cook made of the east coast of Australia.[2] Although the tools have changed from sextants to software, stars to satellites, and magnetism to media interfaces, the cartographic lines drawn on paper were made by early explorers and colonialists – who made these maps for the purpose of navigation and conquest and through the discursive power of the geographical imagination (cf. Gregory, 1994). In this imagination, space becomes a resource, which can be taxonomised categorically, parcelled up and distributed, exploited and capitalised. Thus, the digital transition from cartography as understood by the geographical imagination to the geocoded maps and applications that we find on mobile phones has been made possible by an ambient relationship between geometry, mathematics and cartography at the founding of systems of spatial rationalisation.

As new modes of surveillance and the anxieties they encourage are cautiously criticised (the Apollonian eye of government and capital staring down at its digital subjects), plaudits of increasing democratisation, grassroots knowledge generation and *sous*veillence also appear. The realm of digital mapping is pitched as a battlefield against opposing forces, and a key corner is reserved for mobile personal devices, the most intimate of digital technologies. Such devices are carried on your person, become symbiotic with touch and tactility: personal, portable intermediaries between bodies, memories, situations and locations – and their shadows in the world of networked representation. However, in amongst the complexity of representation and the zeitgeist of new methods and new technology (Marvin, 1990), it is important to ask: What exactly has changed? To what degree is 'the new' *actually* new and to what degree have we accepted the digital and the mobile as the axiomatic and unchallenged avant-garde of a total revolution in cartography, in representation and in space?

1 This is my translation of the term '*età moderna*' from Farinelli, *I segni del mondo. Immagine cartografica e discorso geografico in età moderna* (The signs of the world: The cartographic image and geographic discourse in the modern age, 1992).

2 See, for instance, Pickles, who argues that 'instead of focusing how we can map the subject. [we could] focus on the ways in which mapping and the cartographic gaze have coded subjects and produced identities' (2004: 12).

## Representations, discourses, hauntings

For geographers and those interested in space, it is as difficult to move away from the plan and the map, as it is for media theorists to move away from media. Instead, the world tends to turn *into* the plan and the map as opposed to an iterative coproduction. Pickles (2004) works hard to set up an early discussion of the performativity and fluidity of 'drawing lines' and 'geo-coding the world', yet still falls back on the imaginary analysed through the digital textuality of GIS maps. Massey (2005) cites maps as a key reason that she became a geographer, but chases her experiences of space and place against the lack of temporality in the map. Olsson (2007) teeters on the limits of representation and finds himself at the appearance of the grid in the stories of Marduk and Babylon in the Epic of Gilgamesh. In one sense we can also see how the forms of cartography may be considered mediums that construct their own spatial coordinates – for such coordinates, in the mind of Foucault, are always constructed. If we consider mobile mapping as a performative cartography, what might that mean here, in terms of spatiotemporal coordinates and a 'performative act' for space and memory?

Mobile mapping is an interpretative practice that makes and unmakes worlds in a continuous flow of reading and reproducing, yet in doing so pulls together semi-stable objects like communication infrastructure, policy and language systems that exist externally to the moment of mobile mapping, makes them integral to the process of mapping, and so stabilises them and their power. Mobile mapping defies dialectical rules of formation because it can contain inherent contradictions: it does not present a world view of all spaces at all times, but fragments and snippets of knowledge and experience, as and when it irrupts (Mitchell, 2008). Therefore, this analysis of mobile mapping engages with modes of thinking that are less interested in boundaries and limits between objects, or the ontological limit in its smallest capacity, and instead undertakes an open-ended discussion that points to suggestions rather than conclusions of how such practices unfold in the everyday and what the social, cultural and political consequences may be. Thus mobile mapping is, in Gunnar Olsson's (2007) words, a chiasm of thought-and-action, thinking, being and doing all at once.

This research was originally designed as a way to trace the tendrils of cartography as it wound itself into and around everyday life. I wanted to demarcate how, when and why cartographic discourses erupted into practices in the wake of mobile phones and digital maps. Further, I sought to situate this everyday cartography within a history of scientific and technological knowledges entangled with processes of colonialism and dispossession: not a digital without a past, but a digital made of the past. In much the same way that Shannon Mattern (2017) has recently traced the process of inscriptions in urban media from clay and dirt into code and clay, I wished to revisit the idea of a performative cartography with the simple acknowledgement that the maps that we use are not tabula rasa, but haunted by the past, and this folds into mapping practices. However, it shortly became apparent that the momentary encounter of mobile mapping in practice was supported (and even constituted) by a vast cartographic apparatus of institutions, built landscapes, tools of measurement and calculation, axioms, controls, systems, infrastructures and ideologies (Deleuze, 1992b). From scientific structures of knowledge to the engineering of stone and rock, the labelling of places and demarcation of spaces, the immensity of the ordering of things, people and spaces in these cities was overwhelming. Partly, this stemmed from my choice of a Foucauldian-inspired archaeological method (Foucault, 2002a; Foucault, 2001f) by way of dealing with the lack of representational fixity in maps, while accounting for common underpinning logic. Through archaeology, the fixity of ideas and epistemes could be traced equally across multiple presentations of the same digital map, digital map or data source, as new information appeared, formats changed, data was re-entered and re-aggregated, and localisations shifted between parts of Sydney and Hong Kong.

Despite this flexibility, things – people – kept cropping up and offering regularities to the anterior and exterior of cartographic discourses. These interruptions were unexpected, born of the open spatiality of mobile mapping practices. Each statement has its referent, each digital map has its mechanism in space and its system in time, every digital iteration has its enunciator, and every assemblage has its own unique set of complex components that gather and disperse according to different logics, different rules and different rhythms. Yet, as this research progressed out of interfaces and digital codes into ethnographies and archives, it became clear that the assemblages of maps and spaces and people in situated moments (what we can broadly call mobile mapping) is based not in objects, but in interrelations – both fixed and fluid – across space and time. In these interrelations, discourse and language, geography and history assemble from the far to the near, the distant to the present and into the future: conversations were brought forth which troubled the way in which we thought about the completeness of mediation (or even the way in which we imagine it being localised through networks) (i.e. Thielmann, 2010).

Two central ideas to Foucault's description of the discursive formation – transformation and dispersion (across time and space) – troubled the way in which I had conceived of the digital map as a collection of statements, separate (or at least untangled) from the discourses of cartography, geography and Western rationalism – as inseparably material and a textual processes. First, Foucault does not see the formation of discourse as a teleological process that happens through history: rather, discourses constitute history (2002a). Influenced by Nietzsche, Foucault maintains an antithetical stance against the imagined linearity of time in archaeology. In the context of the digital map and mobile mapping, this means that each appearance of the map is not an individual point on a timeline, and therefore 'the problem is not therefore to ask oneself how and why it was able to emerge and become embodied at this point in time' (Foucault, 2002a: 131). Each instance and each map could be conceived as a multitude of spatial and temporal connections: it was already being formed in discourse before it even came to be, the possibility of its appearance housed within the discourses that produced it. So, what we see in digital maps (and mobile mapping) is not a historical period distinct from others, a digital revolution, so to speak, but rather a phenomenon presaged – to some degree – in the networks of discursivities and positivities as they have stretched across the modern age/world and dispersed through colonial enterprise. Second, this means that when considering the discourses of the digital map, it is impossible to draw a line around the media interface of the phone, or the boundaries of the screen and say 'this here, is a discursive product of cartography', while all around us the shape of the city, the lines on the pavement, the telecommunications networks and the memories that linger and erupt in everyday mapping practices are considered something else, something other.

Digital maps, even in their absences, are revealed in this book to be haunted by the presence of cartographies and their roles in processes of cultural and spatial colonialism, creating uneven textures of experience, which sometimes float across the surface of encounters, and other times pierce into the wounded heart of 'the raw memory of fights' (Foucault, 2003: 8) and subjugated knowledges. This uneven texture can be seen across interactions with digital maps and cartographic discourses, in the strategic field of statements as they appear, and the uneven terrains, paths and traces found in the landscapes and spatialities of both Hong Kong and Sydney. As processes of colonialism, imperialism and capitalism reshape both cities, transformations appear all over the globe, each space producing its own genus and networks of power. This friction produced a mode of disjoint and disequilibrium as the temporally near and far were brought together to stand side by side – media, myth, maps, mayhem – somewhere between space and representation, in what Avery Gordon (2008) has come to call a haunting:

> Indeed, it seemed to me that haunting was precisely the domain of turmoil and trouble, that moment (of however long duration) when things are not in their assigned places, when the cracks and rigging are exposed, when the people who are meant to be invisible show up without any sign of leaving, when disturbed feelings cannot be put away, when something else, something different from before, seems like it must be done. (Gordon, 2008: xvi)

That troublesome presence for this research was a combination of people, and their modes of making-do (De Certeau, 1984) and what Massey (2005) calls the openness of space. What was more important (and somewhere outside that remit of archaeology) was that space, if it is not 'dead and fixed' as Foucault suggests, appeared to be something different again. Space was not a strategic field that faithfully followed the laws of discourse as Foucault set them out, and perhaps even beyond the grasp of the society of control (Deleuze, 1992b), or decentralised protocols (Galloway, 2004). There are many histories written of both Hong Kong and Sydney (Chu, 2013; Chu, 2012; Carroll, 2007; Ashton, 1995; Flannery, 2000; Hoskins, 2009; Patrikeeff, 1989), many of which consider the past in the present as a facet of deep time (cf. Karskens, 2009). This project does not seek to replicate such an endeavour – it is not a history, and it does not present an analysis of deep time, even as it is lived in the present. Rather, somewhere between Massey's quest for hope and Foucault's insistence on regularity, this ethnoarchaeology focuses on *deep space*, the accumulation of the past in space that bubbles up with disruptive force into the surfaces of encounter across which we live our lives: mapping beyond the map.

## Geometries of power

There is no clear consensus on what space is, or what purpose it serves – and there is even less consensus on its relationship with representation, especially in the mutable cartographies of digital mobile media. *Mapping occurs in space-times*, and these space-times are imbued with lingering discourses and, with them, systems of power. This book was somewhat of an experiment in archaeologically tracing the convergence of the digital and the cartographic in space through moments of ethnographic encounter. Yet, from the immediacy of phones tracking locations along streets to the earliest surveys of the urban landscapes of Sydney and Hong Kong, certain discursive regularities appear, folding in upon themselves, as power-geometries (Massey, 1993) that affect people in different ways. Cartography is a power-geometry embedded in geometric representation. Since the modern era, mapping has reasserted its roots in geometric measurement, coordinate geometry, and algebraic geometry through the technologies of surveying, charting, hydrography and navigation: practices central to the development of digital mapping technology, geographic information systems (GIS) and global positioning systems (GPS). Straight lines and curves, distances and depths: cartographies fix the stable image of the world, through the repetition of perspectives and viewpoints inherited from surveyors and the colonial gaze – or what Simon Ryan (1996) calls the 'cartographic eye'.

Geometry is crucial to understanding the regularities between cartographic power-geometries and how they order the world. Geometric thought obeys certain mathematical rules and adheres to strict logics that enable the production of *operations*, systems not just designed to describe *but also to reason and to build* (Farinelli, 2009; Farinelli, 1998; Serres, 2011). Where representations fix, geometries act; where representations are often static,[3] geometries are constructed to be deployed, to calculate, to scale ad infinitum. Triangles can be measured, resized, compared and turned into other shapes, curves have equations that determine their shape, yet the smallest algorithmic change to their function can result in a critical change in their appearance. Digital maps operate according to these logics – through the flat cartographical interface of the screen combined with the operational codes and commands that enable its mutability. When considering the disintegrating fixity of digital representation or text, we can see how cartography works not only by framing and completion of what we currently comprehend as representation but also prescribing how we look, fixing viewpoints through what Verhoeff (2012) has called 'a visual regime of navigation'. This haptic visuality combines embodiment with image, encouraging a navigational 'performative cartography' (Verhoeff, 2012) – a prescription of how and in which way bodies can move through spaces through seeing.

It is the scalability of geometry, its transformability and adaptability according to common rules, that makes it particularly peculiar to this situation. It is not just that the digital map, for instance, tells you how and which way to move through space in an embodiment of cartographic principles: it's that geometry provides the applicability and re-applicability of these principles to reduce all spaces into unified grids, plane figures, and calculations. In this way, cartography is both representational and

3 Even film is a series of static frames run after one another to give the impression of movement (much like GPS maps) (see Wilmott, 2016).

geometric. It represents space, while also ordering it under singular, modular knowledge systems. However, the axiomatic emphasis of Graeco-European mathematical traditions in geographical analysis of geometry, including the work of Farinelli and Olsson, conceals a broader problem. Geometry has never been a uniquely European pursuit. Joseph (2011) details rich geometric scholarship from the Mayans to Kerala and argues that for other mathematical traditions "[t]he aim was not to build an imposing edifice on a few self-evident axioms but to validate a result by any suitable method" (Joseph, 2011: xiii). He claims that this Eurocentric focus instead reifies two ideological positions, even in their invisibility: firstly, that mathematics should be ideal, rather than pragmatic; and secondly, that it should be scholarly rather than tacit, improvised or everyday. Finally, it also enforces an assumption of uni-directionality geographically – from Europe outwards – and temporally – from 'primitive' to 'developed' – in the transmission of geometric knowledges, rather than acknowledging the contrapuntuality of mathematical achievements as they emerged, and especially the influence of Islamic mathematical traditions on Christian scholarship.

What, therefore, is particular to the geometry discussed here is the way in which the European tradition embraced universalities (and infinities) within geometric thought, and used them as reasoning tools to both describe and inscribe space. It is this use of geometry which is the power of what Farinelli (1998) first described as 'cartographic reason', a discourse that is central to understanding how maps operate in digital media environments. Reason, geometry, cartography: bedfellows in the philosophical shaping of this world, and the desire to create interoperable systems (compatible symbols) and increasingly universal narratives in universal languages. 'Cartographic reason', explains Farinelli, arrived out of the advances in scientific rationalism, the cartographic imagination and geographic discourse of modern age from the Enlightenment onwards:

> [O]ur rationality is determined from a cartographic point of view. [...] [I]t is already contained and produced by the cartographical image. Western reason is nothing but cartographical reason, its relentless unwinding and development. In other words, the idea of language as a set of compatible symbols is directly derived from the map. (Farinelli, 1998: 135)

The modern era that developed this mode of cartographic rationality was the time in which René Descartes (1596-1650) developed an algebraic geometry, combining numbers with lines, and after which naval charts, surveys, urban plans played an increasing role in geographies across the globe (Cosgrove,

1999). It was also the age during which Leibniz developed a binary number system, transforming topological and mathematical systems (Serres, 2014) into multiplicities, schemas and fix-points and ultimately producing what we understand as modern computing. Through these epistemological transformations, the history of reason and cartography intertwine in geometry, loose threads melding into shared thoughts, shared points and shared lines that expressed space through geometric and mathematical means.

So, cartographic reason is a discursive path across which we can trace the regularities between old and new, near and far – a path that makes its way through each of the stories in the chapters of this book. It is also linked to other ideas through its participation in the Western geographic tradition or geographical imagination (Gregory, 1994), arriving in the Age of Exploration and repurposed as a colonial weapon crafted by the European academies. The early imperial maps of Hong Kong (from both a Chinese and a British perspective) carefully measured the harbour and cautiously surveyed the mountain peaks (Empson, 1992), while in Sydney, the early images of landscapes became taxonomies (Clancy, 2011; Thalis and Cantrill, 2013). In each city, through cartographic reason, the local populations of the Hakka and the Eora died, were killed, driven away or ignored, and their presence erased, while land allocations were drawn and distributed, roads were built, shorelines were circumnavigated, and the urban form began to emerge. In this mode of reasoning, cataloguing and categorising space was a way to develop more efficient modes of controlling and exploiting both the landscape and the people who live upon it to be more profitable and governable under colonial rule.

How this might be done is based in the way in which discourse operates – at least according to Foucault. Foucault argues that discourse is a practice (2002b). Thus, discourse is open to contestation as a transformative and fluid multiplicity, in constant formation rather than a static group of ideas and concepts. These discursive formations are comprised of 'statements', which are both material and, most importantly, have an 'enunciative function', in that they are *said*, that they are *state*ments, 'speech-*acts*' (italics added for emphasis). Just as Massey (2005) talks of *coformation* of spatial multiplicity, it is important to distinguish between discourse and a *discursive formation*, a far more active terminology that seeks to emphasise the transformational properties of discourse. This means that while, to borrow from Mattern (2017) for a minute, code and data might look and feel different to clay and dirt, they can be linked to a continuity of thought and action which has been dispersed and reassembled across space and time. Therefore, discursive statements do not appear in a predetermined form (for instance, as a map or a piece of code), but as a formation which shares a 'group of rules' (Foucault 2002a: 37), that have an interlocking, interdependent, systematic and transformational relationship. Geometry or mathematics are perhaps two examples of such rules, principles that determine how and where mobile mapping may occur (although, arguably not in totality). Cartography, too, uses sets of instruments and calculations, engages large-scale international institutional regulations[4] to produce such maps, and the many languages of algorithms and codes in software engineering, too, have these characteristics. Increasingly, we can see also how digitalities become collected under systems of binary numbers, algorithmic logics, machine learning and computer vision, and how material urban landscapes are once again reformed to become more hospitable to a digital, as well as cartographic, eye. Under this description, mobile mapping is more than a gathering of technologies, epistemologies and institutions: it is contradictory, situated and performed. Before a phone is picked up, before a digital map is opened, before a search query is entered, statements have already populated the world, articulating and structuring the discourses, which govern lives. Each iteration of the mobile map, each time a phone is touched, a pin placed or a geo-tagged uploaded constitutes one of a group of statements, in an increasingly complex coformation with material and lived worlds.

To understand how this may work in the context of mobile mapping, consider this: mobile mapping is a deeply complex enactment of multiple words and things (statements). You take out your phone and open an application, and before you have even entered in a search query you have already engaged these statements which occur through the code, the interface, the technology and the signal. The map says this is how the world is, the signal says here you are, the interface demands certain modes of engagement and the technology lies silently, yet heavily in your hand, carrying this all along. There have been a number of excellent pieces of research that have already discussed mobile maps on this particular level (cf. Verhoeff, 2012; Farman, 2012; Evans, 2015). But what we are investigating here is not the media of the map, nor its textuality, but the discursive conditions of possibility which have allowed certain constellations of mobile mapping activities to take place. The contemporary iteration of digital mapping is not without history. It was not found, nor did it arise in spaces where humans are not, or in the times before there were people. Thus, this project of uncovering

4 Even in participatory forms of cartography, such as Open Street Map, there is still a complex and highly regulated iconographic standardisation process that occurs (Glasze and Perkins, 2015).

the tender tendrils of material-discursive relations is perhaps more akin Mattern's (2017) work, in which she unfurls a long spatial history of the tools that have been used to mediate urban information.

What we see emerge in this book is that these practices are not so far from the order of things manufactured by new digital databased cartographies. Furthermore, mobile phones become intimate mediators between bodies, spaces and the systems of knowledge that determine the limits of our representations. After the Second World War, cartography expanded from the realm of geographers, explorers and navigators and, through geographic information systems (GIS), became embedded in computing, science and engineering (Rankin, 2016; Wilson, 2017). The shift from space to science meant that cartographic representations, data and calculations embraced notions of authority and truth-as-fact, even beyond the realms of earlier iterations of cartography (Pickles, 2004). The maps we see on mobile phones have inherited this relationship and expanded it into the quotidian, the mobile and the embodied, as digital maps and any number of other kinds of geographic information systems intersect with everyday navigations. The discourses in cartography (transferred to codes) suggest that the information displayed on digital maps *are a higher truth*, truth in scientific, and more recently big data, methods deployed towards the delimitation and calculation of spatiality and experience, and that such information can be trusted more than the perception of the user or the fallibility of the landscape (Wilmott, 2017). Such discourses lean on the authority of cartographic principles that Harley (1992) so criticised for their appearance as a 'seemingly neutral science': taxonomy, measurement, calculation. This authority is palpable when maps and navigational devices make absolute claims about distances between places or the journey time that will be taken through algorithmic practices, and when drivers follow their GPS devices into rivers or the wrong way down streets.

The reiterated relationship expressed through digital and mobile maps between cartography, geometry and rationality is a phenomenon keenly felt in the postcolonial spaces of the world: spaces that have become a tug-of-war between cultures, landscapes and people. As spaces and (power-)geometries collide, postcolonial cities become sites of contestation, where the urban infrastructure becomes a site of reification towards, and resistance to, the rationalisation of space and spatial experience. Sydney and Hong Kong are now complex multicultural[5] cities teeming with contradictory practices,

5 This is intended with the full weight of Povinelli's (2002) critique of multiculturalism – especially in Australia – as reifying liberal regimes at the expense of cultural democracy.

cultures and spatialities (Chu, 2012; Jakubowicz and Ho, 2012). These are spaces that are not at the heart of empires old and new (like Beijing, London or New York). Instead, these cities are fields of contention, constructed out of a sudden rupture at the moment of colonisation (which can be traced back to specific dates of incursion), in which the meaning of the landscape was swiftly reframed in terms of modernity and rationalisation through a clash of epistemes that continues today. Hong Kong and Sydney are cities where digital maps and mobile media are situated in political claims over spatial and cultural meaning that underscore positive absences and negative presences. While Abbas (1997), for instance, draws on the philosophies of Walter Benjamin when this is considered in the situation of Hong Kong, something slightly different appears: 'a culture of disappearance' in the face of global modernity – absences, erasures, forgetting, hauntings – which slips from film to media to literature, landscape and space. The disquiet and the cunning felt and expressed in the post-(and still)-colonial places and spaces of the world is defiant against overarching theories that fix what media and cartographies mean.

The particular kind of research in this book offers an experimental way of comprehending theory and theoretical output not as appearing upon high from an abstract position (much like that of the discourses erupting in cartographic forms) but as experientially grounded and generated in and through everyday encounters between space and representation. Olsson (1988) aimed to undo this fixing of representation, before the map, before the lines of power and the bounding of space, in the indexicality of the finger and the eye. The finger points to what the eye sees (because the eye cannot point and the finger cannot see), and so we have established a set of representational relations embedded in the distance between the body and the object. Furthermore, like Said's beginnings, the line does not begin with the contact between a pencil and paper (or in the case of the mobile map, the application of an algorithm into an equation) but rather begins in the outwards gaze of the eye, a cartographic gaze (Ryan, 1996) and a geographical imagination (Gregory, 1994). The limits of representation are peri-representational, relational and embodied, but become fixed at the index finger of representation. Thus the problem of representation and space comes from two sides, like Olsson's *Birds in Egg/Eggs in Bird* (1980): space enables representation through the fluid possibility of relations, heterogeneity and openness; yet representation expresses space through drawing those relations, its indexicality and the embodiment of an imagination. The ubiquity of the forces of cartographic reason means that such practices become deeply embedded in the subsumed and emerging contestations of everyday lived spaces, which then become represented through cartographic or other means. In situations where space has been a space of conflict and violence, the impact of representations, and the incursion of Western rationalities into the habitual, the embodied and the lived is bound up with historical and geographical struggles.

## The space of the book

How do we find space beyond representation but at the limits of representation itself? This is country in which Gunnar Olsson dwells, where representation dissolves into space, as he follows lines into dark politics (1991b), abseils into the abyss of rationalist philosophy (1980), and traces cartographic reason back to the emergence of the grid (2007). In *Birds in Egg/Eggs in Bird*, Olsson (1980) hopes first to undo language:

> The message is that the society's words are fixed and anchored in the strictures of law and order. But to bring them into full Bloom, the must be so screwed up that their inherent ambiguity is brought forth: the communicable of Leibniz's *salva veritatae* and Descartes' categories yields to the silence of Beckett's manifolds. (Olsson, 1980: 45e-46e)

But he goes on, then, towards a project of truth – towards writing in 'dream-like states [...] for truth emerges when identities are violated and opposites unified' (Olsson, 1980: 47e). Truth, here, we see again in its Hegelian optimism – for at this time Olsson humbly admits that he is 'a coherentist'. But as is the way with such things, the closer Olsson reaches to this asymptotic limit, the more elusive it becomes. By the time Olsson reaches *Abysmal: A Critique of Cartographic Reason* (2007), the imposed Foucauldian limit of discourse becomes tempting, but still, he remains (like Massey) dissatisfied. Pushing these limits towards an unattainable origin, he concludes that he does not know what exists beyond the limit of language, only that something must. Truth, space – what it is we cannot know. Such a journey follows a perilous path; each measure only illuminated as each step finds a foothold in the darkness, as we place faith in increasing abstraction towards an impossible reality. Despite this, he has done his best and that this will always be an unfinished project. Signing off, he says to himself: 'Go home, Professor. GO' (Olsson, 2007: 365)

However, I have often wondered if, by thinking about space from this perspective, we have already determined that heterotopias are not possible – that space is doomed to be structured only by whatever dominant discourses elbow their way to the front of history and geography? Like Massey, I dearly do not want this to be so, if not for the sake of this argument, then for the millions of voices who every day contribute to a multifaceted and heterogeneous exploration of the world and its multifarious meanings. As the map becomes *unfixed* in digital and mobile forms, we need to ask if drawing is an act of spatialisation or, instead, a spatial act that attempts to limit and define our spatial experiences? What Massey asks, and what I wish to question here, is whether space (and time) always an act of drawing and abstraction – or can something exist beyond the code and the coordinates, the lines and the angles of cartographic reason?

So, at Massey's trumpet, we tread cautiously after Olsson, into the abysm, as we stumble again and again through the intrusions, interruptions and messiness that Gordon describes. And we call again upon Foucault's description of subjugation and heterotopia to move forward into a space that is perhaps, prediscursive (in Foucault's terms) or previsible (in Serres's) – a space which is 'other space' (or more-than-space, or not-space).

The first section of this book, *Part 1: Maps, Mappers, Mapping*, deals with the nomadic journeys of theory and methodology. The next chapter, *Tools: Epistemologies, methodologies, anarchaeologies*, focuses on the triad of epistemology, archaeology and methodology to explain the theoretical and methodical underpinnings of this research. It describes how I came to follow seventeen people in two cities, as they chored and explored, with a small action camera, before entering the archive to trace the ghosts of their steps. It makes an argument for experimental or inventive methods, and for both courage and tenderness in pressing forward into the intersections of empiricism, politics and everyday life.

Then we turn to moments of mobile mapping – seventeen moments with seventeen people, to be precise – across Sydney and Hong Kong. These moments have something to say about the way in which we think about spaces, discourses, cartographies and technologies, as they draw together cartographic reason, landscapes, memories, practices, emotions and desires in ways far more varied and manifold than I could ever have expected. These walks are written in the 'dreamlike-state of Beckett's folds' that Olsson describes, through which the heterogeneity of space and the fixity of cartographic reason collide.

*Part 2: Space/Sydney* traces the emergence of heterogeneous and unpredictable spatialities across nine walking interviews in Sydney. It discusses how spaces which traditionally considered settled can be paradoxically unsettled, in tensions that erupt through the ordering of landscapes through urban landscapes, grids and infrastructures through moments with

Marianna, Kyja and Tanija. Then, we turn to affective geographies of this space, as these tensions make their way into the mappings of Sarah, Nick and Shaun – hauntings, intuitions and embodiments, which ripple and burst, linger and ghost through their everyday lives. Finally, we discuss how, between ideologies and affects, spaces might come to be imagined through stories, possibilities and daydreams with Cliff, Ben and Cassie.

Next, in *Part 3: Cartography/Cities*, we have a cartographic interlude in *Drawing the line*, and *Here there be digits*. Travelling across space and time, we chart the intertwining tendrils of cartographic reason as dispersed forms, philosophies and desires become discursive unities which are then dispatched across the globe in modes of new and old imperialism. We trace how binary systems travelled from China to Europe (and back again), algebraic geometry shifted mapping from description to order, as coordinates and code travel from the Age of Reason into our mobile phones, the markers on our screens and the digital maps we use on a daily basis.

Then we move on to *Part 4: Digital/Hong Kong* as we invert the equation, and instead see how digital mapping builds spaces imperfectly, haphazardly and asymmetrically through conflicts between cartographic reason and other forms of knowledge. As Cartesian and Leibnizian philosophies come into contact, the question of rationalist fixity might be rethought as topological as well as topographic. First, we consider how digital systems of representation across grids and numbers stabilise urban fluidities into channels in the stories with Daren, Ellen, Ravi, Taylor. Then, we follow how these discourse stretch, retract and break in political elasticities with Vicki, Camille, Magdalena and Mohammed.

Finally, we conclude in *Part 5: Mobile Mapping*, by way of discussing what it means when cartographic reason, discourse, research and mobile mapping is brought close. Away from the far abstractions of theory and theorists, the distant ivory towers and locked doors of the academy, the institution, the planning office and the corporation, the near presences of memory and embodiment, the wind on a face, the reflection on a screen and the intimate journeys of the everyday and the banal retelling of the story of spaces, cartographies and codes in a practice of making and dismantling relations.

This is a book about mapping and the mobile map, or what I term, mobile mapping, in the wake of a 'digital revolution' of the near and far, of simultaneity, of the side-by-side. The purpose of this term is to open up mapping to a practice that is more than the fixity of cartographic reason, but rather, to interpret the process of mapping as a form of encounter, negotiations between, through and despite spaces and representations. Mobile mapping is mapping with situation and the situated at the forefront of the mind. It is more than maps and mappers, but a heterogeneity of practices of interpreting the openness and possibilities of space through assemblages of memories, institutions, rationalities, spaces, bodies and technologies – which are in constant flux and transformation. Foucault repeated the sentiment throughout his work that '[r]ather than founding a theory [...] my present concern is to *establish* a possibility' (Foucault, 2002a: 128-129). At this point, and after everything we have already discussed, let us try to do the same here and see whether we can establish the possibility for a *spatio*temporal analysis of mobile mapping, which does not shut down possibility but rather rests on the determined (and perhaps irresponsible) desire for openness, for hope without absolutes, for understanding without subjugation. So, let us return to Olsson's work on representation and cartographic reason from the other side, from space, and to Foucault from the geographic and spatial knowledges subjugated in his own work. Let us not start with representation, but let us start with space and let us find a friend by way of Massey, who insists that it exists beyond representation because representation is fallible, fixated and impossible, and let us cautiously tread after Olsson who seeks to find the limits to this representation: Will lines ever conquer the world?

# 2. Tools: Epistemologies, methodologies, anarchaeologies

> I would like my books to be a kind of toolbox that others can rummage through to find a tool which they can use, however they wish, in their own area. [...] I don't write for an audience – I write for users, not readers.
>
> – Foucault, 'Prisons et asiles dans le mécanisme du pouvoir' (2001e: 1391-1392)

What tools can we use to understand mobile mapping? When concerns of privacy and surveillance, of data and algorithms in mobile technologies are at the forefront of the mind, how can we excavate the deeper implications of these practices, the clash of epistemes, people, spaces, materialities and ideologies as they emerge in their particular moments? Before we get into the thick (description) of this book's empirics, this chapter maps a series of epistemological, methodological and archaeological tools that we can use to try to move away from describing the manner and mode in which mobile mapping appears towards an analysis of *how* and *why* it has appeared in that way and the places and situations that it does. In two cities – Sydney and Hong Kong – carrying a small video camera, I walked with seventeen people as they carried out adventures, chores or explorations, and chasing threads of materiality, representation and practice between experiences, landscapes and archives. This strange method cast a warbled light, sometimes moving laterally (and sometimes literally), dancing between lines of inquiry, languages, gestures and geographies. It was this light that formed the shape of this book – an accidentally radical way of inquiring, teased onwards by those whose words fill these pages, and an intuitive reckoning of how it all fits together.

The ambition of this approach appeared, at least in part, because any attempt to map out both mapping and space exhaustively and to say anything concrete about their relationship in contemporary society is met with a pyrrhic victory. The rate of technological change bringing about new interrelations and apparatuses in society, the dissolution of representation

Wilmott, C., *Mobile Mapping. Space, Cartography and the Digital.*
Taylor & Francis Group, 2020
DOI 10.5117/9789462984530_CH02

into mutable, combinable and transformational interfaces and the complex network of relationships that bring forth situated, performative assemblages (especially in the case of geo-locative media) results in differential fixities that dissolve as soon as they catch hold. Therefore, there is a need for new ways to understand this phenomenon of mobile mapping that places the quixotic nature of transformation at the foreground of any analysis rather than simply accounting for it. Making tools is a difficult task and arguably one of the most significant challenges facing contemporary scholarship and made harder by the contrary, ambivalent and asymptotic appearance of everyday *objects*. Digital technologies still place the subject at the centre of a post-human world, fetishise the text in a post-representational age and valorise the consumption of an imagined present, always tumbling on as it formulates the future and disappears into the past before it even comes into being. In the context of Hong Kong and Sydney, even the dialectical oppositions that we traditionally understand between representation/non-representation crumble into a more complex foray between incongruous ways of thinking and being. And so, traditional narratives of now and post-now, mappings of there and not-there, and designations of this and not-this do not reflect the appearance of mobile mapping, or arguably, even contemporary cartographies more generally.

Furthermore, people – as I found throughout – are contradictory and mercurial. No sooner was a meaning interpreted than it was reneged and reinterpreted. This capriciousness comes through constant engagement with material-discursive landscapes (Barad, 2007) as well as pasts and futures. There is no consistent separation between the objects in the world – be they bodies, philosophies, ecologies or ghosts – and so, this became a project of suggesting *relations* rather than defining *things*. In a world where billions of people engage in mobile mapping practices every day, archaeology offers one way to navigate through the contradiction of mobile mapping. An archaeology of mobile mapping is not to analyse texts, per se, but to find statements where they appear, to map the surfaces of their emergence, to trace power as it appears and to find the rules which allow certain things to be said at certain times. In moving away from abstract descriptions of mobile mapping towards investigating how and why it appears, the conditions of specificity in which mobile mapping arises are crucial: it is not just *any* space, or place, or time in which mobile mapping occurs. It is in specific situations, where specific technologies, objects, rules, conditions and infrastructures exist to facilitate that moment. Significantly, it is equally important to consider the moments in which digital technologies aren't used – moments of failure or nonchalance, moments that challenge a media-centred approach. How do we understand how and why mobile mapping occurs, if we do not also investigate it in its full beyond-technology complexity?

As such, methodologically speaking, what I propose to do is to move beyond these debates. Rather than critiquing mobile mapping for not chasing its tail, so to speak, in search of a lost form or origin, or becoming absorbed in a labyrinth of connections and relations, this book aims to gather objects as they fall before us and to trace the patterns and themes that emerge. Mobile mapping, as a chiasm-of-thought-and-action, is enunciative: it speaks as it acts. But in speaking, it is not just what it says, but also what it does not say, the way in which it says it, and the vast array of values and objects from which it gathers its authority. Here, mobile mapping is more than just a map, or a technological device (or lack thereof), or a mapper or a landscape. It embodies more than a history or geography, more than spatial tension or historical conflict, more than its ideologies and its values. Rather, it is a sum greater than its constituent parts, party to an ongoing discursive conversation about spatial meaning, practices and being.

## Epistemologies

Cartography, like geometry and mathematics, has a complex relationship with the notion of 'truth' and transcendence, born out of the Enlightenment through the scientific methods that produced it (Harley, 1988b). This relationship was further complicated in the second half of the twentieth century wherein geographic information systems (GIS) became increasingly widespread and solidified as a practice of science and engineering (Rankin, 2016), and thus embraced notions of authority and truth-as-fact even beyond the realms of earlier iterations of cartography (Pickles, 2000). Mobile mapping has inherited this relationship and expanded it into the quotidian, the mobile and the embodied, as mobile applications, GPS capabilities and any number of other kinds of geographic information systems intersect with everyday navigations. The discourses in mobile mapping, like cartographic reason, suggest that the information displayed on mobile maps *are a higher truth:* truth in scientific methods deployed towards the delimitation and calculation of spatiality and experience – and that such information can be trusted more than the perception of the user or the fallibility of the landscape. This is evident when maps and navigational devices make absolute claims about distances between places or the journey time that will be taken through algorithmic practices, or when drivers follow their GPS devices into rivers or the wrong way down one-way streets. It is also evident in its use of cartographic principles that Harley (1992) so criticised:

taxonomy, measurement, calculation. In addition to occupying the position of a higher transcendental truth achieved through scientific data-based inquiry, cartographic reason also suggests that it can lead you to some other higher truth through the description of the world in image and text. Together, these dual truths claim to be able to transform mobile mapping practices and lead to an externalised cathartic understanding of the space-times and subjects which mobile mapping represents, the metaphysical level of *res mentalis* which Leibniz described, or the dualism between Descartes' mind and body. You are the blue dot, even though in the vein of Magritte's *Ceci n'est pas une pipe*, you are not the blue dot (but yet you are, etc.) (cf. Gamson, 1991).[1] Thus mobile mapping is, in Olsson's (1993) words, a chiasm of thought-and-action: thinking, being and doing all at once. The claims of authority that mobile mapping makes on the world are simultaneously representational, post-representational and non-representational, material and immaterial, and phenomenological and post-phenomenological. This makes its appearance near-impossible to disentangle through mapping either its materialism or the breadth of its objects, or by trying to trace its foundational structure.

The variety of methodologies that surround the current analysis of media have, like mobile mapping, a distributed and discursive relationship to certain epistemic traditions surrounding space and representation. What we see here is a contemporary constellation of philosophies, technologies, representations and practices that are firmly rooted in Western philosophical discourses, as they have transformed and dispersed throughout history and geography. I propose, here, that principles from Foucault's archaeological method offer a productive way forward in bridging the contradictory, heterogeneous and fluid practice of mobile mapping, to look beyond the map, or the phone, or the subject. Foucault had similar questions to Olsson about the way in which discourse operates between bodies, institutions and knowledge. Deeply influenced by his mentor Jean Hyppolite's ongoing engagement with Hegel, he sought to uncover the positivities that structure the world, grand systems of knowledge that seemed beyond question and reproach. In his own words:

> At the moment when the broad system of scientific and philosophical rationality produced the general vocabulary with which people have

1 Leighton Evans discusses this phenomenon of the blue dot and its phenomenological consequences in his ethnography of Foursquare users in *Locative Social Media: Place in the Digital Age* (2015).

> communicated since the 17th century, what happens to those whose behaviours excludes them from this language? This is what intrigues me. (Foucault, 1985: 3)

This is a point of intrigue for me, too, albeit in a digital age. Here, Foucault points to a line of questioning that asks what happens to things, people and events that fall outside of the vocabulary, concepts and systems of knowledge that we use to understand, research and think about the world. What is particular is the way in which he suggests going about exploring these absences. Citing misgivings about the way in which contemporaneous zeitgeists (such as phenomenology) dealt with the perceptual position of the subject while, at the same time, reasserting a fundamental and transcendental search for purity in being, Foucault aimed to try to free history from the grasp of experience, while at the same time, undertaking a 'history of the present' (Foucault, 2002a).

To find these answers, Foucault looks to the archaeologists, who in digging into the ground, encounter remnants and objects scattered about the earth – a clay pot here, a copper coin there, at varying depths and locations. From this collection of objects, the archaeologist must interpret and piece together an ancient history. This means not considering the object alone but as a series of other objects, which have symbolic, linguistic and material similarities (regularities, in Foucault's terms). While cautioning against a linear geological interpretation, Foucault still suggests that this method can be applied not just to a history of objects, but to a history of ideas. Arguing that the etymological fraternity of the term 'archaeology' bears relation to '*arche*' (as in Grand Arche), he puts forward that such a method should focus on monumentality rather documentation, that discourses irrupt as events, words and things. Just as the archaeologists encounter fragments of the past through ad hoc collections of artefacts and relics, we, too, encounter discourses in similar disarray, an archive of similar statements scattered throughout all the things that have and have not been said, and have erected monuments to the shifts in thinking and understanding. This corpus of statements constitutes a discursive formation, that is a continuity of thought and action which has been dispersed and reassembled across space and time, scattered throughout the archive of all the things that are 'already-said' (Foucault, 2002a: 160). As Foucault writes, 'archaeology tries to define not the thoughts, representations, images, themes, preoccupations that are concealed or revealed in discourses' (Foucault, 2002a: 155), but rather attempts to define the discourses themselves, as practices. We find these statements in the formation of the cartographic – the naming of roads, and

GPS tracks – and also in absences, the ghostly spatialities that do not appear but haunt the surface of practice, memory and movement.

Furthermore, the pursuit of discourse allows opposing thinkers to be placed side by side and their systems of thought to be dissected from a lens of contemporaneity: Nietzsche, Freud and Marx, for instance, despite incompatible rifts in their philosophical work,[2] epitomise in the nineteenth century shift towards interpretation as a mode of analytical reasoning: they deploy the same tools, but produce vastly different sculptures. In this, archaeology provides space to look beyond the textual questions surrounding mobile mapping, and to instead deal with it as both historical and material and yet also contemporary phenomenon: to place a seventeenth-century map next to a mobile digital map and ask what here are the similarities in thought and wherein can we find discord. At the same time, mobile mapping practices are lived, they also bear continuity with other parallel systems of thoughts, and even at certain points, intertwine.

The discursive statement has an inherent relation to other statements. It is easy to see how this may be understood in mobile mapping practices, for they are admittedly pastiches of discourses, languages and spatiotemporal performances that draw from many different space-times: coordinate systems are not always expressed by computers, but may be drawn by pen and paper, for instance; a phone has more uses than telephony; swiping and clicking is used for multiple kinds of navigation. Statements also have an *associated field*, which Foucault describes as a 'domain of coexistence for other statements'. In essence, an associated field means that a statement enters into dialogue with other statements in that domain, as they shape and reshape each other. A mobile map on a phone, for instance, does not exist in isolation, but engages cartographic reason and *transforms* it, by providing models of reasoning in new and different ways, through different tools like computation, automation and sensing. A map on a mobile phone is part of a collection of other objects and processes that produces and is produced by it. This might include the form, content, meaning and structure of a map, as it makes reference to, borrows from and contributes to other mappings. Therefore, this field is always in flux. Here, we might find a reduction in the philosophical distance between epistemology and ontology in critical studies of mapping and GIS (Leszczynski, 2009a; Pinder, 2007), a lack of separation characterised by mobile mapping, but has proved difficult to overcome in theoretical work. So, when approaching the limits

2 Even Foucault, at one time describing his position and dalliances with Marxism, said that to be a Nietzschean communist would be laughable (Foucault, 2001a).

of the epistemological in this research, there are also slips into questions of being and experience. As Olsson explicitly states while exploring the concept of representation in geography (of which cartography is a crucial member): 'The braiding of epistemology and ontology is inevitable, even though the former activity tends to dominate during some periods, the latter during some others' (Olsson, 1991b: 205). He argues that by rejecting the power of this dichotomy, as well as its links to both the phenomenon and the subject, the ideas of Lacan, Barthes and Foucault (who we are dealing with here) reject the Cartesian faith of certainty in representation (that cornerstone of cartographic reason). Understanding – or knowing – does not always have to be linguistic, even though its communication must be. And so, the epistemological stance of this research instead embraces the question of representation/reality as a space where we might excavate, critique and rework what Olsson has called 'the revolting ambiguity of the taken-for-granted' (Olsson, 1991b: 121).

## Methodologies: Walking through the archive

This research was gathered from seventeen video-recorded walking interviews (nine in Sydney and eight in Hong Kong), where those-who-walked went wherever they wished and I followed along: chatting, asking, listening. These interviews were followed by a period of archival research, where I traced the patterns and ruptures of these walks in the formalisation of cartographic reason and the materiality of the landscape. As I wandered through space and time with each of these navigators – people who were kind enough to let me tag along, as they went about their everyday lives – mobile mapping proved to be an amorphous and powerful practice. Because of the disintegrating fixity of the mobile mapping, and the increasing rigidity and expansion of cartographic logics, these walks became a series of fuzzy but still political statements – not in dusty documents or books – but in the archives of memories, spaces and landscapes where cartographic reason has succeeded and failed. Furthermore, unspoken unities began to appear, collections that were not necessarily representational, but were embedded in gesture, in practice, in a lack-of-words, or an intuitive feeling, hauntings, ghosts: things that keep messing everything up. As I understand it, these frictions form the membrane between space and the fixity of representation, and by inching towards it through the discourses that irrupt and the wounds that they open we may perhaps be able to get a better sense of what mobile mapping is.

This project is implicitly critical of the restrictive nature of unified theories regarding knowledge and the tendency towards cohesive, univocal epistemologies that act as colonising forces (Foucault, 2003; Massey, 2005). Through searching for ways out of the fixity of representation, this research sought to trace the momentary, multi-pronged assemblage of heterogeneous spaces, cartographies and digitalities. This was the focus of the methodological design – to see if it was possible to trace a path into a mode of research that was one of valuation, not evaluation (Manning, 2015). This process was at once focused on the embedded and porous, sibylline and delicate. Clifford (1997) argues that sociological 'street-corners', or 'sub-cultures', and anthropological 'villages' are no longer isolated, no longer distant enough from the transnational forces of globalisation where the local and global collide in immersive ethnographic work. Humans may be, as Olsson (1991a) suggests, still bound to thrash within the epistemological limits of representation as we struggle to imperfectly conceive and communicate our bodily lives in a world shaped by cartographic reason. Such limitations are also housed in within the paradigms of methods. In a digital age, two lines – 0 and 1 – have come to increasingly define the scope of research and representation, from the archive to the village to the street, in a symbolic exchange that Baudrillard (1993) argues is entirely self-referential. But not all lines are the same; even vectors can be transformed and systems warped. As Haraway (1991) suggests, we still maintain the possibility of shaping our research and our concepts into regenerative politics, journeys towards elsewhere, and relentless artifactualism. Against the fetishisation of modern, rational, scientific methods, and their manifestation in cartographic desires for calculation, categorisation and homogenous systems of order, we can instead focus our methods on *movement* rather than fixity (Sheller and Urry, 2006), *possibility* rather than validity (Denzin, 1989), *knowledges* rather than facts (Saukko, 2003), as they emerge in the course of heterogeneous experiences.

In *Eye of Power*, Foucault writes:

> A whole history remains to be written of spaces – which would at the same time be the history of powers (both these terms in the plural) – from the great strategies of geo-politics to the little tactics of the habitat, institutional architecture from the classroom to the design of hospitals, passing via economic and political installations. It is surprising how long the problem of space took to emerge as a historico-political problem. (Foucault, 1980: 149)

There are two forces at work here. One represents the 'great strategies of geo-politics' as the dispersion of statements across time and space, through processes like rationality and colonialism. The other, the 'little tactics', are the banalities through which the discursive formation becomes spatiotemporal, and which create spaces of surveillance and control, both explicitly and implicitly. For Foucault, space is that which allows discourse to scale between the grand narratives and histories of the Western world and the habits and practices of everyday life. Between open-ended walks and archival research, we can see how, with colonialism, imperialism and globalisation, discourses have travelled across the globe to be situated in landscapes and geographies far removed from those in which they were dreamt: Why have some discourses travelled, while others have not? Why did the flat survey prevail when other forms did not?

Discourse, for Foucault, is a 'series of events'. However, thinking of discourse as 'series of events' is less helpful in its linearity. Foucault attributes this linear framework to his study of history, a discipline that is chronological and deeply teleological (in Wade, 1978), yet it still foregrounds the expansion of Foucault's thinking from the temporal into the spatial (Foucault, 1984; Crampton and Elden, 2007). The complexity of the digital map as interfacial, interactive, graphic and coded means that even within its own systems of representation it may embody multiple discursive statements at once: coordinates, codes, colours, computation. Furthermore, because the map is drawn from a server to be instantaneously reproducible and personalisable on multiple devices – a system of thinking, rather than a fixed representation – when this system flows down onto multiple phones, the same map makes multiple statements *at the same time* yet in different spaces. Finally, each of these statements appears at different points and modulations along a trajectory of transformation: a map on a phone, like those of Lt Cook, for instance, may embody the semiology and hermeneutics of the Age of Reason but may also be coded and recoded, adhering to epistemological logics old and new *at the same time*. Thus, a 'series' is inadequate if it is the only axis along which statements are understood to disperse: this series must have a spatial axis, as well as a temporal one. Instead, I suggest emphasising the spatiality of discourse through Foucault's descriptions of statements as 'archives', 'fields' or 'domains'. The spatial dispersion of cartographic reason – from its first encounters with landscapes to its unyielding tracking of bodies – lies within the residues of space, as well as time, and so for this reason, this method focuses less on the event, but on the moment. Thus, drawing on McFarlane's (2010) writing on comparative urbanism, the question is less about 'when' the moment is buried and exhumed, but 'where'.

This is where we turn to the stories laid out in the coming chapters of this book: these stories are filled with moments and statements that brush the edges of the membranes of our knowledges. Foucault's event is focused on the enunciation of a statement (why here, why now, why not something else) and the conditions that made it possible for it to be said, buried or unspoken. Here, Foucault (2001f) identifies a 'moment of discourse':

> Each moment of discourse must be welcomed in its irruption as an event; in the punctuation where it appears; and in the temporal dispersion that allows it to be repeated, known, forgotten, transformed, wiped out down to its slightest traces, and buried far from every eye in the dust of books. Here is no need to retrace the discourse to the remote presence of its origin; it must be treated in the play of its immediacy. (Foucault, 1998: 306)

The moment at which discourse appears is the 'play of its immediacy', the moment when it is spoken above all other discourses. Immediacy is not interested in the origin, the alluring promise of comprehension that was so tantalising to the thinkers of the seventeenth century. It is interested in the coming together, the conditions of possibility and the surfaces of emergence, the platforms that are built through discourse so that it can be spoken. The play of immediacy is where the dispersion of statements across space and time (geography and history) becomes localised into the personal, the habitual, the encountered and the experience.

Central to mapping 'moments' is an appreciation of shifts in the way in which statements themselves are dispersed: mobile mapping, as a discursive practice, is not characterised by a discursive singularity. In the final chapter of *Rethinking Maps*, Dodge, Perkins and Kitchin (2009b) put forth a manifesto for rethinking the way in which mapping has been studied. This manifesto explores three themes for consideration: modes, or the way in which mapping emerges through interface, algorithms or visual cultures; methods, undertaking approaches that focus beyond the map-text – economies, affect, or visual cultures; and moments, or performative situations of mapping which serve a heuristic purpose. They offer what they term a 'tentative list' (ibid.: 243) of potential kinds of moments: moments of failure, points of change, rhythms of mapping, memories, research processes and moments of creativity. Moments such as these accommodate the processual nature of mapping, and in doing so, they argue, are more likely to allow for critical modes of inquiry. What I want to argue here is that the conceptualisation of mapping 'moments' can be understood as more than a simple tool for uncovering political structures but rather as discursive and imbued within political structures that are thoroughly spatial.

These moments are not evenly distributed terrain. Since the moment is both spatial and temporal, the politics of scaling is apparent in everyday moments of mapping traced through this research. Povinelli describes in a conversation with Berlant that the nature of a quasi-event in a state of late liberalism: 'quasi-events have a different kind of force depending on where they occur in the socially distributed world' (Berlant and Povinelli, 2014). Two events, equally minor in detached comparison may be immensely different in the space of their occurrence, even in the monotone spaces produced by cartographic reason. Where settler-colonialism and global forces construct monuments, a quasi-event which shows little by little how the same trickle of water can create rivulets and canyons, each speech-*act* collecting together. In the quasi-event, the moment becomes more quotidian, more political and fluid. Playing with the idea of the quasi-event, Povinelli explains how she prefers, instead, the term 'becoming-event': 'the moment when peopled places gather whatever creative energies they have left to derange and arrange these kinds of flattening nothings into charging somethings' (Berlant and Povinelli, 2014).

Again, like Massey, Povinelli finds in potential a gathering to 'derange and arrange' openness and positive heterogeneity: Why artificially flatten the world when its uneven textures speak for such possibility? As moments, mobile mapping practices encompass a multitude of scales. However, rather than space stretching between two points – one near and one far, all discursive scales appear at the same time. From feelings to buildings to digital maps to grand visions of universality – all of these elements emerge and speak at once – a conversation in which individual voices are barely perceptible. And so, they must be amplified. Thus, there is also a possibility in space for the moment to be a point at which other knowledges begin to have valence in silent presence and absence. Moments of mobile mapping are filled with friction, multi-temporality and coevalness while being beset by technological failure and communication breakdowns. Each moment is a glimpse of simultaneous and dispersed encounters between the near and the far. Again, this is a particular project to reopen space to possibility and draw it away from being a flat surface of inscription but something that is generative and productive.

What Foucault (2002a) wished to emphasise in talking about enunciation is that speaking is closer to utterance than to creation. This makes subject/author (say, the mapper) and object/creation (say, the map) more ambiguous. We could think, here, about a piece of code that does not have a single author who remains in charge of that creation but its constant emergence as it acts. Similarly, passages from a book may be cited or reinterpreted by another author (as in here), a map may be copied, transported, used in different situations for different purposes, code may be amended, engaged, copied and pasted into different software and transformed by plug-ins, new data or other iterative practices. What we can learn from the moment is a way in which we can imagine an archaeology that reaches beyond the flat statement of a text or a body. Instead, we can begin to define and collect moments together, moments where maps fail, people get lost or remember or discover, moments where space and representation constellate, and consider this in light of discursive formations.

Understanding the impact of the dispersion of cartographic reason, encountering its appearance into mobile mapping practices, and sensing the silent presences and notable absences created in its shadows is central to how we can conceive of an archaeology as it is encountered or as it is dispersed through space and time. At the same time, the ambiguity of ownership of stories, histories, pasts, memories and experiences does not excuse the uncritical capturing of other people's knowledge under the guise of what Gordon (2008) calls 'empirical safety nets'. The question of 'whose voice, whose words, whose image?' is at the forefront of this book. Given the open nature of the interviews, the majority of the stories, experiences, vernacular epistemologies, philosophies and mapping practices are not mine to claim. With their permission, I have used the first names of each of the people who appear in this book or used a pseudonym of their choosing. Names, we will learn, are important, as are words, experiences and memories. This methodology avoided the axiom of anonymisation that comes with institutional research where, in specific situations, vernacular knowledges are set against academic and scientific authority, without recourse for talking-back or claiming knowledge by participants (cf. Nespor, 2000).

I was unprepared for the full force that the stories and moments of other people would wreak upon this research. Gladly, I gave up the roles that I would normally take on, and each person – Marianna, Kyja, Tanija, Sarah, Nick, Shaun, Cliff, Benjamin, Cassie, Daren, Ellen, Ravi, Vicki, Taylor, Camille, Magdalena and Mohammed – were pilots and navigators in their own journeys, and I, a curious co-pilot, being shown the ropes of their lived spatial practices. This inversion was disruptive in more ways than one. I did not steer or guide their journeys, even though I knew both cities quite well. The process of sitting on a bus as we moved past the stop, took a wrong turn or a different street, walked a different way, climbed steep hills, read the map for five minutes when the building was right in front of us (I could go on) created levels of discomfort and disconcertment (Law and Yin, 2009) that were challenging. This discomfort was productive and critical. It sat as a constant reminder of both the politics of research and that subjugation and resistance occur in heterogeneous ways.

Literature in both anthropology (Coleman and Collins, 2011) and the social sciences (Williams and May, 1996) underscores the problems of positionality, gaze and authenticity within interview techniques, especially in light of the ethnographic criticisms of traditional pseudo-objective anthropological research methods (Clifford and Marcus, 1986). The theoretical lens of this research was implicitly critical of how cartographic reason overemphasises calculation and classification in understanding spatial experiences. This concern bled into the empirical design, too. It was difficult to find modes of recording that do not bear the hallmarks of calculation – especially in a digital age. Still, there was potential for reflexivity in this process, too. To 'cut' (Manning, 2015: 58) is to append a kind of fixity in research, either towards organisation or openness, in the hope of generating immanent critique. The decision to use an 'action-camera' (a small digital video camera designed for recording extreme sports) was quite pragmatic, but not perfect. Action cameras are small, lightweight and weather-resistant devices that addressed some of these issues. They can be worn attached to the head leaving the hands free to use mobile phones, to press buttons, to drink water or whatever else was required during the interview. Action cameras[3] have also already been used in field research where researchers and participants were required to undertake active or laborious activities (Brown et al., 2008). The camera required a constant embodied attention, holding the weight in one or both hands and mediating the subject of the film and my movement through space.

However, even in digital video, there is a 'seductive veracity' (Banks, 1990: 16) to the use of audio-visual or photographic recording methods: an illusion of verisimilitude interpreted as 'the pure voice of the "other"' (Banks, 1990: 16). Yet, even at the level of the digital visual rendering this seductive veracity was challenged. The lower resolution of the standard definition

3 I chose to use a Sony® Action Camera because of the 'Steadyshot' shake-reduction technology. The 'Steadyshot' set the field angle to 120 degrees rather than 170 degrees, and artificially smoothed the jarring. Video was shot as MP4 at a mid-range resolution (or standard definition) of 1280x70 with a frame and playback rate of 30 frames per second – any higher in definition and the file size was too large, any less and it was unwatchable and inaudible. A higher aspect ratio allowed more spatial data to be included and reduced the risk of the participant disappearing from the frame. I habitually carried spare batteries and, on rare occasions, had to interrupt the interview in order to change batteries. This led to multiple video files for single continuous interviews that I grouped together and moved to a secure drive after each interview.

recording produced a dream-like quality, blurring lines and undefining visual geometries. The lines of the bitmap appear skirting the edges of clarity. Strangely on the hotter days, the image warbles, steam forms in the inside of the waterproof plastic case and when it is windy, sand, dust and pollution obscure, blur and warp the picture. Imperfect pictures led to disconcertment – the stills you see throughout this book are not pristine, absolute evidence. Instead, I present partial moments, fuzzy and suggestive to give impressions of how space, cartography and the digital might emerge together and apart – even in discomfort.

By way of writing, this discomfort continued. I have chosen not to smooth over any of the disconcertments and tensions. These are productive, for they disrupt both my gaze and yours, reminding us that our knowledge is modest, our practices hegemonic, and our research, always colonial. For the same reason, in the translation of words into writing, the language used in the conversation has not been corrected – people speak how they do, and so I use the words that they speak, in the way that they speak them. Short of letting you hear their voices and see their faces as they were recorded, the best I could do is be reminded of Stewart's use of Bakhtin's translinguistics: 'It is an effort to evoke some of the intensity and texture of expressive forms that voice a cultural poetic embedded in a way of life and the politics of constant subversion and reproduction' (Stewart, 1996: 10).

For perhaps the same reason, some people agreed to have their faces shown – even though I checked twice, and once more again as this book moved into publication. Most were keen to have images shot with the action camera that now accompany their words on these pages. Those who wanted their anonymity preserved chose their own names, and let their hands, their words, and the spaces where we walked might speak for them. Finally, on questions of race, ethnicity, class, gender and sexuality – these were not an explicit part of this project. That is not to say that these social, cultural and economic inequalities are unimportant. Rather, I wanted to give each participant room to shape their own narratives, to let these kinds of macro issues which have been profusely written about in academic literature on cartography emerge in the everyday, under the terms, categories and classifications that each person wished. This wound back into the implicit distrust of the uncritical acceptance of categories and classifications – especially of bodies, pasts and spaces. These emergences have appeared at the behest of spaces, memories and bodies – rather than that of the map, the academe or the desire for clarity. Thus, they, too, are muddy, winding with other experiences, labelled otherwise or not at all, and inchoate in their textures into the world.

In the coming chapters, the writing of these stories is presented as a series of moments, falsified, in a way, into text. But what made these particular emergences important is that they appeared in the stead of something else. Sometimes this was the full force of discourse, shaping the world, and sometimes it was a moment in which the unspeakable made itself known in different ways, casting the powerful to the side. This is a less-traditional reading of Foucault, for whom knowledge and language are intertwined. The discursive practice of mobile mapping, most especially here-now of the statement or speech-act, is at the 'limit of language (*langage*)' (Foucault, 2002a: 126). The limit of language, a precipice upon which Gunnar Olsson made his home, is, in his own words, abysmal (Olsson, 2007). Discourse is always linguistic, language always discursive, locked in a battle that is fixed on the mode of representation that Massey so laments. Unlike Olsson, Foucault suggests that there is no precipice, no chasm and no abyss: even the smallest instances of language remains on this side of that edge: 'the sudden appearance of a sentence, the flash of meaning, the brusque gesture of the index finger of designation, always emerge in the operational domain of the enunciative function [...] the conditions according to which the enunciative function operates' (Foucault, 2002a: 126). For Foucault, there is nothing but language, nothing exists beyond it and so the excavation of something otherwise – space, and perhaps haunting – which enunciates in ways that we do not always comprehend seems perilous. When we consider these limitations of language, perhaps here we are better visiting the teetering house of Olsson and Massey, rather than the more secure one of Foucault. There are always words that are untranslatable from one language to the next, founded on inherently contradictory principles of imagination, discourse and belief. This trouble is seen time and time again in postcolonial contexts – the inability to accurately translate street names between Cantonese and English in Hong Kong, for instance, the mistranslation of the meaning of songlines in Australia, another; and the uncomfortable hybridisations between Indigenous[4] and Western mapping practices that followed colonisation.

4 I use the term 'Indigenous' here following Hostetler (2001) as a way of avoiding prevalent Western narratives of progress in describing mapping practices: the terms 'traditional', 'primitive', or 'early' imply that there is a natural course of cartographic development, and that non-Western societies were slow to develop along this axiom. This is not an accurate depiction. Mappings across the world occupied many traditions and forms, and were replete with diverse values and functionalities that worked in the specific context of those cultures. A cartographic paper map of the terraforma of the Sahara dunes would not have been useful – the dunes shift and change with time: navigation by stars was more practical. In mapping, pragmatism is embedded in

For every word spoken, there is a host of other words which were not. So, the descriptions in this book are about *moments of knowing* rather than a pure archaeology of knowledge: Why and how did they come to be in this space and time? This is where discourse is also material, or 'material-discursive', according to Barad's (2007) reading of Foucault. Foucault specifies that every statement must have *a materiality.* For a statement to be enunciated it needs to enter the world in some material form. The first kind of materiality that Foucault describes is a *substance*, like an image or a piece of film. But, in the complexity of mobile mapping, we might also find materialities in bytes on a memory chip, sound waves, vibrations, the touch between a body and a screen, an element on a landscape like a building or graffiti or a mark, silence, fumbling, a trip or fall, a facial expression. The second kind of materiality is a *status*, a type of longevity with rules for transcription, or re-transcription: use and re-use to become part of a field of statements. It is here that I argue the openness of space and the fixity of cartographic reason come into most contact. Status relies on the potential for dissemination – for a map to hold authority through its form as an (im)mutable mobile against the silence of the raw memories and ghostly matters. Yet, haunted spaces and subjugated knowledges have also have different modes of translation (if not tran*script*ion) through invisibility and hypervisibility. This is a key interest here: matter *matters* (Barad, 2007), for the same reason that the ghostly matters (Gordon, 2008). Cultures have ways of handing down their stories and their fleeting impressions of the world one way or another, in secret or otherwise. Sometimes these are left behind to be rediscovered (sites of trauma, for instance), others are ceremoniously given over to a new era, stories that may be told, or written or drawn or etched over millions of years into the landscapes. So while it may not be very appropriate to call this form of materiality a transcription or inscription when we are not specifically talking about scripts – matter retains information in ways that are deeply cultural. Whether these are landscapes which hold the past and determine, the waves made by voice boxes, instruments, animals or atmospheres or glitches that arrive when circuits malconnect, signals trip and lights stutter and die, discourse *always* has a material form. At the same time, while the discursive must be material, the material does not always need to be discursive: storms rage without human eyes, and stones stand without human words.

discourse: the European need for precision and mathematics came from the measurement models used to navigate ships, and the perils of the triangulation being off. Different practicalities were needed Asian and the Australian continents.

## Anarchaeology

What Foucault's explanation of discourse offers is a stabilisation of sorts between representation and performativity, somewhere between Descartes and Leibniz (while being nowhere near them at all), and, like Massey (2005) between representational fixity and topological fluidity. Archaeology suggests that statements in and of themselves are less important than the rules of formation which they contain – a dissolving map interface, a transforming landscape, even a wandering user, are not superficial texts, but rather profoundly intertwined with other things that have been said and done in other places and times. Thus, in investigating discourses, in trying to identify the politics and grand structures of knowledge and language which appear in mobile mapping, the text and iconography of maps that critical cartographers such as Harley (1988a), Wood and Fels (1992), and Cosgrove and Daniels (1988) once analysed, are not as important as the regularity between ways of thinking. In short, what we see here less a deconstruction of a text (pace Derrida) than the uncovering, mapping and analysis of *ideas*. These ideas are at their root dispersed across space and time, they are processual, building from 'previously formulated statements' – they link between the minute and the massive, between memories and institutions.

But this is not a complete solution: Foucault makes much of words and things as enunciated factors of discourse. Yet, the digital elements of mobile mapping are characterised by the increased velocity of the world, where both words and things are rapidly approaching the asymptote of immediate obsolescence. What I suggest here is to reconsider words and things: to find the rules of discourse that is characterised in mobile mapping *in that moment*. As knowledges and experiences collapse, can we mark out the moment of discursive appearance as both an epistemic and practised at once? Mobile mapping constitutes a performed knowledge, as well as a knowledgeable performance. Can we conceive of mobile mapping as an archaeology of experience, of the moments in which a statement is enunciated, an archaeology of the act of knowledge? De Certeau (1984) certainly thought so, marrying Foucault's work on mechanisms of power with a Bourdieusian analysis of practices. However, much of De Certeau's analysis of the relationship between Foucault and Bourdieu's conceptualisation of 'strategies' rests upon control and the bio-political disciplining of bodies and spaces. This, too, is important in considering mobile mapping. But this particular relationship has already received attention from various researchers interested in the way in which certain mobile geo-technologies produce certain practices (Galloway and Ward, 2006), hybridities (De Souza e Silva, 2006), experiences (Richardson, 2005), patterns of consumption (Hjorth et al., 2012) and social norms (Hjorth and Khoo, 2015). What we need to consider is that the disciplining of mobile mapping is already built into practices, through the discourses like cartographic reason which received and conceived particular forms of language, terms of engagements, technological desires and spatial reasoning. Before mobile phones and digital maps, the disciplining of the body had already begun in equations that fixed the centre point of the world, modes of reasoning and rationalisation and defined the relationality of the subject to it (Olsson, 1991a; Serres, 2011).

Here, the practice of mobile mapping becomes linked again to the textual and the material. These walks were starting points for research, but not its entirety. This was a geographical archaeology in the moment, digital speech-acts *in situ*, a moving archive (Anderson, 2004), where, during the interviews, the cartographic apparatus branched out into time and appeared altogether at once in space and spatial encounters (Dittmer, 2014). The statements of the apparatus formed fragments of a living archive in mobile mapping assemblages. These fragments – cartographic imaginations petrified in landscape, images and architectures, and embodied in contemporary practices – then directed me back towards the archive itself. I drew upon Foucault's writings on Deleuze where he cites difference and repetition, recurrence and phantasm, becoming and return – 'the materiality of incorporeal things' (Foucault, 2001g: 947) – as key modes of considering representation.

The dispersion of statements, across history and geography, across time and space, is a central preoccupation of Foucault, and one of the factors which distinguishes his 'history of the present' from the teleological concerns of traditional historians. This, to a degree, reflects the way in which mobile mapping has integrated multiple trajectories of recurrence into the here-now, in both Sydney and Hong Kong, cities that were the products of a global imaginary from their beginning (Jacobs, 1996; Abbas, 1997). Both cities contain complex discursive interactions as a result of their colonial pasts and presents, germinated across multiple spatiotemporal scales: the immediate, experienced and situated intertwines with the historical, the geographical and the global. Foucault's archaeology specifically highlights this kind of dispersion, providing coherence to the scattered archive of documents, names, places and experiences, moments, memories and landscapes. Significant theorists like Said have extricated a spatiotemporal emphasis from his notion of dispersion. In a time of colonialism, the geographical travels of European epistemes created a new geographical imagination

(Gregory, 1994) which gazed upon alien landscapes with the eyes of colonial rationalities, or to borrow Ryan's (1996) phrase the 'cartographic gaze', via the transportability of 'immutable mobiles' (Latour, 1986) such as Cook's maps of the east coast of Australia used by La Pérouse. This notion of dispersion is important in understanding how Leibniz's calculus or Descartes's grid system comes into being in spaces thousands of kilometres away, several hundred years later, while the delight of the Kerala mathematicians in solving calculations for no practicable purpose (Joseph, 2011) occupies a different realm. It is also important in discovering in the unities of statements made through mobile mapping with maps, images, or stories or writings made in other spaces and times.

As such, the interviews described above were accompanied by a period of archival research in both Hong Kong and Sydney (Lorimer, 2009). Foucault (2002a: 145) writes that an archive is a 'density' of discursive practices made up of statements – that is, a collection of things that have been said. The role of the scholar is to do what Nitecki calls 'making connections' (2008: 37). Through archives, the process of the cartographic inscription into space could also be traced: what kinds of discourses appeared in the archive at the point of 'conceiving' space and how they were then inscribed into the landscape. This focused on the role of the 'representational' in the 'more-than-representational', or 'putting maps back into ethnographic mapping' (Brennan-Horley et al., 2010: 92). Dodge et al. (2009b) emphasise the processual aspects of mapping – or how maps and plans (and in turn, landscapes) come into being. Although many of the early maps of Hong Kong and Sydney were either available online in digitised archives or historical atlases, I was particularly interested in any earlier 'draft' versions of these maps that might be available and the kinds of cartographic techniques that planners and map-makers used. By considering largely forgotten sketches, it was possible to also reconsider the archive as 'epistemological experiments' (Stoler, 2002: 87). That is, in effect, to view the archive as something living (Hall, 2001) which produces varied affects and evokes memories in different spaces and at different times, which can be reworked into a critical tool for reimagining everyday life (Kirsch and Rohan, 2008).

In *Les origines de la géométrie* (2011), Serres critiques the origins of the arch and archaism in European thought, and its links to the hierarchical. From the archaeological to the architectural, to the archive and the archaic, the sacred geometry of the parabola invades so much of European symbolism and materiality, embedded in history and buildings, living and dwelling. For Foucault (2002a), the arch is monumental: a perfect bow, a sublime geometry, an erection to triumph, a rainbow crossing the sky. The curve is repetitious and recurrent, appearing wherever we look. For Serres, the *arche* also demands hierarchies of knowledge, based on reason and the power of visibility: 'power lies in knowledge, the way the invisible lies in what allows seeing' (Serres, 2017[5]: 47). So, in a subtle counter to the monumentality of geometry, and its necessary basis in hierarchies, discursive relations, Serres (2017: 41) questions 'if an anarchical system can be conceived'? This kind of system decries hierarchies of knowledge and decentres the centre – sun, king or model – and does not gaze from above (and forget how we are complicit in making the world) or below (and accept our subjugation as ordinary). Given the back to front aims of this research, the subjugation of the formal to the vernacular, the past to the present, the geographical and geometric to the geo-? (Reichert, 1998), the known to the unknown, could we not think of this project here as an exploration of the anarchive, anarchaic, anarchitectural: an anarchaeology? Can we not flatten the hierarchy, and create new ones?

Thus, by situating this method into the every day, the banal, or what Gerlach (2010) has called the 'vernacular', the epistemological foundations of this approach are not monumental but momentary, not formal but formational, not final but fluid. Like the anarchic, these are conversations about the meaning and experience of the heterogeneity of space – an anarchaeology as it is encountered through discourses and ghosts lingering in space, stirring up memories and shaping practices with their lingering traces. This is a conversation about what it means to live in postcolonial landscapes somewhere between discourse and space. In digging through the present, it is inevitable that other debris, too, will be upturned: landscapes that predate rationality and hauntings of the subjugated knowledges do not exist in lines, or points, or curves or squares. Rewatching each interview and tracing differences and repetitions, recurrences, phantasms, I searched through the archives looking for discursive regularities or dissonances in the irruption of cartographic reason, for material enunciations of abstracted ideas; the difficult border between order and disorder. Such a search was not limited to the form of statements, but rather to epistemic and discursive formations: numbers, geometries, quantifications and taxonomies as they appeared in maps, sketches and plans. The documents obtained from the search, therefore, included journals, newspapers, paintings, sculptures, architectures, correspondence and fiction. They are also sometimes draft

5 All readings of *Les origines de la géométrie* are from the original 1995 French version published by Juilliard. However, given a recent translation has been released, direct quotes in English are taken from the 2017 version *Geometry* published by Bloomsbury.

documents, leaves of preformal knowledge, lemmas in materialisation, cartographies in formation, made with pencil, charcoal or chalk. In Hong Kong, I visited the Central Map Library, the Survey and Mapping Office and the Public Records Office. In Sydney, I visited the Mitchell Library at the State Library of New South Wales (NSW), and the City of Sydney Archives. I also visited the National Library of Australia in Canberra, where I spoke to archivists about their collections and to the curators of a special exhibition of antipodean cartography, *Mapping This World*. Moving through the catalogues of primary materials dating from 1770 in Sydney, and 1830 in Hong Kong, I requested documents from collections that specifically focused on the urban design of each city in the formation of its first 50 or so years, and major events after that which made their ways into the interview dialogues – the culverting of the Tank Stream, the development of the Central-Mid-Levels escalator and walkway system, the production of the Kai Tak Airport, the Great Depression and the building of the Harbour Bridge etc. I kept notes of documents from archives that I had viewed, and information that was given to me by archivists, curators and map librarians about where I could find information if the archives were not available.

These uneven processes created uneven levels of depth. Despite the apparent regularity of a field of statements, such a field is neither whole nor complete – the teleology of statements is not linear, and nor is their spatiality even – in Foucault's words, groups of statements are not a totality, but 'an incomplete, fragmented figure' (Foucault, 2002a: 141). The complexities of colonial archiving (and post/colonial control over documentation), at times, created a frustrating skein, many archives maintained maps that were copies (and sometimes photocopies) of the originals. Many sketches were not digitised, and so no preview was available. Furthermore, the semantic meaning of what a 'sketch' was, changed from archive to archive (and, indeed, from document to document). Given that many of the more official historical maps in Hong Kong had been relocated to Kew as part of the British withdrawal, it was far easier to find sketches and correspondence, because this was mostly what had been left behind. Yet, these abject, discarded and resolutely material items had a power in their own right which appear in each of these stories. Often beyond the ken of the walker, they still emerge and bubble beneath the surfaces of both each moment, as well as the process of research: ghosts of still-colonial hauntings, of the politics of knowledge, ownership of documentation and who has control over history. Across both interview and archive, we find hauntings persist.

Here, hope is offered to us – a wisp of the potential to, however temporarily, grasp mobile mapping practices in the moment of their occurrence, and to begin to untangle the skein of discourses, subjugated knowledges and pre-discursive agents that fill up that moment. The moment is not extra-discursive, it is not beyond discourse itself, yet it *is* beyond a single discourse; it is outside the statement in the singular. The moment is a singular that extends between the pluralities of discourses in space and time, between the distant and the immediate. What the moment allows us to see is the way in which statements are formed and enunciated, across the field of statements, and across the width of discursive formations. As becoming-event, immediate and immense, what the moment does is let flux free (in the mode of Whitehead). This moment is a fluid moment that is not still like a photograph, but rather has the sense of a hand placed in running water, as individual droplets spill and reform, creating different densities of force and flexibility of viscosity as it renegotiates streams, breaks, collects dust and dirt and turns into mist. A moment of mobile mapping is a frame by which we can undertake an archaeology as it is encountered in the everyday, in the banal and the boring: it allows us to move between the near and far, the side-by-side and the dispersed.

Yet, who is the subject and where do they appear? From where are discourses brought forth? This is a key investigation in this book and a key reason for the use of stories and ethnographies – the technology speaks, as does the landscape, as does the user, interfaces, graphic representations, algorithms, law, institutions, data. Mobile mapping has brought about enumerate subjects that speak at once in a cacophony of voices. Part of this project is to map these voices – to consider who, at particular times, is the enunciative subject/s and how their discursive statements enter into dialogue with power. These are discourses which continue to be lived but also need to be situated in the historical and the geographical. They are built into landscapes and languages, through which they come into contact with the ghostly. The formalisation of cartographic reason already has material-discursive residues which linger in the *dispositif*, to be encountered within the mobile mapping assemblage. Such phenomena include urban structures (such as streets, plans and pathways), toponyms, architectures, monuments and landscapes, whose documentary origins may be found within archives and traced into the present space of the research. With similar specificity, a *subject* is not the same as an author, but rather someone (in the vaguest possible sense of the word) who may utter, or bring into being the statement at this particular time and place. The collaborative nature of mobile mapping means that there are multiple invisible authors who speak at once through countless channels: design, engineering, programming, interaction, planning, information, regulation and governance, advertising, philosophy. This is precisely what this book hopes to uncover: the conversations between discourses, between ways of knowing and being which occur in moments of mobile mapping. It sits somewhere between the flash of ghosts in the constellations of bodies, technologies and space-times, that which exists in the pre-discursive, that which cannot be expressed, and that which is expressed instead: an archaeology of mobile mapping.

# Part 2

## Sydney/Space

# 3. Other spaces

> [W]e do not live in a homogeneous and empty space,
> but on the contrary in a space thoroughly imbued
> with quantities and perhaps thoroughly fantasmatic as well.
> – Foucault, 'Of Other Spaces'[1] (1986: 23)

In *For Space* (2005), Doreen Massey bemoans fixity of space that has arisen out of the historical period of scientific rationalism.[2] For Massey, space has been asleep – a still surface upon which political struggles play out, a surface across which time sweeps, but not a surface that has its own liveliness or vibrancy. She argues that when space adheres to the modernist narratives of progress, the spatiality of the colonised becomes framed as backwards – heterogeneity in the Western context is emblematic of progress, but in the postcolonial context, discursive unities govern to the exclusion of other spaces. This is particularly relevant when situating contemporary iterations of mapping in urban spaces, flows and materialities. Unravelling spatio-geographical discourse is not a key concern of Foucault's archaeological method: he aimed to undo history, not geography. As Thrift (in Crampton and Elden, 2007) noted, it has been largely left to others (such as Philo, 1992) to develop spatiality out of Foucault's work, or to trouble his brief interpretations of what space is and what it does (Massey, 2005). Towards the end of his writings, when Foucault did begin to explore space and spatiality in more depth, he produced some of his most influential series of writings on heterotopias.[3] Like, Gordon's 'haunting', heterotopias

1 'Des espaces autres' is variously translated into English with the title 'Of Other Spaces' (trans. Jay Miskowiec, 1986) and 'Different Spaces' (trans. Robert Hurley, 1998). I use the original 1984 version in French for analysis, and the 1986 *Diacritics* translation by Jay Miskowiec for quotations.

2 For instance, as described by Elden (2006)

3 Foucault first describes heterotopia in *The Order of Things*: the description of classifications for animals, written by Borges as an imagined Chinese encyclopaedia reveals the absurdity of taxonomisation and classification. He later expands on this in two more pieces of work, a lecture to the Architecture Circle (1967) and the piece published from that talk, 'Des espaces autres' (1984).

Wilmott, C., *Mobile Mapping. Space, Cartography and the Digital.*
Taylor & Francis Group, 2020
DOI 10.5117/9789462984530_CH03

Figure 3.1. *Nine walks.* January 2-15, Sydney, Summer.

are arguably sites of subjugated knowledges: on the margins and silently seething, places like cemeteries and prisons and asylums are the rubbish tips of human society. But as these ideas came late in his life, Foucault did not expand greatly upon them. This has meant that theorists who have worked with the idea of heterotopias, such as Soja (1989), Harvey (2000b) and Augé (1995), do so in tandem with other thinkers who solidify these spatial ideas more concretely. For Soja, this was the work of Henri Lefebvre and the trialectic of space (Soja, 1996), for Harvey, Karl Marx and class analysis of social space (Harvey, 2000a), and for Augé, Gaston Bachelard and the distinction between space and place (Augé, 1995). The key argument here is that heterotopias, like hauntings, are sites of difference and contestation – and of potential. Heterotopias illuminate the discourses that hide under axioms and shine a light on the absurdity of their rules and the oddities of their practices.

As Massey (2005) notes, Latour (1998), in his proposals for the Left, describes space as the 'series of simultaneity[4] (as opposed to time which is the 'series of succession'), an extrapolation of Foucault's heterotopia into the contemporary zeitgeist. This argument offers an opening up of potentiality, heterogeneity and multiplicity that Massey applauds, and could be mirrored in the simultaneity of multiple different maps emerging on different phones from the same server. Yet, in emphasising the importance of co-existence, of sitting side by side, this description also promotes a somewhat stagnant view of space, a stage upon which multiple trajectories are simultaneously housed, but there is no sign of movement:

> Again, the term coexistence is perhaps inadequate: stress needs to be laid also on coformation, and on the inevitability of conflict. What is at issue is the constant and conflictual process of the constitution of the social, both human and nonhuman. (Massey, 2005: 147)

The nuance that Massey places at the feet of 'coformation' and 'the inevitability of conflict' is crucial to how we understand the fluidity of mobile mapping as a holistic practice beyond texts, representations and discourses. In this quotation, Massey's concern points not just to the way in which things *are* in space, but the *way in which they came to be, together and in conflict* – it is *how things, statements, discourses, objects are constituted.* This conflict is a key concern of *Part 2: Space/Sydney*, as technologies, spaces and people fall into synchronicity and asynchronicity with equal

4 This is also remarkably close to Leibniz's description of space discussed in Chapter 7.

vigour. Conflict highlights a philosophical disequilibrium, one wherein space itself has been conceptualised by 'negative difference' rather than 'positive heterogeneity', opposition as a sign of disunity, rather than a sign of potential. This requires us to radically rethink the relationships not only between representation and space, or, in this case (between the operational discourses of cartographic reason and the openness of space), between new media technologies, digital maps and postcolonial spaces more generally. The process of conflict – as brought to the fore in the stories in this book – is not a sign of the failure of cartographic representation, of algorithmic logics or codes and coordinates. Rather, we can interpret conflicts and collisions in mobile mapping practices as a sign of the potential heterogeneity of space, a sign that cartographic reason and representation has not resolutely and irreparably fixed spatial knowledge and experience. Furthermore, we may also accept the paradoxical, the contradictory and the incompatible as forming together, without need for resolution, hybridity or universality.

The postcolonial city, described by Jacobs is a space of tension between the 'imaginative geographies of reason' and 'stark anti-colonial activities' (1996: 4), leading to an incessant and political socio-spatiality where the ideological coforms with the material. Furthermore, she writes: '[p] recisely because cities are sites of "meetings", they are also places which are saturated with possibilities for the destabilisation of imperial arrangements' (ibid.). Mobile mappings are examples of sites where such meetings occur – somewhere between the ideological strictures of cartographic reason and the everyday living-with the reality of colonial presents. Thus, where Said (1993: 3) speaks of 'geography which struggles', we might also look to these moments of banal contestation as opportunities to rethink how we might make room for the vibrancy of Massey's space in the conversation about digital mapping. This next section, *Part 2: Sydney/Space*, opens up space as a paradoxical force which 'coforms' in constant contest between order and disorder, across both materiality and representation. This is reflected in how we consider space in relation to rationalism and cartographic reason, made worse by the 'persistent opposition of place-as-real to space-as-abstract' (Massey, 2005: 187). Space, here, is a flat, empty and rational model of describing relations in a fashion that is profoundly mathematical (at least in the Western episteme), embedded in the scientific revolution of the seventeenth and eighteenth centuries, about the same time that the Westphalian models of sovereignty and territory were also being established. Elden (2005), for instance, cautions against the conflation of two ideas: space and territory. This distinction is important, he writes, because the birth of territory[5] bears fraternity with the concept of space, as it was appropriated in Western thought as a rational, Cartesian model of thinking – a fraternity based heavily in geometric representations.[6] This relationship was also translated into cartography (Harley, 2001), urban planning (Akkerman, 2001; Biggs, 1999) and the colonial gaze (Jacobs, 1996; Edney, 1997) – structures that we can see spatially and temporally dispersed into the British colonies of the eighteenth and nineteenth centuries like Sydney or Hong Kong all the way through to their contemporary iterations and practices of mobile mapping.

This conversation is also deeply embedded in 'cartographic reason', discussed earlier as a mode of thinking and acting in the world developed out of Anaximander's geometry and perfected during the Enlightenment. Rational, geometric, transcendental, universal, cartographic reason bore the image of the world as both flat and spherical (when it is neither), a world drawn over by straight lines and right angles, a view of the world from both above and across, a world that can be calculated according to mathematical terms, measured according to geometry and made through pure reason: 'After Plato, understanding became geometric and communication phallogocentric; here nobody enters who does not know his geometry' (Olsson, 1991b: 36). Central to the development of cartographic reason is the transformation of the cartographic image in the Age of Reason (and the philosophies of Descartes and Leibniz) during the seventeenth century (Foucault, 2002b). Foucault's (2002a: 135) exposition on archaeology focuses on what is said, rather than what is not said, with ambiguity resting on what constitutes being 'said'. With reproducibility of media, artefacts or objects do not always need a clear enunciator to be able to speak: their existence is an archaeological statement (Huhtamo and Parikka, 2011).

It also houses a league of other associated debates, which, too, are deeply discursive: in planning, in landscape design, software coding and cartography. Foucault (2002b) identifies four modes of order in the European classical period: representation, speaking, classification, and exchange. This, he argues, leads a transition from empiricism to rationalism and later, to the reification of language through history (Foucault, 2002b), science (Foucault, 2001d), interpretation (Foucault, 2001c), grammar (Foucault, 2002a) and the positioning of people in the centre of their own universe. These changes

5 Elden's (2013a) monograph, *The Birth of Territory* addresses this issue in the context of Foucault's writings.

6 Incidentally, Elden (2005, 2013b) argues that it was in the writings of Leibniz that the links between space and Westphalian thinking were best developed.

shift cartographic reason from an empirical observational model, towards an expansionist, transcendental and universal philosophical system that renders the natural world fixed, inert and stable: 'the material substance of physical structures is essentially inert; a body cannot operate where it is not; objects and physical processes cannot think or reason; God has combined natural objects in stable systems'[7] (Farinelli, 2009: 113).

For both Descartes and Leibniz, the limit of infinity – either inwards or outwards – was a Christian God, who had created the world according to stable systems that could be realised through the purity of mathematics. The ordered stabilisation of space – either by this God, or through mathematics – sees cartographic reason determine the landscape as ordered, inert and without agency. Yet, the Cartesian and Leibnizian view of space was more relative than the absolutist idea of space as a 'container' in the mode of Newton, Kant and Berkeley (Lévy, 2012) (see Table 3.1).

**Table 3.1.** ***Four categories of rational space: Newton, Berkeley, Descartes and Leibniz.* Of particular interest is the grouping together of Cartesian and Leibnizian spatiality under a position-oriented, or relation-oriented relativism.**

| | **Position-oriented** | **Relation-oriented** |
|---|---|---|
| Absolute | Newton | Berkeley |
| | 'Classical geography', traditional geopolitics | Sensualism, structural anthropology |
| Relative | Descartes | Leibniz |
| | 'Spatial analysis', 'Cognitive sciences' | Social Sciences of Space |

Source: Adapted from Lévy (2012).

At the same time, we must be careful. There is spatial geometry in the digital map, mathematics of both the Cartesian and Leibnizian variety: coordinates and binary converge in geo-code, in the hybridisation of digital and physical space, in the interaction between numbers and lines, on the invisible plane of triangulated digital signals. Massey describes how, in complete opposition to representational fixity, a new form of spatial thinking has emerged: topological, fluid and non-Euclidean (and quite Leibnizian). This oppositionality is odd because critical cartographers such as Harley (1988a), Crampton (2001) and Pickles (2004) have utilised Foucault's archaeology to argue that the relationship

7 Translated by author.

between space and representation is, in fact, reciprocal. Olsson's many diagrams (Olsson, 1980; Olsson, 1993; Olsson, 2010), too, embody an intricate relationship between representation and space, ontology and epistemology as he attempts to push the limits of representation to the point where the episteme combusts, leading a path towards a more topological mode of thinking. Abrahamsson (2008) takes Olsson's work on lines and grids into an exhilarating expanse of Leibnizian thought (via Michel Serres) by exploring the transformation of representation through stretching and reshaping and elasticity.

Such work is vastly important in understanding how digital representation through equations and geometries is scalable, transformable and intensely spatial. Key to these specific interpretations, I believe, is an approach which considers space, not first and foremost as an axiomatic field upon which struggle occurs, but as equally discursive and contested as language: constituting and constituted by representational practices or mappings (Dodge et al., 2009a). Both the ontological and the epistemological security of cartography have been rejected in favour of a rhizomatic process of becoming and unbecoming. Yet, still, this recent emergence of spatial thinking is dissatisfying for Massey, for the same reason that it is dissatisfying here: it remains within the realm of rationalist and universalist accounts and does not account for the plurality, paradox and openness of space. As we will see in *Part 4: Digital/Hong Kong*, it is in the Leibnizian impulse that the descendants of cartographic reason (with all the splits and branches of this philosophical family tree) reunite for colourful conversations, seeing similarities in their features and their genetics, telling stories of their migration across the world, their name changes, their settlements. It is at this party that digital cartography is welcomed, not a long lost relative but a prodigal child, who best embodies them all.

How then do we deal with the haunting, heterotopic and *spatial* things that kept, at odds to, and away from, the cartographic? At the centre of this debate, and central to the empirical themes of this book, is how we deal theoretically with constant in-becoming, assembling and disassembling, when the language we use to describe processes in flux and transformations is still so often resolutely absolute, fixed and still. Aside from his writings on heterotopia in 'Des espaces autres', Foucault wrote little of space except for some early pieces on literature, architecture and film,[8] and his responses to the geographers of the radical French journal *Hérodote* (see Crampton and Elden, 2007). *Hérodote*, in particular, was a conversation full of tabula rasa,

8 See, for instance: 'Distance, aspect, origine' (1963); 'Le langage de l'espace' (1964); 'La prose du monde' (1966); 'Les mots et les images' (1967); 'Ceci n'est pas une pipe' (1968).

where space is arguably a blank surface of social power, in many instances, interchangeable with spatial representations such as the plan, the map and landscape architecture (see, specifically, Riou in Crampton and Elden, 2007). Space as the domain of Westphalian thinking gets pulled into the unities of rationalism: empty and socially constructed. There is an explicit lack of both potentiality and hope in this narrative of space as a closed and rationalist model of European thought, or as a flat surface for how media connect things together. Even those critical cartographers who have worked with Harley's interpretation of Foucault's archaeological method have been slightly detoured by Harley's easy interchange between Foucault's analysis of statements and discourse, and Derrida's method of deconstruction (Belyea, 1992). This has resulted in a search for fairer representations in a field that is deeply analytical of how power emerges within cartographic texts (and their relationship to the landscapes that they represent) but has less to say about the discursive nature of space itself. So, for cartography and GIS (and cartographic reason more broadly) the question of space and representation has been left largely in the realm of the text, the map, the discursive and the media, the interface – in short, the object. Space, here, is understood through objects of power, and is largely considered to be a political problem, one underwritten by the political structures of space: roadways and freeways, zoning, planning, infrastructure and resource allocation through representation (but not necessarily because of representation).[9]

Away from cartography and into spatial media, Foucauldian-based analysis, too, often rests on this assumption or privileges the temporal over the spatial. Media archaeology, for instance, combines Foucault's archaeology with Walter Benjamin's analysis of media and space, and Guy Debord's work on spectacles (Huhtamo and Parikka, 2011; Parikka, 2013). Media, in this view, have a trajectory across time and space – but are not necessarily produced by or indeed produce, space: 'identifying topoi, analyzing their trajectories and transformations, and explaining the cultural logics that condition their "wanderings" across time and space is one possible goal for media archaeology' (Huhtamo and Parikka, 2011: 28).

However, as Kluitenberg (2011) pinpoints, media archaeology is not quite the same as Foucault's archaeology: there have been criticisms that media

9 This probably accounts for the deeper interest in the biopolitical aspects of Foucault's work in geography, the work on governmentality by Huxley (2006) or Rose-Redwood (2006) on political struggles over toponymy. The relationship between space and representation, a relationship often seen as axiomatically appearing in plans and charts, has not been taken up with as much vigour by geographers and certainly not by those geographers interested in Foucault's writings.

archaeology still focuses on media rather than discourse, tracing the 'geology' (Parikka, 2015) of media topoi to uncover how and why they were formed. This approach has been established in dialogue with Zylinska's (2009) paleontological approach drawn from Bernard Stiegler (1998). Furthermore, undertaking a media archaeology is to follow the relations formed as media mediate through deep time (Zielinski, 2006), in which space is but a supporting actor, or where media *are spaces* (rather than say, discourse or memory of any number of other objects) through which things can be enacted. In this realm of thinking, spatialisation is the act of representation – to draw is to spatialise, a theme which Olsson (1979), too, has taken up, attempting to push the limits of representation to their utter edge and to see how space can be understood within the realms of lines, points, bars and images.

At the same time, it would seem strange to Massey that media like mobile phones or digital interfaces, and not space become the nexus of thinking about action.[10] It might seem strange to Foucault, too, that media is space, rather than one part of space (even if certain ways of thinking govern it):

> [T]he *formulation* is an event that can always be located by its spatio-temporal coordinates, which can always be related to an author, and which may constitute in itself a specific act (a 'performative' act, as the British analysts call it). (Foucault, 2002a: 120)

The formulation of discourse is always situated – in spaces, bodies, materialities. It is event as well as representation. Yet, I also hesitate to use Foucault's 'spatio-temporal coordinates,'[11] since they still fall prey to the same problems we encounter in the rationalist model of geometric space that Elden described: reliance upon epistemologies that fix space rather than open it. Not so Foucault, says Massey (2005), space is open and that, discussing the work of Bergson and duration, '*in the association of* [*space*] *with representation* it was deprived of dynamism, and radically counterposed to time' (Massey, 2005: 21, emphasis in original). We see this slippage in Foucault's work as

10 There is, of course, an ever-expanding definition of what media is beyond communication into the elemental and the atmospheric. But this expansion (which at times feels ad infinitum) seems akin to the Cartesian project of a universal geometry, albeit on a more meditative gauge. Atmospheres and elemental media (Peters, 2015), for instance, is one such expansion.

11 I am not particularly in favour of this specific terminology primarily because of its Cartesian implications, its investment in the metaphors of cartographic reason as discourse-free and an added level of abstraction from space through the representations coordinate geometry. In the case where spatio-temporal coordinates are referred to, this is specifically mimicking Foucault's words in order to highlight his own terminology.

well as Bergson's. While the statement may not be materially defined by its spatiotemporal coordinates, where and how the statement emerges certainly can be. In fact, Foucault directly states that the formulation of statements is performative: it is a speech-act. The problem with Foucault's explanation here is that because he is primarily concerned with the project of history (the subjugation of space to time is another point on which Massey and I agree) he does not account for the other half of this description of spatiotemporal coordinates: the *act* in the speech-act.

Space and the landscape play a profound role in both the expression and countenance to geographic and cartographic discourse. It is a terrain of intermittent epistemological authority – bound equally between experience and representation through its association with space, and also with memory – the kinds of hauntings of which Gordon (2008) writes. De Certeau (1984) traces the dispersion of stories across the planes of space and memory in everyday life away from the strictures (and scriptures) of space as a rationalist tool. He describes memory as an 'anti-musuem' that lingers in spaces: 'Objects and words also have hollow places in which a past sleeps, as in the everyday acts of walking, eating, going to bed, in which ancient revolutions slumber' (De Certeau, 1984: 108). In this interpretation, where there are 'presences of diverse absences' that continue through people and memory and haunting, there remains a possibility for hope, and for a rewriting of the meaning of spaces away from the unified theory of cartographic reason and perhaps more into the ghostly spaces of the world.

Massey writes:

> Equations of representation with spatialisation have troubled me; associations of space with synchrony exasperate me; persistent assumptions of space as the opposite of time have kept me thinking; analyses that remain within the discursive have just not been positive enough. (Massey, 2005: 13)

This is a wilful and persistent endeavour in the search for hope – even in absence, haunting and obliteration – a call to arms that is taken up as the purpose of this book. The same haunting feeling surfaces, too, in Said's (1997) exposition on beginnings, albeit in a temporal rather than spatial analysis. Here, the beginning is not an origin, but a vibrant starting (perhaps even a breaking) point and a re-encounter with the spaces outside of discourse that Foucault dismisses. This feeling again is also expressed in Said's dissatisfaction with the textual emphasis of Derrida and the lack of political will that Said reads in Foucault's defeatist stance on the inescapability of language and discourse (even as it appears through various apparatuses). He places Foucault's work in opposition to that of Frantz Fanon – with specific emphasis on their contrasting stances on imperialism and colonialism (Said, 1978, 1993, 1997, 2004). In Said's estimation, Fanon is spurned on by a sense of change – the kind that Olsson (2007) described as the 'activism' of the Marxists like David Harvey and Massey (2005) sees in the work of Ernesto Laclau and Chantal Mouffe – while Foucault finds himself caught in a web of theory, so much so that although he shares emotional affinities with the subjugation of knowledges and the expanse of biopolitical power[12] he neglects the imperial and the colonial reaches of power (Said, 1993).

And so we have hit here upon a set of key factors which, without too much reproach, suggest that Foucault and the others that have followed and argued with him (Riou, Latour, Deleuze and Guattari, Serres, Harley) and those who preceded him (Nietzsche, Kant, Bachelard, Blanchot, Bataille, Marx) are, simply stated, not enough, not sufficient and not positive enough, especially when we start talking about the relationship between space and cartographic reason in the search for openness and possibility. Let us search for hope in the spaces of Hong Kong and Sydney, away from the centre and into the gateways between competing epistemes. Landscapes, stories, histories and geographies of particular varieties that needed neither Western varieties of rationalism, Cartesian geometries nor Westphalian politics so that they can act and be: the space of settler colonialism was purposefully produced (Banivanua-Mar and Edmonds, 2010). What again is important here is that we walk on uncertain ground in assuming equivalency between space and media, space and geometry/cartography and, importantly, space and reason, especially when considering postcolonial rationalities, because we also assume an uncontested relationship between spatiality and representation, while we afford a lack of relationship between representation and temporality. Why should time be free from this dictum, while we constrain spaces to unenviable status as bland sites of mediation?

Therefore, in the chapters to come, we follow Massey out of this quagmire into open space, even though (and precisely because) she vehemently disagreed with Foucault's interpretation of space: 'For the future to be open, space must be open too' (Massey, 2005: 12). Mobile mapping – as performative and situated – transcends the kinds of stratification that traditional discourses produce between image and space. Mobile mapping is a confluence of both spatiality and representation at once mediated not only through the image but also through bodies, landscapes, emotions, memories and any number of other factors. In doing so, it breaks down

12 Foucault gave a number of interviews on his experiences in psychiatric units in France.

easy barriers between representation and space – between things and discourses – as they may have appeared before the widespread popularity of digital representation in which it was far simpler to methodologically distinguish semiotically between epistemologies and experiences, in which all things are representation. Much of this concern about difference engages with Foucault's writings on heterotopia but with a distinct emphasis on retaining openness where things can happen, rather than closing down the world into discourse and only discourse, bounding all thought into a predetermined Eurocentric political imagination.

# 4. Unsettling spaces

## Marianna/Landscapes

'How did you find it?'
'By getting lost.'

Marianna asks me to meet her at the now-disused brick kilns in the north-west corner of Sydney Park in Sydney's Inner West suburbs. The area where the kilns stand was once heavily forested, but ideal for brick making because of the rich alluvial soil. Brick production started here in the 1840s. By the 1870s it had peaked, and shortly after the Second World War, the kilns closed. During this time, the landscape around the kilns – St Peters, Newtown, Sydenham and Alexandria – saw incredible transformation into industrial, suburban and post-industrial zones. Factories and workshops were established, railways engineered to provide transportation for resources and goods, subdivisions etched into the surrounding suburbs, and the bricks from the kilns were used to build dense housing for the nearby workers and large terraces for rich speculators and owners. Compared to urban centres, this suburban area takes on a more subtle cartography of domestic settler rationalism: gridded subdivisions weathered by urban redesigns and changing demographics; lingering colonialisms in nominal homage to monarchs and settlers, to kings and old countries; parklands, well-ordered with intermingling local and introduced botanies; and domestic buildings in adapted European architectures. This is also a space of lived cultural poeisis (Stewart, 1996; Stewart, 2007) where things, as they emerge and are encountered, produce and are given their own palimpsest meanings (Huyssen, 2003). Such meanings fold in on themselves, not quite like the pastiche appropriation of the baroque described by Deleuze (1992a), but co-dependent, co-productive, co-formational and co-destructive. Oppositional but not hybridised, so too do meanings in this space collide in a multi-spatial poetics of tentative harmony.

I am surprised, however, that Marianna asked to meet – here – at the base of these kilns. Sydney Park is a large park, and the brick kilns are not marked

Wilmott, C., *Mobile Mapping. Space, Cartography and the Digital.*
Taylor & Francis Group, 2020
DOI 10.5117/9789462984530_CH04

Figure 4.1. *Fragments – Marianna, Kyja and Tanija.* (Left) *Marianna's walk* – Thursday, 2 January, St Peters-Alexandria, evening, overcast; (centre) *Kyja's walk* – Friday, 7 January, Broadway-Wynyard-Moore Park, midday, overcast; (right) *Tanija's walk* – Friday, 7 January, The Rocks, evening, partly cloudy.

specifically on Google Maps when I check for the closest bus stop, so I know where to alight. On these cartographic interfaces, the parkland is crisscrossed with the lines of running paths, dog-walking tracks and car parks. It is only because I have specific memories of this landscape that I know where they sit, the tall chimneys in my mind's eye, gleaming with the rose-gold colour of the late afternoon sun as I would drive by on my way south. These kilns are very much the 'image' (Lynch, 1960) of this part of Sydney's space (if not its map), a beacon for a crossroads between multiple suburbs and main streets. They are also, for those who care to remember, a reminder of the long-form redistribution of the landscape, its ephemerality and its impermanence – a timestamp, as much as a landmark. After the kilns became disused, the park became a rubbish tip and the massive pits, from which the clay was drawn, were filled with garbage. Still, the tall chimneys of the kilns remained on the corner, and now that the landfill has been buried and the landscape turned into a park, they remain a lingering reminder of the industrial past of the Newtown-St Peters area. The urban design is a process of folding, memories kneaded by newer, more recent discourses – once a forest, then a brickworks, then a rubbish tip and now a park – an appropriation of meaning and a mixing of the past through its material landscapes.

As the sun deepens into the summer horizon, Marianna arrives. Then, she opens a fitness application on her phone to show me how it works and to explain how it will be tracking our movements. This particular app, Map My Run, is predicated upon the logic of translating locational data into graphic displays. Every 30 seconds, the app records our coordinates and the time. Every half-minute, the digital map tracks our route and provides regular updates on our pace through the microphone on the mobile phone. The data-based fixity and cartographic authority of this digital tracing are at odds with the strange phantasm of the kilns and the park. However, Marianna explains that she likes it, precisely because she does not have to pay attention to it, and she can worry about where she has been and how far she has to go without stopping to play with the interface. In essence, it works because it sits on the surface of her wanderings, as she becomes absorbed into her walk.

As time and locational data are increasingly brought into mobile mapping practices, digital reckonings, too, become furled into the spatio-temporalities of everyday landscapes. The politics of this integration are often articulated as the colonisation of experience by digital, locational data. In itself, this is a settlement and resettlement of the present and very recent past through digital lives, always being overwritten by new, more up-to-date information, shifting data and representational formats to reflect the discourses that shape places at every moment. But, the degree to which data takes root and unearths the lingering materiality of the kilns into digital abstraction – and the degree to which this process is, indeed, different from the spatial and temporal re-orderings of other forms of urban mediation (cf. Mattern, 2017) – is ambiguous.

This ambiguity becomes more obvious, later, as we descend from the bright and busy main roads into the cool suburbia of Newtown. Walking up the southern end of King Street, we dodge people and talk over the buses rumbling past and the planes flying overhead. Music blares from cafes and cars, people talk on their phones as they walk past, and the sun bounces off the pavement. Then, as we diverge down a side street, stillness settles as we wander into an oddball trapezium of unmarked backstreets. It is cooler and calmer in this space, a jumble of narrow roads, stuffed with tiny, terraced, tin-roofed workers' cottages (the kind that were built to house the labourers who worked in now disappeared factories, warehouses and brickyards). Some of these terraces are no more than 4 m wide, colourfully painted and occasionally with florid decorations adorning the front verandas or first-floor balconies. As Marianna and I walk, we must carefully avoid verge gardens and gum trees and wattles, which have broken free of their concrete edgings and are botanising the asphalt. Graffiti is abundant – tags of all shapes and sizes – (illegal) murals and stickers urging uprisings, revolutions and reclamations, cars and bikes cramp along the footpaths.

Most graphic maps make little of the crossing from one street to the next (between orange main roads into the grey swathe of emptiness in-between), with only perhaps a change of colour to represent the rich transformation between spaces. Still, on Marianna's map, this movement looks like even less. The way in which the map reads this landscape transformation is in rows of numbers that gather our location every 30 seconds. Then, these rows of GPS data are re-presented, dispassionately, on a carto*graphic* interface as a generalizable line between two points. So, while the cool air catches our faces as we move away from King Street, the app takes note of a minuscule shift in location from 33.902882°S and 151.179465°E to 33.902508°S and 151.179615°E. Consider this distance in Cartesian terms through the global geographic coordinate system used by Google (which provides the base cartographic data), as shown in Table 4.1.

**Table 4.1.** ***Points*. The difference between the two points on King Street and Angel Street, Newtown, in Cartesian terms.**

| | Latitude | Longitude |
|---|---|---|
| Point A | 33.902882°S | 151.179465°E |
| Point B | 33.902508°S | 151.179615°E |
| Difference | 00.000374° | 000.000150° |

Source: data is tabulated from Open Street Map coordinate data.

Not even four ten-thousandths of a degree to the north we travelled, and only one and a half ten-thousandths to the east – a distance which can only be significant in a realm of ubiquitous calculability yet is vastly different to the landscape. Unless speaking from experience, it's difficult to comprehend the transition from the *hot*, bright and grimy atmosphere of the main road, clogged with sweaty pedestrians and smoggy cars in the height of summer into this quieter and slower space that sits lazily under the shade on a summer evening.

This regimentation is apparent not only in the description of spatiality but place as well (Zook and Graham, 2007). On the corner of this transition, sits an abandoned petrol station and mechanic's garage, decomposing, in a curious nod to the tensions between settlement and unsettlement. This place, viewed in Google Maps when I drop the GPS tracks into the software later, is expressed by three categories of origin as shown in Table 4.2.

**Table 4.2.** ***Origins*. Three categories of origin: street address at the top right, coordinate position middle right, and place_id bottom right.**

| | |
|---|---|
| Origins | origins=536A+King+Street+Newtown+NSW+ON<br>origins=-33.902997,151.179661<br>origins=place_id:ChIJrRDf50mwEmsRZipFiOkKN94 |

Source: Data from Google Maps API, processed and tabulated by the author.

Marianna has a different story. She tells me that the petrol station was more recently a squat. She seems to appreciate the precarity; its fleeting presence only in memory and not ever on her map.

'It didn't last long – the police came ...,' she says quietly.

When place takes on newly coded calculability, where specific coordinates can be given particular names or identities that do not key into monadic digital systems, this fleeting moment does not (and perhaps cannot) make it into the universalising taxonomic structure of cartography. There is no option for an origin that is attentive to the delicate reminiscences of Marianna's mapping practices.

**Table 4.3.** ***Origins II.*** **The origins of Marianna as she tells me her story of this location if it were possible to code ambiguity, vagueness and eccentricity.**

| | |
|---|---|
| origins | origins=We+go+this+way+ON<br>origins=petrolstation,squat<br>origins=place_id:Itdidntlastlong_thepolicecame |

Source: The author.

The functionality of code means that such subjective eccentricity cannot work – or, indeed if it can, as Foucault (2002a) suggests, then it risks being engulfed into hegemonic discourses. Once digital classifications become associated with this location, they *can only be associated with this location* on the digital plane: the heterogeneity of space becomes lost.

With flat maps and top-down views still in recent memory, Marianna's mobile mapping practices through the app seem absurdly abstracted from classic point-line-polygon cartographies. In the settling of the map into our walk, and calculability into landscapes, spaces, areas, paths become just algebraic points, numbers dancing across their own bland landscape geometry. The meaning of these numbers makes no difference to the app or the algorithm, as it works through its numbers, triangulates and calculates. Where Serres (2016: 187) writes 'you will eat codes and numbers', the GPS tracings are a veritable buffet of coordinate points, elevations, times (distance/time = speed), regurgitated onto our screens. This aggregation of numeric data presented on the app appears yet another stage removed from the drawing of the line into the calculating of a line. This Cartesian plane oversimplifies the haphazard obstacle course of garbage bins into processes – tracings through coordinates, calculations and updates, rather than lines or points or curves. This data does not offer the chance to compare the green on the map, with the green of the local park, a waypoint to an embodied moment in space, or sketched line to the shape of our path through the landscape. All the while, once the phone has been set up, it requires no further interaction, and there is no need to return to the screen or the app: all processes are automated, data gathered at evenly spaced points, and then at specified times delivered back to us while we walk.

All the same, this neighbourhood is layered with multivalent and heterogeneous spatio-temporalities. A space like this is *lived in* rather than *looked at* – a landscape given less to the images of the city described earlier (Lynch, 1960) than the everyday business of living (Jacobs, 1962). These streets are familiar territory for Marianna, and so she does not need the map to navigate the landscape, only to calculate it. On the footpath, a small chalk drawing of hopscotch catches Marianna's attention, and she points and laughs – an ephemeral trace left by invisible children, which will inevitably be washed away by the next summer storm (which we can already feel building in the oppressive humidity and darkening skies). She then stops to pick some vibrant pink geraniums (*Pelargonium capitatum* – she knows all the botanical names) she finds peeking through the fence of an unknown gardener – to be planted later in her own garden. The 'ottos' – large green rubbish bins with multicoloured lids – are strewn about precariously, because it is garbage night tonight.

We walk by a small terrace with pale green bricks and red fencing, with a veranda out the front and a car awning to the side. In front of the veranda sits a small garden overgrown with bushes and shrubs and trees. Marianna looks at the garden seriously.

'That house,' she points towards it, 'a couple of weeks ago these two trees had these amazing white trumpet flowers.'

This description is sweet fruit for the imagination – the landscape here, even as it is influenced by cartographic reason and industrial processes, is co-produced by everyday domesticities which leave traces in many different ways. The story of the trumpet flowers, here one week and gone the next, is the simple product of the care and attention of a person invisible in our tour of this landscape. Plants, in this sense, occupy a temporality foreign to cartographic reason. Seasons in the suburbs bring forth new spectacles for the gardener or amateur plant watcher: the smell of damp figs and hot eucalyptus in December, of flowering banksia and floating acacia in September; and the sounds of the animals that they attract: screeching lorikeets fighting over the bottlebrushes, garbling magpies snaring worms from the damp soil at the roots of melaleuca, and laughing kookaburras hunting for lizards as the lizards hunt for bugs as the bugs flock to the sweet grevilleas.

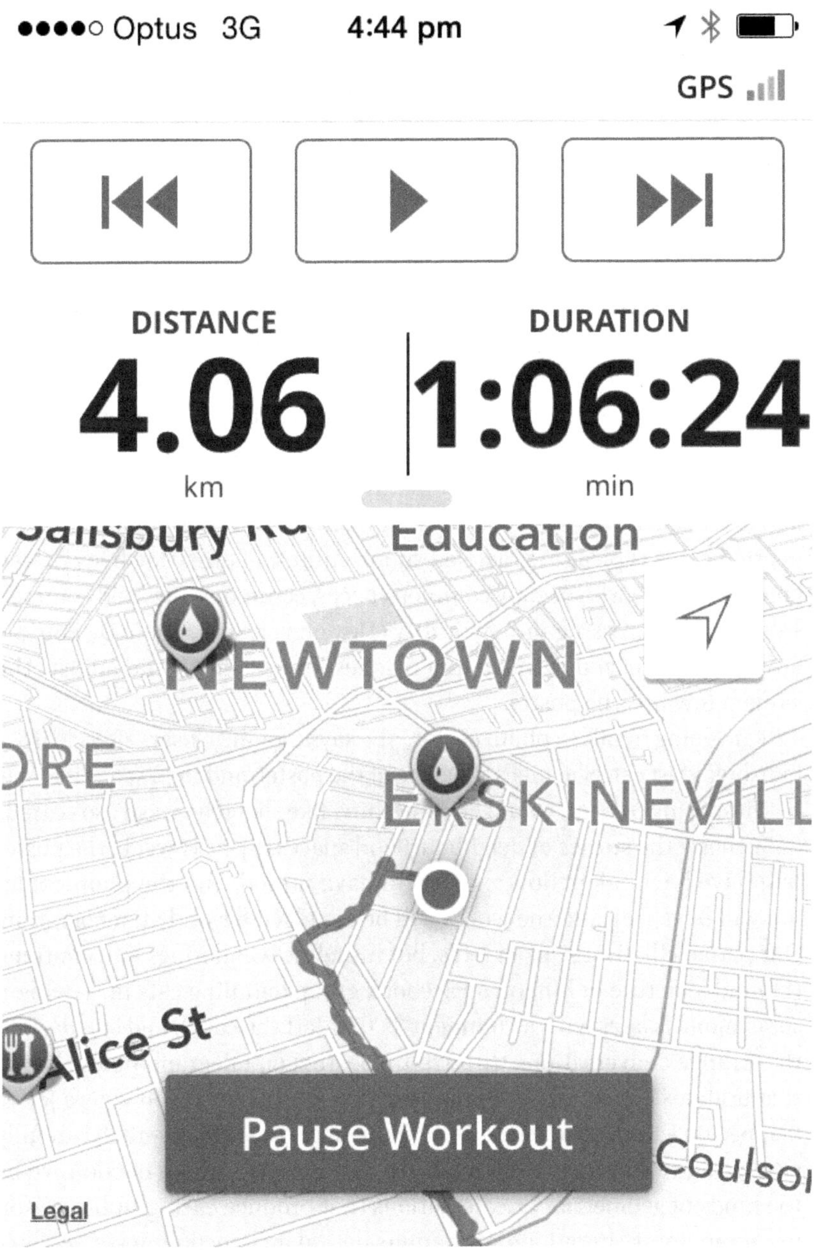


Figure 4.2. *Newtown/Erskineville*. Screenshot of Marianna's phone showing workout information, including distance and overall duration. Of particular interest is the triangulation between the visual cartographic interface and the calculative data. Source: Marianna.

In this vein, the story of Jeff the cat (or perhaps it should be *Jeff the Cat*) emerges along our path, fly-posted to a wooden telegraph pole on a piece of A4 paper, taped up by his concerned owners as a neighbourhood alert. Alongside a picture of Jeff, who is smug looking ginger long-hair, his story has outlined in an imploring tone by his worried owners.

Someone has put a collar on Jeff – but Jeff already has an owner. It seems that Jeff is seeing other people, and charming them into giving him food and attention. However, Jeff is not underfed, and not neglected – *he has two owners and is loved and fed, so please don't adopt him.* In an age of digital spaces, this moment of neighbourly communication appears to be best reached expressed in paper rippled from the damp heat, held precariously together by masking tape. There are no digital coordinates attached to this poster, no tags and no hashtags. This is a curiously analogue event, one embedded in a lived – *living* – landscape that people pass through daily, a material surfacing of every day and habitual space. A poster about an overfed cat is typical of practised suburbanites, of everyday lives shared amongst people who occupy common spaces, common times and common stories. Then, crossing into hybridity (De Souza e Silva, 2006; De Souza e Silva and Sutko, 2009), Marianna reaches for her phone and adjusts the camera towards the poster.

'I am going to take a photo of this,' she says moving closer, 'He's clearly a four-breakfast cat.' She takes a picture of the poster, and then sends it to me.

'My cat, my boy cat, would do something like that if he wasn't so scared.'

Such are the stories of neighbourhood spaces. By next week, the poster will have been taken down, or it will have rained, and the photocopier ink will have run, and the words will be smudged beyond all recognition. Our paths will diverge from Jeff's, but his feline wanderings will continue (I found a picture of him on a Facebook group detailing cats in Newtown some months later with a comment 'Is that Jeff the cat?'), and so, too, will the strange conversations through fly posters on telegraph poles. A map that updates constantly does not track these changes: even where Jeff is mapped on Facebook, this is a deeply human effort – a photograph carefully curated and a comment drawn from Jeff's notoriety – and is not defined by the kinds of geometries or calculations that produce cartographic reason in contemporary iterations. Marianna's digital map records and calculates silently – this moment logged as the crossroads between 33.901878°S, 151.182264°E at 4.44 pm – and is unaware of the briefest crossing of paths that happens here. The digital map does not really know about Marianna meeting the ghost of Jeff the Cat on his daily walks, courting many different owners and starting simmering battles intertwining the lives of people

Figure 4.3. *Telegraph poles.* Marianna uses her phone to take a photograph of the *Jeff the Cat* poster (seen bottom left).

who do not know each other through his nondescript undocumented feline space/territory.

This kind of mobile mapping is embroiled in settlement and unsettlement. As we continue down the road, Marianna gestures towards a typical suburban cul-de-sac.

'This street here,' she says, 'it's called Pleasant Street, and I walked down this way on – just before Christmas, and the whole street was closed off, which was late-ish afternoon, and they were having a very late lunch, evidently. So they had tables, the whole street had tables, and I thought, yeah, that's pleasant.'

Her description of the Christmas street party is evocative. It is not difficult to imagine how the street could be closed off, the cars moved to make way, and plastic garden tables and chairs would migrate into the middle of the street for a holiday feast. The close-knit plan of these suburbs facilitates a community closeness as well, an everyday sharing of space that culminates in end-of-year parties. Yet, the difficulty of imagining this moment on the maps that have unwoven throughout our walk – either as graphic or numeric representations – remains. Street party or simply 'street', the cartographic image remains a steady yellow, and though the numbers of nearby devices, or of people wandering through or gathering together, may ebb and flow, the digital cartography remains brutal in its ambivalence.

Marianna's wonderment is also centred on the serendipity of encounter – that she should be walking this way and find this moment of pleasantness and celebration. The residue of this party lingers in (this) space, revived, or perhaps, evoked, by Marianna's memory of it. Her association links back with the name of the street, too, and the heuristic moment when she found its toponymy lived by its residents. The richness of association and the textures of experiences layered into Marianna's fleeting recollection do not translate to the kinds of mediated mapping systems that she uses to record her walk. No amount of distance or duration, and no abstracted cartographic representation can adequately express the complexity of Marianna's relationships with space and memory as it rests less in image, and perhaps more in after-image (Resina and Ingenschay, 2003). It is clear that the affects (Massumi, 2002) of the neighbourhood – the atmospheric and intangible elements that can trace the everydayness of spaces that are lived in – deeply embeds itself into Marianna's experience of space between digital maps and landscapes. Even the most minute shifts between one day and the next, trumpet flowers, hopscotch paths, maverick cats and surprise street parties, alters the texture and surfacing of her experience. Across space, these moments are distributed, and this neighbourhood becomes an archive that can be traversed, recombined, restructured and reencountered. Memory and discourse hold *in space*, as Edward Casey suggests, 'in its countless alveoli, space contains time' (Casey, 1993). This is a lived archive, infinitely heterogeneous and *always shifting*. Paths change and spaces are encountered in different states and at different stages of the manifold stories that fold and unfold within them. Rolling together, these multiple temporalities interact as the ephemeral becomes encountered and reencountered. As Marianna recounts each minor discovery, and as we find new ones, they blend in space to become lived, relived and reinterpreted in the irruption of this moment, here, at this time.

'How did you find it?' I ask Marianna.

'By getting lost,' she replies.

How can cartographic reason comprehend the paradox of space when its discursive ambition is to eliminate inconsistency, incompatibility and contradiction? To find something by getting lost – and to weave it into the patina of spatial experience in such a way that when reencountered, it always appears slightly different. It is possible to outline and colour a space, and then to give it a name – but, as Massey (2005) suggests, to represent a space is to fix it in one way or another. Marianna's encounters in space, however, are absolute *un*fixity, and when they are portrayed, even in this retelling, become mere approximations. I cannot write or draw enough to explain the uplift at Pleasant Street or the ghostly image of the white trumpet flowers, or the sudden barrage of realisation, shock, at other non-human lives that are traced across a space that have suddenly become visible in their potential. At the limits of representation, where Olsson writes, we find no clearer answers either (Olsson, 1991b). There is a dissonance between the writing of space and the living in of space. This is evident in the distance between the discourses of Marianna's phone digital map, and how she engages the spaces that it represents. It is evident in affect and emotion, and in the atmospheric forces that attempt to understand how the invisible and permeable circulates through the world (Anderson, 2015). It is also evident in the haunted, which Avery Gordon writes as 'seething presences and muted absences' that linger on the shores of colonised landscapes in which space becomes commoditised, calculated and controlled (Gordon, 2008).

We can return to the kilns – which have no one meaning and perhaps are not any place suffice the present in which we encounter them – and find that they are not so much a mere footnote to the spatial stories that Marianna and I live. Even though the terraces hold a longer grasp on the material longevity of cartographic reason, these brick houses are still eroded and decomposed slowly as dust and grime brushes away new paintwork, the cast-iron lacework on verandas turns into rust, and the heavy brick foundations subside back into the clay ground. The brick kilns foretold this metamorphosis of the earth, from one site to another. In the concerted efforts of colonial industry, small amounts of clay were packed into regular rectangular cuboids, fired, and then transported a few miles and stacked up on top of each other to become the houses that we pass. In the movement of the landscape from one kind to another, and as the brickworks dug into the earth, remnants were uncovered – in 1910, a full-skeletal fossil of a *Paracyclotosaurus davidi*, a prehistoric amphibian, was discovered here, the only kind believed to have lived in Australia. The earth itself contains such stories, maps, perhaps, to the past – but in such a monadic form that transfigured products (once settled) become axioms, and the traces of earlier endeavours to reshape the landscape persist only in memory by way of anachronistic remnants, like the kilns themselves. These pasts, like the *Paracyclotosaurus davidi*, only speak through the process of unsettling.

Rather, the kilns also hold potential ephemerality encased in the disappearance of the brickworks, of the earth that surrounded them, and the rubbish covered over with new soil. The kilns occupy a space that is *lived in* and *lived past*, 'storied spaces' that have their own trajectories that we encounter in the domestic narratives of that we weave. And so, too, all elements in Sydney, even those that do not have the obvious beatific monumentality of colonial dreams. Hopscotch becomes crumbed over by dropped gum nuts and geraniums intersperse with banksia and wattle. Jeff the Cat gets fed by many, but also possibly hunts lorikeets and budgerigars in his own silent space of feline colonialism. Christmas is celebrated in the late afternoon, when it is cooler and nicer, traditions of holly and snow sweating under a December sun. In all spaces, especially those that are postcolonial, paradox reigns. While these inconsistencies may be carefully ignored, no matter how tall or imposing like the kilns, or how habitual and domestic, like the flowers, they can never quite be forgotten. Thus, there is already an internalised ambiguity towards the cartographic discourses and this impacts on how digital maps are engaged. Marianna uses her map, but unlike the story of Borges (1998), she does not live it: her map is not her territory.

## Kyja/Grids

'It sort of exists outside all space and time. It's like its own little island.'

Sometimes people who live in Sydney dream of Melbourne's perfect rectilinear grid system. Kyja is a relative newcomer from Melbourne to the Sydney landscape but knows the area well enough. We are heading to Wynyard together, and Kyja is using her phone to navigate because she is unsure of when we should get off the bus.

'I know it has a station,' she says.

The transition from the wide gridded urban plan of Melbourne to the haphazard pastiche of Sydney is a struggle for Kyja's navigational skills. This is a spatial struggle as well as an ideological one, folded into the urban plan of Sydney by the slippages, misdirections and naivety of the British colonialists who settled on the shores of Warrane, known also as Sydney Cove and Circular Quay. As Thalis and Cantrill state:

> Sydney has witnessed dramatic interactions of public places with its site, landform and geography. The material evidence of the dialectic between nature and culture, between memory and erasure, marks and makes the city to an extraordinary extent. Although this foundation lies submerged beneath today's city, its presence underpins the layout. (2013: 24)

Travelling across this landscape, Kyja and I sit on a bus heading down George Street, the main spine and thoroughfare of the Sydney Central Business District (CBD). Staring intently at her phone, Kyja watches the little blue dot skip down past Town Hall and the Queen Victoria Building towards Wynyard, in the north of the city. Muscles tensed, she expects Wynyard to creep up and surprise her, forcing her off the bus without a moment's notice.

'The problem with Wynyard,' Kyja explains, ' – and this is why I really need maps to go to Wynyard – is that is that I don't really understand where Wynyard is in relation to anything.'

Early maps of Sydney emphasise the Tank Stream to such a degree that, in comparison to contemporary renderings, it warps the harbour towards it. The earliest known European map of the Sydney colony was drawn in 1788, the year of colonisation, by Francis Fowkes, a convict, and shows Sydney Cove as the mouth of a large snake.

In this map, the Tank Stream dwarfs the landscape towards the landscapes needed for settlement – fresh water in the middle of summer in a drought-ridden country. This landscape also reshaped the process of settlement, unsettling ideology, reshaping habitat and forming modes and practices of dwelling. One of the early British soldiers, Captain Watkin Tench, noted in the first month of settlement that the Tank Stream served as a spatial divider between the east and west sides of the Tank Stream, fed from the south into the cove:

> [January, 1788] Into the head of the cove, on which our establishment is fixed, runs a small stream of fresh water, which serves to divide the adjacent country to a little distance, in the direction of north and south. (Tench, 1789)

Captain Tench's comments already point to an emerging relationship between landscape and the forming city. This relationship remains tense and fraught. Again, a common lexicon is that the shape of Sydney (compared to Melbourne) is down to accidents, forces of nature, strange geologies, haphazard architectures and vernacular planning. However, architects Thalis and Cantrill (2013) argue differently:

> Recently, the proposition that Sydney is essentially unplanned, even *accidental*, has been given undue currency. [...] What has been misrepresented as 'accidental' should more accurately be described as 'mistakes, errors and poor decisions', which some confound as 'chaos'. (Thalis and Cantrill, 2013: 24)

For, Thalis and Cantrill, there is no possibility for an 'accident' of urban planning in Sydney, and Kyja's fragmented Wynyard experiences are not the result of 'chaos'. What lies beneath these spatial experiences and the uncertainty of her mobile mapping is poor decision-making, and most importantly, poor planning. At the same time, given Carter's (2009) suspicions of

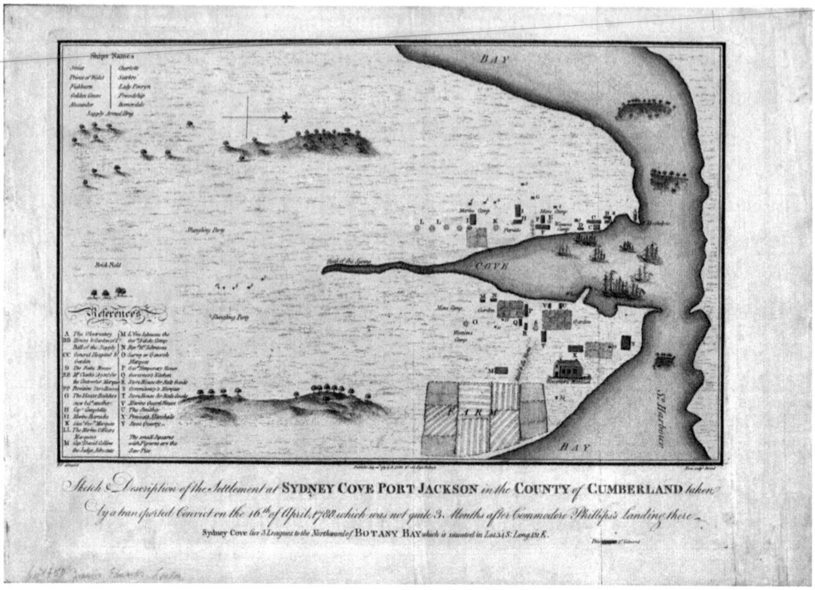


Figure 4.4. *Sydney Cove*. Frances Fowle's 1788 map of Sydney Cove, Port Jackson, in the County of Cumberland. This is one of the first maps made by the new settlers and shows the Tank Stream feeding out into Sydney Cove. It also contains pictographic elements, including the First Fleet in the harbour and some of the surrounding hills around Sydney. It is also peculiar in its directionality – north is pointed towards the right of the map, suggesting that this map was drawn from the perspective of a westward approach along Port Jackson from the Pacific Ocean. Source: National Library of Australia.

the geographical myth of a rational landscape, we should also ask if Sydney could ever have been successfully planned? This is especially crucial when the same stream of fresh water that was at once responsible for assuring the survival of a new colony in a drought-ridden country also created urban spatial divisions which still resonate today. Was this a failure of planning, or was it a fatal error, in which cartographic reason and the materialities of the Australian landscape were fundamentally incompatible?

We sit directly next to Town Hall, perhaps one of the most significant landmarks in the centre of Sydney, and yet the foregrounded worry is, in her mind, that Wynyard is not really a place at all. If the captains of the First Fleet anticipated an uninterrupted settlement on these shores, nowadays, as we inch closer towards the map point, Kyja anticipates interrupted unsettlements.

Looking up again, Kyja sighs.

'It just seems to exist, sometimes you just pop up there – I often get the train there – and sometimes you just pop up there and its got these fancy streets – shops – and it is on one street, isn't it? It just doesn't exist according to general logic,' she murmurs.

Kyja's description of general logic is largely anticipatory, resting on her ability to establish a pattern of expectation about what comes next in the space. However, Sydney is what I have often humourlessly called a 'trick-grid', a rectilinear system that is not quite regular enough to be predictable, lulling unwitting navigators into false senses of security before quietly betraying them. On the bus, we pass the Queen Victoria Building, and continue on north, moving into the older end of the city, the first place of 'settlement' (not contact) of the fledgling penal colony.[1]

'It's like its own little island, according to my brain.'

Suddenly, the signal drops out and as the dot relinquishes its acrobatics in favour of an unnerving stillness. Kyja frowns.

'It doesn't seem to know where we are.'

North of Botany Bay, Sydney Cove was chosen for two primary reasons: first, the harbour itself was deep enough for the ships to make a landing, and, second, there was a source of fresh water running down the hills, a small stream which would be called the Tank Stream. This initial decision – a moment of planning that, according to ships logs, took no longer than three days – was the first step in which cartographic reason began to be materially settled into the Australian landscape. Incidentally, it also brought forth the first rupture between the materiality of space, the corporeality of the body and the ideology of reason. Common lexicon in Sydney's vernacular history is that the city wasn't planned at all, that it was put together in a desperate hodgepodge of survival as the members of the new regime of colonial settlement first prioritised their own safety and control: from both the local Eora population, and the resentful convicts who outnumbered them (Hughes, 2003). Later attempts to go back and redress the maze of passageways and alleys around the first settlement areas in The Rocks, Circular Quay and Wynyard, and to help them conform to a more modern nineteenth-century grid pattern was largely unsuccessful due to the lack of adaptability of the geological formation of Sydney.

Not taking her eyes off her phone, she tells me about Wynyard, describing how a train station is there, and how she used to go there – but she has never really managed to cross-reference Wynyard's position with the rest of Sydney.

'So what's usually at Wynyard when you go there?' I ask.

'I think, well there's the train station there. And, if you go to the North Shore then I think you pass through Wynyard. A couple of times I've gone

1 Original British settlement was planned for Botany Bay, where Cook landed, further south. However, after arrival it was deemed unsuitable, and Sydney Cove (now Port Jackson) was chosen instead. This is outlined in further detail in Chapter 6.

there for New Year's Eve celebrations,' she pauses and looks at her phone. 'This is where it's going to creep up on me, now – because of the way it's, like, extricated from normal space and time there.'

As we get closer and closer to Wynyard, the map starts to skip.

'And how would you describe this area here?' I ask as we are travel up George Street past Martin Place.

'This is a kind of a nothinglessness space. Well – not a nothingness space – this is going to be thing you quote me on, isn't it?' She laughs.

'I think nothinglessness is a perfect word,' I reply.

We pull into stop at Wynyard Station and Kyja smiles.

Kyja looks up and notices that we are at the stop next to the train station. However, our position marker on the phone has not caught up to the marker on the map.

'We must be getting pretty close, now,' she says. 'There seems to be a train station there, which would be Wynyard more than anything else.'

Furthermore, cartographically speaking, it seems on the map as if the bus would naturally continue down the yellow-coloured George Street towards the Harbour Bridge, while the navigation shows that the bus leaves the stop and turns right towards Circular Quay, crossing the area which was once the Tank Stream. This makes it difficult to navigate, and the lack of coherence translates into contemporary mapping practices as we sit on the bus, at our stop, frowning at Kyja's phone. Although the Tank Stream is now buried under the urban infrastructures of Sydney, the geomorphology around Sydney Cove continues to maintain a fundamental role in shaping the urban design of Sydney. Further, the formation of a city is more than a simple and pragmatic intersection between imaginary and landscape. Instead, the geological, hydrological and ecological landscapes of Sydney interminably structure and restructure urban space, and in so doing, they also structure spatial experiences, and thus, the unfolding of everyday mobile mapping practices. This is certainly the case for Kyja. As we watch the screen intently, waiting for the blue dot to reawaken, the cartographic spectacle encompasses all of her attention to the detriment of a more tacit reading of the landscape.

We take off and suddenly, the blue dot skips.

'I actually think ... crap,' Kyja yelps, stands and presses the button. 'Oh-ooh, the next stop is not for ages.'

While explaining where we were headed, she missed the fact that we had arrived, and the map – slipping from accuracy in the urban infrastructural confusion of Wynyard – had not caught up.

She sighs.

'Oh no. That's okay, we'll have to walk back.'

Around the corner at the next stop, we laugh as we disembark and retrace our route back towards Wynyard.

'This is fun,' she says happily, 'it's like having your own personal geographer.'

'It's really hard,' I reply, 'particularly when you know where something is, not to direct as well. I just sat there and watched you go past the bus stop.'

Kyja chuckles.

'I can imagine it would be 'cos I didn't know where the bus stop was, there, and I was just like, 'there's the shopping centre,' better hit the thing, and then I just imagined there would be a stop between there and here – which obviously, there wasn't.'

'You just fell off the edge again…,' I reply. She smiles.

'Into the swamp.'

I laugh and tell her that strictly speaking, she's not far off the mark. As the Tank Stream came down the hill and reached Sydney Cove, it broached outwards and downwards into a marshy wetland. Thus, the area around Wynyard where we find ourselves was indeed once a swamp, and lingering references to the old Tank Stream can be found scattered about: a public artwork which marks the original route of the stream, street names, and a bar. Further up, in Hyde Park, a fountain runs to memorialise the source of the Tank Stream, and near the harbour shore in Circular Quay, another public artwork sits to acknowledge its end.

The 'dialectic of nature and culture' (Thalis and Cantrill, 2013) is better understood as a form of rationalist thinking which seeks to enforce a peculiar and totalising visual aesthetic of settlement and dwelling upon a landscape in the form of urban planning. And so, when this vision fails, the resulting friction appears chaotic but is actually underwritten by irresolvable spatiotemporal conflict. Arguably, this is a failure of the very principles of urban planning to take into account the tenuous and unpredictable nonconformist landscapes which cannot be understood through the epistemological structures of cartographic reason. For everyday mappers like Kyja, attempting to navigate these spaces in which this conflict still resides, there erupts a sense of confusion in the legibility of the urban landscape (cf. Lynch, 1960). As Kyja notes while we walk back, following the phone's redirection, Wynyard does appear to be a place at all – when you search for it, it does not appear with the nice bounded lines that Pickles (2004) notes delineate the spaces that we live within. And so, when later governors of the colony returned to the first streets around Wynyard and attempted to use cartographic discourses to redraw the crooked streets into straight lines, it resulted in and a skein of streets – incoherent on the map and incomprehensible to those trying to navigate. And without lines, Wynyard remains for Kyja 'a magical land where nothing makes sense', forgotten by the map and lost to digital signals, a place which does not work with any of the cartographic logics in which she follows.

Where Fowkes's 1788 map depicts Sydney Cove in a serpentine formation, nineteenth-century maps emphasise streets rather than geology. The desire for lines enacted in this era of planning was presaged in the early attempts by colonisers to etch geometry over uneven hills:

> The great road from near the landing place to the governor's house is finished, and a very noble one it is, being of great breadth, and a mile long, in a strait [sic] line: in many places it is carried over gullies of considerable depth, which have been filled up with trunks of trees, covered with earth. (Tench, 1793: 97)

Tench's comments point to an emerging relationship between pre-colonial landscapes and the forming city. In particular, his comments suggest that the structure of the landscape even in 1791 was already giving shape to the way in which the city was developed as straight lines began to culvert over water catchments and the Sydney basin was reformed into an asymmetrical and macabre rendition of the grids of North American urbanism. Thalis and Cantrill state:

> The material evidence of the dialectic between nature and culture, between memory and erasure, marks and makes the city to an extraordinary extent. Although this foundation lies submerged beneath today's city, its presence underpins the layout. (2013: 24)

And yet, to counter to Thalis and Cantrill (2013), the lack of cohesion in Sydney, then, has nothing to do with a lack of rational or good decision-making – rather, it seems that the same principles of planning which apply in European cities quite simply are not working in this instance. Freshwater for a new colony is essential, and there is not much of it to be found along the east coast of Eora land: terrain recommended specifically by Cook for settlement in 1770. Rain is scarce, the water is salty, the shores are swampy and the soil sandy. But, Cook came by in April, when the weather was already cooling towards winter, and landed on the soft shores of Kurnell at the mouth of the bay. The First Fleet arrived in the scorching heat of January, with more than 1480 people, seven cows, a bull and a bull calf.

I often think of the story of the wild cattle of the Sydney basin as a simple parable, a tragic-comedy, how poorly the First Fleet comprehended both the landscape and the local Gadigal people. In June 1788, about six months after the First Fleet arrived, these bovine companions (less one who was killed because she became dangerous) were put out to graze. The account is that while the herdsmen were having their lunch, the herd promptly wandered off. As Tench wrote: '[T]he whole of our black cattle strayed into the woods.' The colony searched intensely for three weeks before Governor Arthur Phillip concluded that they had probably been hunted by the local Gadigal people, and eaten. Over the next ten years, conversations between the Gadigal and the British brought stories of cattle being seen near the Nepean River, in thriving herds. In 1795, the newly appointed governor, John Hunter, set out with a small party to investigate, and found a herd of hundreds of cattle, living happily on nutrient-rich grass, some bearing the brand mark of the fleet. They renamed this area the Cowpastures and a government hut was settled nearby. By 1805, when John Macarthur was given a large land grant of the area, with no natural predators, the numbers of cattle were in the thousands. These herds did not need grids and lines to survive and settle: the desire for order is a very specific condition.

This reacquaintance became an example of how favourable the conditions in south-western Sydney were for cattle raising and kick-started what has now become one of Australia's most profitable industries. From their non-consensual arrival in Australia as seven to their ability to self-organise and sustain into the thousands when the colonialists could not, the abundance and health of these herds of free bovines was also the mechanism of their own reimprisonment. After their reacquaintance with the colonists, the calves were domesticated, the bulls were shot and salted for food, and the cows forcibly inseminated and their descendants became subjugated under the industrial logic of one of Australia's biggest industries (Boyde, 2013). Further, those Eora people who saw and reported the herds, also inadvertently started a process of mass dispossession of local custodians of the land westward and northwards across Australia under policies of land acquisition for cattle grazing. This process has wrought large-scale environmental destruction – from water shortages to land use emissions, greenhouse gases and soil and ecological impacts of pastures. Still, in the 1930s, 150 years after Cook stepped onto Kurnell, a herd of wild cattle – probable descendants of the inhabitants of the Cowpastures – were found to the west in a remote and rocky area of in the Blue Mountains, in the Kanangra-Boyd National Park.

Later, Kyja and I walk back down George Street from Wynyard to the more ordered rectilinear space of Martin Place. Having completed our first mission, we have moved on to our second – to navigate out to the Eastern Suburbs to purchase some roller skate wheels for Kyja. On first glance, the clearer gridded structure appears to be better landscape for her. More used to navigating along Melbourne's predictable grid, this more regular 'southern end' of Sydney make more sense for her navigational style. But still, it remains deceptive, haunted by the Tank Stream, and the attempts by the material to unsettle the ideological. Archival documents from the early years of the City of Sydney (1842-onwards) suggest that access to the Tank Stream defined urban planning through the city during the 1840s and 1850s. During this period, the Tank Stream was gradually paved over in an attempt to redress the maze of passageways and alleys around the first settlement areas in 'The Rocks', 'Circular Quay' and 'Wynyard', and to help them conform to a more modern nineteenth-century grid pattern – with limited success. Such layout alterations resulted in incoherence on the map and were incomprehensible to those trying to navigate. The geological formations of Sydney resisted transformation: engineers struggled to blast enough rock from the surrounding quarries to fill the stream. Indeed, even where it was paved over, the contours formed by the stream continue to define the topology of the landscape in Wynyard.

Ignoring the convoluted suggested route from Google Maps down through Hunter[2] Street, Kyja instead elects to follow the grid along a slightly longer, but simpler path up George Street – the way we arrived on the bus. This path takes us up Martin Place, a major pedestrian thoroughfare, which paves above the buried Tank Stream. Despite this, Kyja stands in the middle of the long promenade extending from our position, tapping her phone and sliding the Google Map under her fingers.

'So now I'm just being lost,' she says. Looking up, she squints at a street sign ahead.

Looking closer at Kyja's map, the blue dot of our position is nowhere near the blue line of the suggested path. Rather, the dot hovers on the screen, south of the jagged blue inscription, just above Martin Place with a little arrow pointing east towards Elizabeth Street. Kyja almost crashes into nearby pedestrians as she twirls around, trying to figure out if this crossroads is Pitt Street, and whether she's heading the right way through Martin Place.

The shift towards a French nineteenth-century ideal of geometric accuracy, which emphasised relationships between, not qualities of, landscapes (Picon and Ponte, 2003) meant that the spaces *in-between places* became

2 This was named for Governor John Hunter, the first European to meet the free herds of south-west Sydney.

homogenised and subdued. Rossi (1984) describes how, once certain places, structures or features are instituted within the urban designs, cities tend to continue along those axes, no matter how anachronistic they may appear now. Sydney is one of those particular examples (Thalis and Cantrill, 2013). Through repetition and intersection, the historical axes of the city are revealed; even in absurd correlations between bus lines and polluted streams – and, it seems, unique interpretations of navigational instructions. For example, after a fire destroyed an entire block between Pitt and Castlereagh Streets in 1890, a new street was marked out perpendicular to where the Tank Stream once lay. On this street, plans were also made for a General Post Office (GPO) to be located on the new street, with a grand frontage on what was the widest city boulevard at that time. Combined with the GPO, Martin Place could be understood as 'a tour de force of public architecture and public placemaking in Sydney' (Thalis and Cantrill, 2013: 112).

Martin Place was slowly extended throughout the nineteenth and twentieth centuries, all the way between George Street, where we now stand, and Macquarie Street, where the governmental buildings sit at the top of the hill. Through these transformations, it has become a more complicated site of rationalist planning where the tide of pedestrians has now all but erased the tide of the Tank Stream.

'So, it looks like, it's Elizabeth there,' says Kyja.

The green sign on the corner shows 'Pitt Street' in white letters. Elizabeth Street is several streets up the hill past a fountain and the Anzac War Memorial. The colonnade of the post office (sitting just to our right) is now dwarfed by the skyscrapers that surround it. Still, completely absorbed by the phone, Kyja continues in her navigation.

'The little blue dot seems to be pointing in the right direction,' she murmurs, 'but I don't trust that little blue dot.'

'Is Pitt Street on the map?' I ask, pointing towards the sign.

Kyja increases the detail with her thumb and forefinger, and replies.

'This is the annoying thing about, the annoying thing about this is that the little streets don't have their names on it until you zoom in really close ... like the laneways, or the pedestrian streets ...? Like, Pitt Street doesn't have a name on it. You have to zoom in that far just to find Pitt Street. And I needed to find Pitt Street to figure out if I was going the right way.'

Peering over Kyja's shoulder and dodging oncoming walkers, I do see that Pitt Street isn't labelled until the scale is increased so far that Kyja's little blue dot has disappeared off the screen and out of view.

She sighs.

'Now I have to zoom right out.'

Martin Place embeds itself in the spatial imagination: it holds gravitas that not even the 'little blue dot' can shake. Martin Place dominates the spatial orientation of the city. But once there, it appears that it has more influence attracting people to it, than directing them through and away. The first major waypoint on Kyja's suggested path was a bus stop on the corner of Elizabeth Street and Martin Place. Yet, despite the comparative simplicity of the gridded path Kyja has decided to take, the complicated instructions of the Google Map through the old swamp of the Tank Stream may well have been easier.

'Obviously, this would have been much more straightforward if I had followed the walking path as it suggested,' she murmurs. She spins again, and a man in a business suit dodges to avoid her.

'Why didn't you?' I ask.

'I don't know. I just like ....' Her eyes widen in memory, 'Oh – because it said Elizabeth Street near Martin Place, and I was like, I will go to Martin Place, and Elizabeth Street will then be nearer. I felt like I didn't need directions to Martin Place because I already know where Martin Place is.'

The Tank Stream still unsettles that part of the CBD, and so the streets are complicated, unevenly planned and were never fully integrated into the rectilinear patterning of this part of the city. So, wandering up perhaps the most well-known thoroughfare in Sydney, we find ourselves trying to make Kyja's little blue dot meet the lost blue line, awkwardly integrating the enduring axes of the near and far as they criss-cross through space. Looking up, finally, Kyja decides just to go straight on.

'The way I went isn't really slower anyway.'

## Tanija/Infrastructures

'I'll recognise it when I get to it.'

Tanija walks quickly up George Street, step by step, barely pausing for breath while talking energetically about a place she once found. We are heading north towards The Rocks, one of the first landscapes transformed after 1788. Tanija's aim is simple: to get to Sydney Harbour Bridge. Monumental (it takes 81,000 litres of paint to coat it) and iconic, the Harbour Bridge is an agglomeration of design and engineering. Spanning the harbour north to south, the bridge is constituted by a single steel arch pinned up by two sandstone pylons standing on each end. The Harbour Bridge is perhaps the most recognisable landmark of Sydney. It has been interpreted by artists, writers and commentators as a symbol of Australia's industrial and social achievement, the progression of the Australian urban imagination into the 'modern age' (and the high expectations it bestowed on the Australian public to live up to its grandeur) and, more recently, as a postmodern symbol to reflect upon how processes of modernity have shaped and reshaped Australian imaginaries, psyches and identities (Genoni, 2012). In her biography of Sydney, Australian writer Ruth Park writes:

> During the years of the Depression, the Bridge was known as 'the iron lung', for it kept so many people breathing. It gave work to a fairly constant number of 1400 men on the site, as well as thousands more in the steel, cement, sand and stone trades which supplied the immense quantities of materials. (Park, 1974: 74)

In its immensity, the bridge stands as both a social and a spatial symbol. Stories of its production tend to be hinged on the story of its material qualities (steel, cement, sand and stone), and their entanglement with the social processes of labour, working-class histories, political scandals and global economics. Here, the Harbour Bridge becomes synonymous with the story of the settlement of Sydney itself – its final stage – as the two sides of the harbour are connected, and the distance between landmarks and lived spaces become dissolved as earth is reformed into infrastructure. The image of the Harbour Bridge and the freeways which join it is somewhere between the modern notion of symbolic progress and the fluidity of post (or late) modernity (Soja, 1989; Jameson, 1991). Their experience is acutely volumetric, made of different levels and perspectives, shifting their affective qualities depending on who is looking, and from where. This sense of scale provokes intensities of feeling, as they tower above the spaces in which ordinary pedestrians walk. When driving along them, the freeways themselves are as high as halfway up the skyscrapers that line their route. The impression here is of a smooth choreography that could only be dreamed by the modern imagination: a frictionless connection of steel and stone, floating in the sky above.

Back on the ground, Tanija grasps her phone in her hand as she races onwards towards the bridge. On Google Maps on Tanija's phone, the bridge stretches from the south shore across the harbour. Volumetrically compacted, the highlighted freeways spilling out from the Harbour Bridge north out onto the bridge and east and south into the CBD dwarf the tiny perpendicular streets running between Circular Quay and the Hungry Mile through The Rocks below, as the overpasses cut through Milsons Point on the map. It's a distinct shift from the landscape imaginary of Sydney, which seeks to render some amount of legibility to the city. Here, the arched form of the Harbour Bridge is flattened to two lines bisecting the harbour. But despite the relative clarity of the map, the route is less simple. Cartographically level, it is easy enough to follow our position on Google Maps up George Street, highlighted in yellow. However, in the space directly beyond the Cahill Expressway into The Rocks, navigation suddenly becomes more complex and far more vertical. In the cartographic imagination, as it appears on the Google Maps, the flatness of the representation means that it can only show streets at the point of extremity between emphasised freeways and tiny streets, resulting in The Rocks peninsula being depicted without topography. This obscures a diachronic and dichotomous three-dimensional landscape that characterises The Rocks, formed by the flows into the Tank Stream and Sydney Cove, and scarred by the spatiotemporal layering of settler colonialism in its overlapping iterations of colonialism, modernity and postmodernity.

As we get closer to The Rocks, the Cahill Expressway looms overhead, along with the City Circle train line to and from Circular Quay. Its aspect, combined with the Western and Eastern Distributors that also feed off the bridge, suffocate any view we might have of The Rocks or the Harbour Bridge. Open to traffic in 1958 to allow road vehicles to flow quickly and freely from the North Shore, across the Harbour Bridge and into the Eastern Suburbs, the design of the Cahill Expressway (and, later, the Western Distributor) was met with criticism and resistance because of its impact on the urban landscape. As architect Jan Gehl states in a report for the City of Sydney on the topographic peculiarities of Sydney: 'These views are important in terms of understanding distances, creating a sense of place and in significantly characterising the individual streets. Thus it is unfortunate that some of these views are effectively blocked by the Western Distributor or by the Cahill Expressway' (Gehl et al., 2007: 27). As the Cahill Expressway cuts across the reclaimed land where the Tank Stream swamp once lay, it also effectively severs the north part of the city into two, creating a gloomy and dark undertone around Circular Quay by blocking any vantage point through the city from either side. On the map, like the landscape, it also underscores a spatial composition of the discourses of planning and cartographic reason that have shaped the northern part of the city. The Cahill Expressway serves as a boundary between two different kinds of cartographic spaces: the urban plan south of the Expressway adheres more strongly to the grid system that was developed and redrawn in Sydney during the nineteenth century; north of the expressway in The Rocks, the layout becomes deceptively simple and surprisingly illegible.

As Gehl notes, because the expressway obscures our view of The Rocks as we walk down George Street, it is difficult to measure distance, and we cannot see the Harbour Bridge. Furthermore, while it's possible to reason from memory that the Harbour Bridge is quite high rising somewhere above us on our left, and Tanija and I are currently at sea level, so I struggle to imagine how we might scale up to it from where we are now, somewhere below.

'How do you know when to turn left?' I ask.

Tanija hesitates.

'You need to turn left and go up some stairs, and then walk around a little bit and then go up some more stairs. There's lots of stairs.'

'Which is the left?' I ask again.

'Which is the left?' she echoes, hesitating.

'Do you know off the top of your head or do you have to see it?'

'No, no, no, I know…,' she pauses, 'But I can't tell you how many.'

Her hand moves forward as if laying out the streets and her lips count silently.

'I don't even think there is – if there is an "actual street"', she makes quotation marks with her fingers. 'I think it *is* the next street but it's a walking street, it's where the markets are – cars can't normally turn up it – but it's like on the opposite corner of the MCA[3] …. I'll recognise it when I get to it,' she laughs. 'Yes, I navigate by landmarks.'

Remembering the map from earlier, I know that it's not the next street, or even the street after that (or after that). But arguably, for Tanija, it *is* the next *important* street – a street that I can't necessarily discern, but one that she knows tacitly, and which stands out in its recognisability against the anonymity of all the other streets in Tanija's memory, if not the map.

As we emerge from the darkness under the Expressway, The Rocks, Circular Quay, and the Harbour Bridge manifest, before my eyes have time to adjust back to the light. The suffocation of being on the ground, while under several overpasses, is replaced by a blinding chaos of people, a hodgepodge sandstone buildings in the style of the early colonial era, advertisements and signage. The echoed noise of trains and cars that can be heard but not seen is replaced by the horns of ferries coming into the quay, the chatter of people in many languages, the clinking of glasses and the cracking of cutlery

3 This is the Museum of Contemporary Art, which sits on the western foreshore of Circular Quay.

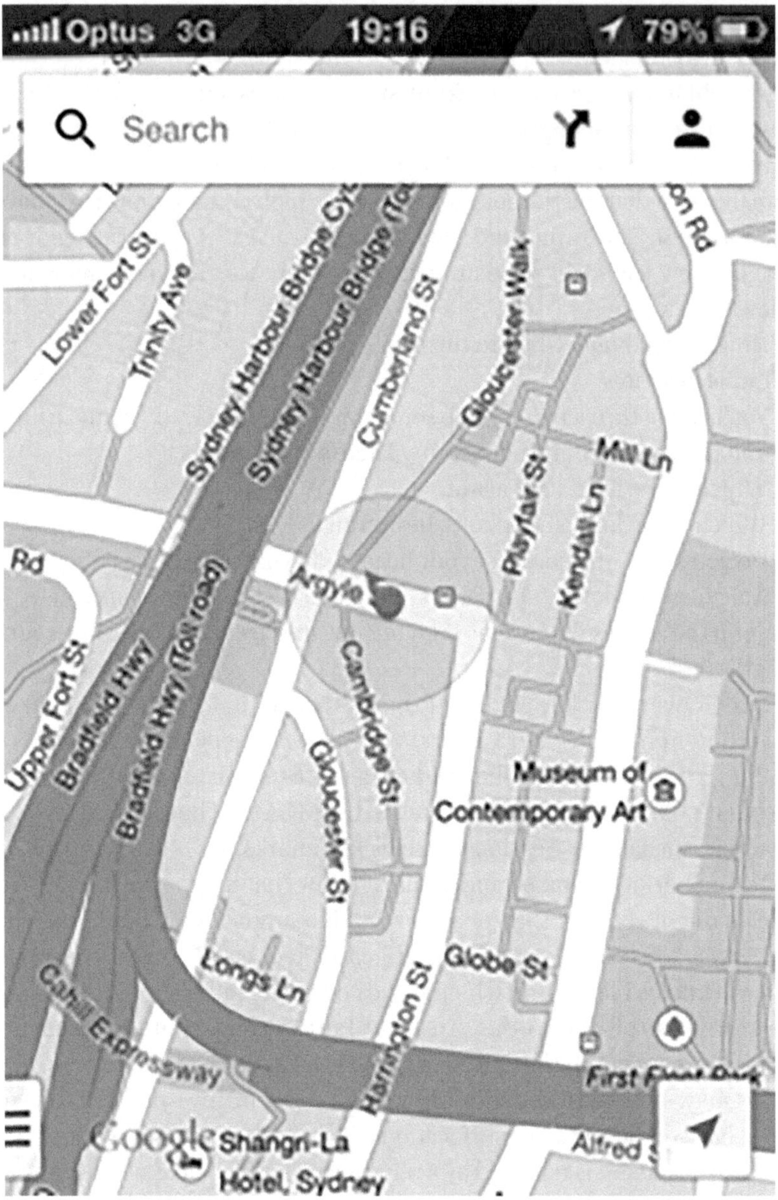


Figure 4.5. *The Rocks*. This is a screenshot from Tanija's phone of the Google Map of the Rocks. The Argyle Cut is at the bottom of the Argyle Stairs at the top of the map. Freeways in orange, the Harbour Bridge at the top, and the Cahill Expressway cutting across the bottom. The far left white road, unmarked, is George Street, and the pedestrianised section of Argyle Street is the thin grey strip between the two.

on crockery. Onwards, we are suddenly captured by throngs of tourists pouring out of souvenir shops (weighed down by cameras, sheepskins and boomerangs). Men and women wearing corporate dress smoke cigarettes outside renovated pubs, laughing loudly, beers in hand. Into the throngs of people, we continue along the steadfast guide of George Street, and Tanija completely abandons the map on her phone. Holding it loosely in her hand, she attempts to explain our path further.

'I, like, picture things literally like a Google Map,' she says.

Although the literal map is now ignored, the cartographic imagination retains a visual power not dissimilar to that of our destination, the Harbour Bridge. Tanija talks about her path as a 'snake', winding along a system of streets. This image seems at first orthogonally top down, but when she explains, her hand makes a surfing motion *through* the space in front of her, an amalgamation of mapping and touring in both representation and spatial embodiments. It is steadfastly situated, reaching out from her body into her future path. Joking, I ask her what colour her 'snake path' is, and she replies immediately and seriously that it is 'blue or green' – the colour of the navigation line on Google Maps.

The tools for finding spaces – maps, memory, mnemonic systems, intuition, wayfinding and collective discovery – both reflect space and also produce it. Umberto Eco writes: '[R]emembering is like constructing and then travelling again through a space' (1986: 74). Memory is spatial: it holds experiences that can be reconstructed and retemporalised. Tanija remembers and encounters these spaces around us through multiple temporalities: her past experiences, her present embodiment and her future reencounter. The folds of space are complex – both imagined and embodied, personal and social while at the same time, deeply interwoven with the fractures of the Tank Stream and the early settlements that we encountered with Kyja, and the social, botanical and unexpected that we explored with Marianna. Tanija's hand movements irrupt an attempt to articulate introspective translations between the embodied experience of *moving through* the geometries laid out by planning and waylaid by landscapes, and their graphic representation as she imagines it 'literally like a Google Map' on her phone. Effectively, she navigates her way through the distance between images and experiences, as well as the heterogeneous constellations as they have been spliced by cartographic reason, in a landscape that is always in the process of settling and unsettling. This becomes clearer as she explains further: Tanija's navigations retain a certain register of memory – landmarks or maps, she moves easily between both.

As we make our way up towards the Museum of Contemporary Art, the Harbour Bridge imminent, Tanija reminisces about how she has always been good at maps, because it was 'her job' to read the map and give directions whenever her parents drove somewhere.

'Mum would give me the map and be, like, tell me where I'm going,' she ruminates. 'She was *so* bad at driving that you had to tell her, like, y'know, in three turns you'll need to turn right,' Tanija makes another hand gesture to the right.

The relationship here in Tanija's navigation between the map and space is, perhaps, what Del Casino and Hanna (2005) might call 'map-space', but I disagree with this easy synthesis. Here she is not merely hybridising representation (the map) and space, but working on a far more performative level of translation between multiple logics, affects and imaginations. Telling these stories, she translates between the powerful image of the map with its attractive iconography and cartographic rationalism, and the everyday, tacit and interminably bespoke assemblages of desires, practices, socialities, encounters, embodiments and landscapes. Tanija's gestural descriptions are more apparent as an embodiment of this translational effort within mobile mapping. Here, the tensions between un/settling in materialities of the landscapes become corporeal in the lived liaison between space and cartographic reason in her memory. This is not a hybridised map-space: this is a series of micro-translations, as the space of the city is settled and unsettled in materiality and discourse ad infinitum, between ordered and disorded space.

Google Maps annoy Tanija now because she'd never been 'one of those people who need to turn the map', and now it often turns itself, with her as the axis, and the direction she is facing as the orientation.

'It shits me,' she says vehemently. 'The map doesn't move – I do!'

The map is fixed, settled on the phone, and Tanija is unsettled, moving, disrupting.

And so the map has been deserted now. Even though I am not convinced, Tanija has decided that she does not need it and so her phone continues to lay in her hand, better put to use as a prop for explanation than a tool for navigation. She is working from a different set of navigational tools, such as experience and memory, to those that she used, ten years old, reading the street directory in her mother's car and having to tell her when to turn right. Tanija and I occupy a heterogeneous set of spatialities and temporalities, assembled somewhere between embodiment, memory, space and cartographic reason: we share a local space, an immediate experience, but have different corporealities, memories, and ways of translating. The here-now of multiple spatialities, made all the more complex by my presence, irrupts into a constellation of representations, spaces, discourses and experience.

Between material and imagined bridges, spaces embodied now, in the past and into the future and the space coforming here, we encounter many open Massey-esque spaces of possibility of over there, the next turn, on the path, towards the bridge, and weaving through this, the space-time of the map, previously open now closed, once paper, sometimes digital, showing other spaces at other times, bleeding into back into our separate and combined here-nows. Back there-then also weaves into this space, shaping our paths and bringing us together and apart, an implicit reckoning that haunts our movements. This moment – quasi-event, if you will – of translation also differs to what Lynch (1960) or De Certeau (1984) might call a 'path', which emphasises movement *in* space, the performance, or practice, of what Tanija is currently trying to describe. So, already we have heterogeneity of space-times, into which our ever-close conversation with cartographic reason continues, now in lieu of absent maps in present memory.

The Rocks is a difficult area for landmarks, largely because, like the bridge itself, it is already a landmark. Small, damp sandstone cottages (like those found in northern mill towns in England), line ramshackle alleys and passages. Furthermore, to the uninitiated, any landmarks on the urban landscape or on the map are overshadowed by the bridge up ahead. Yet, Tanija confidently turns us west at the Orient Hotel, pausing mid-rant about heads-up wayfinding signs in London.

'We go up that way,' and we flow seamlessly onto the pedestrianised section of Argyle Street. Here, in the oldest built parts of Sydney, the urban landscape has been written and rewritten, a geography rendered grey by the reductionism of the map. It sits between the palimpsest geographies in gardens and neighbourhoods that Marianna encountered, and the colonial imaginaries that Kyja navigated through the Tank Stream and Martin Place: a lived space, dwarfed by the Harbour Bridge. The bridge is unambiguously present, the back alleys, arcades and other secret thoroughfares ambiguously absent: how Tanija will navigate this dichotomous space between monumental and quotidian and between down-here and up-there, phone in hand but not in use, calling instead on a constellation of memory, maps and imaginations, I do not know. The map shows no road that goes to the bridge from The Rocks, and looking up towards the bridge, the relative distance between us – and it seems insurmountable.

Before us, through the cliffs, sits the Argyle Cut, with the recognisable bridges spanning its width. The lowest bridge is Cumberland Street, and above that, the Bradfield Highway runs north towards the Harbour Bridge. When the First Fleet arrived, they found this landscape as a peninsula jutting out into the harbour, with tall, craggy sandstone cliffs running up to the ridge along the centre. Although, as we saw with Kyja, there were some plans to lay out a rectilinear grid pattern across the peninsula, efforts were hampered by the sheer cliffs and the uneven sandstone terrain. Yet, Argyle Street, originally in two separate sections on the east and the west of the cliffs, was to be connected by the Argyle Cut, a road cut straight through the cliffs. To realise that vision, planners and engineers then designed and reshaped the craggy landscape (for which The Rocks were named) through a deconstruction that took sixteen years (Ashton, 1995). These cliffs, which were once described in 1839 by James Maclehose as 'exceedingly steep – so much so that it is almost impassable for wheeled carriages of every description' (Maclehose, 1977: 80), ended up cut by brutalised convict labour (Karskens, 1999, 2009). It was a long, dangerous and laborious task to cut through the cliffs, and at the time it was considered a feat in engineering. Furthermore, the geological refuse from the cliffs as they were cut into and through was used to culvert the Tank Stream down the hill. This is a cartographic history – Argyle Street is a straight road, but it did not necessarily have to be so: only a cartographic imagination staring from an imagined planimetric angle (an angle of contemporaneous impossibility) at the shape of the shoreline and hatchings on the peninsula could conceive of a road straight through the cliffs.

This transference from imaginary to landscape is the domain of cartographic reason, that ambitious Cartesian project to reform space in line with geometry, to think in cartographic terms, is to cut through with cartographic reason. Here we see that processes like the Brick Kilns, the Tank Stream and the Argyle Cut are not isolated, but part of a dispersed network conceived through the map, arteries which transfer the landscape resources of the city from one part to another, to serve multiple purposes,: the combinations of these 'feats' of engineering meant that the Tank Stream, abused to the point of pollution, disappeared and forgotten only to leave traces in artworks, bars and street names. To date, the cut has surpassed this forgetting, remaining singular and unwavering in its function bridging The Rocks and the western side of the peninsula, with the Sydney Theatre and Barangaroo – but for how long?

The cut is precisely why Tanija knows to go this way. Dodging trees along the footpath up Argyle Street towards the cut, she talks enthusiastically about the first time that she walked through The Rocks when she had an exhibition in a nearby gallery a few years earlier. She didn't have a smartphone then, so it was with a paper map that she navigated – and Argyle Street appeared to be the only street that went under the thick lines of the freeway. Tanija became familiar with this space as she made her way between the east and west sides of the peninsula through the cut, the same purpose for which this thoroughfare was originally intended. Again cartographies and spaces collide in this mobile mapping, between her original paper map, the phone in her hand, her memories of being here and the peculiar formation of this perforated space. This is a shuffling of discordant discourses, as Tanija navigates her own ontic positioning, her memories both near and far, and the landscape with which she has marginal, but not quotidian familiarity. She has both read and remembered a map of The Rocks, with its freeways and flat representations, shapes but not toponyms, and she has walked through it, under the shadows of the bridge and together, the two statements in memory and cartography do not quite interpolate.

From our oncoming position up the hill, there is, to the right, a strange flow of pedestrians who seem to appear and disappear into the rock-face of the Argyle Cut, taking pictures as they go. As we near the mysterious crowds, and just before the Cumberland Street Bridge crosses the Argyle Cut, an unobtrusive sandstone archway reveals a staircase, the words 'Argyle Stairs' above voissiers and a keystone perched in the middle of them. Without pause, Tanija hustles us up the stairs, and when I've had time move past my surprise and gather my thoughts, I turn to her.

'How did you know to go up these stairs?'

She laughs.

'I was with somebody else who knew where they were going. So, I was following them.'

The stairs are bustling. The first set up leads to a small pedestrian street that tentatively clings between a series of terrace houses on one side, and the steep cliff on the other, with only a cast-iron railing to prevent a fall.

As I turn and look back, it strikes me that I have seen these stairs before – even if I have not been here. Later, as I write, my thoughts cast back to a photograph portrait I encountered of artist Tracey Moffatt, taken by Greg Weight in 1995. In the photograph, Moffatt stands facing down the stairs to the arch, the Cumberland Street Bridge in the background, holding a handheld mirror. In the mirror, the top half of her visage can be seen, a glimpse, perhaps, of connection between her and you, filtered through the mirror as she looks both backward and forward. It seems a pertinent portrait, not just of Moffatt herself, but of the place that I now find myself – perhaps dichotomously tranquil in the photo, but still jarring – what Garbutt (2015) might call a 'stutter' in the landscape. The appearance of the Argyle Cut unbalances temporal proprioception. It presents a disarming distance between the cartographic – an acutely and precisely designed vertical system across three levels adorned with decorative sandstone, beautiful cast-iron

Figure 4.6. *The Argyle Cut.* Pedestrians and tourists mill about under the Argyle Cut with the Argyle Stairs to the left. Its keystone and engraving can just be made out above the arch.

bridges and elegant lamp posts – and the haunting – a trauma reduced now to a nauseous, vertiginous, stutter made present by the worn crevices made by unwilling labour forcibly sent from one side of the world to another as they sliced through cliffs owned by a people in the midst of dispossession. Too quickly we move up these stairs, glancing briefly at some calligraphic graffiti quoting Henri Matisse, and at the houses, pushed up and onward by the eagerness of visitors behind us as they find the Harbour Bridge now within reach. That Bridge, which some half an hour ago seemed impossible to reach, and until a minute ago had revealed no path to it, suddenly opens up into space as we reach the top of the stairs, above the bustle of The Rocks onto Cumberland Street.

At the top of those stairs, Tanija points across the road towards a more grandiose staircase. This staircase is completely contained – protected from the rain by a concrete roof and edged by a neoclassical balustrade. Cartographies collide as the map now abandoned reveals another cartographic space in the carefully planned and levelled terraced paths as they ascend up to the bridge, side aspects and elevations. This is a structured imaginary – perhaps not flat like traditional maps, but certainly within the discursive bounds of cartographic reason. Rethinking Cartesian space into the third dimension, measurement has height and breadth as well as length. The cubic and volumetric geometries that form the architecture of Cartesian thinking become transformed into cubic and volumetric geographies that Tanija and I now find ourselves navigating. Such geometric geographies sandpaper against the planimetry of the map, but not against its discursive structure. Rather, together, they become complicit in the cartographic impulse, envisioning three-dimensional space as a volumetric resource that can be categorised, calculated and controlled. Referring back to the image of Tracey Moffat on the Argyle Stairs, we can see the way in which a geometric imagination engineers its material transformation into flat-surfaced terraces (like stairs, bridges or cuts), and dislocates the landscape in the process of spatial transformation.

A clear path can be seen now – up the stairs and along another ramp leading up towards the bridge overpass. The open space above us brings us full circle in this archaeology of monumental encounter from the imagined path and the icon retained in memory and culture to the imposing shadows and refractions cast off the steel structure of the Harbour Bridge as it sits before us, resoundingly material. The bridge, dreamed, designed and built by engineer and planner John Bradfield, is a vision of modernity, designed to leave behind the angel of history in a model of progress that moves forward – but that cannot erase the cuts on the landscape, nor undo the epistemological interventions into the spaces that have produced its possibility. Bradfield did not just design the bridge: his imagination etched downwards, too – into the subterranean tunnels of the underground City Circle line. Kyja missed Wynyard underground station as the blue dot on Google Maps slipped past, the Cahill Expressway obscures the raised platforms of Circular Quay Station, and I almost tumbled over the staircases leading up from the ground plane towards the bridge. Upwards and downwards, these vertical geographies and geometries are obscured by maps, and the full extent of Bradfield's vision is muted when the bridge is so prominent on the landscape. Jack Lang, the premier of New South Wales, who oversaw the construction of the Harbour Bridge later wrote of Bradfield in his memoir:

> I realised that he was a dreamer. But behind it all was his belief that he was planning the greatest city in the Southern Hemisphere. He wanted to be the Wren of Australia. As he talked you could almost see the new city emerging. He wanted to get away from the old bullock tracks. (Lang, 1956: 226)

Urban geographies are imagined into being – regardless of possibility and diversity of landscapes, and the heterogeneity of space – as Bradfield's Sydney continues to define the axes of the city not only in area but also by volume. But their appearances are obscured under the trickeries of cartographic reason, which can at once order disordered landscapes but hides its workings under the flatness of its representations. This means that finding spaces in volumetric geographies becomes a multiheaded task, interpreting between memories and experiences, and imaginaries and cartographies. The reinscription of this path in Tanija's memory unfolds as a series of steps – waypoints – punctuated by landmarks and secret archways. Cartographic reason pretends omniscience: it offers the entire path laid before you, a blue snake writhing through a volumetric grid flattened into two dimensions. Yet, in this moment of illumination, as we can finally map our entire way visually to the bridge, blind corners and blocked vantage points are revealed.

# 5. Feeling spaces

## Sarah/Hauntings

> '[Hyde Park] is full of statues of white men who kind of came here, and colonised, and erased the history of my grandmother and my grandfather's people.'

Where spaces can be found, they can also be lost. Sarah takes me on a walk through the CBD after work. Walking from the Lindt Café in Martin Place, we weave through an area filled with law courts and clothing stores towards Hyde Park. Eventually, we end up on the pedestrianised section of Pitt Street – exiting from a shopping centre onto the bright street below. This section of Pitt Street is closed to vehicular traffic and has now become one of the most expensive shopping strips for rental prices in the world – nearly as expensive as Fifth Avenue in New York City, and not far behind the Avenue des Champs-Élysées in Paris. As we walk along, dodging buskers who draw massive crowds, Sarah and I talk of the Tank Stream. Where our feet fall, the Tank Stream once flowed. The source that fed it is in Hyde Park – our destination – the oldest public park in Australia that sits within eyesight of Market Street where we now stand. As Sarah talks about it, she describes how the Historic Houses Trust still runs tours through the storm water drains, but, she laughs wryly, she believes that barely a trickle exists now because 'Europeans ruined it'.

We turn onto Market Street, and I ask her why we are headed to Hyde Park. Nodding at St James Station (another of Bradfield's stations), Sarah responds that the Sydney Festival is coming soon and that she's read about a large inflatable Stonehenge that is occupying the north-eastern corner of the park near the Archibald Fountain. She turns to me.

'Apparently, you can jump on it – which adds to the whole cultural inappropriateness – and it might be – although I might be dreaming – it might be called Sacrilegious.'

We stand on a street corner, waiting for the lights to change, looking at St James Station towards Hyde Park. St James is designed in the art deco

Wilmott, C., *Mobile Mapping. Space, Cartography and the Digital.*
Taylor & Francis Group, 2020
DOI 10.5117/9789462984530_CH05

Figure 5.1. *Fragments – Sarah, Nick and Shaun*. (Left) *Sarah's walk* – Friday, 8 January, Hyde Park, evening, overcast; (centre) *Nick's walk* – Saturday, 11 January, Chippendale, morning, sunny; (right) *Shaun's drive* – Saturday, 11 January, Chippendale – Collaroy, afternoon, sunny.

style, reminiscent of the Paris Metro, and with upscale boutique Hermés on the opposite side of the corner, the desire for a cosmopolitan Sydney speaks again. Between these two institutions of aesthetic desire – one architectural and the other high-end consumerism – two eras appear side by side and become merged into the present, a narrative generated over decades. This narrative is tinged with the same desires that built the Harbour Bridge over laneways and sandstone cottages and into the imaginations and the everyday life of those who inhabit Sydney. It is also the same desire which built the Brick Kilns, the Argyle Cut and Pitt Street Mall over the forgotten Tank Stream – buildings to generate capital, promenades in which to promenade: symbols of commercial and ideological ambition. The constellation of urban discursive monuments becomes further populated and slightly rearranged as we continue on into Hyde Park, yet another site of Sydney's ambition and another example of the strange shift between the top-down cartographic eye and the volumetric structuring of cartographic reason.

Sarah doesn't remember her first time in Hyde Park, possibly a school excursion many years ago, or perhaps with her parents when she was even younger – like so many things in Sydney it is as if it has always been here, and for her, it maintains a presence beyond memory, a kind of mythology. This is why she doesn't use maps – landmarks have a certain prominence, and it seems that she resents their intrusion into her own sense of space and time.

'They tell you where to go.'

'And you don't want to be told where to go?'

Deadly seriously, she replies, 'Not unless I want to be told where I have to go, which is like, most of the time, no. If I'm, like, going somewhere and I don't know where it is and I've got to be there by a certain time, then I might look at a map on my phone, but otherwise, I don't use maps.'

That's it, *finito*. Curious about her stern rejection of maps, I ask Sarah how she gets about on a daily basis.

'I have a set routine in the city,' she replies. 'Sometimes I go to other places, but, like yeah, I'd probably explain it in a way that would be, like, totally confusing.'

What about places she doesn't know, I ask. 'For instance, if I said ...,' I cast about for a place where she is unlikely to stumble, '... Barangaroo?'

Sarah gets excited.

'Uh, yeah ... I know where it is! And I know the history of it,' she sobers, 'but I've never been there.... If I've never been there then it doesn't really exist in my mind, as a place that I can give directions to.'

Barangaroo (on the other side of The Rocks from where Tanija and I found our way to the Harbour Bridge) is, for Sarah, a location that paradoxically exists but doesn't exist. It is somewhere that, for Sarah, has both a temporality as a transforming space – a past as rocky cliffs, shipyards and contest – but also a strange fluid geography where she can know where it is, but not how to get there. Barangaroo is a space of both consequence and ambivalence for Sarah, negotiating between the apparatus of the cartographic imagination and the power that it exudes, and her own lived space. Sarah's Barangaroo is both on her map and off *the map*. The distance between the map and the tour, the imagination and the path, between here and there has never seemed greater. Or perhaps, better, Sarah's Barangaroo is away from the map, away from the cartographical logics of seeing, of navigation and away from the simplified dialectics that we find in paradox. This aura of separation surrounds us as we head past St James Station. The bubbling fountain that memorialises Busby's Bore – the replacement water source for the Tank Stream which pulled water from Centennial Park – trickles gently to our left, and we dodge commuters rushing into the station to make our way up the western entrance to Hyde Park. At this place, the Bore still finishes some few metres beneath the ground in amongst the abandoned railway tunnels that lie dormant, flooded and only marked by the etchings of the urban exploration groups.

Ahead, the neo-gothic sandstone architecture of St Mary's Cathedral stares down at us, with the whimsical mythical figures of the Archibald Fountain in the foreground. It is a formidable building, architecturally gifted with both the political will of the Catholic Church and a clear line of sight running through the trees towards us. Looking up, Sarah tells me how her grandparents were married in the catacombs of St Mary's.

'I think that's the story. Well, I don't know if it's actually true ....'

A family mythology then, one which has been handed down through two generations with enough emphasis to reappear here, against the formidable architecture and landscaping that surrounds us. Her grandfather was in the army, her grandmother was from Cowra in the central west of New South Wales, and was heavily pregnant. Sarah is from up north in New South Wales near Lismore, and so I ask her how that happened, how they came to be married in the catacombs of a Catholic cathedral. After some thought she responds.

'Well, both my grandparents were Indigenous but fair skinned. Technically, my grandfather would have been considered white by the standard of the time, which meant I don't think he could legally marry my grandmother. Technically. Because she wasn't legally considered to be white. So –.' It is a long 'so' that she says at the end, more a sigh scaffolded by her breath than a fully formed word. It is also a sad 'so', which reaches into her eyes. I point towards the cathedral.

'But the church was prepared to marry them?'

Sarah turns towards me.

'She was eight and a half months pregnant.'

The politics of discourse and truth begin to emerge here in a surprising diversion from the kinds of exploration that Descartes and Leibniz undertook. Away from the map, the discursive power of cartographic logic, truth and reality dissolve into a realm that seems beyond the Cartesian grid or the Leibnizian universal characteristic. This story, which she can't know for sure is true, holds a weight that is, perhaps not greater but certainly more important than the well-known histories of Old Parliament House, Barangaroo and Pitt Street that she has colourfully discussed with all the enthusiasm of a vernacular historian. Where Bachelard (1994) searched through his house to uncover the poetics of space through his own memories and encounters with objects in attics and cellars, Sarah reiterates a memory that is intrapersonal, hers and someone else's, from outside rather than inside the cathedral. On the one hand, we have a cruciform building, regulated by the gothic revival architecture and strict spatiality of religious space, placed according to invisible longitudinal and latitudinal lines, near perfectly in line with the north-south axis. By the same token, Sarah explains how the qualitative taxonomisation of people and race led her grandparents to arrive here, to be illegally married in a church because, while her grandmother was fair enough to 'pass' in Sydney, she could probably not have done so in her home in Wiradjuri country near Orange or Cowra. And yet, despite the fierce oversight of discourses that uphold the hegemony of rationalist logic, and the apparatuses of cartographic reason, like architecture and parish registers which translate them into spatiotemporal dominance, Sarah's is a story to which the epistemological rules of cartography don't apply, where verifiability, taxonomy and calculability hold less domain than meaning, myth and emotion. She holds this story preciously, so much so that despite my own academic desire to search the parish registers for marriages, and to speak to the keepers of the cathedral about shotgun weddings in the 1930s and 1940s in the crypts below, I promise myself not to – because it seems somehow discourteous to the story of her grandparents, to misread it so badly to think that it is about history rather than about the past, to think that it is about a misconceived notion of truth rather than about something else, something spatial, something ghostly.

What else this story could be, if not about truth and history, is still little more than a barely articulated apparition on both Sarah's part and mine – and how that relates to Sydney and mapping, is still less well-formed again. It is at this juncture that we have wandered far enough up the hill that the life-size Stonehenge, *Sacrilege* (2012) by Jeremy Deller, comes into view between the cathedral and us.

*Sacrilege*, described by Deller as 'a way to get reacquainted with ancient Britain with your shoes off', premiered as part of Glasgow International Festival of Visual Art in 2012, then was shown during the Olympic Games in London, and now in 2014, we have stumbled upon the preview event in Sydney, before the season starts the next day. We can barely see it through the curious onlookers amassing nearby in this contemporary repetition of the Sydney International Exhibition in 1879. The exhibition was the first in the southern hemisphere and sought to emulate and parade the grand European cultural products of the time. The practice of cultural importation from Britain and Europe seems to have changed little in Sydney's yearning for cosmopolitanism. The media release about *Sacrilege* by the Sydney Festival was featured with a long quote by the Mayor of London, Boris Johnson – more words than from the artist himself – and the absurdity of the colossal European monuments resurrected and juxtaposed in this place is revealed in their discursive exteriority to Sarah's solemn and delicate story. The lifetime of *Sacrilege* (9-26[1] January 2014) is a

1 It should not be lost here that the finishing date is Australia Day, a national holiday commemorating the arrival of the First Fleet into Sydney Harbour/Port Jackson. This day is marked by increasing critique, with the political renaming of the 26th of January as 'Invasion Day' becoming more common.

Figure 5.2. *Hyde Park*, north-eastern corner, with *Sacrilege* (2012) by Jeremy Deller in the foreground and St Mary's Cathedral in the background, 2014. Port Jackson Figs intersperse with Moreton Bay Figs and Hills Figs.

much shorter than that of the Garden Palace that housed the Sydney Exhibition and stood not far where Sarah works, lasting from 1879 to 1882, before it burnt down (but we can only expect that in a world, as David Harvey and Anthony Giddens have pointed out, that is getting faster). Looking at *Sacrilege*, and then around at the public artworks that litter the park, Sarah sighs.

'[Hyde Park] is full of statues of white men who kind of came here, and colonised, and erased the history of my grandmother and my grandfather's people.'

White men, in all their modalities, have made their way here ever since Cook surveyed the east coast in 1770 and now, his statue stands nearby to our left, surveying the flocks of people gathering around to gawk mawkishly at this surreal inflatable monument. This, Sarah thinks, is 'pretty normal' for Sydney.

'I mean, you don't consider that [points to Stonehenge] of our own [Australian] identity,' she breaks off. 'Or, we do consider it to be our own identity because everyone here is Anglo-Celtic – so this is their history.'

As we walk nearer, we can see better how the Stonehenge vibrates and heaves with the numbers jumping gleefully from side to side.

'Oh, see you can jump on it,' she says, but then she adds, 'I don't think I want to jump on it.'

I don't want to jump on it either. The spectacle of *Sacrilege* has lost its glamour for us, at least, cast aside by our odd mood and this unrelenting sense of 'something else'. We stare at it for a while, and then Sarah speaks up and starts talking about Uluru,[2] a massive sandstone rock formation in the centre of Australia that has become a major tourist attraction.

'The thing is,' she says, 'people still climb it – and they die. They go back to their hotel room, and they just die. Like, people find them, like they're people who have climbed the rock, or have bits of the rock in their room and I don't know why that doesn't scare white people, but that scares me.'

For Sarah, the last vestiges of distance between original and the referent (absolutely crucial to the delighted squeals of the people bouncing up and down on the jumping castle/artistic intervention) have suddenly disappeared. Near and far become the same: a rock from Uluru is the same as Uluru, not different and not a smaller part, but the same – with the same power and same consequences. In the same way, for Sarah, this inflatable sculpture of Stonehenge is very not distinct from that which sits 20,000 km away on the Salisbury Plain – still a sacred site, as a representation, just like Uluru.

As Sarah and I depart from *Sacrilege* and head south through the park, I ask, 'Does it scare you in Sydney, or is Sydney too far changed to really contain that?'

'It scares me that I don't necessarily know where there are sacred sites in Sydney.'

'Because they're not demarcated?'

'Because we don't know where they are. Well, people know where they are,' she sighs. 'Everything has been changed, and so it's hard to identify the markers.'

Sarah's position defies what we know about simulacrum, about the space between maps and landscapes, and about the abstractive process of representation. Land, site and country, in Sarah's understanding, is neither reducible nor abstractable. The meanings and powers of a landscape or place are transportable and transferable in multiple modes across multiple contexts, imbuing itself into different spaces and times, into hotel rooms, into cities. *Sacrilege*, Hyde Park, the Tank Stream, the Brick Kilns and St Mary's Cathedral are now subject to a discursive inversion: not to think of Stonehenge through *Sacrilege*, but to think of *Sacrilege* through Stonehenge, to find a monument in this particular landscape archive and to think it

2 Uluru is the name given by the Pitjantjatjara people of the Anangu, for whom the rock is sacred. In 1873, surveyor William C. Gosse named it Ayers Rock to honour Sir Henry Ayers, the Chief Secretary of South Australia, which would remain its official (governmental) name until 1993, when it was changed to dual name status Ayers Rock/Uluru. In 2002, after a request from the Tourism Association in Alice Springs, the names were reversed to Uluru/Ayers Rock (Northern Territory Government, 2016).

through from position of subjugation, rather than hegemony, and to give that position the full discursive weight of power. Borges (1998), famously, describes an emperor who desires to map his territory, and eventually, the world becomes mapped so completely that it is 1:1, and the map becomes the territory, a simulacrum as argued by Baudrillard (1994). Sarah arrives from the opposite direction, which at first glance subordinates the map to the power of the landscape. Rather than the map becoming the territory, the territory becomes the map – Stonehenge becomes this absurdist dirigible in front of us, and Uluru is embodied in the rocks that have been taken away. And so, in Sarah's position, meaning persists, more forcefully and more vengefully the further and longer it travels, rather than being lost in representation.

'White people don't care,' she says. 'They like it if they can go on holiday and see a sacred site then that's cool, but when it gets in the way of their day-to-day life, they've got this sensibility, like, you know, it's irrelevant. We've got a couple of those sites, and it doesn't matter if that site isn't Gadigal or – if it's Wiradjuri then it's okay, they're all the same thing. But it's not. It's like saying so, we've got this thing in France, and so we don't have to have this same thing in Norway, or, the Norwegian version of it, because we have a version of it in France. Which I don't think Europeans would be happy about.'

We walk under the Port Jackson fig trees down the large avenue that forms the spine of Hyde Park, and it now seems completely transformed, rewritten by a cartographic imagination over several iterations, designed and redesigned in the form of triangles, semi-circles and straight lines. Now, more than 75 years later, it emerges as if it has always been there, worn into normalisation by new, more modern buildings that distract from the temporal shifts of space.

I ask, 'If you could regain a way of reading the landscape or it were possible, how would you, like if you could find a way to read whether or not particular places were sacred or not? Are those stories completely lost, or – ?'

'I don't think those stories are completely lost. I know there is an Aboriginal burial mound under or next to Central Station. Like, that said, I would say Europeans don't really care about Aboriginal cemeteries and if it was a European cemetery then they might care, but then Wynyard is on top of one of the first, if not *the* first cemetery in Sydney. Central, across the road from Central – Devonshire Street – has the precursor to Rookwood necropolis was there prior to Rookwood, so I suppose Europeans don't even care about their own cemeteries so why would they care about a burial mound? I don't know how you reclaim those things ... like, Hyde Park has completely overwhelmed something that was sitting here before – this,' she gestures around at the footpaths, the Port Jackson fig trees and the large skyscrapers surrounding the park, 'is all made – this wasn't what it looked like. Even the green spaces of the city have been flattened and restructured irreversibly.'

Crossing Park Street into the south end of Hyde Park, she frowns at a statue of Queen Victoria.

'They haven't just gone and put footpaths through what was originally here – they got rid of what was here and then created a park here in the European sense, even though there might be natives [plants].' She cranes her neck looking at the trees. 'I don't know if there are that many natives. There might be, I dunno. But they've used them anyway so it's been destroyed and you can't really reclaim something that's been destroyed.'

This sentiment of troubling the way in which space and spatiality have come to be conceived in the context of cartographic reason becomes a theme of this walk. As we walk along, Sarah talks about the way in which the park has been built – neat promenades laid out in geometric patterns. This, she iterates, is a space of leisure that is also heavily policed to remove homeless or disruptive people. The park becomes a site of biopolitical control between ordered and disordered bodies, an abstraction away from the underlying stories of the landscape. The relationship between the discourses of colonisation and natural/unnatural in Sarah's estimation is still unclear.

I ask, 'Do you think it's been fractured by colonisation? Do you think it was going up on this process where it always does change but slowly and builds and then something happened – or do you see the city as being somewhat natural?'

Sarah sighs and stares at the mowed grass (unusually green for the summer) and the hotels that surround the park.

'The city's not natural – I mean – the British came here 226 years ago like, it's sprung up in less than that because they didn't start building straightaway. All of these buildings have come, and all this damage has been done in a really short period of time. And so it's not something you can reverse – it's just going to keep getting bigger, and there's not enough room in Sydney.'

Her claustrophobia is palpable. The questions of the natural and the urban become decentred in Sarah's interpretation. Her experience of the park is one of relentless progress, of building on top of histories and spaces, of the implementation of order into the landscape. She speaks more quickly this time.

'There's like 5000 new people every week or every month – it's already overcrowded so they're just going to keep building and building until you can't see the sky.'

Curious, I turn to her.

'And the sky is important?'

'If you can't see the sky then everything is dark. I mean, you can't see the stars at night. The stars are important. The stars show you where to go. And you can't see them, so ....'

'Why do you think the stars show you where to go?'

''Cos they've always shown – like you follow the constellations.'

'So, like navigation or do you think it's more of a future thing?'

'Well, traditionally Aboriginal people, among other way used like a lot of other people used the stars to navigate all the places of the world. But also I think it's important to see the sky. If you cover it with buildings.'

'You've got no future. You've got no direction?'

'You can't go anywhere. You can't go anywhere,' she looks up at the overcast weather, 'if you can't see the sky anymore – everything is filled. Some things need to be unfinished. You can have a future. You can do something with that future.'

Curated ideologies rewrite the landscape, the landscape becomes the map, and space becomes the domain of cartographic reason. Sarah has not given up on space, or the future. But with every increment that is filled further, space is denied its heterogeneity. As Sarah says, some things need to be unfinished.

'And eventually Hyde Park is gonna be a series of apartment buildings. You don't really value land as somewhere to hang out if there is money involved.'

New colonialisms, as the landscape becomes the map, it subsumes it and rewrites it, again – from colonialism to capitalism: expanding rationalities, expanding cartographies. Nothing is lost, it is only forgotten.

## Nick/Intuitions

> 'Can't you tell where you are by the feel of the road, like the general slope and the degree?'

'Do you want to try to find one?' asks Nick.

We're walking about in Chippendale, another leafy suburb in Sydney's inner west. Sandwiched between Sydney University to the west, the University of Technology, Sydney (UTS), to the north and Central Station to the west, Chippendale is an odd mix of terraces and converted warehouses, a mixed-use area with homes interspersed with design studios, art galleries and start-ups. Nick and I met up in Broadway Shopping Centre not far away, and after a brief discussion about his new-found enthusiasm for cycling by way of getting fit, he's offered to take me on a tour of the bike paths in this area. He explains how he uses his phone to track his route as a way of gauging how much exercise he's undertaken (helpfully sending me a .kml example of one such route), and how a proposed series of cycle paths through Chippendale will result in him being more connected to the city, and able to cycle more on the paths. He directs us towards where the proposed path will be placed on Shepherd Street ('possibly the next one'), and as we walk deep into Chippendale, Nick explains how the path here will connect up with the new one near his house, at least according to the plans he's read online.

At the same time, he isn't sure if all the paths marked on the plans have already been built because he's only seen the plans released by the local council, the City of Sydney. But, he reasons, bike paths have their own temporality, since the newly completed bike lane outside his house has been furnished with a 'Don't Ride' sign. He tells me that this is presumably because they're waiting for the rest of the network to be built. Interested in how a completed bike path with a 'Don't Ride' sign would appear on his mapping data, I turn to him.

'So, with the bike lanes that are on Google Maps – are they marked as closed or open?' I ask.

It appears that I have misunderstood.

'It's not on Google Maps,' he says, 'I found out about that information on the Cycleways network where they talk about how they're building it.'

This is a reference to the Sydney Cycleways website coordinated and run by the City of Sydney. The City produces their own maps and navigation tools to encourage residents to cycle to and from work and in-between suburbs in order to address congestion problems in the Sydney CBD (City of Sydney 2011). Nick appears to be keeping himself conscientiously up to date on where the cycle paths will be built and how he could use the new routes to get from here to there.

As we reach Shepherd Street, he speaks again.

'So this is where they're going to build it.'

There is no sign of a bike path on Shepherd Street yet, but in-between the leafy trees and terraces, for Nick, the promise of it has been drawn into being through the plans and images online. He seems disappointed that there is no path here by way of comparison to the internal image he describes to me, but, given the presence of a new path near his house, Nick reasons that there should at least be one cycle path in production somewhere nearby.

And so, he offers me the adventure of trying to find a bike path somewhere in Chippendale. Ushering me on (coffee in hand and wheeling his bike), he motions forward.

'Let's wander up to the new development where the old brewery used to be.'

The old brewery, once Carlton Breweries, is now a massive housing development named Central Park, with the manufactured space and time specific to post-industrial residential developments and narratives of the global city (Sassen, 2001). His logic follows as such: where there is construction, there are bound to be new bike paths. This isn't a terrible logic – but it does seem to be borne from the generic nature of planning documents. A connoisseur of artist impressions and architect's drafts, Nick ardently describes the information they contain.

'Tree here, tree here, tree here. This road will now be right turn only.... This parking spot will be lost and new trees planted.'

These documents elicit profound imagery of the future construction of Sydney for Nick – not because it is wishful thinking or even misplaced anticipation, but because his understanding of the city, of the way in which it connects, is so deeply embedded in his chosen mode of transportation. For this reason, he expresses dissatisfaction with Google Maps, preferring instead to meticulously plan out his route using the Sydney Cycleways maps. When I query why he does so, he responds: 'Because I like to plan it myself, that's why – Google doesn't tell you a sensible way to ride, so there's no point using that feature of Google.'

Cartographic reason maintains an authority (Crampton, 2003) in mobile mapping practices through technological omnipresence and the normalisation of the cartographic mode of thinking about space. Furthermore, it also conceals other ways of reading space and producing spatial knowledge. I was expecting Nick to tell a similar story to Kyja, a destabilisation of vernacular wayfinding from here to there by the insistent and didactic recommendations of the map. Instead, I am confronted with Nick's outright rejection of the normalisation of digital mobile map use, simply because Google Maps does not work in this instance, and so does not offer anything useful. Nick prefers to take control of his own navigations, 'to plan it [himself]', and so sets up his receipt of the spatial knowledge that maps provide according to his own systems of importance, resonating with Sarah's rejection of the cultural authority of cartographic logics. He explains his position further.

'There's nothing to make me want to use it [Google Maps] over the paper one,' he says, 'they're exactly the same. They [Google Maps] are not more accurate, the predictive doesn't work, so why – I'll look at the paper one and then while I'm riding, if I want to check where I am, I'll pull up the Google one.'

Not only does Nick disrupt the normalisation of mobile map use for navigation, but he also problematises one of its key pillars: accuracy. Accuracy, arguably, is one of the key sources of a priori and axiomatic authority that cartographic reason enjoys (Crampton, 2001). A feature of online mapping platforms that has been significantly touted in cartographic literature (cf. Sui and Goodchild, 2011) is that digital maps have the ability to be updated regularly. This means that, regardless of when you pull up the map, it will always be the most up-to-date version. Long gone are the days when last year's street directory turned you incorrectly down a one-way street or failed to take into account roadworks, new streets, closed streets and changes in street toponymy. But, as Nick has just laconically identified, that only matters if the map already contains the information that you need to get from here to there (or there to here). If not, you need to find another map or another source of knowledge. The notion of accuracy between different cartographic technologies is predicated upon a discourse that suggests that, first, accuracy is contextual to need, and, second, that technological progress should apolitically reify the pillars of cartographic reason by affording them greater might, rather than questioning and destabilising them.

Curious, I ask Nick to expand on what he means about there being no difference in accuracy between Google Maps and the Sydney Cycleways map, despite one being constantly updated digitally and the other being immutable on paper. After a moment he replies in a matter of fact tone.

'They tell you the quickest way to ride. They don't say, 'You could spend an extra five minutes on your 30-minute ride and ride along this bike path.' They say, 'You can save five minutes by riding along this road.'

And so we have hit upon the crux of the deficiency of Google Maps compared to the static ones provided by the City of Sydney: Google Maps does not know what it is like to cycle in Sydney (a perilous and heart-racing task). Despite the overarching discourse of digital cartographic platforms being more accurate and up-to-date, they are not necessarily more sensitive to Nick's needs as a cyclist. There is a disconnect between the discursive dependence of cartographic reason on the stability of meaning of 'accuracy' and 'up-to-date information', and Nick's humble dismissal of these discursive interpretations in favour of his own needs, knowledge and navigation. At first, Nick's seemed to be a different political reasoning to Sarah, whose resistance against Google Maps, and maps more generally, was an intense mixture of anger and personal defiance towards the epistemological failings of cartography and cartographic reason, and the discursive power it holds over her, the landscape and the past. It was also deeply embedded in the history of colonisation, and the brutalities of erasure and forgetting that have been intertwined with the development of Sydney (James, 2013). But there *is* a relationship between Nick and Sarah's misgivings. Somewhere in the translation between cartographic reason, the heterogeneous and complex landscapes and the lived spaces of Sydney misunderstandings arise. These misunderstandings arise because of incompatibilities of need and value, and because axioms established by cartographic reason in the primacy of its emergence have become an opaque quagmire of values – truth, enlightenment, and transcendence.

Accuracy holds a key conceptual role in the development and valuation of GIS and other digital cartographic technologies (Goodchild, 2007, 2009). Furthermore, a large body of research questions the hegemony of accuracy in cartography by pointing out that maps lie (Monmonier, 1996) and hold secrets and silences (Harley, 1988b). This critique has carried on through to critical analyses of GIS and digital cartography, especially analysing the results of crowdsourced or volunteered geographic data (Haklay, 2013). Yet, what Nick presents to me is a discursive questioning of the meaning of 'accuracy' itself. In Sydney, for Nick on his bike, accuracy means something different and is instead allied with the ability to describe and recommend a particular experience of the world, rather than a Cartesian aim to capture and order it under one system of geometry. Nick prefers the bike paths over main roads and has less interest in shortest distances or faster speeds (those portents of Virilio-inspired modernist desires) than in establishing his own rhythm and modus operandi of moving through space. On that question, he says that he prefers the cycle paths.

'They're nicer – it's more enjoyable. I guess because they're safer, they're more enjoyable.'

It's the checklist theory, Nick argues, that connects enjoyment and safety. He describes how checklists were introduced into doctor's surgeries, 'not because doctors are stupid', but rather, to free up their mental space so that they can think about other things. In practice with cycling, this means that you don't need to focus on worrying about cars, pedestrians and other cyclists, and so it becomes more enjoyable.

'Less things to hit, less things to hit you,' he concludes.

Thus, it is important for Nick that when he plans his journey, poring over the dotted lines on his paper maps, that his route is enjoyable. At odds with his enthusiasm for plans and visualisations, Nick approaches space as a terrain to be moved through, and so carefully curates the journeys that he makes so that in the future moment where he embodies other spaces, he enjoys them. This is not a cartographic impulse, like that which Said (1993) describes, to calculate, conquer and control: instead, Nick's movements reveal themselves to be far more multidimensional than blue dots on screens. He doesn't even use maps for walking and when I ask him 'Why?' he responds in that same decisive tone.

'You don't plan your journey when you walk.'

You just walk. Or, at least, Nick does.

Underlying the politically ambivalent concerns of accuracy and interoperability is the fundamental question of reading space itself and the way in which the axioms established by cartographic reason limit how we conceive of every day and lived practices where people read and produce and negotiate all the open possibilities of space.

'I think it's more how someone grows up,' he states pensively, 'how they memorise routes.' Pre-empting my next question, he goes on.

'I say that because I met someone from Canada who couldn't tell where they were because the streets didn't have the north and the south on them – and I went, 'What? Can't you tell where you are by the feel of the road, like the general slope and the degree?' and he had no idea. I was dumbfounded, but I guess, we're in Sydney, in Australia, and we've got hills and everything everywhere and so, just by the general slope of the land you kind of go, oh yeah, I'm here and you can look up and you can see UTS[3] as you get closer, and stuff like that.'

It is an unexpected, but not altogether unsurprising, return to this odd intuitive feeling of how you know where you're going, especially when you're busy not using maps. Like Marianna, who just gets lost but always knows where she is, Kyja, worrying over the map but figuring it out through memory and luck, Tanija, who couldn't tell me which turn was Argyle Street (but just knows), or Sarah, who worries about different landscapes (for fear of what might happen), Nick returns, too, to this other idea (the feel of the road and the general slope of the land). What is it about the landscape of Sydney that evokes such particular 'feelings' – of hills and flowers, of sacred sites and secret staircases?

We are getting close to Central Park now, and it strikes me that as he said it, Nick's waypoint, the UTS Tower, comes into view behind the new development. Until the development of Central Park, the UTS Tower (also known as Building 1) was the only skyscraper to grace that part of Sydney's skyline, earning it fondness from some (particularly those, like Nick, who studied there) and ire from others like journalist Mike Carlton, who wrote:

3 This refers to the University of Technology, Sydney, based in Ultimo.

> In any competition to name Australia's ugliest building, the University of Technology, Sydney tower on Broadway would be right up there at the top. It is a menacing concrete monolith in an architectural genre that the old East German Stasi brought to perfection. Every time I pass it I half expect to hear the cries of the damned being tortured in dank cells. (Carlton, 2012)

Far from the dense and disciplining image conjured by Carlton, the UTS Tower landmark across the sky acts as a guide for Nick as he cycles. These beacons, if you're a cyclist, are important because they moderate and structure the rhythm and route of your path through space when you don't necessarily have the time to stop, check a map, and reconsider. But, as Nick emphasised, I now realise that the tools that cartography offers to help you determine what kind of path you'd like to take are limited and limiting.

The breeze drifts past, and I turn to Nick and ask him about the relationship between the City of Sydney map and his method of 'feeling the road' and navigating by slopes. How does he work between the cartographic view and the space and landscape of Sydney? Most maps, I argue, don't have slopes unless they're topographic.

'No,' he returns, 'but the slopes you can feel.'

He starts making motions with his hands and head as if placing himself on a bicycle somewhere unbeknownst to me.

'Yes, I'm continuing in this direction, because I'm continuing up this slope. I haven't accidentally changed around, or this road hasn't secretly curved on me, and stuff like that.' It's an acute method of navigating an acutely deceptive landscape. The craggy hills of Sydney combined with the indefatigable intentions and defeatist realisations of urban planners have resulted in an odd jumble of roads in this area. Following the remit of pragmatism, some of these roads twist, turn and obscure any clear sense of the path ahead, but they do tend to provide a soft gradient up the cliffs and down the gullies of Sydney. Others, occupying remit of geometry and planning, provide gloriously clear vantage points down their length, so you know exactly where you are headed, but can be perilously steep and near-impossible to cycle down safely. Either way, there is a risk of getting lost or of losing control of the bicycle. Furthermore, the hills provide a distinctive topography that is useful for vernacular navigations, often branching out along the spine of the numerous peninsulas that pierce Sydney Harbour, much like the cliffs that Tanija and I scaled to find the Harbour Bridge. These hills are difficult to gauge on maps, and often the only sign that they exist is irregular winding roads echoing their contours. Straight lines, on the other hand, obscure the texture of the landscape and effectively silence this vernacular mode of getting about, and make the route appear deceptively straightforward. To clarify, I say again: 'So, actually, you use the hills to feel your way?'

'Yeah – not north-south,' he replies referring back to his Canadian acquaintance, 'To feel that I'm going in a constant direction.'

For Nick, the hills provide a truer estimation of direction (and the consistency of direction) while he's on the move. Without the opportunity to stop and pull out Google Maps to check where he is, he relies on a combination of memory and his off-the-cuff reading of the terrain along which he cycles, and it is this mapping practice that is formative of his experience of Sydney. Sydney, like Los Angeles, is a city for cars. This is reflected in the ubiquity of the street directory, the prominence of roads in maps and the emphasis on freeways and overpasses (and even tunnels) without space given to other landscape features. The relationship between cars and cartography has been inherited by Google Maps, if the lack of information for cyclists is any evidence. Central Park looms ahead. As we move into its manicured grasses and blinding pale pavements, Nick points to signs that suggest a bike path will go through here: shared cycle ways, low-speed limits, speed humps specifically designed for cyclists and ample public space. Still, I notice that the UTS Tower is all but obscured by the new development. I ask Nick if he thinks his experience of Sydney, as a cyclist non-driver, is reflected in Google Maps.

He pauses. 'I don't think my – I don't think drivers' experiences are reflected in Google Maps.'

'What do you think *is* reflected in Google Maps?'

'It feels more factual, it feels really old now. Lots of the street views have buildings that didn't exist – like this part [gestures around] isn't even on Google Maps, it's been the brewery, still, and there's the old brewery there.' He points behind us where an old brick building has been renovated into an art space, the words 'Carlton' still faintly printed onto its chimneys.

The old Carlton Brewery, which typified the grimy, crowded industrial history of Chippendale, sits in its new iteration as an art space, designed to support Sydney's new, young creative class (cf. Bennett and Beudel, 2015). The Google cars that log Street View and the algorithms that create routes haven't quite caught up to the present, which slips past us as we stand near the brewery. The limits of spatial representation are being eaten by the limitlessness of temporal curation, or more accurately, by a designed, branded and consumed future full of all the Kantian dreams of cosmopolitanism (Harvey, 2000a). This is a different kind of cartography, but not as far as imagined from the halls of cartographic reason. The Central Park website is littered with references to Chippendale's dark past – stories of Pig Mary scrabbling about for offal and struck down by poverty, of boxers and sleazy underground gambling dens, and of notorious criminal kingpins and the lives they lived here. It seems history is now a major selling point for those looking to capitalise on the future (a studio apartment now sells for a minimum of A$800,000), and the promise of cultural capital now includes the designs and dreams of architects from Paris and Copenhagen, as well as London and Sydney. However, the cosmopolitan, modernist dreams that built Bradfield's Harbour Bridge and the art nouveau architecture of St James Station have changed a little in this contemporary iteration. We now find the aesthetic architectures that structured the landscape transformed into a zealous consumption of past and of place – living without feeling. This is as much the case with cartographic reason as with architectural design, especially at the point where they emerge as allies in the pursuit of an ever-evolving process of colonisation that now irrupts through 'creative' gentrification and white-washing in Sydney's inner suburbs (Gibson, 2006).

Nick argues that Google Maps doesn't represent knowledge – rather, it just presents data, however old. In doing so, I would argue that it instead proposes one kind of knowing: of the didactic navigation that almost had Kyja transfixed as we made our way up Martin Place. Further, it suggests that data consumption, in itself, is perhaps more about mirrors to the cartographic imagination than about reflecting ways of knowing. By the same token, Central Park doesn't fully construct Nick's, or anyone else's, understanding of this space, but rather proposes how it should be understood: of progress-driven creative hubs that refuse to look carefully and see the cycles of colonialism in their grout. But, like Google Maps, Nick rejects the explicit framing cast by the new development on the past and the present and instead favours the tacit, the intuitive and the habitual. Despite its metamorphosis as an imago of art and creative enterprise, Central Park, for Nick, remains 'the old brewery'. In doing so, he also rejects the narrative that newer knowledge is necessarily better and that technological development for the sake of newness doesn't necessarily marry with social and cultural knowledges embedded in practices and the everyday: the intuitive knowledge of doing, rather than the cartographic knowledge of looking. Google Maps, he says, does public transport really well. But, he says it's a commuter map, and he wouldn't necessarily use it to find cafes or other places like that.

'I don't know who would,' he adds.

Nick's easy suspicion of the schism between old breweries and new developments is translated into his experiences with maps and movement. He wouldn't be persuaded to use a GPS device on his bike, or even when he learns to drive.

'I think people should learn – if they're going to drive around the city, they shouldn't use the GPS. I find it, people that I have seen use it, they don't seem to know where they are – so, I think people need to be more intuitive as they drive 'round and get directions.'

Intuition, here, is important for Nick because people should know where they are, and by association, know the city. If you don't strike out on your own and insist on using a GPS regularly, then you don't discover the city or get 'a feel' for it. You don't learn which paths to take and which roads lead to which. Eventually, Nick says emphatically, this feeling is lost altogether.

'That you don't know how to – what's a one-way street and how to turn right and you end up scared of the city and stuff, like that.'

Devices like the GPS take cartographic reason a step further: by way of a combination of Cartesian reasoning and Leibnizian systems, the GPS doesn't just represent the landscape; it takes the implicit directions embedded in the map and makes them explicit. In doing so, it shapes mapping practices, and, according to Nick, makes people compulsively subservient to cartographic reason by making the city a place of danger, rather than of exploration and enjoyment. Using a GPS while moving through the city means that '[p] eople don't get instincts', they think the roads are too narrow and there is too much traffic. He describes how he's seen drivers not realise that if they miss a turn, then they can just go 'around the block' and try again.

The city, says Nick, is not like a software program.

'It's more like intuition, y'know, feeling and this kind of, yeah, gut feeling. That type of thing.'

People become embedded in technology, in a way in which Nick resists as he carefully plots out his route, commits it to memory and then traces it through his intuition and the feel of the hills.

'It's just a personal personality, and how people treat technology and how they want to use it and some people just have the mindset that "I want to listen to the GPS".'

But what drives that motivation? What makes his wayfinding different? What makes him navigate the way that he does and understand the landscape in this intuitive way? He's not sure.

'I dunno,' he says 'I know what you're saying, but I can't think of how to word it exactly.'

That's a fair point; I can't think of how to word it either. So I ask him about Sydney around us instead, hoping to sit on the edge of the limits of representation: How does he produce his own spatial knowledge when it is all feeling and intuition? How does this relate to the strict conditions of possibility placed by cartographic reasons? He looks at me, sighs and then looks around.

'In terms of just knowing, I mean, as I stand here, I know Pyrmont's that way and the Fish Market is just down there and I know roughly how far North Sydney is – because I know those things I can, you know, navigate in-between them, or left or right of them, 'cos the sun's there, you know.'

He's right; those places are that way, just down there and North Sydney isn't too far. Central Park all around us obscures any visual reference that we could see, the UTS Tower barely peeping out from behind its glass façade. No hope of seeing the tall buildings down near Pyrmont, or the view down to the Fish Market, or the Harbour Bridge that leads to North Sydney. But these are relational spaces that he has constructed in his memory, and as he describes them, like Tanija, he maps them with his body – arms pointing and curving, careful not to spill the coffee that is still in his hand.

'And I guess, it's, it's being less observant. Like surely if someone knew where the sun was and knew something was in the direction of the sun, then they wouldn't have to – and they knew where North Sydney was, surely they wouldn't really have to rely on GPS that much.' Looking at the road, and paying attention to the GPS breaks the rules of the checklist theory. If you're too busy thinking about other things, then you don't look around, and you don't begin to read space. Hills, trees, coasts and sun combine in Nick's personal topography, embedded in the seasonality and shifts of Sydney, a navigational method that is fluid as he rides down the streets and relies on his own subjective fix-points to help him navigate.

Looking up, he smiles ruefully.

'Although I don't know with this stuff,' he waves around at Central Park, 'if it,' he points now to the UTS Tower, 'will still be a landmark because you can't see it now.' Nick lets out a huff. 'Which annoys me.'

It seems a shame that after such a carefully established vernacular knowledge of the space of Sydney that one of Nick's anchors, an ugly titan of the brutalism era in Sydney architecture, should be hidden behind the beautiful, carbon-neutral, green-edged folly of neo-liberalism, with its uplifting words and art and its dubious agenda. But, Nick glances at the construction site next to the UTS Tower and brightens.

'Although,' he says happily, 'they're building that new ugly building, so maybe that will become a new eyesore landmark?'

## Shaun/Embodiments

'Why won't she talk to me ...?'

The GPS directions on Shaun's phone are broken. That is, they work, flawlessly moving from a top-down to a heads-up mode with the recognisable blue line streaming along the streets that we will drive down, but the audio isn't working, and there is no tinny voice telling us which way to turn. We're starting in Darlington in the backstreets of Sydney University, not far from where Nick and I walked in search of the cycle paths. Tapping the phone screen, Shaun suggests casually, 'Why don't we go to Collaroy?' and starts typing the destination. Shaun has never been to the North Shore before, but he wants to go because a man he once worked with came into a fortune and bought a large house up near Dee Why Beach.

'Birthplace of Sarah Murdoch,' Shaun says. 'She fancies herself as a scrubber from Collaroy. Bear in mind, the local member for Pittwater, Bronwyn Bishop. And then in Warringah, Tony Abbott.' A conservative heartland, then.

It is an extraordinarily hot summer's day, and the glaring sun cuts through the windshield, reflecting off the smooth glass of Shaun's phone as he tries to set up the GPS.

'So, we will start now,' Shaun turns up the car radio and starts pressing buttons. 'So, um ... I'll just get her to talk.'

'Okay. Her?'

'Woman's voice.'

'Woman's voice,' I repeat, 'Does she have a name?'

Impatient to get going, he puts on his sunglasses, starts the car and does a U-turn.

'No.' Shaun replies, 'However, we have an American GPS when we go overseas, and she has *such attitude* ... and when you miss a freeway exit she'll be like' his voice deepens and becomes robotic '*recalculating*'.

The fluid interplay between bodies – humans, machines, landscapes – is typical of automobilities (Sheller and Urry, 2000). In the motions of navigation, direction and recalculation, the GPS extends the more-than-human hybridity of car-driver-road (Thrift, 2004a) into an embodied hybridity between maps, motions and materialities. As we drive faster, the street takes on a different momentum. The driver's side window is open, a contrived draught that garners a slight breeze against the hot-to-touch heat of the car, tickling our skin and letting in the sound of the engine and the tyres on the road.

Watching the phone, and feeling slightly ill between the movement of the car and the iPhone's visual gymnastics, I ask Shaun if the GPS gets annoyed if the route has to be constantly recalculated.

'Well,' he responds, 'You sort of anthropomorphise her, don't you?'

The act of driving, as Katz (2001) argues, is a personal and subjective act. Shaun's arms flex as he changes gears, fingers dancing over the scorching steering wheel, and feet bend and extend to speed up and slow down, as his body co-pilots us forward. At the same time, the hybridisation of Cartesian and Leibnizian geometries when recombined to form a technological interface that we can approximate as a map reader, sitting next to the driver, telling them where to go, becomes humanised into a quasi-passenger in the car. This produces a complex reality, with multiple more-than-human meanings folded together in Shaun's subjective and bodily interactions.

'You sort of, you know, you think, oh yeah, she's got attitude now, but really, it's the same monotone,' Shaun explains, and not without cynicism.

As we drive, the 'monotone' is strangely absent while the GPS map on the app shifts and transforms as we change direction and turn corners. Shaun went to no special effort to choose this voice – it is, as he says, the one that comes standard with the Google Maps GPS phone software.

'Oh, well,' he says. 'She's a means to an end, really.'

As we stop at a traffic light on Cleveland Street, he picks up the phone as and starts pressing the screen.

'Why won't she talk to me ...?' he murmurs.

Cars and trucks lumber through the crossing, making it difficult to hear, and the sun bears down through the windshield, making the dashboard steam.

'Being, like, born and raised in Sydney, I always thought that I would never use one of these things,' he motions with his hand towards the phone. 'But they are really fucking handy. It wasn't so much the Google Maps that came with iPhone 3G, I think it was really, I think it really came into its own – why don't we just have air-con on and the background less noisy.' Shaun presses a button and the window goes up, dimming the noise of the passing vehicles, and the air-conditioning begins to blow lukewarm air. This quick move creates a further barrier between interior and exterior, with us inside a semi-detached, climate-controlled shell (Laurier et al., 2008), and the noisy infrastructure muted outside. Shaun gathers his train of thought again.

'Um, I think it really came into its own – I had an Android phone last year, a Samsung Galaxy S3 and it really had the turn-by-turn directions, and it was the first time that I saw that on a phone. And you know how it plots, sort of, multiple ways of going.'

As we stop at some lights, he picks up the phone again and starts tapping it impatiently.

'Why she's not talking now, I'm not really sure.'

Between windscreen and phone screen, the GPS navigational system has a deictic thrall. The screen places Shaun at the centre point of a distance between here/now and there/later and promises to guide him, step by step, via audio to get there. This technological affordability means that the visuality of the map becomes reconfigured as a list of instructions, triangulated between geographic databases, GPS coordinates and audio files. This is a small but crucial shift in the way in which mapping is performed. As Dodge, Perkins and Kitchin (2009b) argue, maps are performative – they invite doing as well as looking (Lammes, 2017). Verhoeff (2012) describes the relationship between image and movement as a 'visual regime of navigation', in which the deictic becomes navigational by agglomerating movement and image. Yet, after this visual engagement, the map becomes a set of audio instructions, guiding the user step by step: going, looking *and listening*. This becomes crucial in driving practices as they are increasingly understood to be navigational mobilities: no longer just a visual regime of navigation, but a mobile, hybrid regime of navigation based on sound-image interfaces. Driving occupies a different navigational geometry to walking or cycling. Furthermore, Shaun's multitasking embodiment of driving is distinctly different from the absorbed Kyja's embodiment of passengering. The digital and mobile evolution of cartographic reason diminishes the distance between the map and its embodied performativity, and Shaun, despite growing up in Sydney, is relying upon it to tell him the way.

'Well, the voice is on ...,' Shaun says distractedly.

At this point, we have only travelled 500 m. Suddenly, the lights change to green, and Shaun drops the phone, pushing the gear stick into first, and hurriedly turning right. Despite the absence of instructions, he drives on confidently pulling up at another set of lights.

'So, presumably you already know the way?' I ask. We're properly in Chippendale again, ready to start cutting across the CBD towards the Harbour Bridge and into the North Shore. I ask him because, from memory of the Harbour Bridge with Tanija, the freeway to and from the bridge is *fast* with no lay-by lanes, and the roads ahead on the map look complicated and labyrinthine.

'Vaguely,' Shaun replies.

'Oh, right, and so you use a GPS because – ?'

'Well ...,' he drifts off, watching a cyclist walking with a white whippet on a lead cross quickly at the lights.

We fly out through the lights and onto the freeways that will lead us across the harbour. On the left, the tall glass buildings of the CBD glint in the sun, the blue sky reflected on their panes like a mirage. Driving is also different sensation – and a different mode of navigation – to sitting on the bus, staring at a phone, as Kyja and I did earlier. The act of driving, of guiding a vehicle through space is far more active and more prescient. Driving is an embodiment of modernity: always forward, even in reverse; and the freeway pulsates along, no chance to stop, to look back or return to the past under the voracious and unceasing flow of the traffic. The shapes of roads between here and there, the wide berth of the curve and obtuse angles accommodate not necessarily the car itself, but rather its speed. Merriman (2007), drawing on Urry (2004), suggests that driving practices have established the conditions of their own expansion across the space of the road. Roads and capitalism have been as much intertwined throughout the twentieth century (Soja, 1996, 2000), as steam engines and industrialisation were in the latter half of the nineteenth.

The relative speed and demand for fluidity produce a spatial order which, at first, appears to be contrary to the static grids of cartographic reason. On closer inspection, as we weave seamlessly across lanes, as freeways merge and part, movement has become bound progressively by roads, and then freeways. The intensity of speed and intuitive bodily reactions demands that the space of the road must be uniform, predictable and standardised, ensuring the primacy of landscape homogeneity over the heterogeneity of paths, materials and memory.

The reflection of the car pelts off the glass skyscrapers which stand sentinel on either side of the freeway as we continue along the freeway system rising high above the city. On cue, the curve of the Harbour Bridge appears again. As we pass by where Tanija and I reached the second staircase to the bridge, ahead we can see where Jack Lang, the premier of New South Wales, insisted on opening the bridge himself, before Francis de Groot rode up on a horse to cut the ribbon before anyone had the chance to stop him.[4] It is difficult to change lanes, here, the patina of light adding another complication to the driving assemblage. After the bridge, as we pull into an off-ramp positioned to the right of the lanes, we hit the first traffic light that we have seen since the other side of the city. We pull into a stop, behind a growing line of traffic.

4 Francis de Groot, a member of the New Guard, a short-lived proto-fascist military organisation in 1930s Australia, achieved notoriety at the opening of the Sydney Harbour Bridge on 19 March 1932 by intervening on horseback during its official opening, cutting the tape before Lang could do so.

Exasperated, Shaun huffs. 'I mean, look at this now, if you point the camera here,' he becomes directorial, and moves the camera towards the line of traffic backed up ahead of us, 'we're about to turn onto Military Road, and the traffic is banked up all the way back here. It's probably because there's a boat going through the Spit Bridge.'

'How far away is the Spit Bridge?' I ask, looking at the map on the phone.

'From here, um, about seven or eight ks,' Shaun responds. 'When I mentioned earlier that my commute from where I live to work can be from between 35 minutes and two hours – that one day it took two hours, two sets of traffic lights went out on the Princes Highway and it just, it was just like fucking infuriating.'

The change in pace jumpstarts more frustration. Since the traffic is moving nowhere, pulling up the handbrake, he takes the phone.

'Why isn't she talking?!'

As he plays around with it, he hits the wrong button, and it zooms back out of navigation view into the map view.

'She is suggesting I go a different way because it's traffic.' The radio swells again. 'She's actually glowed a little bit red where it's ... yeah.' He shows me the phone, pointing out the angry red lines that indicate where the traffic can be found. 'Heavy traffic via the A8. Should we go a different – yeah, I've never been that way.'

Shaun puts the phone down and turns the wheel to merge into traffic again and indicates left.

I'm going to be one of those annoying people,' he says. 'I don't like to change lanes, it's not part of my world view.'

Shaun pulls out into the lane and speeds back up. The directions recalibrate, but still no sound from the GPS.

'Why isn't she talking?!'

I ask if it's turned up.

'Yep,' he responds. 'So, fuck. I don't know why it's not working. If you want to have a play with it? I think we're going on Willoughby Road.' I can see the off-ramp up ahead, so I quickly grab the phone and read what's on the screen.

'Yes – you're going 800 m, and then you're turning right after that.' Suddenly, I become part of the assemblage: phone-me-Shaun-car-road.

'Great.' Shaun's voice is quiet with ire. Hesitating, I play with the dials on the dashboard and press buttons.

'And we're certain it's not this machine here?' I point to the radio, which ostensibly says that it is connected. Button.

'Probably is.' He quickly glares at the flashing lights, as he drives onto the off-ramp. 'It can be a bit cunty actually. So,' he puts on the indicators again, 'turning right?'

'Yep – and then you've gotta merge,' I reply.

'Was that you or did it just talk?'

'That was me,' I say. He laughs. Sighing, I juggle the role of technician and navigator, watching the phone with one eye, and the dashboard with another. Switch.

'In 1.5 km you're turning left,' I tell him. Button.

'What usually happens is that she'll just come up,' Shaun explains, keeping his eyes on the road, 'and it'll just look like a phone number. Like, unknown phone call.'

Dial. Button. Blaring pop music comes on, and I panic. Eyes still on the road, Shaun reaches out and presses an ambiguous button. The sound disappears.

'No, we shan't listen to the '90s handbag house.'

I press another button. The lights go off. Swearing quickly, I press it again. The lights come back on. Shaun's eyes flick to the dashboard as we stop at some lights.

'That actually might work,' he says, grabbing the phone. 'Wait, it's initialising. Line active.'

Suddenly, a tinny monotone bursts out of the cars speaker system in stereophonic array. 'In 400 m, turn left onto Mowbray Road.'

'There you go,' Shaun says, merging into the left turning lane.

The GPS has changed our conversation. Up until this point, Shaun has supplied a lively commentary of city politics, inequalities and histories. Now, the GPS interrupts in spurts, inconsiderate of the rhythm or the flow of the traffic, the car, or the conversation, driven by geography rather than sociality. As the GPS increasingly begins to infiltrate Shaun's navigational styles, we turn onto Boundary Street, and he points to an overhead road sign that displays the name of the street as well as a numeric code, 'A38'.

'That's the other thing, too,' he tells me, 'they're bringing it into line with this 'A' nonsense and 'M' nonsense, and they've ... it's the renaming of main-major streets and roads and stuff, and it sort of happened about a year and a half ago. They didn't – they just sort of did it and didn't really tell anyone. Or, actually, they might've. I just don't watch TV.'

This reclassification is part of a national roads initiative to bring road toponymy into a standardised form across all Australian states by creating a hierarchy of importance according to a national framework. Each alphabet code is supplemented by numeric designation, which has been decided either

Figure 5.3. *A road of national importance.* This shot is taken at the intersection where Boundary Street ceases to be the A38, and Babbage Road instead takes on the marker, where Shaun first comments on the new alphanumeric system.

based upon pre-existing road numbers or because of their relative proximity in road hierarchies to other more important roads (Austroads, 2013).

**Table 5.1. *Austroads alphanumeric road system.* Designation and roads in NSW.**

| Alphanumeric Designation | Type | Meaning |
|---|---|---|
| M | Motorway | Motorway |
| A | Main road | National importance |
| B | Lesser main road | State importance |

Source: Austroads (2003).

Importantly, the spatial and historical restructuring involved in the renaming of streets, for instance, has long been in play. Shaun's observations that 'they just sort of did it and didn't really tell anyone' is astute, delving into the complex way in which the reclassification of roads is occurring between governance and the embodied experience of driving across them. In fact, according to the peak organisation of Australasian roads and traffic management (Austroads):

> [T]he new signs have been 'cover-plated' from view, awaiting the roll-out of the new system. Given the high percentage of the State road network that is now ready to unveil the new signs, Roads and Maritime has decided to commence the implementation of the new scheme. (Austroads, 2003: 9)

One of the key selling points of this system was its interoperability with GPS devices and GIS data systems. The new road names had been rolled out to major cartographic stakeholders well before they were available to the public (Austroads, 2013). Local planning increasingly cooperates with global standards of cartographic communication and best practice (Söderström, 1996).

Thrift (2004b) describes the increased territoriality of identification systems and the way in which space itself is being rearranged in order to accommodate and optimise these systems. The 'track-and-trace' evolution, Thrift (2004b) argues, results in a '*standardisation of space*' (Thrift, 2004b: 175, emphasis added), brought about as a result of the availability of geolocational technologies, increased the formalisation of sequential knowledge systems and the expansion of calculative capabilities. I ask Shaun if he finds the switchover from the current toponymic system to the new alphanumeric one confusing?

'I understand why they're doing it,' he responds. 'I mean, Victoria has it, Queensland has it. They're just sort of bringing it into line.'

Ostensibly, this reclassification standardises names into machine-readable logics, thereby assisting the efficiency and productivity of planning regimes and government systems. It also translates the taxonomic and toponymic systems of cartography into coded and digital systems. Even though the GPS shows both the toponymic name of the road, 'Boundary Street', and its alphanumeric equivalency, 'A38', the two are not quite the same. The 'A38' is, in fact, comprised of a number of different roads, only one of which is 'Boundary Street'. This is evidence of gradual standardisation of road names, which can be traced back into the early nineteenth century. Consequently, the toponymies that retain the specific temporalities of development in postcolonial urbanism – from the Brick Kilns, to the Tank Stream, the Argyle Cut and the old brewery – become replaced by governmental and commercial interests through a reformation of the past under the same logics of progress which have spurned the city since 1788 – a logic that we painstakingly and labouriously invited into the car with us.

The redraft isn't necessarily symptomatic of the digital turn and technology itself. The desire to standardise is simply a different manifestation of the same discourses of order and reason that resulted in the production of grids and infrastructures, parks and maps (Foucault, 2002a). Rose-Redwood (2012b) traces the history of geocoding into its earliest archaeological forms, arguing that there are discursive and political links between contemporary modes of geocoding, toponomy and governmentality. He terms this 'governing by numbers' (Rose-Redwood, 2012b: 626) through a vast array of systems: social,

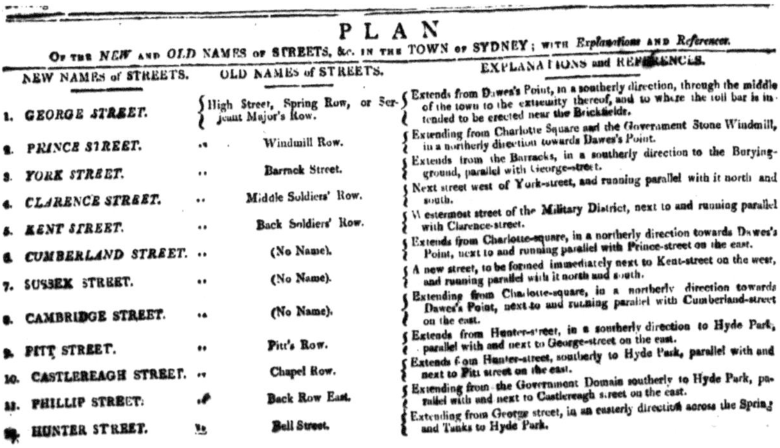

PLAN

OF THE *NEW* AND *OLD* NAMES OF STREETS, &c. IN THE TOWN OF SYDNEY; WITH *Explanations* AND *References*.

| NEW NAMES of STREETS. | OLD NAMES of STREETS. | EXPLANATIONS and REFERENCES. |
| --- | --- | --- |
| 1. *GEORGE STREET.* | High Street, Spring Row, or Serjeant Major's Row. | Extends from Dawes's Point, in a southerly direction, through the middle of the town to the extremity thereof, and to where the toll bar is intended to be erected near the Brickfields. |
| 2. *PRINCE STREET.* .. | Windmill Row. | Extending from Charlotte Square and the Government Stone Windmill, in a northerly direction towards Dawes's Point. |
| 3. *YORK STREET.* .. | Barrack Street. | Extends from the Barracks, in a southerly direction to the Burying-ground, parallel with George-street. |
| 4. *CLARENCE STREET.* .. | Middle Soldiers' Row. | Next street west of York-street, and running parallel with it north and south. |
| 5. *KENT STREET.* .. | Back Soldiers' Row. | Westermost street of the Military District, next to and running parallel with Clarence-street. |
| 6. *CUMBERLAND STREET.* .. | (No Name). | Extends from Charlotte-square, in a northerly direction towards Dawes's Point, next to and running parallel with Prince-street on the east. |
| 7. SUSSEX STREET. .. | (No Name). | A new street, to be formed immediately next to Kent-street on the west, and running parallel with it north and south. |
| 8. CAMBRIDGE STREET. .. | (No Name). | Extending from Charlotte-square, in a northerly direction towards Dawes's Point, next to and running parallel with Cumberland-street on the east. |
| 9. PITT STREET. .. | Pitt's Row. | Extends from Hunter-street, in a southerly direction to Hyde Park, parallel with and next to George-street on the east. |
| 10. CASTLEREAGH STREET. .. | Chapel Row. | Extends from Hunter-street, southerly to Hyde Park, parallel with and next to Pitt street on the east. |
| 11. PHILLIP STREET. .. | Back Row East. | Extending from the Government Domain southerly to Hyde Park, parallel with and next to Castlereagh street on the east. |
| 12. HUNTER STREET. .. | Bell Street. | Extending from George street, in an easterly direction across the Spring and Tanks to Hyde Park. |

Figure 5.4. *Toponymies*. 'Plan of the new and old names of streets, in the town of Sydney; with explanation and references.' This notice taken from the *Sydney Gazette and New South Wales Advertiser* in 1810, which describes the renaming of the streets around the Tank Stream, concurrent with the urban redesign of the area around Wynyard and Circular Quay. Notable in this list is a loss of geographic markers, such as Chapel, Windmill and Barrack to more austere, English and colonial markers such as York, George and Cambridge. Source: National Library of Australia/State Library of NSW.

such as the census and statistics; spatial systems, such as street and house numbering; and material, including the grid (Rose-Redwood and Tantner, 2012). Whether functional aesthetics, or systems designed to improve the calculability of disordered landscapes, the result of renaming of names, paths, and places into alphanumeric taxonomies is a loss of toponymic history and memory – one that is embodied through the act of driving.

I'm curious about the impact that this may have on Shaun's everyday driving and navigation practices. Does he feel that loss? I ask him if it will be easier for him to remember 'A38' as opposed to 'Boundary Street' – and again, he responds by shaking his head.

'Nup, nup. But I mean, generations after me probably will.'

Shaun seems resigned to the formalisation of these systems in the future. Yet, his off-hand comment also hints towards how these seemingly minute shifts become embedded in the production of history. For generations after Shaun, the heterogeneity of these names will be absent, and the qualities of space and place that they trace – such as boundaries – become forgotten.

Further north from Boundary Street, the name A38 has also replaced Warringah Road. According to the local council, 'Warringah' is derived from a Guringai word for 'Middle Harbour', although it is also associated with words from other Aboriginal languages meaning 'sign of rain', 'across the waves' and 'sea' (Warringah Council, 2015). It was retroactively and somewhat arbitrarily applied to the council area in 1906. As we turn onto Warringah Road, now on the homeward journey, the GPS speaks up again, mangling the pronunciation and the intonation of the name.

'We're turning onto WORingae [Warringah] Road ....' Shaun laughs, mocking the pronunciation of the GPS.

Warringah is pronounced War-RING-gah. Throughout the trip, several instances occurred when the GPS struggled to pronounce the Aboriginal words that were adopted for particular places and paths. Similar names exist all over Sydney – markers of the European interpretation of an Aboriginal past, ghosts of the people who were disappeared from the landscape so that roads and skyscrapers could be built and named after them. Toponyms like Warringah Road carry a complicated and tense history, reminders of the devastating destructiveness of the colonial process and the death of millions at the reckoning of invaders small and large. However, while they acknowledge that colonial past, it also becomes pushed so far into the light that in its hypervisibility – its ubiquity – it becomes invisible again (Gordon, 2008).

'Is it mostly just the Aboriginal names that it has problems with ...?' I ask curiously.

'Probably,' he replies, 'And don't you love that, too,' he points to the car next to us, occupied by two young women. Noticing the small action camera in my hand, the young woman who is driving moves awkwardly.

'Look at these white blonde girls,' he continues. Shaun's anger is palpable in contrast to his earlier philosophical mien about the GPS and the changes in the road names. These shifts have seen a change in the nature of 'the address', argues Thrift (2004b), beyond people and objects to anything that can be calculated. However, what the national shift to alphanumeric systems signifies, even in the localised spatiotemporal event between Shaun, his GPS and the A38, is arguably a continued reassertion of the cartographic imagination (as an ordering device) over landscapes that ostensibly belong to others.

'Y'know they're the only –,' Shaun's voice rises, 'the street names of the people that lived, that used to own, walking through this land 60,000 years ago – the only thing that remains, we have these blonde, y'know .... Bitch, we're not filming you!'

She can't hear us, because her windows are up for the air conditioning. The traffic moves, and she drives off, oblivious to her role in our conversation as an unknown assailant in an ongoing history of injustice, an injustice perhaps returned by Shaun.

But, where names like Boundary Road and Warringah Road still link the social history of the Sydney landscape to the present, the name 'A38' no longer references Aboriginal people, nor the process of colonisation – nor even its own cartographic processes of drawing lines. The new alphanumeric road names effectively remove that past, becoming solely referential of the planning systems and ideologies that produced them. Carter (2009) describes how the journeys erased from documentary memory linger on in the names of places. Other erasures linger on, too – stories that form part of Shaun's identity. But what appears particularly brutal with the arrival of this new system is that even this seething and complex past is brushed aside by institutions that care less about the reconciliation of the past, than about inducing rationalities that suit future calculability. The A38 all but hides any cartographic or toponymic trace of planning boundaries (Boundary Street), of colonisers (Babbage Road[5]), and of the original inhabitants of the land (Warringah Road), both on the landscape and on the map.

The renaming of the roads in line with these logics heralds a present-future where cartographic reason attempts to define and territorialise spatiality – not just in its representational symbolism and iconography, but in its discursive logics and ideologies, too. Many of the city's roads have already been reordered 'behind the scenes', through invisible cartographies designed for geographic information systems, data analysis and transport strategies. As these reclassifications become implemented into the landscape, the road systems of Sydney are shaped and renamed accordingly. The A38 is calculated against the hierarchy of roads, and under the gaze of the GIS map in determining their numeration, enacted in line with transport planning and institutional data-gathering systems. Hence, this coded and ordered landscape is filled with simulacra, where the original referents of colonialism are lost through an endless cycle of representation and re-representation. To calculate a route draws upon a hybrid discursified space that is distinctly algorithmic and geometric, Leibnizian and Cartesian, where the connection of the car to the asphalt and the freeway (Featherstone, 2004) becomes encompassed under a calculative space different from the intuitive 'feeling' of space that Tanija struggled to express and that Nick so loved. The GPS calculates and recalculates under incredible pressure, translating between multiple planes of experience: top-down Cartesian grids, egocentric apexes and the flatter, bird's eye view that takes on the view of a driver with its long blue line. What Shaun's observations discuss is the formalisation of this discourse to the point where these logics have been so naturalised

5 Babbage Road was named for Eden Herschel Babbage (b. (c. 1844-5 February 1924), a resident of Roseville. A memorial proclaiming him 'Father of Roseville' can be found on the corner of Babbage Road and Ormonde Road. He was also a descendent of Charles Babbage.

that their systems are being made visible, concomitantly, to ordinary road users and navigators. This would suggest that cartographic imaginations, rather than diminishing in use, import and power, are in fact becoming more prevalent – but less visible than ever.

The alphanumeric system does not, however, pay homage to erased past and the continued conflict in the present. Tench (1789: 102) describes the 'calamity' that overcame the local Aboriginal population in the summer and autumn of 1789, as they died slowly from disease, dispossession and violence. The Eora nation, annihilated by smallpox and dispossession, haunt this landscape in a constant reminder of the brutality of imperial conquest and the erasure through abstraction of the cartographic imagination. The words of the Eora in place names, no matter how cynically attributed, are ghosts of the people who were erased from the landscape, and increasingly, from geography and history. Such stories are perforations in the straight Cartesian lines of cartographic reason and gaps in the folding over of the past into the future. With the standardisation of spatial toponymy under universal systems of classification, these stories suffer yet another erasure.

# 6. Imagining spaces

## Cliff/Stories

'We are a nation of aliens, postulating timidly on alien shores.'

Walking along the south-western shore of Botany Bay, a warm wind with cool edges blows around us. Sand grains on the shore whip up onto the grassy promenade with each gust of wind, and the waters are choppy, the white pinnacles of the waves catching the shine of the sun. Cliff has recently moved nearby and is happy for a walk along what has become one of his favourite beaches. It's a typically Australian beach promenade: a foreshore wall three feet above the water leading to a wide expanse of grass between the beach and the car parks. The lawn is a browned in the summer heat and decorated with trees, scrubby bushes and blinding white footpaths. Families gather around wooden picnic tables, and brick barbeques and children run euphorically between the sea and the crowds dripping wet and then drying in the sun.

Before us, Botany Bay sits, its north and south heads like two pincers trying to grasp the ocean. First calling the inlet 'Stingray Bay', Cook later renamed it Botany Bay due to the rich and diverse landscape of flora around the bay, meticulously documented by Joseph Banks, botanist aboard the *Endeavour.* We stand now in the shorefront between the Cooks River and the Georges River. Once called Seven Mile Beach, then Lady Robinson's Beach after 1874 in honour of the wife of the Governor of NSW, Sir Hercules Robinson, the foreshore has been renamed again to Cook Park. This time, the name was not for the first Cook who set foot on the shores of Botany Bay, but for Samuel Cook who worked towards developing it as a leisure area for residents. This area was developed in the post-war period in the 1950s and 1960s, a busy time in shaping the Australian imagination, and took on a number of very British toponymies: Brighton-Le-Sands, Ramsgate and Scarborough Park, for instance, a change in pattern from the Coogee, Bondi, or Maroubra of the pre-war period. To our left, beyond the northern shore, Cliff shows me how you can just see the city through the hazy air,

Wilmott, C., *Mobile Mapping. Space, Cartography and the Digital.*
Taylor & Francis Group, 2020
DOI 10.5117/9789462984530_CH06

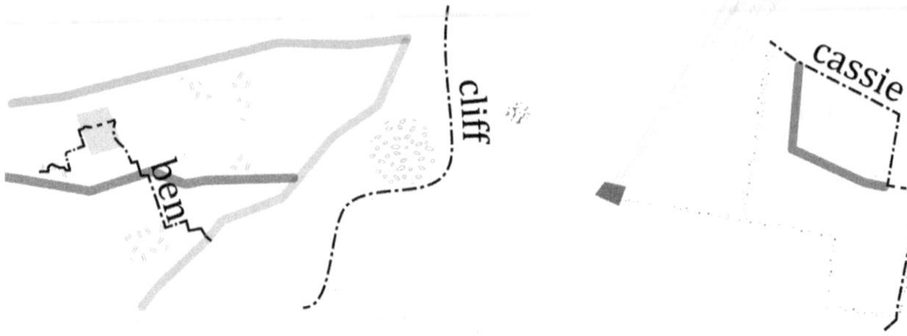


Figure 6.1. *Fragments – Cliff, Benjamin and Cassie.* (Left) *Cliff's walk* – Sunday, 12 January, Botany Bay, morning, sunny; (centre) *Benjamin's journey* – Wednesday, 15 January, Newtown-Camperdown, midday, sunny; (right) *Cassie's walk* – Wednesday, 15 January, Redfern-Surry Hills, evening, sunny.

its skyscrapers, straight like the pines, rising out of the skyline. Gesturing towards the northern shore, he points to the runway from Sydney Airport that spills into the bay, planes tentatively landing against the wind, and the ships from Port Botany just behind.

Cliff says when he first moved into the area he didn't spend too much time down at the foreshore, but it was the place where he introduced his granddaughter to the beach because it is safe, has few waves and a shark net for swimming. It has plenty of shade, too, afforded by the rows of Norfolk pines planted by the first Europeans because their straight trunks made excellent ship masts.

'This is the birthplace of the nation, if you like,' Cliff says, gesticulating out across the bay.

This is a profound claim, pregnant with hundreds of years of dispossession and erasure, combined with uneasy but defiant nationalism. It is also a peculiar claim – 'the birthplace of a nation', a natural time and a place in which a nation emerges into the world, a moment that can be etched out and settled in the colonial imagination to resonate through history and geography, erasing conflict and the struggle with a natal inevitability. He points to the south head, Kurnell, where the dunes can just be made out under the pines.

'This is where Captain Cook came, and he looked at the Aboriginals, and the Aboriginals looked at him.'

This is not quite the story as it happened – the awkward encounter inscribed on an epitaph sitting on the shore in Kurnell. This is a powerful revisioning of a moment which ended in gunfire, and which was mired in written accounts that emphasised material exchange of goods, protection of territories and accounts of weaponry from the three shots of a musket (one of which embedded itself in the arm of an Eora man) and bark shields (Schlunke, 2013). Captain Cook is, of course, Lieutenant Cook, captain of the *Endeavour*, the first British ship that sailed up the coast. He is also a colossus in the pantheon of biographies that form the national imaginary: 'The Great Navigator, The Original Invader, The Marker of Modern Australia and The Discoverer' (Schlunke, 2008). Despite his mythical status in the Australian imaginary, Cook and his crew did not stay long – pausing briefly to gather water and supplies, and scout the area for a possible future colony. This is not so much the birthplace of a nation as the start of violence and resistance, dispossession and theft.

As Cook's journal elaborates:

> [Anchor, Botany Bay, New South Wales], Sunday, 29$^{th}$.
> Saw, as we came in, on both points of the bay, several of the Natives and a few hutts; Men, Women, and Children on the South Shore abreast of the Ship, to which place I went in the Boats in hopes of speaking with them, accompanied by Mr. Banks, Dr. Solander, and Tupia. As we approached the Shore they all made off, except 2 Men, who seem'd resolved to oppose our landing. As soon as I saw this I order'd the boats to lay upon their Oars, in order to speak to them; but this was to little purpose, for neither us nor Tupia could understand one word they said. We then threw them some nails, beads, etc., a shore, which they took up, and seem'd not ill pleased with, in so much that I thought that they beckon'd to us to come ashore; but in this we were mistaken, for as soon as we put the boat in they again came to oppose us, upon which I fir'd a musquet between the 2, which had no other Effect than to make them retire back, where bundles of their darts lay, and one of them took up a stone and threw at us, which caused my firing a Second Musquet, load with small Shott; and altho' some of the shott struck the man, yet it had no other effect than making him lay hold on a Target. Immediately after this we landed, which we had no sooner done than they throw'd 2 darts at us; this obliged me to fire a third shott, soon after which they both made off, but not in such haste but what we might have taken one; but Mr. Banks being of Opinion that the darts were poisoned, made me cautious how I advanced into the Woods. We found here a few small hutts made of the Bark of Trees, in one of which were 4 or 5 Small Children, with whom we left some strings of beads, etc. A quantity of Darts lay about the Hutts; these we took away with us. 3 Canoes lay upon the beach, the worst I think I ever saw; they were about 12 or 14 feet long, made of one piece of the Bark of a Tree, drawn or tied up at each end, and the middle kept open by means of pieces of Stick by way of Thwarts. (Cook, 1770)

We see here how stories travel, where the taxonomic language of the navigator and the explorer in the time of cartographic reason becomes the evocative language of landscape and memory for those who live those stories. Questions of obligations and causations arise, of orderly behaviour and the expectation of subjugations – stories held entirely in the eyes of the beholder. As Healy argues, Cook is not a just an historical figure, but 'an enduring icon, a huge network of narratives, images and ceremonies' (Healy, 1997: 11). In Cliff's retelling, there irrupts a discourse wherein 'Cook's role shifted from reporter to convenient symbol of a well-intentioned, orderly and yet adventurous, commencement of the colony' (Schlunke, 2013: 22): 'The birthplace of a nation.' Cliffs factual tone belies this shift, as landscape both transcends but also reinscribes what it means to both gaze from across the sea and also from the land: to be the progeny of discourses that have settled far and travelled near, and travelled far and settled near. Cultural remanence continues, irrupting in new stories and retellings, the gravity of the past gathering here in Botany Bay, around Cliff, as he tells me that the local Aboriginal clans thought the pale men who appeared on their shores were the ghosts of their ancestors. Botany Bay, too, holds the past, a place which is always in occurrence and continually contested by an enduring Aboriginal presence (Nugent, 2005) and the mythologies of nationhood.

Cliff also has his own ghosts here. He tells me how did not even realise the shore existed until he was old enough to remember seeing the sea for the first time. He grew up in Western Sydney, and after moving to Revesby, his world was 'a mysterious river, because the main strip of road was called River Road'. One day, in the mode of explorer, he walked the length of the road down to the Georges River, whose outlet flows into Botany Bay a few kilometres south of where we stand. But this river was nothing compared to the first time he ever saw the sea. He recounts the story of heading out to the Eastern Suburbs through the heat of summer towards the eastern beaches. Down Bondi Road, he reached a peak in the road and which the landscape melted away downhill exposing the vast expanse of the Tasman Sea. His voice holds a tremor as he describes the 'huge rollers' dumping water onto the sand in rhythmic continuity that echoes across the seaside valleys of the basin.

For Cliff, both these discoveries underscore a relation between the land and the sea. The first, finding the river at the end of the road, opened up meaning about where he lived – to find out the mysterious waters that bounded his life, preambling their existence memory, well beyond where they could be seen. But the second, hitting the edge of Australia on Bondi

Beach, to see the powerful and fierce intersection between land and sea as water and sand merge into the breakers, made him think that 'the land has an end, that there are boundaries'.

This moment, between land and water, is perhaps what ties the stories of Botany Bay and Cook together. Cliff came at this turbulent boundary from a different side to Cook, from land not sea. But the spaces he inhabits, the maps and the imaginaries, at one point, did come from the sea and seeing this edge brought this shock to the fore. Where the birthplace of a nation occurred for Cliff, was on the moment where a British foot stepped on Eora country. The meeting of these spaces is barely a glance between two cultures.

We happen upon a wayfinding map at the boundary between Ramsgate and Dolls Point. The map outlines the shape of the shoreline and tracing his finger across the width of blue that represents the bay; Cliff emphatically reiterates this position.

'This is the history of discovery whereas Sydney Harbour has a history of development.'

Botany Bay was not deep enough for the First Fleet to anchor close enough to shore, and so they scouted ahead, following the coastline etches that Cook had drawn out earlier. French explorer La Pérouse and his men made the north head their home for a brief period, following those same maps by Cook. Immutable mobiles (Latour, 1986), they were re-embodied by La Pérouse's ships as they navigated between the latitudinal and longitudinal lines, the final note of the ship's passing made by the new settlers of the Colony of New South Wales as they saw them between the headlands of Sydney Harbour further north. These are not lines in the sand or the earth, but cuts in the water redrawn upon paper – resolute and fixed without being subject to changing currents and shifting tides.

'The first settlers here,' Cliff says 'were English. And they wanted it to be like home.'

And so, while some of the first settlers were also Irish, with new stories, new reinscriptions appear in the palimpsest landscape: that north head is named La Perouse, and the beaches are renamed, and the shoreline is redrawn and refigured into two long buttresses that form the airport runways. However, the lines of Cook, or their rereading by La Pérouse, or even the pantone colour blocks in front of us at this map of Dolls Point cannot entirely reshape Cliff's experiences. The first thing Cliff did when he got his first GPS device was to hold it and see how fast he could run. But it wasn't that accurate. Speed for a GPS is based upon triangulation between distance and time, and he discovered this when the speedometer on his car, which is based on mechanics, often contradicts the GPS speed.

Cliff loves the aspect of computing in location. The first web browser he ever had was Mosaic, credited with popularising the Internet, and he has a wistful nostalgia about how he 'saw it all unfolding'. And now, computers that were once so large have now become the size of a smartphone – and the same impulse that had him running down River Road to the source of its mysterious toponymy is now one which is embedded in his desire to explore beyond the edge of the continent.

'I like to travel,' Cliff says. But then, motioning towards his phone he adds, 'I like to know where I am. I like to see myself.'

The tension of being from both near and far, between sea and land, is somewhat resolved. It is easy to feel lost in a world that only exists in the imaginary – to find boundaries all the time and to know that your place in the world is only as wide and as settled as your knowledge of it.

'Maybe it's identity, too ….' He's philosophical about how the map helps him to anchor his place. 'Here I am, this dot here, moving in this direction on this huge planet etc. etc. on this size solar system, on the outer spiral rim of the Milky Way galaxy, in this huge and expanding universe. That's me.'

Cliff's lived spaces of boundaries and beyond them, vast abysses of uncertain and disruptive possibility. Seeing himself against this chasm settles that, to a degree, by locating him within the networks of scale between not just near and far, but massive and minute. It's telling then, that although he trusts the location – his spatiotemporal coordinates – he doesn't trust the map at all or the information that resides within it.

'Because I know damn well that it's not aware of stop signs, one-way streets.'

Cliff's separation between location and spatial information becomes more apparent.

'The phone has more or less replaced paper maps.'

Google Maps, he says, are 'like the holodeck on the USS *Enterprise* – the floor keeps on unfolding under you'.

This analogy explains how Cliff finds Google Maps unsettling in their ambiguity and precarity. To be located, for Cliff, is a metaphysical question: when the information dissolves and rescales, you occupy multiple levels and scales of being, juxtaposing and contradictory spaces, located across the ever-ambitious expanse of cartographic reason through Cartesian structures outwardly, and Leibnizian structures inwardly. Cliff takes out his phone and wiggles it.

'It's not a whole lot different except that it helps you locate yourself more precisely.'

Walking along the fuzzy edge of the Australian shore, and the limits of the past, he points to the line on the edge of his screen where the pixels stop and the black border begins. This line is a point of frustration about wanting to see beyond the boundaries of the screen. Despite the lauding of the slippy map, of Möbius strips and never-ending rhumb lines, the screen still bounds the map, curating and limiting the view that he could have. To see beyond the boundary means sacrificing another part of the map, to zoom in and out, the same: be it a part of the location or the depth of information. Even in its digital form, the map is still not the territory. This, Cliff explains, is the same frustration that he had with the book directories, hurriedly turning pages to find the adjacent maps in peculiarly distant parts of the directory.

There was a storm last night, and up ahead large portions of sand have been blown ashore completely obscuring the dunes and the footpaths. The sand trails into the front yards of the large concrete-rendered houses that sit stalwart between the sea and the suburbs with large plate-glass windows consuming and reflecting the sea views. The noise of a small engine can be heard behind the mounds of sand and Cliff looks at the houses, regarding their absurdity with squinted eyes.

When he was a boy, he used to collect oysters from the salty waters of the Georges River. The oysters now in the Botany Bay are not clean enough for his granddaughter to eat, and so she will never have this experience. He never felt quite at home in the Australian landscape: the old European cities that he read about in books were not places where oysters were gathered, and so seem bereft of the ancestral connection to Europe that he feels. The sand along the footpath squeaks under our feet as we walk. This feeling lingers in the Commonwealth relationships that maintain the queen as the Australian head of state.

'Of course,' he clarifies, 'the queen has no power. But the symbolism is powerful.'

It is and is possibly the reason he feels so disquieted at the vagrancy of squatting in the world at large.

'I grew up hating gumtrees and dust and people. I loathed them. I thought gumtrees were the most horrible stunted looking things.'

The stories of afar – of Cook and his landing party, are steeped in an English imaginary that does little justice to gum trees and dust. To be on land while looking over the sea, across the boundary, subdued by the waves pounding against the shore. Up ahead, a small motorised digger emerges from the dunes. It is working hard to shovel up the sand that has blown over the bank and dump it back onto the beach. It comes towards us, stiff

Figure 6.2. *Sandringham*. A small digger blocks the footpath while it carries sand into the bay, while the wind blows more sand back onto the footpath. Facing southward, Botany Bay is to the left of the image.

in its objective to decolonise the footpath from the disobedient shore, and forces us to stand aside as it passes, up against the fence of one of those gargantuan houses. It scoops up a pile of sand, some of which flows through the claws and back onto the path, and it does a quick U-turn and hurries off down the path towards the beachfront. As we follow it, it stops on a corner, blocking our path again, and moving towards the brick tidal wall that separates the path from the beach, lifts its arms and dumps the sand back on the beach and into the sea. As it does so, the wind continues to blow, and the half of its load is blown back towards the path on its journey downward.

It was only as Cliff was leaving Australia, lifting off from the runway by plane and staring down at the traced shores of Botany Bay, that he began to appreciate the landscape of his childhood.

'I didn't think much of the suburban Australian landscape, which was all I knew. But when I came back after living in the States for ten or eleven years and went out to the bush, I felt much better then. It felt much more like home.'

Home is a recurring theme for Cliff. But despite his practice of using maps to locate himself, his description of home is strangely non-cartographic.

'The smells – the sorts of things that make you think about home, that I think about – the sky.' He points upward with both his hands. 'It's different.

It's higher and bluer. It's the weirdest thing – you think, mmm, southern skies again.'

Across the sky, Captain Cook Bridge spans the Georges River. Cliff is surprised that the road he lives on comes out here.

'I would use my map for this,' he says, 'to figure out where I was. To see which way north, south, east and west was.'

He pulls out the compass on his phone. It needs to be calibrated. As he moves his handset in a figure eight pattern, he looks back out at Botany Bay and points towards the sea.

'I know damned well that's where east is.'

The compass calibrates, and he points it north towards the city. The eastern arrow points towards the sea. Looking at the phone, Cliff faces becomes serious.

'We are a nation of aliens, postulating timidly on alien shores.'

I ask him about home again, about what it is like to leave the land and then come back across the sea and resettle on the shores. The bush 'is alive' he says.

'It hums and throbs … like a giant living thing and you're sitting on its belly in the dark.'

It has 'a heartbeat and a pulse'.

He's come a long way from the birthplace of a nation – and gone a long way from home. The heartbeat of the bush, the belly of the Australian terrain and the euphoria of southern skies operate on scales beyond the cartographic imagination, beyond a little blue dot in a universe of numbers and the mysterious boundaries of the river at the end of a road.

We have returned to the same place, where all these things happened, the sky high above and the confluence of the Georges River with Botany Bay. But it is a different landscape on which Cliff treads. He tells a story of how he, a city boy, went out to the bush once, after hitchhiking all the way to Perth and then travelling out to the Swan and Avon Rivers into the bush, and suddenly the many Aboriginal stories and ways of understanding the landscape made sense.

'Spirits being everywhere,' he waves his hands around, 'in the trees and the rocks, and for them, it was self-evidently true. It wasn't something that needed empirical verification. There it was, in front of you. You felt it. I felt it. I was terrified, frankly.'

Where was he was when this happened, I query – what persuaded him to travel all the way to the other side of the country, to another boundary at land's end, and to then move outward into the bush? By his own admission, he was a city boy unable to locate himself between stunted gum trees and brown dust.

'I had this notion in my head,' he smiles ruefully. 'One of my favourite books of all time, I read it when I was young, was [Mark Twain's] *Huckleberry Finn*, and I had this vision of floating down a wide river on a raft of some kind and lazily chewing a grass straw of some kind and watching the clouds go past and – ah – I had no idea that the Avon River or the Swan River were nothing like the mighty Mississippi.'

'So did you actually get a raft and try to float down the ...?' My face must have shown my incredulity.

He smiles. 'I got a rubber raft – inflatable – and a couple of paddles and a backpack and a bunch of dried food and canned food and a little gas stove and a tent and all this crap. Stuck it in the backpack.' I laugh as he continues. 'Got friends to drop me 8 km up the coast, up the river, on the Avon and then I hiked inland to the river. Found it. There it was. Nice water and put it out.' He makes a pumping motion with his hands. 'Ch ch ch ch – pumped up my raft, stuck all my stuff in it, got in, laid back and watched the sun and the sky wielding overhead.' Southern skies again. 'I did that for all of 6 minutes and then, suddenly, the river disappeared, and there were all these rocks and rapids, and I thought, "Ah, shit." So, I got out, deflated my raft, dried it off, rolled all it up and stuck it all back in my backpack and hiked overland until I found some more clear water, and then got back in, pumped it all up, floated for about another 500 m or maybe even a kilometre, and then had to get out and do it all again.'

'After three days of doing this I was exhausted. I had diarrhoea because of the river water which was not good to drink and all the dried nuts and berries I was subsisting off – so cramps, diarrhoea, exhaustion. I gave way.'

He has an expression that suggests he knows he was lucky, that other people who were so deceived by the discrepancy between the map and the Australian landscape in their search to live a foreign imagination have not been so fortunate – that the process of inscribing someone else's imaginary into this landscape is dangerous and fraught.

'But the first night I pitched my tent, and the sun fell, and that's when I noticed the bush was alive. You could hear roos,' his hands move again, this time in a rhythmic bounce, 'phwmp, phwmp, phwmp, phwmp. I'm in there in my little tiny tent thinking, "God almighty, if they don't see me – pfft."' He slaps his hands together. 'They'll flatten me in the dark. And the second night I pitched the tent and, um, it was the weirdest thing. There were high trees – a lot in the forest where I was – and I could hear the wind coming through the tops of the trees.' He puts his hand either side of his face. 'Phww, phww, phww, phww, phww – getting louder and louder and I realised that it was the front of the wind – you've seen those old cartoons of the wind like a face – phww – blowing? It was like that moving across the land, and the trees were snapping over as – bending over – as the wind gust hit it. I could hear it coming towards me. And so, phwmp, my tent flattened, and I was rolling around on the ground wrapped in a tent like a blanket, y'know, and then suddenly, whoosh, torrential rain came ripping down.'

He pauses before continuing.

'No tent, torrential rain, middle of the night. I thought – this isn't anything like *Huckleberry Finn*. And so, on the morning of the fourth day, I packed it all up and got out my compass, figured out where the highway was and started walking across – through the bush. And then, stuck my thumb out and hitchhiked back to Perth.'

I don't know what to make of this story, at once absurd but still so familiar.

'On the map,' Cliff remembers, 'it looked like a big blue strip the way it ....' His eyes fog over as if seeing the map again, and remembering being in this small, destroyed tent in the middle of a storm in an unfamiliar landscape that he had lived in all his life. 'See, this is for your thing, maps mislead you.'

From some people being scared of the city to others being scared of the bush, maps have a deceptive quality that is not just smoke and mirrors but dislocating and disorienting. Cartographic reason provides inadequate tools to understand the diversity of landscape – it makes the Mississippi look like the Swan and Avon Rivers, and it makes the bush look like a forest.

'So,' I reply 'when you were planning it, you actually went, and you found the rivers on the map and thought – oh!'

'That's right.'

This is the trouble with the promises of cartographic reason: it suggests that it can locate you in knowable universes, that its system is generalizable across all spaces and times. But every time Cliff traced the map to the edge, he found a greater expanse beyond that which was recognisable or readable through the stories and maps that Cook brought with him and set down here in Botany Bay.

Cliff continues.

'I saw that's a big water going down there. I thought, oh, it looks like a wide river, it's a wide blue strip, it's easily navigable.'

Sometimes, these stories come to the fore, even for those enamoured with European cities and who embody the dislocated identities and tenuous imaginaries of settler-colonies.

'But it wasn't. I lost about eight kilograms.'

## Benjamin/Imaginings

> '[I]n some respects you can actually get more lost with a map than without, maybe.'

There is a difference between Camperdown Park and Camperdown Memorial Rest Park, Ben explains. Camperdown Park is a large green square and, as for Camperdown Memorial Rest Park, 'it's not even green on this map'.

On the other side of suburban Newtown to where Marianna and I wandered weeks ago, it is hot and bright, the cast-iron work on the terraces glinting in the sun. This afternoon, Ben has nowhere particular to be or to go, and so he wants to explore somewhere that he hasn't been before. Looking at the map on his phone, he touches Camperdown Park with his thumb and moves it around on the screen.

'So how about we walk over there? So this ...,' Ben pauses, 'I'm also in the wrong maps application.'

'You're using Apple Maps?' I smile, 'do you do that often?'

'All the time! Especially since the latest OS, which is infuriating because it feels like a power struggle between two companies.' His eyes light up. 'Actually, I can show you something really interesting which I thought was ... where *were* we?' He looks off into the distance searching for a memory unseen. 'Oh, it will be in my recent searches. Do you know how to look in previous ones? Ah, okay,' he taps the phone twice, 'so GOMA in, uh ....'

I look at his map, which is centred on Africa, 'Africa?'

He looks at me with serious eyes.

'No – in Brisbane. The art gallery. So, we were in the centre of Brisbane, and I searched for GOMA in Apple Maps, and it went to Goma, the DRC, whereas in Google Maps it took me to the Gallery of Modern Art in Brisbane. That's to say, there's a very subtle difference.'

It is a slightly more than a subtle difference between a town in the DRC, and an art gallery in Brisbane. But the difference between them, at least regarding Benjamin's experience, has less to do with geographical distance than the consequences of discourse that generalises all places through taxonomies and calculation. Google Maps provides search results based on the nearest places, indexing between coordinate locations and the geo-tags attached to place names. Apple Maps doesn't appear to have this function (yet). Instead, it builds a place-based hierarchy on size and importance, rather than proximity. Each system provides a different result: Google Maps, GOMA in Brisbane; and Apple Maps, Goma in Africa.

Further to this simple error, however, is the way in which the heterogeneity of space is filtered out under cartographic reason, where geometries are built based on universal characteristics. Goma and GOMA are almost the same in a database of place names. Furthermore, attaching coordinate positions to these place names forms calculative territories through which various places can be attached. GPS devices, like smartphones, form roving agents within these territories, as their position shifts and needs to be retriangulated and recalculated every 30 seconds. Within the framework of calculative territories produced by cartographic reason, the 'subtle difference' between GOMA and Goma is merely a matter of numbers, and how well the algorithms are coded to take into account certain factors within this Leibnizian-Cartesian space. It is not so much a matter of which search ranking is better, although Google provided a more accurate result, but consistent valences given to the belief that the fallibility of cartographic reason is best solved through the application of more taxonomies, more indexes, more tags and more calculability. The appearance of cartographic reason as situated calculation is not total discursive transformation: there is little evidence to suggest that a break has occurred and a new way of thinking is nigh in digital mapping. What we see here is the way in which certain codes anticipate and deduct meaning from inputted information, like GOMA, but at the same time, like cartographic reason, denies the complexity of the way in which meaning is formed.

As we stand there, and Ben explains how he uses maps, the repercussions become clear as he intertwines his own spatial imagination with the cartographic imagination of the mobile digital maps. Usually, when he's navigating, he just finds a place and walks towards the 'dot', preferring to shape his own route between here and there, and allowing space for detours and explorations. As he switches from Apple Maps to Google Maps, however, he points out how mapping platforms differ in representing and taxonomising space.

'This is interesting,' he says, zooming in on the park. 'It's actually green on this map.'

This seems to fit better with his image of the park and contributes, too, to the reason he uses Google Maps, rather than Apple Maps. Maps, for Benjamin, bear a special relationship to the way in which he imagines the spaces that he inhabits. Parks should be green because parks are green. However, like the others before him, speed and mode of transport play a large part in determining precisely how the relationship between imagined spaces and embodied spaces unfolds. Following the 'dot' and trying to find his way on a bicycle, for instance, poses bigger problems. Laughing, Benjamin explains how he had a different experience to Nick trying to navigate with the phone while on his bike.

'I had to put [the phone] in my bag because my pockets are really big and so it falls out. So I'd have to stop every time I would lose track of where I thought I was.' The expression on his face suggests that this was more often than he would like.

'Of course,' he continues, 'it would be that difference between having an actual map versus the actuality of the environment versus the map,' he pauses as we cross a road, 'so, of course, like, my imaginary world, which was what the map showed me, was not accurate.'

Where Nick *feels* his way, Ben *imagines* worlds: somewhere between image and embodiment each interprets cycling through the city according to their own logics, and with unique mediations between cartographies, bodies and spaces. There is a difference for Ben between encountering spaces or maps first. In exploration, Ben's 'imaginary world' is drawn from the map at first encounter, unlike Sarah who declares that, for her, an unvisited space does not exist in her mind. Ben's mind is filled with images, drawing between cartographies and spaces, between fixed and unfixed, as it warps and derails his imagined worlds. This means that while cartography assists in interpreting in the distance between the environment and Ben's imagination, it also disorients. It is a futile promise that cartography gives Ben, and leaves him cold and unsure at every corner as the route disappears from his mind and 'the actuality of the environment' detours and changes. Despite their ability to situate and contextualise information, the abstract and remote cartographic nature of mobile digital maps means that their authority falters in interpreting between material and imagined worlds – even as they become more precise and better replicates of everyday mapping practices.

Originally, Benjamin tells me, he had intended to take me on a drive for this interview – much like Shaun had, to discover new places. His girlfriend has recently bought a car, and he has become fond of playing navigator in the front seat using Google Maps. He describes how the 'car function' uses the 'blue line' to determine the route, but also helpfully, there is a setting for step-by-step directions. This is down to a feature that he has just discovered, the 'slide left – slide right' instructions that pop out from the side of the screen, in which he can specify what kind of transport he is using, enter the leaving and arriving time and how he wants the navigation aids to be displayed. But he 'couldn't get the car', and he doesn't drive, and so we are wandering down through the backstreets of Camperdown in search of a park that he hasn't been to before. At every corner, we pause on a footpath beside a telegraph pole (safe enough from cars, but far enough to read the street signs). He won't use the blue line or the step-by-step instructions for walking.

'It's unnecessary,' he says, 'but once again it's that ambiguity, right?'

Ben's wording also has a double ambiguity: hinting at the surprises that irrupt in mediating between maps, spaces and imagined worlds, as well as the ambiguity of the map itself. It is, if anything, a fascinating way of reconceptualising the abstraction of cartographic reason. Although discursively, cartographic reason strives to erase ambiguity by developing epistemological systems that are calculable, predictable and universal, in the midst of the process of abstraction, ambiguity emerges. Walking is a different pace and a different kind of experience to driving or cycling. While the cartographic assumes an axiomatic translatability of relative speeds and rhythms, the ambiguity of how things fit together, the fragmentary nature of space and how imaginary worlds are constructed through cartographies and memories assembles differently in a walk compared to a drive or a cycle. This becomes apparent as Ben calls me to a pause at another street corner pungent with mimosa, to discuss which way to go. To pause without fully stopping is the indulgence of the walk, to glance at the map without becoming absorbed and to find our way, without becoming beholden to its authority.

Ambiguity is part of Ben's modus operandi in imagining Sydney. Like for Kyja, Sydney is still novel for Ben, and so piecing it all together, drawing lines between places and discovering the osmotic potential of space has been a thoughtful project for him. He describes his imagined Sydney as a series of partial thoughts, beset by an alluring vagueness. Sydney, he says, has a philosophy of 'being scattered'. Little suburbs thrown together between the coastline and the mountains, inward-looking neighbourhoods bounded by intimidating roads that discourage traversal across them. When he first moved to Sydney, Ben was based at the Museum of Contemporary Art down at Circular Quay – across the road from the Orient Hotel, where Tanija directed us to turn right up Argyle Street towards the Harbour Bridge. The route between home and work becomes formative in his imagined Sydney – down the spine of George Street and into Circular Quay, along the main roads that are painted yellow on the maps. This journey retraces the hegemonic structure of the transport system, yellow roads quickly sliding through the city through spaces that hold the city's history. These spaces, as we have seen with Kyja, and Sarah, Marianna and Shaun, gather themselves together, and take the people who inhabit them with them into their skeins.

'When I used to come and visit,' Ben tells me, 'I used to travel everywhere and go everywhere, and friends would say, like that [it's hot!]' – he fans his face with his hand – 'that, uh, Sydney is really notoriously bad for forming small cliques around geography – that once you move somewhere it just becomes, like geographically centred. But I would always counter that and say, "Well, no, I wouldn't do that because there is just so much interesting stuff happening everywhere. How can you become geographically stuck?" And the most hilarious thing is that I pretty much live within, like, three or four spots and it's a struggle to leave.'

This, Ben reasons, is because transport maintains an integral and powerful role in structuring lived geographies of Sydney. It's near impossible in some parts of the city to avoid buses, and if you cycle, you are more than likely to encounter very aggressive drivers who loathe sharing the road. Furthermore, walking in the heat or the rain is very difficult, and so public transport becomes a necessity. Even though the train structure is fixed as Kyja noted, it is also quite erratic and without full coverage for the planning reasons and vested interests that Shaun sketched out. This means that if you don't drive, like Ben, the image of the city is not based necessarily upon wayfinding signs or architectural distinctions, but the path and rhythm of moving through the city. These connections are heterogeneous and transformative. In the lived-in spaces of the suburbs, people flow through in modes of exploration and habitus, traversing the patterns left by subdividers, seeing the neighbourhood as it changes every day. But then, on buses or trains, planners etch transport routes from an impersonal eye and a rational logic, glancing down at the map and defining the flows of spaces and carving up the urban imagination into sections (Söderström, 1996). This is precisely why the discursive formations of cartographic reason rather than the textuality of cartography are central to understanding how mobile mapping practices shape, and are shaped by, spatiality. Cartographic reason classifies and quantifies – it draws odd boundaries around suburbs using main roads which then seep into cartographic imaginations: the small cliques around geography bound and define spatial practices, and the more segmented the city, the more difficult it is to transcend those boundaries.

Yet, we also see how everyday practices unsettle the ambition and illuminate the limitations of cartographic thinking. Ben describes how he intuitively navigates while he walks. To get to this point, he has only looked at the map once or twice, to check where we are, but not to decide the route. He's connecting the dots between his scattered geography of Camperdown Memorial Rest Park, which he visited recently, and is then figuring it out from there. But now that I've brought it up, he's struck by a crisis of confidence, incidentally on the corner of a street which slices through the heart of Camperdown, effectively separating the neighbourhoods that centre on King Street in Newtown and those on Parramatta Road in Camperdown.

'Sydney streets often diverge,' he says, checking the phone. 'How badly did I go? Oh, not too bad .... So let's just keep going up and turn – left, right?'

'Right, left,' I nod.

Out of the heat of the main road, we turn down an alleyway overshadowed by the cool perfume of eucalypts. This is a strange and unfamiliar part of Camperdown for Ben, and he takes his time looking at the houses and reading the graffiti on the wall. As we stare at it, Ben muses.

'It's kind of funny, the strategy that I use for finding my way.'

As he discusses his strategies for navigating and how he decides which way to go, he realises that he prefers 'narrow streets'. He also describes how he has to imagine what he does because he's not checking his phone as much as he normally would because he's too focused on the conversation. I laugh and point around the laneway.

'So when you walk, do you prefer laneways as well?'

'Yeah,' he replies 'it depends. It really depends on that, like, the area and the feeling of the place. And I think sometimes, like, silly enough, I get a little afraid of laneways or dark places as well ....'

'Where, in particular?'

'Any place that is kind of unknown with a demographic that I'm not sure about or not.'

'Do you find when you navigate there is a correlation between the way the laneway appears on a map and the way it feels or is there a disjuncture? How does that relationship unfold?'

'That's the interesting thing about Google Maps – it has no social demographic, right? So it can put you down a path where, like, more, like, streets that would normally be avoided by ....'

Ben is emphatic on this point. Google Maps doesn't show people – it doesn't show atmosphere or ambience, and it doesn't show areas that are safe or dangerous. All spaces are part of the same system under Cartesian geometry and cartographic reason (Olsson, 1991b). While the map might be able to locate us at a particular moment in space and time, the meaning of our position, the experience of moving through space and the intuitive and affective relations that form in mobile mapping assemblages are uncannily erased. Regimentation through cartographic reason fixes space and obscures the manifold spatialities that exist across space and time. It presents an 'imagined world' wherein all spaces become like ours: the connections and meanings that the map makes for us, in our specific space-times, are assumedly transferable through the map to other spaces.

Ben already imagined an a priori relationship between the green on the map (and even switched maps to reinforce that imaginary) and the cool, green and leafy parks that he sees in his personal geographies. After crossing the road towards a large oval with sun-browned grass, rugby goals at both ends, and a few trees scattered around the edges, Ben looks at his phone.

'So we are at that park. And it is boring.'

'Did you think it would be more interesting?'

'I did think it would be more interesting.'

'Why?'

'I don't know. Because it was green. I thought there would be more shade, and less, sort of, sporting grounds.'

It would be oversimplified to read this moment of disappointment as a mistake made by Ben in accepting the hubris of cartographic authority. The colonising power maintained by cartographic reason is exerted by inscribing spatial imaginations with cartographic iconography, resulting in a cartographic imagination. Then, by using the power of cartographic systems of representation, it expands its discourse by universalising the interpretation meaning of personal experiences across all spaces and times. In this discourse, space can only be understood through the imagination, and that this imagination is formed solely through mediating between the abstract representations of the map and the embodied experience of space: or, what Ben thinks should be represented by a green block on a map. At the same time, the discursive power of cartographic reason is neither deterministic nor absolute, and Ben is disappointed when it is less green and more 'sporting grounds', browned by the summer sun.

As Ben scrolls across the screen, he tries to find somewhere that may be green and the kind of park that he was hoping to find. To our north, he finds the green spaces of Sydney University, before concluding that, from memory, they, too, are all sports grounds and probably full of rugby players.

'We are there,' he explains, pointing to his phone. 'Where are the little green patches? I think we may be at – tch – this is the biggest green patch around.'

His disappointment is evident. Eventually, he decides to take us down to the waterfront at Glebe, continuing our path out of Camperdown, to a park that he knows will have enough space and a cool breeze to walk and chat. As we continue out of the park, Ben spots a street sign indicating that there is an art gallery down the road.

'It would take us right off course,' he ponders. 'Is it okay to change course? I think maybe it is.'

He checks his phone again, squinting at the screen in the sun, despite the sign clearly indicating which way the gallery was.

'Why did you check your phone?'

'I don't know. I guess I wanted to see what was around me.'

He does the same thing wherever he is, he explains. He likes to have 'a radar', to be able to check what lies around him and sense how the environment might unfold. Through the map, he is afforded a partial imaginary of the space, which he supplements with his own experiences. All the same, the radar is not quite accurate, and since the park was bright and dry rather than green and dark, he resigns himself to the fact that it is probably best to gather a sense of spatiality between places, and not as an omniscient descriptor of how places may look or feel. He puts the phone back into his pocket and Ben reflects on how Google Maps instils a sense of 'needing to constantly check the phone'. But it doesn't make too much of a difference when he is walking. It shows what is around him, but he moves by intuition, feeling his way and choosing streets to walk down.

The sign has directed us to a dead end, and Ben inspects a possible pedestrian thoroughfare. Ushering me on, we stumble through an overgrown footpath that connects two roads, narrowly housed in on the left by cricket practice pitches attached to the park and penned in with chicken wire and the end of a terrace row on the other side. He explains how he likes to 'stay away from main roads', and it is precisely this kind of footpath that he enjoys encountering – a footpath that was, notably, not on the map. As we emerge, we find ourselves deep under some large figs, with some inscrutable warehouses running down the other side of the road.

'It's just kind of interesting seeing all these buildings and not knowing what goes on in them,' he says.

'What do you think goes on in them?' I ask.

'Industry.'

We turn the corner and head on to another park, O'Dea Reserve, without sports fields, but still sparsely forested. From our perspective, the footpath curves in a horseshoe, rising up the hill before descending back towards the bottom of the park. There is a set of exercise equipment cemented into the grass and covered over with bark chippings. Ben looks at it strangely and then pulls out his phone to check that the path won't take us too far off course, but then puts it back without looking at it. Eventually, we will get to the same place, even if there is a marked difference in the mode and manner of walking between A and B. We don't necessarily know where this path will take us – but it matters less when you have nowhere important to be.

'I think there's a very big difference between' – he pockets the phone – 'when you're using a map to just wander versus wandering without a map versus using a map to find something.'

'How so?'

'Well, I think when you have directions to go somewhere you use a map to specifically find that point, right, so you don't care about anything in-between – like, it's just the shortest or quickest journey. Whereas, if you're using a map to wander, then you're interested in whatever is around the place and how you are situated in the larger, kind of, possible surroundings and places that you could explore. Whereas, if you're exploring without a map you don't care really where you are, and you constantly have to keep sort of, or you don't really *have* to, but you do, keep track of more, be more conscious of where you are so you know how to get back to where you possibly have to.'

Two ways of imagining space: one centred on the exploration of possibility, of imagining and discovering the infinite openness of space; the other about placing points on a map and navigating between them, closing down options and fixing space and limiting possibility. Looking back now, I can see how this path took us – an undulating detour that resulted in us arriving much where we had planned to be. One route – that of the map – suggested that we should walk straight through the park on the quickest route as Ben returned us home; the other path, which we took, was less efficient, but more interesting to Ben, as we wandered through the streets of Camperdown. In the end, we never found the kind of park that Ben was looking for, and we never found the art gallery that we detoured to see. Standing on the south-western corner of the park, Ben stopped again, hesitating about whether he wanted to check the map on his phone and find which way to go. Yet again, putting it away without looking at it, he sighs.

'But that's more internalised,' he says, referring back his second mode of mapping, 'so in some respects you can actually get more lost with a map than without, maybe. I don't know.'

## Cassie/Dreams

> 'Yeah, so that's literally how I do it. Write down the landmark, and where I'm turning.'

A cyclist zips ahead of us along the Bourke Street cycle path, while Cassie and I dodge trees and discuss peeking into houses and imagining who lives there. The cycleway is separated from the footpath by a thin garden bed, filled with flowering bushes and wood chippings and overhung by tall trees in one of the oldest suburbs of Sydney. It's a cool journey under the canopy along Bourke Street on a January evening, as the tall terraces crowd in and stop the glare and the trees lower the ambient temperature reverberating off the road and the paths. Travelling home from work in Waterloo, Cassie decided to take me to Central Station, rather than Redfern, because this route is a longer walk and it will give us more things to see. There's a poetic reason, too. This way, she can take me from her new job to her old job, a journey that she describes as 'fitting' because she's looking for work – again.

Redfern and Central Stations are prominent in Cassie's Sydney.

'I tend to judge everything by train lines because that's my main form of transport. So I kind of have rough ideas that the city is that way and the train line curves around that way. Redfern's that way. My home is kind of more that way.'

As has been revealed again and again, movement influences how the city is mapped out, how connections are drawn and spatiality constructed. With Cassie, this is not necessarily a cartographic imagination. Like with Nick, curves and shifts, landmarks on horizons and hills forming contoured terrains render an intuitive, material legibility to the spaces that Cassie inhabits – a gaze that is embodied, an epistemology that is experienced.

'It's not the map,' she says, 'so much as the line itself, kind of looking out the window and seeing the city in the distance and seeing whether we're going on a curve.'

'Okay.' An ambulance can be heard in the distance, getting closer, disrupting the tranquillity of the street.

'Sort of by landmarks.'

'And the city's a big landmark?' I ask.

'Yeah, Centrepoint Tower is my landmark.'

Centrepoint Tower, rising above the city at 309 m tall, is the second-tallest building in the southern hemisphere. Designed by Donald Crone (it is rumoured on the back of a napkin) it is a tall turreted structure, an observation tower perched on a high steel limb. Fifty-six steel cables stabilise it against the strong onshore winds, anchored into the Sydney bedrock. It sits between Pitt and Elizabeth Streets, where Sarah and I walked along the invisible threads of the old Tank Stream to St James Station and Hyde Park, in the centre of the CBD. It's never been officially known as Centrepoint Tower – Centrepoint was the building from which the tower rises. First officially known as AMP Tower (as AMP owned the building and adorned their logo on the outside of the observation deck) it was recently bought by Westfield, who replaced the old logo with theirs and renamed it Sydney Tower. But it has always been Centrepoint Tower in the vernacular of those who live around it. Corporations may come and go with their authoritative toponyms and vagabond branding, but the tower itself holds on as Centrepoint, as other buildings are built, and views are obstructed.

'So the city is a big landmark?' I clarify.

'Yeah.'

'So what are the main landmarks along here?'

'Along here,' the ambulance is rushing towards us now, dominating the space of our conversation, as Cassie pauses and waits for it to pass.

'Along here I tend to look at the houses.'

'Okay.'

''Cos I'm a sticky beak, and I like to look at houses.' She laughs. 'Ah, so, I might notice a house that I particularly like or just a section of street that I think is attractive so yeah, I just tend to remember I guess the way the street kind of works.'

From here, we can't see Centrepoint – we are too deep in the urban landscape to be able to see the city. Different landmarks open up this space for Cassie in different ways. The spaces that are *lived in*, which Marianna and I first encountered, offer a less architectural and more social terrain, defined but not dominated by cartographic reason.

'I like to go for walks on my lunch break and walk around the streets where the houses are – look at the houses, kind of daydream a bit about, you know if I had that house, you know if I lived there what the place might look like inside, or whatever. Yeah, I just like houses. It's disturbingly domestic of me.'

Not all daydreams are of iron bridges, transport networks, pedestrianised walkways, entertainment quarters, manicured parks and the landscapes that are found in literature. Back here, to end the final walk in Sydney in a space of suburban domesticity is coincidental, but also profound. Walking through someone else's spatial lives as their houses, and parking spots, and street parties mingle and intertwine with your own spatial life evokes possible, imagined spatialities that perhaps speak better to Massey than to Olsson or Foucault. In this daydream of Cassie's, space is open to reinterpretation – being denied knowledge of inside, the lack of representational fixity that lurks far away from planning documents and maps, opens up possibilities for Cassie, so that she may reimagine what a life there would be like to live. Of course, social imaginaries like modernity and postmodernity bleed and structure how we think about things (Soja, 1989) – but the kind of knowledge which is barely known, subjugated because it is lived but also muted – occupies the realm of open space, away from drawing lines, and the indexicality of fingers and eyes. Cassie's daydream, Marianna's evocations, and Sarah's never-forgotten geographies are space with*out* the realm of cartographic reason.

As I discover, later on, this is not a momentary lapse or a minor resistance against an unyielding discourse – it merely *is* for Cassie, a spatialisation that is habitual, and until I brought it up, completely unconsidered.

'When I was up in Queensland for Christmas,' she ruminates, 'we went to look at the Christmas lights – it's as much looking at the lights but also if they have to have a tree in that window, then it's a good excuse to look through that window and see what kind of house they've got.'

It would be erroneous to interpret this as a kind of competitive living, or anxiety based on social climbing – and Cassie's tone is one of curiosity, not envy. Rather, inside houses are spaces that are not catalogued and mapped – they are private spaces and within the curtains and window screens that mediate between public and private space, space, as Massey (2005) states, is always open. In the rare times where those curtains are open, and the rooms are lit up, Cassie can see that possibility come to life, away from her daydreams into someone else's lived world, and the immense heterogeneity of being.

Certainly, she uses maps. When I ask her how she chose the route that we are walking along now, she replies earnestly.

'Yeah, this is the way that I would normally go. I looked it up on Google Maps because if I'm walking somewhere that's not, sort of, my everyday thing I do like to check. Yep. You know, where I'm going and write it down. But also there's a bus that I catch that goes along this way as well, so ….'

But it's not quite as immersed as it could be.

'So, you'll look at a map and write down the instructions rather than looking on your phone?'

'I will have my phone. I've got it here,' she waves the phone in her hand, 'But I really prefer to write things down because I can get disoriented with a map, and with numbers and even with a map on my phone, it'll have the little arrow but sometimes I might walk 100 m before it kind of catches up, and I might have gone the wrong direction. If I've got it written down, you know, I can look at the map and think about which way to turn and what street and write it down.'

Cassie's method is inexplicably analogue – but also signals a discord with the way in which cartographic reason represents the spaces in which Cassie lives.

'Like anything, even involving numbers and budgets, I will write it as if I'm talking to myself rather than actually having numbers and figures.' And so, it is a discursive objection, as well as a practical one.

Maps, for Cassie, are like numbers, and budgets and figures – deeply situated in mathematical modes of reasoning and drawing connections. But this order of things is not the way in which Cassie thinks. Cassie daydreams and glimpses into possible lives – she creates stories, and so translates the abstract realm of figures and shapes into conversations with herself, into epistemological structures that are more meaningful, and so more memorable, to her. It is curious how Cassie's analysis strikes at the ambitious heart of cartographic reason, and how lackadaisical her contrition appears.

'So you wouldn't use the sort of thing on Google Maps where you can go for directions, and it'll take you step by step?' I wonder.

'Um, oh, I'll use it. I did it for this, but the directions it gave, they weren't familiar to me. So I moved the little cursor back over to the way that I know. But if it's somewhere I've never been before at all, then yeah, I'll definitely do that.' Cassie likes to choose a route and stick to it – and it is up to the map to accommodate her habits. She does not shy in the face of cartographic reason, nor does she embody the map as Kyja did, or take it into her imagination, as Tanija did, or trouble it, as Sarah did – Cassie merely steps around it.

'I get into routines really quickly, really easily,' she continues.

'Yeah?'

'Um, I'm probably only inclined to change it, really, if somebody else kind of, y'know, suggests or takes me. And then, I can really quickly fall into their routine.'

We pass the police stables on our left, as the colourful terraces give way to large red brick walls and imposing barbed wire. It is a strange institution, nestled into another gentrifying neighbourhood, the residue of the working-class past of Surry Hills that Ruth Park wrote about so vividly. The rail workshops and factories in Eveleigh which employed the residents of Newtown, also employed the largely Irish community in Surry Hills, as well as rag trade garment factories. After work, the class structures continued, police cultures melding with drinking cultures, the social scars of far-off places carved into new territories, over other cultures.

'I used to walk home of an evening, like to Redfern Station, with, um, one of my co-workers. And, they sort of, they get sort of near the bit with Redfern Park, and there's a couple of different ways you can go. And he would always go one way and y'know, would keep going straight down, um, I think it's Young Street whereas I walk – when I was walking by myself – I used to, there's like a little a basketball part/area, and kind of, behind that, and go kind of down this dead end, kind of go through this dark, lonely street, you know, where there were broken bottles and things like that, but it was just habit, it's the way I go.'

A cultural poetics of space (Stewart, 1996): everyday romances formed through routine. Dark, lonely streets with beer bottles become familiar spaces – and the surprising textures of space that are made uniform in the map become familiar. Ben worried that Google Maps didn't show what spaces are like – that all spaces look the same, regardless of their social and cultural variations.

'But then, in the mornings, I notice, he goes another way, he kind of goes up this big hill near this apartment block – so yeah, if I'm walking with him, then I just tend to fall into his routines.'

Cassie worries less than Ben, while she negotiates her route with her co-worker.

'I'm very happy to let other people navigate.'

A space that is not defined by strategies or tactics (De Certeau, 1984), but rather by lines of flight (Deleuze and Hand, 1988) and tours (Sadler, 1999), Cassie does not protect her spatial imaginaries but leaves them open to opportunity and intervention. There is a subtle difference here that does not attempt to fight or undermine the discursive power of cartographic reason as it has been etched into the landscape and the imagination. Rather, Cassie simply denies cartographic reason the power that it claims, and seeks other stories and other possibilities instead. Maps intersect and structure Cassie's tours, but as she translates them into space, the hegemony that they at first occupy slips, and space is revealed to be far more complicated than cartographic reason would portend. She explains how she navigates through space, dissecting Cartesian geometries and reconstructing her own.

'It's by points,' she looks around, 'and actually, this is Cleveland Street, so I think we have to go ...' – the engine of a motorcycle drowns out her voice – '... left .... Yes, we do. Yes, it's points.'

'How did you know to turn left? You didn't use the map .... What did you see to make you go, "Yes, we do"?'

'Actually, it was by memory, so we sort of double – let me check it. Because I don't trust myself.' She pulls out a tattered Brita-branded sticky note. On it, in scratchy black ink, is a list of bulleted instructions hastily written step by step. Carefully, she reads it, 'Yes, left on Cleveland.'

'Left on Cleveland?'

'Umm ... yeah, so that's literally how I do it. Write down the landmark, and where I'm turning and ....'

'From Google Maps?'

'From Google Maps.'

'What did you do before Google Maps?'

'Oh, god.' Cassie looks horrified as her memory reaches back.

'Use a street directory?' I laugh.

'No, honestly, before,' she tucks her hair behind her ear, 'before Google Maps I probably wouldn't have needed a map, to be honest.' Another siren sounds in the distance, 'I wouldn't have been going to places where I had to navigate. Umm. Yeah, I really can't think of anywhere, actually.'

'So, you never went anywhere?'

'Um, I went to places, but I don't think I had much reason to go anywhere that was – kind of – different. I mean, I'm trying to think. I would have started using a kind of Google Map and navigating myself around when I moved back to Sydney.'

'Yeah?'

'And by that stage the Internet – er, Google – was there with its maps and I could look up directions – although Google Maps didn't look the same as it does now. And I didn't have a phone, so I'd just have to write everything down. Um, but before that, while I was living in Queensland. Um, yeah, I would have only ever gone to the same places in the same way, and public transport dimensions would have to be really exact.'

We pull up on the corner of Cleveland Street and Crown Street, the Crown Hotel sitting prominently across the road. Cassie squints at the intersection and then nods her head and points.

'Yeah, we go down here.' She grasps the sticky note in her hand and continues talking. 'Public transport connections were really exact because if you missed it, there might not have been another train for another half an hour. You might have to walk another 20 minutes to somewhere else. Whereas in Queensland, if I couldn't get public transport somewhere, I just couldn't go there, you know. I couldn't drive, so there were just lots of places that were just out of bounds to me.'

Her description of the need for accuracy in negotiating the public transport system is at odds with her current directive.

'So what's the next one? Right onto Elizabeth?' I ask.

'Yep, which is down here,' Cassie replies. The issue I've spotted is that we aren't on Elizabeth Street, we are at Crown Street, demonstrated by the large lettering of the hotel across the road.

'So,' Cassie continues, 'I know where we are because I've eaten dinner down there a few times and I've walked down this street with people I used to work with, so it's all sort of memory and familiar landmarks, and things like that.'

This is an example of the slippage that I described before. Even when Cassie follows the map she instinctively detours without even realising it. This is a familiar landmark, so she presumes that, of course, it is the waypoint that the map means. She has memorised the next step – Elizabeth Street – but when that collides with her own memory, the map and space become entangled.

'And so, if I said to you where does Cleveland Street end up, would you know?

'Um, Cleveland Street goes ... all the way down, I think, towards, um, Chalmers Street, which goes along the train line. So I think I could, in theory,

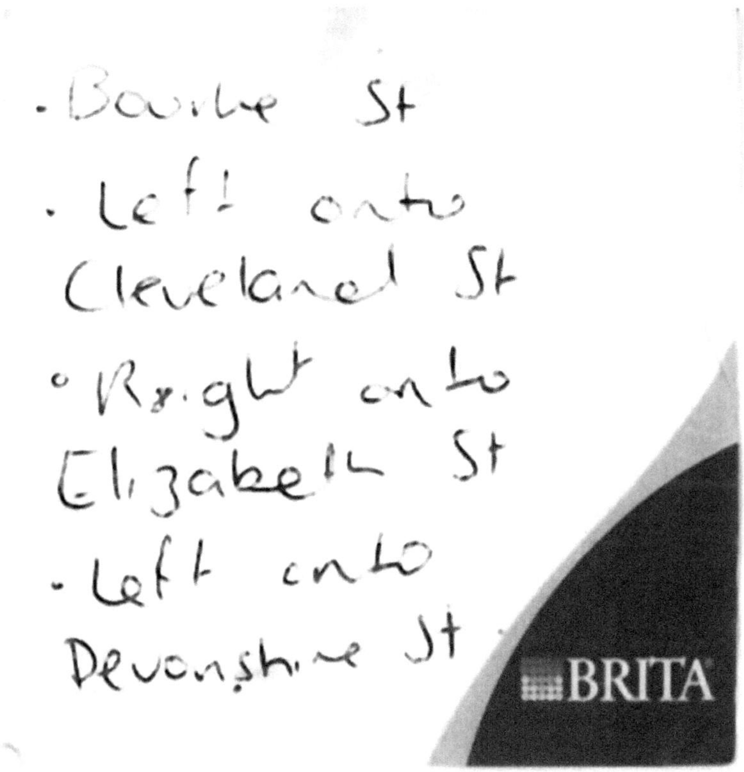


Figure 6.3. *Brita note.* List of instructions written on sticky note by Cassie from Google Maps before the start of the trip.

follow Cleveland Street all the way down and get back down to the train line. But I prefer this walk because – I just like this street – I like to walk and look in the windows and stuff. And think about places I'd like to eat.'

The street is busy, filled with boutique delicatessens, independent design stores and charcoal chicken and kebab shops. It is also markedly different from Elizabeth Street, which is more functional and less trafficked. The distance between taking Elizabeth and Crown must be minimal, yet even the most minimal distance is enough for Google to try to carve new goat trails into the everyday routines of Cassie. All the same, she walks along her own path, firm in the belief that she is following the map's instructions all the while following her intuition. Between places lies space, and this is where Cassie unties and reties paths.

'I probably only know the centres of suburbs, like their main hubs or their main transport points,' she says.

'And then you'd move between them.'

'Like the nodes in a network?'

'Yes, exactly. Like little nodes.'

'So, when you wander, do you see a relationship between where you are and street names? For instance, what street is this?'

'This is Elizabeth. But the only reason I know that is because I had to look it up and write it down. Otherwise, I'd have absolutely no idea.'

'Even the walk I do to work every single day, I couldn't tell you the names of most of those streets. Which is terrible, because people ask me for directions, and I'm like, I walk here every day, and I have no idea.'

'And so how did you find how to get to work for the first time? Google Maps?'

'Google Maps,' she nods, 'Yeah, I wrote it down and then I just had it committed to memory.'

'But it's not actually the street names that you commit to memory?'

'No, it's the, um, the landmarks and just the way the street looks and feels.'

'The kind of ambience?'

'And I actually kind of have little landmarks along the way. Like, I know when I get to a certain pub or park or something, kind of how much further I have to go to get to the station or to get to work. See, from here, this is all fine. This is the walk I do very often, so we just go down here. I am probably the least geographically minded person.'

It's a strange comment for Cassie to make to define herself as 'the least geographically minded person'. Geography, she concludes, is a mindset – a way of thinking. In this, she also concludes that geography is distinct from space, and on a different epistemological footing to her intuitive, paper-based and habitual navigations. Geographically minded implies an intuitive understanding of how a geographical imagination (Gregory, 1994) shapes paths and tours through space, reshapes landscapes and imports an extrinsic imaginary into material reality through the process of colonisation. Cassie's space is not geography – and so she does not subjugate her knowledge to what Carter (2009) calls 'geography's myth' – the myth of equating lived space with Euclidean epistemes and Western rationalities (or I what call 'cartographic reason').

Geography's myth is equally cartography's myth, and perhaps even geometry's myth – the achievement of perfect angles and divine vanishing points inscribed into spaces that are then lived. The lines of geometry as materialised through cartographic reason are what create the hard boundaries of the police stables, brushing up against the fuzzy borders of cycleways, footpaths and gardens. Cartographic reason irrupts in spatial and representational statements that define main roads against backstreets, emphasise freeways over alleyways, and prioritise speed over ambience and longevity against ephemerality. But such absolute statements are antithetical to the way in which Cassie moves through space. As we approach the corner of Crown and Devonshire, she points us left – both her sticky note and her phone, forgotten. She chooses to go one way rather than another not because the map tells her, or because it is quicker or perhaps a more major road, but because of the landscape. These are old colonial spaces, decorated with the Old World nostalgia that spread from Botany Bay and returned again: names like Devonshire, Wilshire, High Holborn and Marlborough again intermingle with Elizabeth, George and Crown and Pitt. Yet, it is not the nostalgia of England that draws her to these spaces: it is the architecture.

'It's usually to do with the kind of style of houses,' she shrugs, 'Like, it's purely aesthetic. Um, I like old houses.'

As we cross the road, we move onto another similar area, turn of the century terraces with shopfronts on street level.

'Um,' Cassie continues, 'I like murals and graffiti and things like that – I like cities, basically. So, the more urban an area is, or if it's a bit old, or even if it's a bit run down – that's what I like.'

There is something of the sublime here that cartographic reason cannot contain or represent. It is not so much an aesthetic representation, but an aesthetic experience – the rapture of certain types of houses, of certain kinds of streets and the affective process of moving through that space, imagining and reimagining possibility through sites of difference, of time passing through space, of resistance. This is completely counterposed to her experiences in the western suburbs, the landscapes in which both she and Cliff were raised.

'Whereas out there, you just get totally suburban. You know, like three-bedroom, red brick houses built in the 60s – it all looks the same to me.'

Structured space, like that of the 1960s, little, red, off-the-plan houses built a certain dream of conformity, which for some, like Davis (2006), resulted in emptiness. This is something that Cassie feels – and something that she also thinks impacts on her ability to navigate through space.

'I think I just like big and full. And the bigger and the more crowded a city is, and the older that a city is, the more I tend to like it. And, I think I probably even find that easier to navigate as well because they tend to have, again, better public transport and more interesting stuff.'

And so we return to spaces that exist in, around and through cartographic reason, representation, conceptualisation and the map. Space, space that is open, is not a subjugated knowledge as Foucault would describe, hovering around the margins of hegemonic discourses. By the same token, cartographic reason is not a discourse that unequivocally and unyieldingly delineates what space is and what it means by pushing all other knowledge to an abject and inaccessible space. Rather, like powder shot sprayed through a wall, the boundaries between representation and experience, fixity and openness, discourse and that which exists beyond it, are revealed to be permeable.

In each of these walks, cartographic reason has irrupted in statements that are harsh in form and message. Erased cultures, rewritten pasts, cliff sides cut in two and dominating transports are supplemented by affective relations with space, paths that can be felt and an embodied custom to the waxing and waning of the landscape. We walk up to the highest point of Devonshire Street, one of the many hills in Surry Hills[1] and Cassie stares down towards Central Station, past the Gaelic Club, and somewhere across where the burial mound that Sarah described would be.

'The route that I mentioned that my co-worker takes in the morning goes up a pretty steep hill. I would never go that way. I go via a gentler hill. It would never occur to me to walk up a steep hill right into the sun – because that's the direction that the sun is in the morning.'

The sun is different in Sydney, the sky is bigger, and the light is harsher. These claims are not quantifiable, and perhaps not even provable. They may even be wrong. Yet, the enduring stutters between cartographic reason and the landscape of the Sydney basin irrupt in these moments of disconnect, where people struggle to explain why they do not follow the map, or logic, or reason. And so the landscape, while it might be melded to suit a European gaze, still encourages certain spatial practices that move beyond the grasp of cartographic reason, a mathematical transcendence or abstract space. Somewhere between the fixity of cartographic reason and the openness of space lies a social and cultural negotiation between discourse and *something else*. Cassie stops outside the stairs to Central Station on Elizabeth Street. Even though she thinks she has followed the directions she wrote out on her sticky note, she has strayed from the cartographic into the habitual, and without even knowing it, made her own way. Why does she think, then, that she has so little understanding of geography?

'I will just automatically blame myself,' she says, 'because I accept the fact that I have a terrible sense of direction.'

But she doesn't. It turns out that she probably didn't need to check the map or write down the directions at all. But this is entirely geography's

1 Surry Hills, however, was not named for its hills. It was named by Joseph Foveaux after Surrey Hills in Surrey, UK.

myth and the discursive power of cartographic reason: it suggests that you do not know. The hegemony of numbers and categories, of calculations and taxonomies, subdues and subjugates the fleeting, the memorial, the felt and the haunted aspects of spatiality. Furthermore, it suggests that there is only really one topological way of comprehending space beyond the subjective – a geometric, mathematical and monadological abstraction which can show us the way through the spaces that have been lived in, evoked, unsettled and troubled, felt, driven, misread, imagined and reimagined.

# Part 3

## Cartography/Cities

# 7. Drawing the line

> What does it mean to draw and interpret a line, to make and use a map, to dwell in the cartographic imagination?
> – Pickles, A History of Spaces (2004: 9)

From coordinates to code, mobile mapping has undertaken a tremendous journey in form and function. Trigonometric calculation transforms into automated triangulations and the assemblage of the map has expanded into new wings of the apparatus – digital infrastructure, technology, software and data networks. The mobile phone has embedded the map into a powerful two-way radio that can send and receive signals to satellites and through trilateration of the GPS satellites, using certain kinds of codes and automation, the phone/map can determine its coordinate position. This capability can be replicated across all kinds of map-based applications – from adding coordinate tags and time stamps to photographs to marking the position of the user in the map interface with a small blue dot to tracking users in near-real time if they've not been careful enough with their privacy settings.

When Franco Farinelli, Gunnar Olsson and Dagmar Reichert wrote of 'cartographic reason', they did not write of the manifold mapping applications that appear on a mobile phone, nor did they write too much of the disintegrating digital cartographic image that updates and shifts as a user walks through space. At the same time, in *La crisi della ragione cartografica* (2009), Farinelli speaks of a crisis of cartographic reason – with its emphasis on the rules and logics of modernity – arising from the network-based structure of the Internet: 'The structural logic of the Internet is, in fact, spherical, not tabular' (Farinelli, 2009: 200).[1]

The shift from grids or tabulation to spheres, Farinelli argues, reflects the transition from intersecting grid lines seen in modern cartographic images

1 Translation is my own. Original reads: 'La struttura logica di Internet è insomma sferica, non tabulare' (Farinelli 2009: 200).

Wilmott, C., *Mobile Mapping. Space, Cartography and the Digital.*
Taylor & Francis Group, 2020
DOI 10.5117/9789462984530_CH07

towards a networked, decentralised and protocol logic characterised by digital communication systems:

> But the only law of the Internet is its codes, the architecture that emerges from the whole of its hardware and software, and the Internet is a network defined by a set of protocols that are open and not subject to private property, of which access and use does not require any prior personal identification.[2] (Farinelli 2009: 201)

Virilio, Lessig and Castells have critiqued the dependent relationships between software and hardware, networks and signals, Farinelli notes. This has resulted in a crisis of the modern conception of space as territorial, earth-bound and finite in favour of a hybridised spatiality, with no centralised point, at odds with Cartesian rules and logic. He goes on to explain that this has created a new form of public space – self-determining, self-organised, free from the systems of private ownership and governmental oversight – and auguring something different from the modern conception of space: the death of distance, and perhaps even the end of geography and geographic discourse. Because the Internet has its own logic based in codes and hardware, the programmers and users who create the architecture and infrastructure of the vast digital networks that span the globe are bound to work within those coded logics rather than the geographic discourses of cartographic reason that preceded the development of the net.[3]

Thus, the space of the Internet and its operations occupies a different mode – or even plane – of conceptual existence to the modern idea of earth and territory. Networks rewrite the relationship between subjects and objects, spaces and people, and so, according to Farinelli, resemble more of an opaque postmodern skein than a visual order of modernity:

> The components of this collective are members more representative of a mixed body [...] in the age of the Internet, the age in which public space, to the extent that it survives, becomes in some manner chthnonic: not because it disappears under the face of the earth, but because it seeks to take the place, benignly, of that matrix that, entirely subterranean

2 Translation is my own. Original reads: 'Ma l'unica legge della rete è il suo codice, l'architettura che risulta dal complesso del suo *hardware* e del suo *software*, e Internet è una rete definite da un insieme di protocolli che sono aperti e non sottomessi a proprietà privata, il cui accesso e uso non richiedono cioè nessuna preliminare personale identificazione' (Farinelli, 2009: 201).

3 Translation is my own. Original reads: 'Perciò chi produce I programmi a sorgenti aperte produce la legge di Internet secondo la logica stessa di Internet' (Farinelli, 2009: 201).

> and invisible, has always ordered [disposto] the earth's form, but that modernity, precisely because it concentrates fundamentally on the visible, never managed to grasp.[4] (Farinelli, 2009: 201)

For this reason, Farinelli argues, cartographic reason is perhaps no longer an adequate concept to describe the acceleration, dispersion and fluidity of the current era. Yet, the rule of the skein, the binary space and the cyborg is not necessarily as distant (or distinct) from the Cartesian space that Farinelli describes. In his first discussions of the cartographic image, Farinelli focuses on a transformation in political and philosophical thought that occurred in Europe during the early years of modern age. This period of transformation was within the bounds of the same period that Cosgrove (2003) has focused on as the formation of an Enlightenment cartographic image, that Foucault (2002b) in *The Order of Things* calls the 'Age of Reason' and that Deleuze (1992a) discusses in *The Fold*. This was a time of upheaval, in which systems of thought were radically transformed, reified, or both. It was also a period in which there was significant desire to use philosophy, mathematics and geometry towards a transcendental ordering of space. It was during this period, in which Descartes created a *mathesis universalis*, or a universal science, Leibniz sought a *characteristica universalis*, 'a universal encyclopedia providing a common global language composed of clear, universal signs for primitive concepts' (Batchelor, 2004: 231), a universal taxonomy.

However, although the forms have changed from paper to digital maps, although the transference of information has become faster (and some would say, less reflexive), as the image has become reproducible, and now mutable, and space and time have become compressed, the logics of geometries, rationalities and taxonomies of this period are not as distanced as we might think. Farinelli (2009) describes the matrixes of the Internet to be invisible, like the creatures that dwell in the underworld, and cartographic reason, when faced with the unapologetic focus on the visible, cannot account for the complexity of the manifold logics. However, such codes and such logics are not as opaque, invisible or 'blackboxed' (cf. Latour and Woolgar, 1979; Callon and Latour, 1981) as they first appear. Beneath the high-resolution

4 Translation is my own. Original reads: 'I component di questi collettivi sono i membri piú [sic] rappresentativi del corpo misto ... dell'età della Rete, l'età in cui lo spazio pubblico, nella misura in cui sopravvive, diventa in qualche maniera ctonio: non perché scompare sotto la faccia della Terra, ma perché cerca di prendere il posto, a scopo benigno, di quella matrice che, del tutto sotterranea e invisibile, ha sempre disposto dell'ordine della forma terrestre, ma che la modernità, appunto perché concentrata fondamentalmente sul visibile, non è mai riuscita ad afferrare' (Farinelli, 2009: 201).

representations and smooth scrolling images on the screen, we can find that digital maps continue to work according to both the logics of this mode of geometry and reason, of visibility and invisibility, of process and picture.

*Digital* is an ambiguous term that opens up more meanings than it defines. Digits are the fingers that you count upon, one by one, the numbers that you add together to produce sums. In their most historical meaning, digital systems are simply systems of counting with limited signs, from the tally system to semaphores, Braille to Morse code. Before computers, geometry was already using digital systems of representation to make geometric calculations (such as the size of angles and the length of lines), to discover and problematise inconsistencies (such as the quadrature of the circle), establish the rules of its own discursive formation. Furthermore, as the iconography of the map became more formalised during the Enlightenment and later, cartography took on certain digital systems of representation. Grid lines etched across the world to regulate the representation of distance, sets of universal signs and colours that represented roads, rivers, churches and property as calculable, apprehensible data: all of these systems, whether metonymic or numeric, operate on digital logic.

But what we mean when we say 'digital' is the most recent iteration of this phenomenon – the computational technologies and logics that have evolved from this history but seem to sit without past in our everyday semantics. This is a peculiar forgetting that privileges the description and analysis of objects and technological progression over the discourses that frame the world, that takes the most recent phase of progress as new, even if the ideas are not and which allows us to pretend that digital thinking is much more contemporary than it is. This focus on newness distracts from broader concerns and makes it more difficult to see how hegemonic ideologies continuously transform and reify their hierarchies, processes and resources to produce more amenable structures. Thus, we should not consider the mobile map as a lone stranger without an oeuvre. Rather, the present and future of mobile mapping are also parcelled in its past discourses and logics. Cartography has always been a digital system of representation, and so before it was even conceived, mobile mapping was already a digital *object*.

In the digital world, is it not better to consider cartographic reason not as insufficient, but as the ultimate expression of its roots in the Enlightenment: both mathesis and taxonomy, number and language? It is the compass points that were set up to navigate between longitude and latitude to move ships across the world, and it is the GPS algorithms which triangulate between phone antennas, cell towers and satellites in space. If cartography is such a powerful amalgamator, then mobile maps have inherited and invested enthusiastically in this dual role between geometry and imagery. Geometry makes spherical globes appear on flat atlases, but representation fixes our imaginations to a world that always been represented in the mode of cartographic reason: it was only ever one globe that stated *Hic sunt dracones* (Here be dragons).

**Cartographic ambitions after coordinate geometry**

Cartography is not necessarily equivalent to mapping; rather it is better understood as *a mode and method of mapping*. Cartography is often conceptualised to have a natural ally and axiomatic synonym in 'the map' or 'mapping'. However, cartography and mapping have subtle differences in meaning, and perhaps do not share as strong a fraternity (historically or spatially) as supposed. Crampton (2001; see also Gregory, 1994; Braun, 2000) makes it clear that the word cartography came into popular use as terminology in the nineteenth century and has been retrospectively applied to describe certain geographic practices, including geometrically informed mapping, as has been done here. Cartography is to draw, to inscribe surfaces with images, or, in the words of Gunnar Olsson, the drawing and reading of lines. Cartography is a graphic act, testament to a Western reliance on the perceived permanence of the written word, the sketched image and the countable object. Mapping, on the other hand, simply refers to a sheet, a surface upon which relations can be traced. A blank sheet is a tabula rasa. Like Euclidean space, it is full of potential; all starting points may be equal, all axes possible.

At the basest level, it could be said that mapping is the expression of spatiotemporal relations, and a map is merely the sign of that expression, however impermanent or recognisable. To this effect, Deleuze noted that 'lines are the basic components of things and events. So everything has its geography, its cartography, its diagram' (1995: 33). Under the structures of representation, what we understand to be cartography or the cartographic (the harbinger of Cartesian thinking and gilder of rulers, compasses and sextants) has a much more scientific purpose. Foucault (2001c, 2002b) describes how the discontinuities in the West between the seventeenth and eighteenth centuries, and the nineteenth century, the pendulum swing between interpretation and formalisation (and then back again with the writing of Nietzsche, Freud and Marx). Mapping also shifted from interpreting the world to formalising it – through images, lines and reason (Farinelli, 1992). Accompanying the map-makers in this transition was cartography, a faithful stalwart of the scientific order and commodore of capitalist colonial enterprise (Edney, 1997). As De Risi states:

> If during the scientific revolution a number of new sciences were born, surely geometry was then born again. [...] All of a sudden geometry took a radical turn, and in only fifty years, it changed beyond recognition. (2007: 4)

So, what was this turn and what did it mean for maps, mappings and cartography as they appear today? Let us not pretend there were no maps before there was cartography, and so let us not say that all maps are burdened by this cartographic tradition.[5] At the same time, let us also not say that mapping and cartography are easily interchangeable and that 'the map' is an axiomatic term that always means the same thing. Rather, emphasis on the map object (as material and representational) has distracted from the broader question of its ontic power (Dodge et al., 2009a), the way in which mapping is performed, deployed and practised.

There is a distinction between mathematical and lived spaces, between geometry and what Dodge et al. (2009b) have called 'ontogenesis'. Serres (2014), who specifically terms this understanding of space as 'Euclidean space',[6] wherein all points can be considered equal. The regularity of mathematical space means that it is easily malleable – all points on a number plane are, in theory, of the same standing as others. Each point is merely a conceptual marker, which can be assigned and reassigned in the equation hierarchy as the 'coordinating zero point' and every line can be formed to be the 'coordinating axis'. Thus, the relationality between centre and node is purely functional; a method deployed to solve some greater problem, without consequence as long as it coheres to the rules of the mathematical episteme.

5 See, for instance, a number of hand-drawn mapping projects aimed at interpreting the affective and personal experiences of the city in *Mapping Manhattan* (2013) by Becky Cooper, or *From Here to There: A Curious Collection* (2010), edited by Kris Harzinski

6 The term 'Euclidean space' is not without its critics. Elden (2005) claims that 'the Greeks had no word that equates to our modern notion of "space". Despite regular use of the notion of "Euclidean space", this is a term that finds no parallels in his writings ... and is a rather modern invention' (Elden, 2005: 12). At the same time, despite the notion's contemporaneity, it is arguably an important conceptualization, if only as a marker to distinguish Aristotelian philosophy (which, according to Elden, made clear distinctions between algebra and geometry) and Cartesian philosophy (which considered the geometric as a form of applied algebra, made modern through the development of the Cartesian coordinate system). Thus, 'Euclidean space' could be seen as invention that is particularly Foucauldian in nature, because it aims to distinguish epistemological discontinuities, rather than pay heed to the contemporaneity of historicity itself. For those purposes and the importance of understanding the transformation of geometric thinking, I have, for the clarity of this argument, adopted the popular usage of the term, and forgiven its status as a modern portmanteau.

Euclidean space, as Serres understands it, differs to the spaces described during the Age of Reason by both Descartes and by Leibniz. This difference is underpinned by a geometric transformation – by which a clear centre point was established – but also a philosophical transition from bounding and description to expansion and ordering – a shift that is central to what we can understand as an underpinning impulse of cartographic reason. For instance, Olsson describes the difference between Cartesian thinking, which dominated the philosophy of consciousness characterised by the Enlightenment, and the Euclidean principles that proceeded it:

> The major difference between Euclidean and Cartesian geometry is [...] that whereas the former deals with the things of the finite world, the latter is occupied with the relations of infinity; while Euclid proved theorems, Descartes solved problems. (Olsson, 2007: 134)

What Olsson points to here is not canonically a historical discontinuity or a discursive rift. Rather, here we see an expansion of geometric discourse into new epistemological territory: *Euclidean geometry sought to understand and reify its own conditions of possibility; Cartesian geometry sought to push the limits of its own representation and impose its order on the world.* This is what formed the crux of Farinelli's (1992) work where, instead of focusing on maps or space, he turned his critique towards the epistemological trend 'cartographic reason',[7] a 'mode-of-thought-and-action' (cf. Olsson, 1993). Cartographic reason is not simply a way of drawing lines or representing objects: it is a set of principles that are at once logical (and yet thoroughly discursive) that mark the gateposts of cartographic authority as we understand it in contemporary terms. Farinelli (1992) traced the emergence of the cartographic imagination through the establishment of a body of recognisable signs, which represented the features of the world during the early stages of modernity leading to the discursive formation of cartographic reason.

Geometry and cartography, then, have an epistemological relationship, codified in trigonometric thinking, borne out of Enlightenment thinking. In

7 Cartographic reason is also sometimes referred to as 'cartographical reason'. Gunnar Olsson in *Abysmal* writes at length on the origin and continued usage of the idea of 'cartographic reason' in a footnote on his chapter on Kant (Olsson, 2007: 482-483). It is well-worth reading as a personal homage to the history of this particular group of geographers and their lasting contribution to the field of critical geography.

the work of Descartes, cartographic reason can be found in the application of mathematical principles of thought to describe the world and understand our sense of existence. Olsson (2007) describes how Kant codified Cartesian geometric reason, and later, how Wittgenstein codified Kantian reason into cartographic reason. According to Olsson's (2007) reading of Wittgenstein's *Tractatus*, cartographic reason contains the following set of principles, with Olsson's interpretation in parentheses:

- the problems of representation (the picture is a model of reality);
- the fix-points (a picture is a fact);
- the scale (the picture is laid against reality like a measure);
- the mappa (every picture is at the same time a logical one, logical laws are about the net and not what the net captures);
- the projection (the senses proposition, the act of pro-positioning, literally the act of positioning oneself, of moving from the perspectivists' vantage-point to his vanishing-point);
- the pointing and the naming (the picture reaches out to reality, the end-points of the graduating lines touching the objects they measure);
- the legitimation of power (saying that God is illogical is impossible). (Olsson, 2007: 218)

Cartographic reason in its Cartesian dress reveals the desire to be omniscient, omnipotent and omnipresent in all matters representational, but most importantly, it reveals ambition – the will to expand its understanding, to bring the world into its own discursive fold, to push its epistemological limitations farther and farther afield. Thus, as Olsson states frequently, cartographic reason is both thought *and* action, and its foundation in Cartesian principles means that its specificity of meaning hinges upon its desire to act and form into lived space.

## Drawing ideology into space

For many philosophers, time, space and number have an integral relationship. We must not forget that number, too, is an abstract concept conceived from the minds of humans, not a natural, fixed entity that predates human thought. There are also many ways to use numbers: mathematics, arithmetic, geometry, calculus, binary. It is number that binds together cartography and digitality under the banner of reason – number positions the world, objects in relation to other objects, which together amount to more objects – it is number that allows for geometric reasoning at all. Number reaches beyond knowledge into experience and ontology – being-through-calculation. Elden

(2006) describes how Heidegger found number to be crucial in his study of the ontic as being human emerges through technology. He investigates how Heidegger's thought was influenced by the topology of numerical practices throughout the ages and by the calculation and calculative principles. This is what makes geometry so powerful: Olsson (2007) chased the ur-form of the grid back to the Babylonians and to Marduk, and already we are chasing it into the future of algorithms and mobile mapping. Contra-Farinelli and pro-Olsson, it is, perhaps, not the age that describes cartographic reason, but the manner and mode through which it operates – the desires, the impulses (Said, 1993).

To turn circles into squares, Farinelli (1994) describes how the problem of the quadrature of the circle wracked ancient Greece. As Farinelli outlines, so sacred a discourse was geometry to the ancient Greek mathematicians, that as geometry was inscribed into the classical urban form through the city plan, between radial and quadratic interventions, so, too, was the problem of the quadrature of the circle. The issue, simply put, was how to transform a circle so that it would occupy the same area as a square, as its circumference gradually comes to mirror the quadratic form. As urban planning in Ancient Greece became more political, so, too, did the geometry of the city. The solution to this problem of the quadrature would be cathartic – a lost link between two different modes of classical measurement, the circle and the square, the compass and the ruler. By association, Farinelli implies that, in this way, the limits of thinking cartographically about the world were already political:

1. In 1882, F. Lindemann proved that the quadrature of the circle could not be solved with a compass and a ruler, because π (*pi*) is transcendental (Hobson, 1913);
2. City planning in classical times involved geometric urban forms derived from both the compass and the ruler wherein 'within the circular city the civic distance is *equal from the centre, unequal between citizens*; within the quadrangular city it is, exactly the opposite, *equal between citizens, unequal from the centre*. It is precisely in this inversion that we have the passage from isonomy to democracy' (Farinelli, 1994: 25);
3. And so, isonomy and democracy are bound up in spaces that are beheld to different ideas, with shapes that could not be amalgamated with rulers and compasses.

But does it matter anyway? Herodotus laughed at the map-makers drawing parts of the world they would never visit (IV, 36, quoted in Farinelli, 1994) and we may well laugh at those trying to turn circles into squares to find a transcendental order in reason and to build cities that cannot exist. Circles are not European inventions, nor did they start with the Greeks (Joseph, 2011). *Pi* can be traced back as far as the Egyptian Ahmes Papyrus (c. 1650 BC), Babylon and India. Compared to the rudimentary tools and anti-experimental environment afforded to Archimedes (c. 250 BC) who estimated π to 3.14, Joseph (2011) argues that the later work of Chinese mathematician Liu Hui (c. AD 260) – an estimate of π = 3.1416 – and Zu Chongzi (c. 480) – π = 3.1415927 – in estimating pi were the result of 'mathematical culture sympathetic to computation and offering methods that made its mathematicians far better equipped to carry out complicated calculations' (Joseph, 2011: 270). Furthermore, in c. 1400, Madhava of the Kerala mathematicians estimated π correctly to 11 decimal places, and Al-Kashi in Persia to 16 decimal places. By comparison, and reacknowledging both the contrapuntuality of cartographic forms and the non-linear development of mathematics, in 1579, French mathematician François Viète correctly estimated π to 9 decimal places. However, once again desire, discourse and ideology come to the fore. This desire to solve the strange incompatibility of epistemological structures rails against anomaly and casts heterotopia into the shadows. What the quadrature of the circle shows is that the desire for universal order is a particular and peculiar tradition, that rationalism is the tool of an impossible order, and, perhaps radically, that the rules of formation were already flawed before the first line was even drawn in the sand.

These flaws can be seen in early interactions between Western and Chinese geometries, birthed from similar mathematics (Serres, 2011). The rise of the Qing Dynasty (1639-1911) saw the modernisation of ethnographic and cartographic endeavours in China (Hostetler, 2001). This coincides with the arrival of Jesuit missionaries into China, Westerners who bridged an epochal gulf between the advancements of the east and west of the Eurasian continents. Chinese mapping before and during the Qing was multivalent, with many cartographers employing different methods and emphases on particular aspects of their maps. This is so much the case that it is very difficult to say anything concrete about what did and did not constitute a typical Chinese cartographic enterprise during this time: some maps stayed true to scale while others disregarded it completely, some used annotation and others did not – and there was no coherency of iconography.

In the late sixteenth century, in the final years of the Ming Dynasty (1368-1643), a small number of Jesuit missionaries arrived in Beijing, China, one of whom was Matteo Ricci, a prolific maker of maps (Joseph, 2011). During the period of Qing rule, Chinese maps did begin to transform, relinquishing the narratives and descriptions found in their margins and across their artwork. As, too, did European maps: *mappae mundi* gave way to navigational charts, colours to grids, with ever diminishing ornamentation. Hostetler (2001) argues that contemporarily in the Anglophile academy of the history of cartography, oppositional descriptions of European and Chinese cartography are still too closely imbued with insinuations of differences between 'traditional' and modern, scientific modes of cartography. So rather than attributing the role of the Jesuits in bringing European traditions in cartography to China and 'educating' the Chinese, producing maps in Mandarin, such as those by Matteo Ricci, she proposes that instead, it is the formation of the state that led to the gradual decline of earlier mapping pratices, a process which forms a nation 'predicated on an ideology of sameness' (ibid.: 17).

Maps are key to nation-building (Anderson, 1991), just as they are to empire-building (Edney, 1997). Same maps, same toponyms, same standards. This is at once an argument about the relationship between modernity and cartography as it is about the ever-present orientalist gaze which assigns a colonial progression to technological development that it believes is axiomatic in its own experience:

> [I]t was not so much a departure from *Chinese* tradition as a departure from premodern to early modern forms of representation. A similar transition occurred in Europe, but we do not express the transformation in terms of where the new technology came from. (Hostetler, 2001: 20)

Drawing from Anderson (1991), the main qualities of what Hostetler calls the modern map are crucial: first, that it is predicated upon territory, namely the formation of the nation-state; and, second, that it transcends autochthonous knowledges, rendering standardised geographic information available to anyone who is trained to read it. The modern map heralds a settling of cartographic reason into the political world: an earth with limited space, navigated by the stars, and territories unclaimed upon which imperial powers – China, England, others – could make a grab for their corner of the territorial sandpit.

However, Hostetler takes care to remind us that while the Qing (especially in the nineteenth century) employed numerous European and North American scholars, cartographers and scientists to make specific maps for specific purposes, this did not result in a total transformation of Chinese mapping. Rather, she argues, '[w]e need to distinguish between making use of techniques introduced by Westerners and adopting "Western" technology' (Hostetler, 2001: 24). For the Chinese dynasty-crafters, cartographic reason as it appeared in Western hands was more than the infallible episteme of global enlightenment that we have believed it to be – an oddity, curiosity, or tool. Maps are cultural more than anything else – and the Chinese did not need the promise of Christian enlightenment that the tools of the Jesuits offered (Pegg, 2014).

## Quantitative vs qualitative

We need an interlude here. There has been much discussion over the past half a century of a quantitative revolution in geography – starting with data sets more than 50 years ago through to geographic information science (GIS) (Pickles, 2000) and what we might contemporarily call 'spatial big data' (Leszczynski and Crampton, 2016). This 'revolution' towards quantitative data sets and number systems has been met with a qualitative resistance against positivism, which is sometimes post-structural (Leszczynski, 2009a, 2009b) and sometimes theoretical (Crampton, 2011a). However, the discussion that we are having here, between Leibniz and Descartes (and between fluid and fixed planes), and between the qualitative and quantitative, could be seen as the wrong bout in the wrong ring – and so we need to set it straight.

(Let me be a little Foucauldian here for a moment.)

Foucault (2002b) outlines two shifts that emerged from the Age of Reason, which were not defined by language, but rather by discourse. The first, *mathesis*, was what we see in the Cartesian desire to expand mathematical models across the world, and the Leibnizian desire to find universal principles: it is quantitative, fixed and deeply mathematical – a precursor to the combinatorial mode of algebraic geometry, whereby space and number converge. *Mathesis* is what we see in the lines of locational data that mobile phones collect every day – it is the triangulation between signals to determine coordinate points and the calculation from one point to the next. Most importantly, *mathesis* is the desire to quantify, to stretch numbers all over the world to achieve order, so that data can be captured and aggregated – numbers are simply numbers through which meaning is inferred. The second type, *taxonomia*, is what was more concerning for Foucault. *Taxonomia* is the ordering of things, the classificatory systems through which phenomena, objects, spaces and people are categorised and arranged to produce order. *Taxonomia* is a qualifying order, imbued with the desire for regularity based upon description: location A qualifies as a place, and so can be expressed in numbers and aggregated into *mathesis* principles; location B, however, does not obey the rules of qualification, and therefore, remains uncategorised, in the terrible miscellanea pile of geography and history. Qualification is the translation between numbers and spaces. So, the debate between quantification and qualification is largely one of appearance – what is concerning, as Pickles (2004) rightly noted, is that the coding of the world into numbers and categories is not about what representations look like, but the unfurling power of cartographic reason to impose order, regularity and calculability.

## Lines, real and imagined

In geometry, there are two modes of lines: those that are drawn and those that are imagined.

Those that are drawn are made with rulers and compasses. They represent all points together that we cannot see, but they cannot represent all points individually. Infinity is impossible to draw with a single stick of chalk. Any line that is drawn is always a reduction of the imagined line, a generalisation of immeasurable points and an approximation of infinity so that can be seen by the human eye.

Those that are imagined are made up of infinite numbers of points, expressed one after the other. Even within two points, there is still an infinite number of infinitely small points.

In theory, the space between two points can be divided by two. And then divided again. And again ad infinitum. And yet, the space itself is still limited, bounded by the points P1 and P2. This is addressed by Zeno's dichotomy paradox[8] and the Argument on Infinite Size[9]: How can the finite be infinite[10]?

*(Should we search at the limits of representation? Hegel argued that the point cannot be compared to measurement, Whitehead that space and time are not structured as a mathematical continuum: they argued that the way to preserve the reality of motion was to deny that space and time are composed of points and instants. However, we have clearly seen that the tools of standard modern mathematics are up to the job of resolving the paradoxes, so no such conclusion seems warranted: if the present indeed 'becomes', there is no reason*

8 This particular paradox – the Dichotomy Paradox – involved the motion of a moving object towards a fixed point, by a sequence of halves. Aristotle claimed in Physics (IV) that it was analogous to the Achilles and the Tortoise paradox, which featured two objects moving at different speeds in the same direction.

9 This argument, also described by Aristotle in *Physics*, involves the halving of an object, again and again.

10 To resolve this paradox, mathematicians in the nineteenth century created limits to the sequence of numbers and defined the asymptote as the limit of an equation.

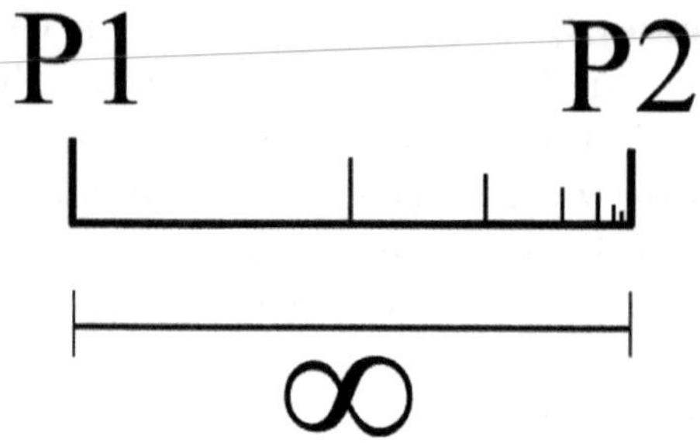


Figure 7.1. *Zeno's paradox.* An infinite space between two points (P1, P2). If you were to halve each distance ad infinitum, would the distance ever equal zero?

*to think that the process is not captured by the continuum. Bergson argued that motion is not divisible.*)

Later, during the seventeenth century, Descartes developed an analytic geometry. In doing so, he converged algebra and geometry through a fixed coordinate plane upon which lines could be drawn. On the horizontal lies the *x*-axis and on the vertical, the *y*-axis. Each coordinate is a pair – (x, y) – designating a place on the space of this Cartesian grid. These axes of indeterminate numbers cross at the *origin* at (0, 0), vivisecting the grid into four quadrants, counted counter-clockwise. Space had found its fixed point and its regularity of division.

Descartes' geometry meant that lines were no longer simple sequences of points, but series of points that obeyed a common law, a continuity or regularity expressed through algebraic substitution ad infinitum. Lines were now defined by equations, which could substitute a single point with a linear representation of all points that obeyed a certain rule. For instance, where *x* number, transformed by *f* function, would result in *y* point. With algebraic geometry, lines ($x = y$) and curves ($x^2 = y$) were now able to be expressed as equations taking on a new ambiguity and a new mode of infinity. Through the coordinate system, it was not the point, but the function which came to the fore, as lines became calculable, transformable, and reproducible: the line became systematic in a space that was systematic.

Of course, in the seventeenth century, there were still two modes of lines. While lines that were imagined had undergone a massive transformation, lines that were drawn were still hazy and imperfect. But the Cartesians had a universal desire (Foucault, 2002b) to encompass the world in their geometry, to express all things according to mathematical principles, an existence which comes first and foremost from the mind: *cogito ergo sum.*

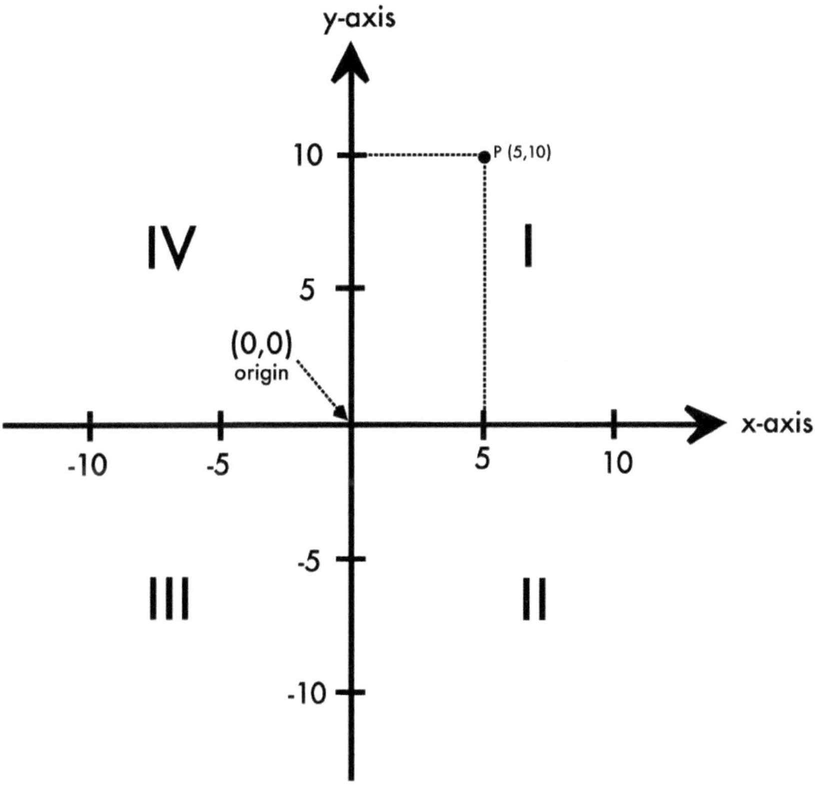


Figure 7.2. *Cartesian coordinate plane*. This graph shows a basic coordinate plane with the *x*-axis running horizontally, and the *y*-axis running vertically. A point (P) is comprised of two coordinates (x, y) corresponding to their position on each axis.

And so the task was set to draw lines all over the world in cartography and the imagination. Flat or spherical, the earth was reconceptualised as a grid that could be stretched and squeezed and the points upon it triangulated and measured. This grid formed the basis of navigational coordinate systems that European ships used to move throughout the world: from the paper map and the sextant through to geocode and the GPS. Boundaries in maps work as law on land. To draw a square property on a map is to draw ownership on the earth. Once a border between sea and land, between nations or between people has been drawn, it takes a great force to make it shift.

## Lines on screens

There are two types of lines that appear on mobile screens: lines made up of tiny squares, and lines made up of equations. The first is a line designed for description – an approximation of an image, a shape or a colour. These lines, like the lines drawn in chalk, or graphite or ink, are limited by resolution. But this resolution is not determined by the human eye. Rather, resolution is determined by the size of a file, how many pixels by how many pixels can be displayed. The pixel is the monad of the digital image, and its size depends on how many colours it can display. The second kind of line is made up of equations, and as such, they are infinitely scalable. No matter how large or how small they do not lose resolution, do not pixelate, do not abstract.

There are two kinds of representation on a digital map, which interlock together over geographic coordinates.

A raster layer is a grid of square data cells. Raster layers can be satellite imagery or the polygon tiles that form the base map. The raster layer depends on a grid, a series of pixels that make a series of images or tiles, which join together to make a map. In Mapbox, for instance, these tiles are organised by a coordinate system for each layer, which is interoperable with the geographic coordinates:

(z, x, y) / (zoom, x coordinate, y coordinate)

Sometimes, when you zoom in or out too fast, or when the signal on your phone is poor you catch a glimpse of the underneath, a blue dot sitting lonely in a landscape of brown squares. But even without a visual referent, there the blue dot still sits. It is not keyed into the raster landscape, but the geographic coordinate system that lies underneath used by the phone receiver, radio towers and satellites (depending on the app) to determine where you are.

A vector layer is made up of points (nodes), lines and shapes (polygons). Each line is a path that moves through and between nodes. Each node has a position (x, y) and each line an equation (x = y). Vector layers sit separately to the raster layer, infinitely scalable and unrelated to the raster map underneath. But more and more, digital mapping platforms are embracing vector base layers, too – layers not made of squares, but of equations, parks coloured through coordinate geometry. Vectors navigate between points, not places (places are placed on points – places are just points). Perhaps in this debate about territorialisation and maps, we are, as Elden (2005) suggests, missing the point.

The computability of the line in the digital map depends upon two points on a gridded coordinate system, which each has an x and y coordinate – the same philosophical system created by Descartes. Like in the Cartesian system, the line between two points can be expressed as an equation, which expresses the possibility of all points along that line. Yet, unlike the lines drawn hazy on paper or the lines in Descartes's imagination, the digital line

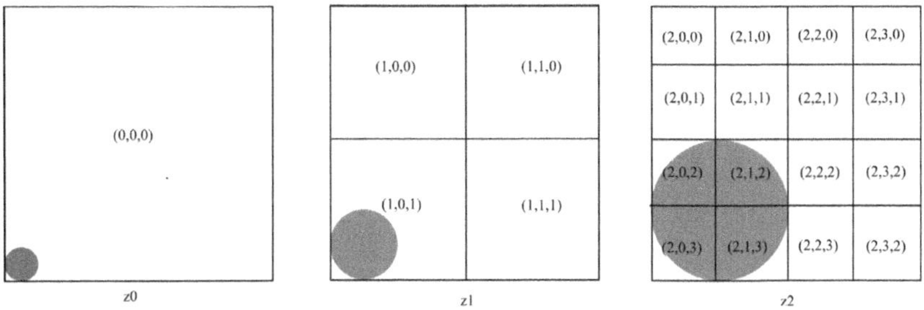


Figure 7.3. *Zoom and the* z-*axis*. Mapbox tile layer coordinates (z, x, y) at three zoom levels z0, z1 and z2, showing the relative size of a symbolic object.

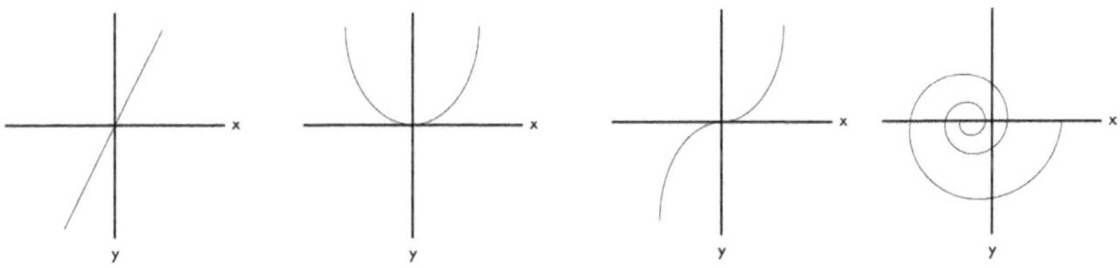


Figure 7.4. *Linear equations*. From point to point, changes to linear equations allow vector lines to transmute. In order from left to right: straight line, parabola, differential equations, spirals.

is neither entirely real or imagined. Sitting somewhere between the two, it is merely representative of a calculation, transformable and transmutable between digital and material worlds that find themselves connected through Cartesian coordinate planes.

## Drawing the *y-axis* on the Earth

We all know the story of longitude thanks to Dava Sobel (1998), but I'll tell it again here. When you are a small European explorer in a small boat navigating across the enormous grids of the world, it is important to know where you are. Latitude could be measured with a quadrant and a compass according to the sun and the stars, belted around Africa and Asia, navigators had long known how to tell if they were in the northern or southern hemisphere. Longitude, however, was a more difficult operation – not knowing if they were closer to South America or Africa, boats disappeared, sailors starved and cargo was lost. A prize was set up in 1714 via the Longitude Act enacted by the British Parliament for large sums of money depending on the accuracy and applicability of solutions to those who could solve the problem of calculating longitude.

The largest prize given in 1765 to John Harrison, a clockmaker from London, was an answer of a temporal, not a spatial, nature. The key, it seems, was not knowing 'where you are', but 'when you are'. A marine chronometer: two clocks

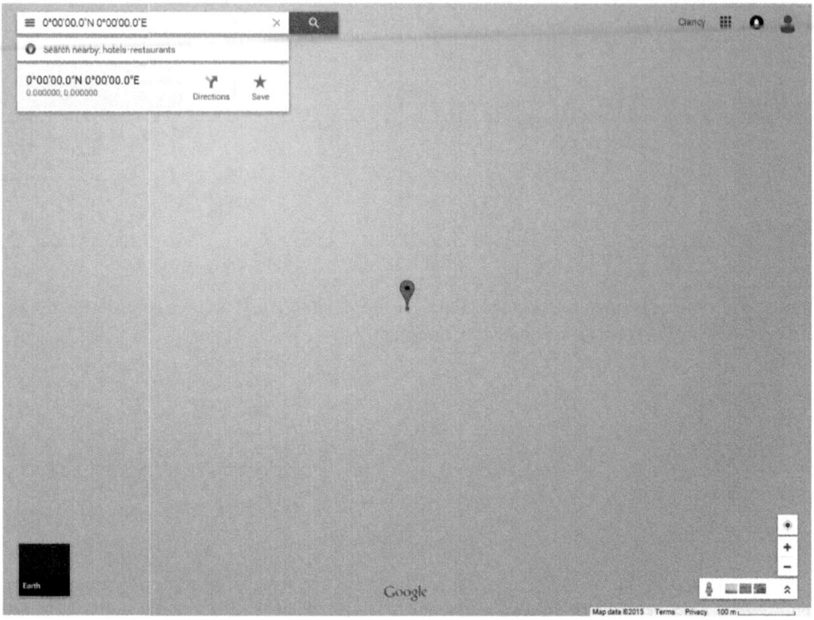


Figure 7.5. *Hic sunt draconis*. Google Maps: 0°00′00.0N, 0°00′00.0E – where the Prime Meridian crosses the Equator.

that show the same time, one that sits at a fixed latitude, the prime meridian, and one that travels with you. The clock that travels is measured against the local time at the prime meridian, and so distance is measured. In 1884, the prime meridian was voted to be located in Greenwich, UK, at the Royal Observatory. It divided the world up into two hemispheres, East and West, and so the Cartesian quadrants had finally found their origin. It seems strange, that for all the arbitrary and rational decisions that were made in the process turning imagined lines into drawn lines, the most deliberate would prove to be at once the most and least arbitrary, and by far the biggest statement of power.

Later, in the early twentieth century, wireless radio transmission replaced the marine chronometer, and more recently a combination of global positioning systems (GPS) and radar: the same technologies used in mobile telephony to find your location on the map. Despite the advances in technology and representation towards fluidity, however, some statements remained resolutely fixed. Boundaries in maps work as law on land. To this day, the prime meridian continues to run through Greenwich at the Royal Observatory. To draw a line on the map is to secure a line along the world. To draw a square property on a map is to draw ownership on the earth. Once a border between hemispheres, between sea and land, between nations and between people, has been drawn, it takes a great force to make it shift.

# 8. Here there be digits

> You will eat words, but more often these days you will eat codes and numbers. So you will gorge copiously, and still more, always more. Nothing goes down quite so easily as code, nothing grows as well as numbers. You will gobble up quantities of them. Your body will overrun the space around it, just like the word itself, carried on the wind, just like a society founded on the word.
>
> – Serres, *The Five Senses* (2008: 187)

The Age of Reason in Europe, writes Foucault (2002b), was enveloped in universal desires to understand the world. As the world got smaller as philosophers and scientists peered through telescopes and saw the face of cosmic massiveness, so they turned their gaze earthward (while keeping the heavens in their peripheral vision) to find some sort of regularity or reason amidst the chaos. In the Age of Reason, what we understand as rationalism is inscribed by thinkers who found answers through reason, rather than empirics: Descartes who drew the grid, Spinoza who developed ethics and Leibniz who chased infinity.

As Descartes algebraised geometry, mathematician and philosopher, Gottfried Wilhelm Leibniz worked steadily on the *analysis situs* – a *science of forms* or a *formal geometry*. While he embraced the algebraisation of geometry, later becoming one of its major proponents, he also recognised the shortfalls described by Newton, whereby some problems were simply more easily solved using a ruler and a compass, than the mechanics of coordinates. De Risi (2007) suggests that where Cartesian coordinates had left the question of the quadrature of the circle obscured and forgotten, Leibniz kept them in mind – for Leibniz, imagination was important, especially in mathematics. Cartesian coordinates had succeeded in turning a curve drawn with a compass and a line with a ruler into mechanical shapes, determinable, transformable and producible by algebra. Descartes arranged his geometry around a fixed coordinate (0, 0) at the intersection of two lines and created a system of coordinates and pushed its applicability further into the world: Cartesian geometry had produced the quadratic formula. In

Wilmott, C., *Mobile Mapping. Space, Cartography and the Digital.*
Taylor & Francis Group, 2020
DOI 10.5117/9789462984530_CH08

doing so, Cartesian geometry distanced itself from matter and produced a cosmos that was 'a network of invisible gyrating fluids in which the heavenly bodies are swept along' (Rynasiewicz, 1996: 284), a relational space.

Leibniz's *analysis situs* brought up the question of a situated analysis, an analysis that needed to occur before the operation of synthesis – one that, like Descartes, was opposed to absolute time and space. This was a mode of thinking that could transcend the dichotomous Cartesian relationship between imagination and coordinates, between representation and geometry, between process and fixity. For Leibniz, his opinion of space and time was thus:

> I hold space to be something merely relative, as is time, that I hold it to be an order of coexistences, as time is an order of successions. For space denotes, in terms of possibility, an order of things which exist at the same time, considered as *existing together*, without enquiring into their manner of existing. (Leibniz and Clarke, 2007: 9)

Rather than working from an arbitrary fixed point in space, as Descartes did, Leibniz slowly developed a calculus that would be able to analyse space from any point and in any form. He aimed to uncover the 'veri Numeri Characteristici rerum', a true characteristic number of things (Batchelor, 2004). He set about doing so through various techniques including infinitesimal calculus and binary arithmetic in order to 'try and reopen the Cartesian institutions of algebra and geometry to the philosophical question of number itself' (Batchelor, 2004: 234). The relationship between Leibnizian space and mathematics can be found in this sentiment – a further expansion of the Cartesian *mathesis universalis* (universal mathesis). His life's work constituted the pursuit for a key to unlocking this universal characteristic of the number of things, and eventually upon the exhaustion of that search, the development of a new characteristic that could calculate just that.

Like Descartes, Leibniz was not content with simple measurement or comparison. He, too, sought a universal model – but unlike Descartes, this was not of measurement between lines and numbers, between points in space but 'a mathematics of qualitative orders', an insular and contained mathematics which could describe all things. Leibniz was troubled by how the Cartesian schools were defined by a geometry that specifically sought to recoil from epistemological questions, from the imagination (and by association, the imaginary and imagery) and settle on an algebraic, calculative mode of reasoning. He sought out another answer to the problems of space, time and matter. One of his earliest solutions was 'phenomenalistic' (Rescher, 2013), divided into two realms. The first was that of the metaphysical, the monad. Monadology, in Leibnizian thought, was the most fundamental and irreducible object of being, set apart from the second realm, that of everyday experience, of physics, wherein lived space, time and matter.

Later, in what Hartz and Cover (1988) term the 'transition', Leibniz started ruminating on the relationship between metaphysical mathematical objects such as a perfect circle or straight line, and his realisation that they do not exist anywhere in the physical realm: they are concepts without a phenomenal referent. The ontic status of these perfect objects is in a realm that Leibniz describes as the 'ideal', 'mental' or 'imaginary', and begins to argue that space, too, should join the monads there (Cover and Hartz, 1994). Eventually, Leibniz's thinking begins to form a three-tiered system of metaphysics (Hartz and Cover, 1988), as shown in Table 8.1.

**Table 8.1.** ***Metaphysics.*** **Table showing Leibniz's levels of metaphysics from the top tier (III) to the bottom (I), detailed in Hartz and Cover's (1988) explanation.**

| Three-tiered Leibnizian Metaphysic | |
|---|---|
| III | Ideas (res mentalis or entia rationis) |
| II | Bodies (quasi-substantiae or entia semimentalia) |
| I | Monads (substantiae) |

At the top, is the world of the ideal and the imagined – in which perfect circles and infinite lines can be found. In the middle, the phenomenal – where exists bodies, and discrete objects and things that we encounter every day. At the bottom, the monad, the smallest substrate of being, it is its own representation, is indivisible and irreducible. In parallel with his metaphysical questions, Leibniz also began to experiment with the binary form, a base two system of thinking based upon two digits: 0 and 1. He developed this in contrary to the Base 10 counting system, which had developed in Western mathematics, writing in General Meditations:

> At a glance, we can see the reason for the *famous property of the double Geometric progression* of whole Numbers, which provides that if we only have on of these numbers to each degree, we can make all the other whole numbers less than double of the highest degree. (Leibniz in Chabert, 2012: 41-42)

This was a concept of representation which could operate and calculate – the simplest description of things. Batchelor (2004) describes how binary furthered the Cartesian project of a *mathesis universalis*, by creating a *characteristica universalis*, a universal characteristic or common language. Here, the numeric and the linguistic converge in Leibniz's thought, as he seeks to apply systematic models through formal logic (Serres, 2014). It also solved the problem of infinite series and irrational numbers through the tabulation of numbers. Binary operated in a tabulated format, counting upwards by twos. For instance, Figure 8.1 shows the simple tabulation that Leibniz demonstrated as part of his 1703 explanation of binary numbers.

Thus, with binary, Leibniz (in an unfinished text composed in his final months) declared that he had basically created an automatic calculation, since the model of columns could be extended upwards and outwards ad infinitum. It was this system that laid the path for digital computing as we can understand it today. Rather than a Cartesian (0, 0) coordinate from which all things could be measured, Leibniz creates a 0, 1 binary from which all things could be ordered.

Where Kant and Wittgenstein later passionately embraced Cartesianism, the work of Leibniz was, perhaps, equally as passionately elided. The works of Leibniz, which were largely to be found in his notes and correspondence, lay dormant in the library of Hanover and did not become accessible until 1830. Yet once the gate was opened, the influence began to filter through. While the Germanic academies were scrambling to catch up and debate on the subject of Leibnizian logic, George Boole (1815-1864) was devising a method of algebraic or symbolic logic. This system was, at first, inspired by contemporaneous debates on quantification. It was designed along a binary system of yes and no (where yes is 1 and no is 0), and rather than using traditional mathematical functions such as multiplication or division, used conjecture: either, or, and. His wife, Mary Everest Boole – a mathematician in her own right – claimed that Boole developed much of this algebra independently of knowledge about Leibniz, although he did discover similarities afterwards (Boole in Laita, 1980). Peckhaus (2009), however, has traced citations through the early nineteenth century: Erdman prepared two volumes of fragments of Leibniz's writings published in 1839.

It was not until the early twentieth century that scientists and mathematicians rediscovered the work of Leibniz, and Leibnizian ideas once again entered the discourses of the world unequivocally. The formal languages of Leibniz's binary and calculation machine together with Boolean algebra

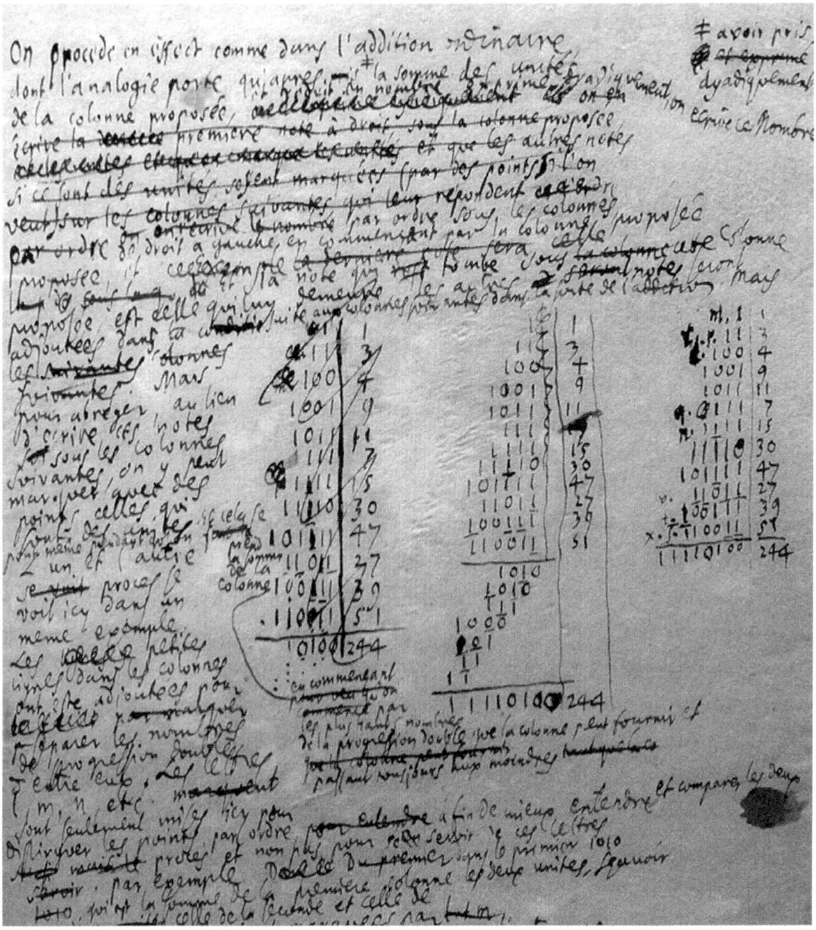

Figure 8.1. *Calculating binary.* This figure explains a basic calculation in binary code (*Binärcode*) from Leibniz's (1697) writings.

became to be the basis of the *Entscheidungsproblem*, the problem that Alan Turing (1912-1954) proposed to solve via his theoretical computing machines (known colloquially now as Turing machines).

In the current world of mobile mapping – in algorithms and code – we have to ask once again if it was only through Descartes that cartographic reason is reified. Bytes and binary, computers and calculation – the ideas of Leibniz have reconnected again in the cartographic, in the applications and algorithms that draw everyday cartographic navigations into being. Let us pause for a moment and consider if, in mobile mapping, cartographic reason has been laid bare as a product of absolute rationalism, at the point where grids, ethics and infinities intersect.

## Automated navigations

Automation is a matter of important distinction in the crisscrossing history of binary code and cartographic coordinates. Not all binary computing is digital, and not all digital objects are binary nor computational. There is a large body of literature that delves into the history of computing (cf. Ceruzzi, 2012), tracing its roots in the mathematical work of Leibniz and Boole, in set theory and the history of analytical science and engineering. The origins of the computational machine can be found in Lovelace's (1942) Note G, the first algorithms designed for a machine, Babbage's (1837) Analytical Computer, and Turing's (1939) Bombe. Yet even before that, some scholars have argued that computing has its origins in Egyptian and Babylonian algorithms, abacus devices and other tools of calculation, such as Leibniz's calculating machine (Ausiello and Petreschi, 2013). What sets modern binary computing apart from other digital systems, and from its historical roots, is a twofold discursive shift based upon two facets. First, the coupling of computation with binary logic, which affords a silent primacy given to a two-tone system of categorisation, a foundation upon which digital cartography, images and datasets germinate. Second, *mechanics* have facilitated a shift from a logic of calculation by human labour to the establishment of systems of *automation*. The combination of this dual transformation has resulted in an abstraction of human labour from the processes of calculation (and, increasingly, even measurement), wherein the discursive logics of binary systems are masked by the production of automated systems that quasi-independently mine data, categorise it and use it to calculate various outcomes.

This material abstraction is paralleled by a related discursive shift from the logics of data production to data reproduction. Dijkstra's algorithm – one of many examples to find the shortest distance between two points – is a set of instructions. It is not necessarily digital, and it is not necessarily coded. Figure 8.2 shows the diagram.

The instructions are complicated, but basically thus – to find the shortest distance between A and F, the distance between each node needs to be calculated cumulatively. Any calculated node as the shortest distance is labelled 'solved', and given a distance from A. First, the measure distances between A:B = 3 and A:C = 5. Thus B is solved as the shortest distance, 3. Then, identify all unsolved nodes connected to the solved node B. As such the distances B:C = 6 (cumulatively), B:E = 10 (cumulatively) and B:D = 7 (cumulatively). Each time you have a solved node, then you find all nodes attached to that and repeat. And so on.

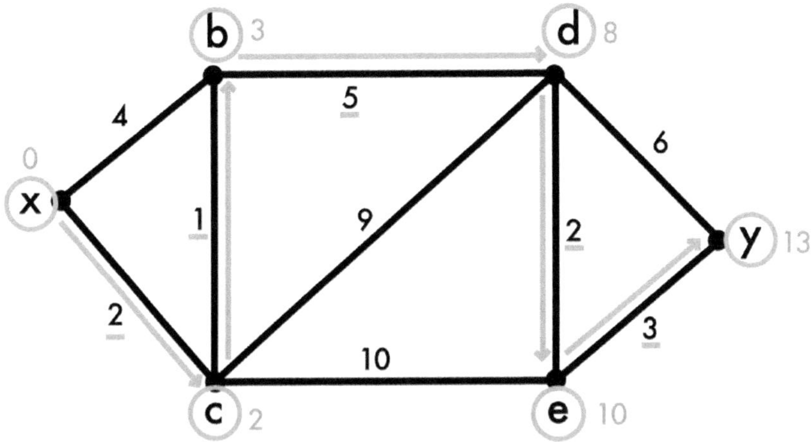


Figure 8.2. *Dijkstra's algorithm*. This is one of the most common algorithms used to find the shortest path between two points.

What makes Dijkstra's algorithm so powerful is arguably not the proliferation of algorithmic practices (Kitchin and Perng, 2016), nor the determination it maintains over the selection of places, routes and directions that mapping applications give to users (Zook and Graham, 2007): what makes it powerful is the automation of the algorithm so that problems can be solved by computational means. Algorithms, like any set of instructions, are designed to be written and read. The first step is writing the algorithm into pseudo-code, designed for software engineers and web developers, who then rewrite the algorithm into whichever programming language (C++, PHP, HTML etc.) they are using. The charm of the algorithm is that it is processual (Rossiter, 2003; Galloway, 2004), in the same way that maps can be considered processual (Kitchin et al., 2009). Algorithms, like Dijkstra's, are designed to carry out calculability over a linear temporality, like a musical score: if yes, proceed to the next step, if no, *dal capo al coda*. Algorithms also maintain both a structure and a fluidity which rests usefully between the grid and the monad: the instructions provide a skeleton to navigate through an idea, which can, in turn, be shaped through a heteroglossia of linguistic and semiotic formations.

The digital map occupies multiple languages that operate under common discourses: vectors and rasters, lines and points, polygons and choropleth colours. The algorithm stands near this summit of digitality and computability: as the world is increasingly turned into numbers and letters, the algorithm can happily and automatically work between *mathesis* and *taxonomia*, between a *mathesis universalis* and a *characteristica universalis*.

## Ordering colours after code

One can imagine the mappers who hand-painted the first maps, grinding pigments and mixing the colours together to produce the blues and greens and browns that coloured the world. Then, as cartography allied with expansion, inks spilt as ships lurched, or tinctures dried unexpectedly quicky in tropical climates – and colour became bound up with lines in the Age of Reason and order. In the late eighteenth century Abraham Gottlob Werner, a mineralogist, created a comprehensive scheme to describe and classify colours. This system was modified and translated into English in the early nineteenth century and was purportedly used by Darwin on his voyages. *Werner's Nomenclature of Colours* (Syme, 1821) became a colour dictionary – a universal and transcendental system for the chromatic world to numerate, name and describe colours according to where they are found on animals, vegetables and minerals.

In *Chromatic Algorithms: Synthetic Color, Computer Art, and Aesthetics after Code* (2014), Kane explains how, when colour computer monitors were first developed and popularly purchased, most screens could only display 216 (web-safe) colours. Many systems were developed to make sure colours stayed true across platforms – that the green on one person's map was the green on another. The most prevalent system was the trichromatic colour system that had some success in early colour photography. RGB was comprised of three colour channels or bytes – red, green and blue – and, linguistically, was structured by a three-set, hexadecimal system of designation which specified each channel separately. The RGB decimal system runs from 0 (0%) to 255 (100%). In RGB, black is the absence of colour (zero saturation or percent in each of the channels), while white is the complete saturation of colour. HTML 3.2 officially adopted the hexadecimal system based upon the RGB channels, now a major backbone for all maps coded in HTML.

Digital screens are the opposite to paper in chromatic terms in that they are subtractive, rather than additive. Open a notebook and start with a fresh sheet of paper. Paint on it and see it get darker. Use inks in a printer – cyans, magentas, yellows and blacks (key) – see them blend to produce chromatic darkness upon white canvas. Turn on a screen and see black. Populate it with pixels, red here, blue there and green elsewhere. Combine the colours and see lightness etch across the surface of darkness, black turning into white.

**Table 8.2.** ***Hexadecimal and decimal colours.*** **This diagram shows the different digital compositions of basic colours in RGB (red, green and blue) and HTML.**

| | HTML | Red | Green | Blue | Percentage |
|---|---|---|---|---|---|
| Black | #000000 | 0 | 0 | 0 | (0%, 0%, 0%) |
| White | #FFFFFF | 255 | 255 | 255 | (100%, 100%, 100%) |
| Red | #FF0000 | 255 | 00 | 00 | (100%, 0%, 0%) |
| Yellow | #FFFF00 | 255 | 255 | 00 | (100%, 100%, 0%) |
| Blue | #0000FF | 00 | 00 | 255 | (0%, 0%, 100%) |

The worries of the cartographer have changed. Today's digital cartographer is no longer troubled by finding the most brilliant shade of blue, the most available shade of yellow or the deepest shade of red with which to designate their travels and their advice – with which to supplement and ornament their lines of power (Kane, 2014). Instead, such concerns in the digital era centre on the translatability between different screens – monitors to phone screens to touch screens, finding colours that are safe, standardised, and which operate in the same language. And they are now freed from the chemical choices of compounding coloured dyes: 'In order to use colour on the internet, one *must* adopt the standardised hexadecimal system of colour values' (Kane, 2014: 143).

The Google Maps API now allows cartographers to change the colours on their base maps. This is the code for yellow, against Werner's model. Sulphur Yellow (from sulphur) and Wax Tallow (from the greenish parts of a Nonpareil apple) become numeric qualities of saturation, hue and gamma.

There are four stylers – four taxonomies – in which the colour yellow is understood by computational devices displaying Google Maps: hue, or where it sits along the gridded spectrum of web safe colours (represented originally as a cone cell that replicates human vision); saturation, or the intensity of the colour compared to white; lightness, or how light or dark is the colour; and, gamma, which preserves bit-memory by presenting differentiation in darkness (where the human eye can see it) and ignoring it in the lighter tones that we cannot see. The digital colour model is predicated purely upon human eyes, designed by the Cartesian systems, triangles of colour laid on grid planes. At the same time, colour was a phenomenon widely perceived as unruly and wild – deeply subjective and vivid it was always 'something deeply historical, material and ideological, at the core of the always already Other that perpetually threatens to unveil and undermine the notions of truth, purity, origin and order that underwrite Western culture' (Kane, 2014: 31).

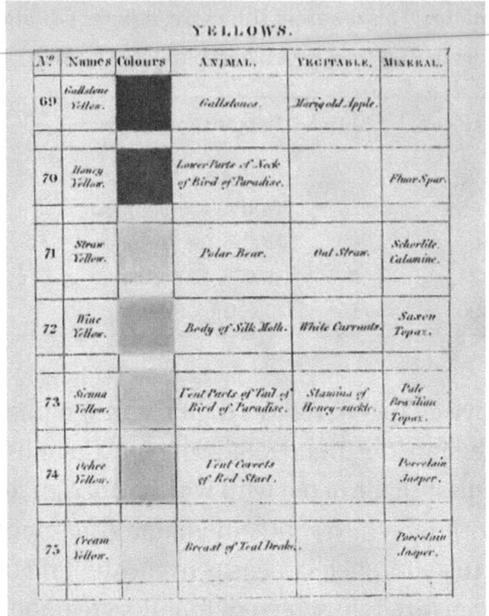

YELLOWS.

| Nº | Names | Colours | ANIMAL. | VEGETABLE. | MINERAL. |
|---|---|---|---|---|---|
| 69 | Gallstone Yellow. | | Gallstones. | Marigold Apple. | |
| 70 | Honey Yellow. | | Lower Parts of Neck of Bird of Paradise. | | Fluor Spar. |
| 71 | Straw Yellow. | | Polar Bear. | Oat Straw. | Scheelite. Calamine. |
| 72 | Wine Yellow. | | Body of Silk Moth. | White Currants. | Saxon Topaz. |
| 73 | Sienna Yellow. | | Vent Parts of Tail of Bird of Paradise. | Stamina of Honey-suckle. | Pale Brazilian Topaz. |
| 74 | Ochre Yellow. | | Vent Coverts of Red Start. | | Porcelain Jasper. |
| 75 | Cream Yellow. | | Breast of Teal Drake. | | Porcelain Jasper. |

```
stylers: [
{ hue: "#ffff00" },
{ saturation: 0 },
{ lightness: 0 },
{ gamma: 1.0 }
]
```

Figure 8.3. *Nomclemanture/stylers.* On the left are the shades of yellow from *Werner's Nomenclature of Colours*, with names, colours and examples of where this colour might be found in the taxonomy of animals, vegetables and minerals. On the right is an example of Google's styler for the base colour yellow based on hue, saturation, lightness and gamma.

In digital colour, curves and triangles become translated into letters and numbers, leading to a remarkable homogenisation of colour values and experiences in the digital realm. In digital cartography, colour has lost its viscerality and become monadic, numeric and calculative.

## Cartography, calculation, control

But what does this desire for digital order mean for cartography and a critical politics of mapping (cf. Crampton, 2002)? In a letter to Foucault (in Crampton and Elden, 2007), the geographers of *Hérodote* threw an accusation towards him that the story of the map has not conformed to the chronology of the three thresholds of Foucault's work in *Les mots et les choses*: the measurement of the ancient Greeks, the inquiry of the Middle Ages and the examination of the eighteenth century onwards. Foucault responded that the each of these techniques did not remain isolated, but informed the other: from the measurement of the compass and the ruler to the questioning eye of medieval *mappae mundi* and the calculative examination of eighteenth-century charts and nineteenth-century choropleth maps. While maps may transcend these thresholds, and, indeed, contain all three at once within their confines in a contrapuntal cartography (Sparke, 1998), cartographic reason is a particular kind of articulation that hinges upon the action of measurement, questioning and calculations within the operations of geometry and using them to examine the world. Cartographic reason, too, has links through all these ages: it is firmly based on the principles of measurement, of inquiry and of calculation.

The theoretical relationship between cartographic reason and cartography can be at best described as tumultuous. As noted in the introduction, cartography is a relatively recent invention (Crampton, 2011b) – far more recent than the philosophical shifts during the Age of Reason that we have discussed. This has broad-ranging consequences. Cartography occupies a peculiar position, bridging both mathematical spaces and lived spaces in the way that metaphysics did during the Age of Reason. Since then, the relationship between geometry, cartography and 'space' has become somewhat clearer, and so has become embedded in cartographic reason by way of understanding the positivities that developed during this epistemic shift. With the advent of digital cartography and counter-mapping, some have declared the end of cartographic reason as it becomes submerged under new representational forms that are more fluid and less linear. Pickles (2004), for instance, accuses cartographic reason of reducing cartography to a hegemonic, Western practice, underscored by scientific positivism. By reinterpreting cartography through Deleuze, he also argues that cartography can as equally be found in the Enlightenment maps (and their critics) as the renaissance of Indigenous or First Nations mapping projects outlined like those documented by Eades (2015). Farinelli (2009) has heralded the Internet as the harbinger of a crisis of cartographic reason that new practices and modes of cartographic communication have been brought into being. Mitchell (2008) describes the undoing of rationalism and modernity in postmodern literature and art through cartographic strategies aiming to subvert modernist narratives of progress and truth.

But what the discursive practice of cartographic reason does is to take data from a heterogeneous, living, spatiotemporality – data that may or may not hold equivalency in that space – and transform it to conform according to the homogenous principles of a determined mathematical space geared towards specific hegemonies. Cartographic reason describes the positivities of this process: one in which reason, inference and formal logic can be used to mathematically describe phenomena to calculate, predict, structure and control. This transformational function of cartography and cartographic reason gained particular currency as modernity unfolded, bleeding forth from the Age of Reason: Biggs (1999) describes how the modern city was built to be a bastion of control through cartographic principles; Stone (1949) describes the essential role that cartography played in establishing global, imperial merchant routes where people, goods and resources were traded to bring wealth to European empires; Edney (1997) focuses on the emerging relationship between cartography and military power in building the colonial world; and Pratt (1992) accounts for the production of a cartographic imagination through the travel writings of Alexander von Humboldt. Hence, the emphasis on the functionality of cartography beyond its representational qualities: cartography homogenises space and time so that it can be controlled, exploited and conquered. Despite this, cartography afforded a false objectivity to these processes – as Bollnow (2011) argues, all points in mathematical space are equal, and all axes equivalent, and so upon looking at a map, the inequalities and power imbalances in the world are made invisible. Without lived indexicality, each axis of latitude is only as meaningful as any another, each location point indecipherable from the next. And so, cartography as it emerged during the Age of Reason, and as it became ratified in the Age of Exploration, Colonisation and Empire served the expansion of capitalist enterprise, colonial conquest and governmental power. At the same time, it rendered invisible the hierarchies of discourse and power that these processes inscribed on the world (Harley, 1988b), and so, removed itself beyond the reach of those subjected to its authority.

In the first maps of New South Wales, numbers lie dotted across the harbour, echoing the shape of the coastline, paced apart regularly. Similar numbers, too, can be found in along the northern edge of the island, by the city of Victoria, in the early 1848 ordnance maps of Hong Kong by Lt Collinson. These soundings, which map the sea floor, hint at the landscape, unseen by the eye, but made apparent on the map. They construct a particular reality, based in numbers, that allows us to imagine and navigate treacherous terrain that banks and wrecks ships. Furthermore, these numbers are not lines; they are not cartographic shapes or geometric drawings that trace boundaries and give a graphic form to the landscape. Instead, they are catalogues of an invisible terrain with secret codes for reading and understanding their logic of measurement. There are multiple forms of bathymetry, where depth is measured in different systems – fathoms or feet, at high or low tide – these numbers that appear so sturdy on the map are measured against an ever-changing sea that constitutes the point of reference. To make these numbers make sense, the landscape *must* be fixed in space and time. The kind of representational fixity that Massey

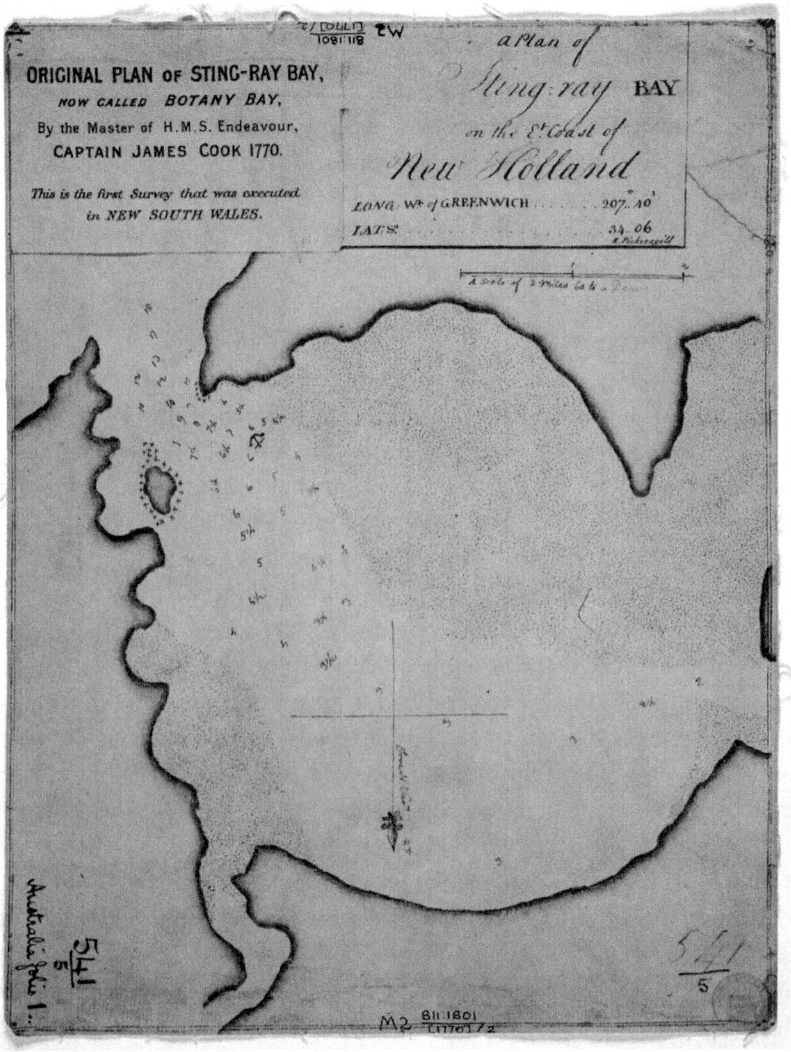


Figure 8.4. *Numbers*. Later reproduction of Lt Cook's map of Stingray Bay, now called Botany Bay. Of particular interest is the numbers outlining the depth of the bay as a series of measured points. Source: State Library of NSW.

describes is not enough; this representational fixity *must* be inscribed into the landscape to freeze it so that the geometry makes sense at once, without further measurement.

In Hong Kong in 1866, the crew of the survey vessel HMS *Rifleman* drove a copper bolt into the wall of the naval dockyard to determine the mean sea level. The *Rifleman*'s Bolt now sits in the Hong Kong Maritime Museum, on loan from the Survey and Mapping Office. It is surprising how such a small object placed in an arbitrary place at an arbitrary height, an object no more than a few inches in length, could so affect the determination and measurement of some of the tallest buildings in the world. But this bolt is imbued with the epistemological authority of an empire based on reason, in which numbers are given a weight that belies their instability, and such numbers build cities. Years later, in 1995 (Nissim, 2011), when a new mean sea level was established according to the Hong Kong Principal Datum, the height of each building was altered, wherein K.-C. Dung suggests: 'Hong Kong's actual elevation is perhaps a little lower than the one of our imagination' (2012: 137).

In Sydney, the Obelisk of Distances was constructed[1] in 1818 to mark the point from which all roads in the new colony were measured. It is difficult to know whether it was wholly necessary because the land does not shift at the same pace as the sea. Is it fair to say that it is less a milestone than a monument erected to valorise the incursion of Western epistemes into this unfamiliar landscape? According to the NSW Government Office of Environment and Heritage (2008), it holds multiple symbolisms: the transition from a penal colony to a planned city; the edge of the British Empire at its farthest reach; and, evidence of the continued colonial expansion into the interior of the continent. It is strange irony then, that this anchor between representations, geometry and landscape remains one of the few surviving remnants of the original topology of Sydney Cove – the rest has been planned beyond recognition. It alone has survived its own intent.

Historically, ordnance means military equipment such as artillery and weaponry. Yet, increasingly, maps, too, were deployed as a form of ordnance, culminating, in Great Britain, with the first Ordnance Survey Act of 1841. The 1841 act situated ordnance maps as both a civilian as well as a military pursuit. What it resulted in was the cataloguing and numbering of the landscape methodically and systematically, which at once characterised the discourses of military and colonial order favoured by the British Empire, but also normalised the objectification of landscapes through a colonial gaze as a necessary, ordinary and perhaps even patriotic practice. The early maps of Sydney and Hong Kong maintain complexity in negotiating these two roles, being both bathymetric but also topographic, giving shape to the shoreline, while hatching contours, affording authority to angles, while also drawing houses and farms. Thus, these combined logics of reason and aesthetics facilitated the translation of space into numbers and images, building places through geometry and representation.

1 Designed by convict Frances Greenway and built by stonemason Edware Cureton.

## Travelling philosophies, travelling binaries

The *I Ching*,[2] or the *Book of Changes*, is an ancient text, the oldest of the Five Classics in Chinese philosophy. It is a book of divination, often associated with Fu Xi, but also King Wen of Zhou, and is a significant influence on Taoist and Confucian philosophy (Wilhelm, 1967). The text of the *I Ching* is marked out in a hexagram system of six broken and unbroken, stacked and parallel horizontal lines.

The upper three lines of the hexagrams are derived from Fu Xi's trigrams – eight glyphs of three lines each of broken and unbroken lines – which signified heaven, lakes, fire, thunder, wind, water, mountain, earth. Fu Xi's trigrams, and so the hexagrams, too, could also be expressed as binary numbers (*bagua*): unbroken lines are *yang*, while broken lines are *yin*, the founding binaries of the *I Ching* philosophy.

In 1907, Gorai Kinzō visited the library in Hannover as part of a study into the influence of Chinese philosophy on German thinkers. While he was there he happened upon a diagram of the *I Ching* hexagrams dating to the early years of the eighteenth century, drawn by Fr Joachim Bouvet, and sent to Gottfried Wilhelm Leibniz. The document consisted of the Fu-Hsi arrangement of the hexagrams, an 8x8 square, encircled by a ring of 64 hexagrams threefold wide. Gorai made a copy of the diagram and published it in his book (upon which his doctorate in political sciences at Wasada University was conferred) *The Influence of Confucianism on German Political Thought*, published in Tokyo in 1929:

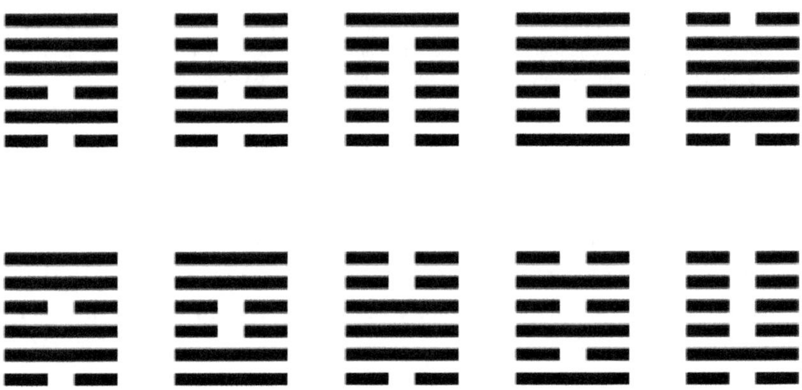

Figure 8.5. I Ching *hexagrams*. This is an abstraction of the basic principles of the *I Ching* hexagrams based on the presence or absence of lines.

2 *I Ching* has been written in the Latin alphabet variously as *Yi Jing* or *I Ging*.

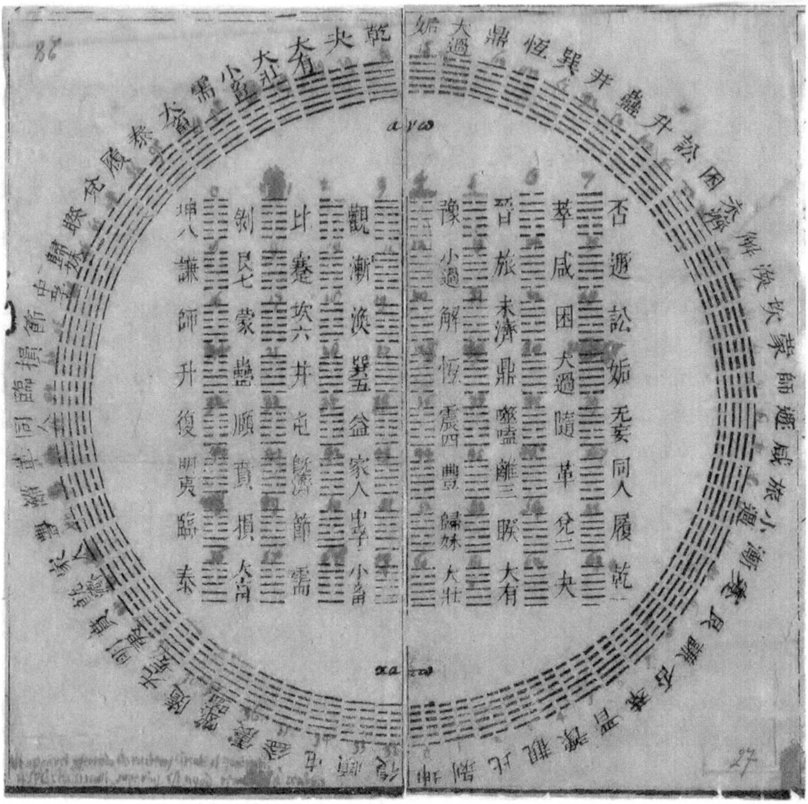

Figure 8.6. *Fu-Hsi arrangement*. This is the arrangement of the *I Ching* hexagrams sent by Jesuit priest Father Joachim Bouvet to Wilhelm Gottfried Leibniz in 1701 (GWLB Bouvet to Leibniz, 4 November 1701, AA I xx: N 318), as it appears in Perkins, *Leibniz and China* (2004). The Arabic numerals written around the outside appear to have been written by Leibniz himself, and were in the same order in Leibniz's binary arithmetic. A full, annotated English transcription of the entire correspondence, and specifically this letter, appears in Leibniz and Bouvet (n.d.).

> We see Leibniz's stroke of genius in the idea of expressing all numbers with a 0 and 1. The idea of expressing all the universe by two symbols *yin* and *yang*, in the *I Ching*, also needed a flash of genius. The two geniuses contacted and recognized each other through a universal and intuitive method of mathematics, and shook hands. (Gorai, 1929, quoted in Aiton and Shimao, 1980)

In 1689 Leibniz travelled to Rome, where he met Jesuit missionary Claudio Filippo Grimaldi. Enthralled by the culture that Grimaldi described, Leibniz edited a series of articles titled *Novissima Sinica*, prefacing it with a concept of universal culture based on the complimentary philosophies between Chinese and European thinking (Aiton and Shimao, 1980). Joachim Bouvet, who had been commissioned by the Qing emperor to undertake a survey of the Manchu Empire (Pegg, 2014), obtained a copy of this new volume and wrote to Leibniz to say he was impressed by its contents. So followed a correspondence between Bouvet and Leibniz. As the conversation developed, Leibniz had been working on his binary arithmetic, writing his 'Essay on a New Science of Numbers'[3] and describing it to Bouvet, who immediately connected it to the Chinese *I Ching* hexagrams (which had been in his thoughts since it also bore relevance to an earlier piece by Leibniz on Chinese writing and language). Bouvet responded to Leibniz with a copy of the hexagrams, exclaiming that he had found their true meaning, which had been lost long ago. According to Aiton and Shimao:

> In his [Bouvet's] view these represented in a very simple and natural manner the principles of all the sciences, or rather a complete system of a perfect metaphysics, of which the Chinese had lost the knowledge a long time before Confucius. (Aiton and Shimao, 1980: 74)

This binary ideas, stretched into a 'perfect metaphysics' by Bouvet, were adapted by Leibniz who along with François Quernay, Joseph argues was at the 'forefront of promoting a universal system of national philosophy based on Confucian writings' (Joseph, 2011: 306). Leibniz published them as 'Explication de l'arithmétique binaire [...] avec des remarques sur son utilité, et sur qu'elle donne le sens des anciennes figures Chinoises de Fohy' in the *Mémoires de l'Académie Royal des Sciences* in 1703. It was not reproduced in any form until Gorai's publication, over two hundred years later.

## For space and other mappings

In the first series of the Japanese animated television series *Ghost in the Shell: Stand Alone Complex* (Kamiyama, 2005), Tachikoma, an artificial intelligence device, says to Batou, a human, on the concept of the spirit, the 'Ghost':

> [Y]ou know that 'existence of God' thing that I had trouble understanding before? I think I am starting to understand it now. Maybe, just maybe, it's a concept that's similar to a zero in mathematics. In other words,

3 Read to the Académie Royale des Sciences, 23 April 1701.

> it's a symbol that denies the absence of meaning, the meaning that's necessitated by the delineation of one system from another. In analogue, that's God. In digital, it's zero. what do you think?

Over the years, the question of God in mathematics, Leibniz's *creatio ex nihilio* and Descartes' universal mathematics, has been forgotten – but their ghosts haunt us still.

Chatwin (1998) made a mistake, drawn by the colonial eye to privilege the inscription over the ephemeral, the visual over the vocal. Marcia Langton (in Perkins, 2008) reminds us that the songlines are less song*LINES* than *SONG*lines – melodies that rise and fall in pitch and rhythm as the songs sweep across the landscapes of the Australian continent. Songlines are embodied paths, too, traversed and experienced through the songs of the landscape and the history of each route. Each nation was the custodian of the songs for country. Songlines have been traced across countries that connect up for thousands of kilometres, mapping out the paths according to the songs. Can a song be a map? What kind of geometry is this?

In the illusory artwork of M.C. Escher, a Dutch graphic artist known for his realistic prints and woodcuts inspired by mathematical concepts, the sacred geometry mystifies, presenting in the image an impossible reality. Reason says it could be so, and representation says that it is. Like the mobile map, this work casts a veil over the workings of the world. Cartographic reason does not merely fix the world in geometric order – through its surface images; it makes cruel promises about what we can know and what can exist. Where the images created by Escher show impossibility in reason (a space that can be depicted and imagined but that cannot exist in reality), cartographic reason shows only the opposite in infinite possibility in reason: that all existing spaces can be drawn and imagined, and that within its own logic, a cathartic clarity may be achieved, a spiritual understanding of complete existential coherence.

The numbers that lie beneath the lines, the equations which govern their relations, the people who drew the maps, and those that aligned them with the stars, the ruler and the compass – none of these things are present, and so the process of fixing the world is given a mystical status within a mythology of reason.

## New technologies, old discourses

Over a period of a few centuries (a relatively short time in the history of mathematics transcribed in the texts of the Babylonians, in the philosophies of the ancient Chinese and the methods of the ancient Greeks) the extensive epistemes of reason and geometry found themselves radically transformed. This was only, in part, a linguistic or mathematical transformation, where the Cartesians dotted numbers over space and the Leibnizians over objects: it was also a discursive transformation, where geometric thinking found itself expanded into a philosophy of being, a quest for transcendentalism and universality which could be achieved through number. Cartography found itself implicated in this quest, backed by a powerful ally in cartographic reason, which beckoned it forward as cartographers surveyed new shores with imperial eyes, parcelled up the land into marketable properties and developed systems of order, surveillance and control. With the enlargement of European imperial networks into new continents, this quest became an axiom, inscribed and re-inscribed into geographic imaginations, colonial societies and narratives of progress – as new colonies found themselves to be the first global cities (Jacobs, 1996). A menagerie of discontinuities has punctuated these few centuries, from the Age of Reason until the present day, where shifts and changes in technology and theory have become the norm rather than the exception: 'Discontinuity – the fact that within the space of a few years a culture sometimes ceases to think as it had been thinking up till then and begins to think other things in a new way' (Foucault, 2002b: 56).

Discontinuity – a break, a transition, a shift: from the quadrature of the circle to Descartes and the *x*-axis and *y*-axis, Leibniz's dusty correspondence unearthed by Gorai, a map made by Lt Cook of the east coast of a new continent, another made by Lt Collinson of a small mountainous island in the South China Sea, a formal logic created by Boole, and an algorithm by Dijkstra and Lovelace, an automatic computing machine by Babbage and a digital one by Turing, the establishment of standardised global coordinate systems, and of HTML, of lines made of squares and equations and of mobile phone telephony. But these are, perhaps, better understood as methodical discontinuities – the convoluted genealogy of the Age of Reason, or cartographic reason with its twists and its branches, its folds and its fusions.

The mobile mapping practices that we see today, the interactions with maps, technologies and landscapes – and the apparatuses which support them, tenderly, as their geometries reshape space and time – are folded in with cartographic reason, even though their interfaces and the languages may appear more convoluted and abstracted from this distant waypoints in space and time. The proposition being forwarded here, before we even begin to think about what mobile mapping *means* and what it does (not

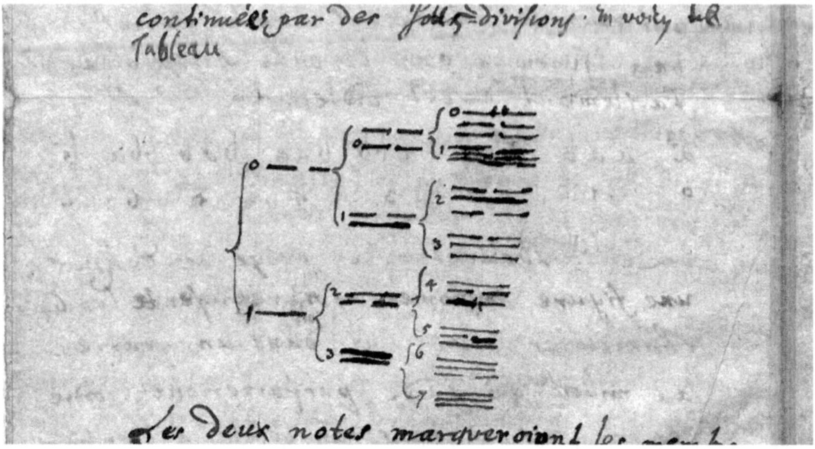

Figure 8.7. *Binary logics*. Taken from Leibniz's *Handschriften*, this basic demonstration of binary thinking between lines and numbers shows the evolution of basic numerals represented by complete or broken lines (Leibniz, 1705).

just what it *is*), is that although the language and system have changed, the discourses that saw the foundation of modern cartography – order, reason, transcendentalism and universalism – have not. The originary impetus of the digital map lies in the discursive formations of Enlightenment philosophy. What makes the discourses arising out of this philosophy particular is the transition from geometry-as-tool, as the ancients used it, to geometry and mathematics as ordering devices, reaching beyond the realm of the sciences into philosophy, and what we now understand to be social science and even, in their digital engagements, humanities and the arts. But there was a methodological break in the Age of Reason, a discontinuity between discursive formations within the same episteme, two trails of geometric thought, two lines of cartographic reason, two different kinds of representation, one of cartography and one of calculation.

Lévy asks: 'Can we construct a Leibnizian cartography?' (2012: 4). With mobile mapping, arguably, we already have.

Two lines – Descartes on the left, Leibniz on the right (Leibniz on the left, Descartes on the right).

On the right we have Cartesian coordinate geometry, an evangelising force that drew lines all over the world, making its own playing field according to its own rules. This geometry navigated the world, one angle, one triangle at a time, working between numbers and lines, calculus and compasses to create and reshape the *terra*, to build a world in which all things could be understood in relation to fixed points in space. And on the left, we have

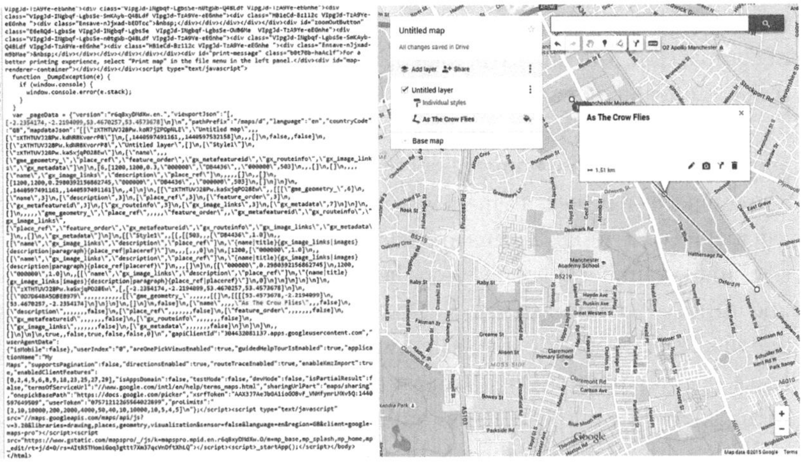


Figure 8.8. *Leibnizian and Cartesian cartographies.* This figure shows the difference between the cartographic interface (right) of a digital map, and its underlying HTML code (left). The name of the line 'As the crow flies' and its coordinates have been highlighted in the code on the left.

Leibnizian monadology, relational, fluid, a fixed point in form, not in space. What a search, to find the smallest base of all forms, an object that cannot be reduced or dissolved, an object that is ontically fixed. To try to find this in binary thinking despite resisting dialectics, and for centuries, to set about populating the world with numbers, denominating spaces and times, attempting to reduce it to a cohesive, interoperable, enumerative language: two numerals, 0 and 1.

Over the centuries, these narratives had many a secret (and not so secret) rendezvous. Their trysts can be found intertwined in words and things, on charts and maps, in plans and structures. They have come together to navigate all over the world, to expand, to colonise and tame non-Western spaces and to build European cities on hostile landscapes. Wherever there has been cartographic reason, there have been modes of geometric thinking borne again, transformed again, subtly sculpting the episteme towards mathematic epistemologies and the ontic towards rational ontologies. In mobile mapping, the Cartesian and the Leibnizian have once again met, and perhaps even become the same. We can now move all over a coordinate grid with a fixed axis on our mobile phone that continually transforms the maps that surround us. Sometimes we are the centre of the grid, other times in the periphery.

Still, regularity remains in discourses of cartographic reason and spatial order, and discursive continuity goes on: algebraic geometry still aims to order the world, and the same binary system still tries to find universal structures of interoperability. As Foucault writes: 'There exist two forms of comparison, and only two: the comparison of measurement and that of order' (Foucault, 2002b: 58).

The discontinuity, this uneven and jagged break from the Euclidean geometry towards the geometries of Descartes and Leibniz, constitutes both. The comparison of measurement is found in sizes or numbers, arithmetic and calculability. Cartesian algebra and Leibnizian calculus combine number and size, and so number space between the imagined planes of intersection (0, 0) and infinity. According to these logics, it is possible to both spatialise an idea and then to enumerate it: from a new world to a digital colour spectrum, such logics of comparison through measurement can be applied and reapplied to an expanding empire of phenomena. The second form of comparison, order, is, perhaps, more subtle. Where Descartes sought to draw order into the world, Leibniz sought to bring the world into order. His mathematics of qualitative orders, where all things can be expressed as numbered elements, has exploded into the digital systems that are ubiquitous in late urbanism. This kind of order does not require an external qualifier; it goes on without reference to any exterior and establishes its own rules in binary, in code, in coordinates. In the world of the digital map, two elements are ordered, given a common denominator of description and then measured. In the world of the mobile map, comparison, measure and order are the same things:

> Such, then, are the two types of comparison: the one analyses into units in order to establish relations of equality and inequality; the other establishes, elements, the simplest that can be found, and arranges differences according to the smallest possible degrees. (Foucault, 2002b: 59)

But the mobile map and the mobile device are not the same things as mobile mapping. The project of order and reason is never completed. The inequalities established through the relations of measurement become distorted through the establishment of elements: people are not made of binary codes, our places and locations lose flavour when reduced to coordinates, and so the paths and spaces between such abstracted inferences (such odd logics), journeys and space-times which are measured and calculated, are already hollow. Within mobile mapping, these discourses jar with something else – something intangible and inexpressible, *something not quite right* – as we use phones and signs to navigate but still end up lost, stare baffled down impossible inclines on roads that should never have been built, mirthfully note the numbers all around us describing slopes and trees and swells, and wonder why that bit of town *just doesn't make sense*.

What we must ask now is how this discursive relationship folds and unfolds in the everyday digital city, with people who live beyond numbers, who have voices that are earnest, and experiences which are always poetic. What does cartographic reason mean in mobile mapping in a digital age, and how can we trace its past trajectory into the present and the practiced?

# Part 4

## Digital/Hong Kong

# 9. Other digitalities

> But every time I returned, I saw more surrealism. Everything was tied to everything else. Nothing was what it appeared to be. The mask conceals and the actor hides behind it. It is impossible to break out, for the fetters are our own.
> – Gunnar Olsson, preface to *Birds in Egg/Eggs in Bird* (1975: i)

We have come this far already. We have discussed how we can pinpoint and trace the interlinking strands of cartographic reason through methodology. We have found emergences of heterotopic and haunted spaces of affect, of struggles between rationalist ideologies and material disobediences in Sydney. Then, we walked a dangerous path, unpicking uncanny resemblances between lines and numbers across space and time, and the course of their transmission. We have some idea about how anarchaeology might help to follow the path of cartographic reason across history and geography, as it irrupts in different places at different moments. Tracing cartographic knowledge might also help us disentangle how these different kinds of mappings – spaces, cartographies and digitalities – are linked, even if on the surface they appear to be very different.

So what then for the digitalities in mobile mapping? In the situated spatial choreography of the *dispositif* across digital technologies, signals and bytes, screens and sensors, starting from these mappings is a more difficult task. To begin, we need to trace how transformation of cartographic reason during the Enlightenment has resulted in ongoing continuities across both analogue and digital cartographies: a remodelling of space from an absolute to a relative extension; a rethinking of the line from a series of infinite points to a series of infinite numbers; the development of the idea of universal basic matter; and the resurgence of the illusory representation of the baroque image. These changes are foundational to understanding the contemporary structure of digital mobile cartography as a geocoded, position-oriented and trickster medium, which carries on the principles of spatial order and spatial rationalism established during this period. The encounters throughout this section, grapple with cartography in its

Wilmott, C., *Mobile Mapping. Space, Cartography and the Digital.*
Taylor & Francis Group, 2020
DOI 10.5117/9789462984530_CH09

Figure 9.1. *Eight walks*. February 2-15, Hong Kong, winter.

digital forms, in the translation between a *series* of fixed points, scalable ad infinitum, and *building blocks* of codes, equations, and functions that are recombinable and fragmentary. These encounters are less interested in the location of points than the relationality *in-between* the points: the translations, velocities, accelerations and redirections. This is the realm of Leibniz and his philosophy, of what Baudrillard terms the 'metaphysics of the code' (Baudrillard, 1994: 57).

Furthermore, even in their representational or performative forms, this version of mobile mappings does not occupy a fixed plane. They invert Foucault's reasoning of the 'speech-act', wherein speaking itself has become an incessant action which does not pause from its transformation, nor allows itself to be captured long enough to be considered 'speech'. What we meet in mobile mapping is a fluid, shifting set of statements, unified by rules, but near impossible to delineate into a discursive formation because of their ongoing disruptions, reworkings and resistances. For Pickles (2004), the production of images through digital technologies illustrates how geocoding, in tandem with cartographic reason, becomes central to the geographical imaginations that produce spatial identities through social inscription. But, he also asks for investigation into 'the ways in which we can live in them' (Pickles, 2004: 23). In digital realms, distinctions between real and virtual are dissolved through of socio-techno-spatial configurations, or spatial media/tion (Leszczynski, 2015). Here, the constant formation of cartographic reason, and the assembling and disassembling of mobile mapping instead comes to emphasise the hybridity of speech and act. So, this next section, *Part 4: Digital/Hong Kong*, considers both the speech and the act, and their ongoing interrelations in a world that has been founded on digital logics for much longer than we often remember.

Although we are limited in what we can describe here – in terms of the affects, monadism, intensities and feelings of digitalities – in this section, digital technology does not become the entire story of mobile mapping: in the social, the spatial and the material, other digitalities survive and thrive beyond the universalities of Leibnizian desires. My biggest concern is that, under the spectacle of the device, cartographic reason becomes an a priori without history (Foucault, 2002a). Its existence is an unquestioned condition of reality, and the stories that might exist beyond scientific, speakable or deictic rules, ghosts that linger on the landscape and the body, remain subsurface and cththonic. In the space-time of settler-colonialism typical of Hong Kong and Sydney, universal foundations of knowledge, experience and being are up for contention and contestation. In this setting, absolutist determinations on the meanings of space and knowledge tend to create more injury than healing. In ways of thinking that place a certain level of faith in Western desires for epistemological coherence, and, further, draw to this the possibility for geometry and mathematics to provide clarity in questions of experience and being, a particular threat is posed. It is precisely this desire for universality that characterises some of the crueller brutalities of cartographic thinking, specifically in postcolonial contexts: what Said (1990) calls a 'cartographic' impulse to conquer, categorise and control. What danger, then, lies in searching for unified explanations of theory or practice, of experience or of language – this same question that intrigued us earlier? When subjugated, abject or 'other' knowledges are pulled into dominant discursive formations they become transformed into alignment with hegemonic structures and unified with the models of thought characteristic of that postcolonial space (Foucault, 2003). In mobile mapping in a postcolonial context, this presents a danger of space becoming synonymous with territory, mapping with cartography, and digitality with code. In the first instance, then, should we not hope for the opposite to order – to disassemble, scatter and fragment the unities that have sat idle, and then see what lies amongst the rubble? Space, if we agree with Massey (2005) is anything but unified and so, I ask, might we say the same for the digital?

In an era of digital cartographies – and apparatuses of digital architectures, infrastructures and logics – to what degree are cartographic impulses resurrected in the networked, topological and relational structures of everyday digitalities? Topological thinking in cultural and spatial research is designed to grapple with the fixation on the subject and challenge the hegemony in Euclidean geometry across all disciplines (Shields, 2013; Parisi, 2013; McFarlane, 2016). It draws deeply from Michel Serres's reading of geometry (Connor, 2004) and his subsequent theories on topology: specifically, Serres's (2014) doctoral work on Leibniz's geometry, systems and monadology. Leibniz was at once fascinated with the relational potential of Cartesian geometry yet also wary of the absolutist nature of the intersection of the axes (Evangelidis, 2018). Thus, Serres proposes a different way of thinking geometrically based in Leibniz's geometry, predicated upon relationality between objects, rather than relationality to an absolute point. This is a different way of imagining the world through metaphors that he uses to understand the worlds created by the virtual – from the origins of history, existence and the map: 'How can the three [origins] be conceived, in effect, if not as innumerable multiplicities of states of things [choses], attached or not by inestimable quantities of relations?' (Serres, 1994: 101).[1]

The ideas of an innumerablity and inestimability are crucial to understanding the complicated relations of digital systems. Parisi (2013) has called this 'incompleteness in [computational] axiomatics', in that the desires of algorithmic structures are never completely nor fully formalised. In topological forms, infinities are continuities that can be broken up into parts, and parts which can be larger than a whole (Parisi, 2013). She argues that infinity, discussed in the last section, in computational terms is that which is *incomputable*. Infinite data is incompressible, inconclusive and attuned to randomness in the outputs, structures and folds that it produces. The point at which the world becomes entirely digitised is dependent upon the (perhaps unachievable) capacity to calculate infinite probabilities from infinite data: 'The age of the algorithm therefore involves the construction of digital space conditioned by incomputable quantities of data' (Parisi, 2013: 18).

In short, the flipside of the growing desire for determinative forms of governance through more information – like big(ger) data – is increasingly incomputability, and therefore, indeterminancy. We have already seen indeterminancy in the material architectures of Sydney, where the ongoing insistence towards a rational Cartesian urban form creates unexpected loopholes, fragments, fractures and ruptures: blue dots bounce all over screens, Africa appears where Brisbane should be, GPS devices can't

1 This has been translated by the author, as (as far as I am aware) no prior translation exists in English. The original is quoted here: 'Comment concevoir les trois, en effet, sinon comme des multiplicités innombrables d'états de choses, attachées ou non par d'inestimables quantités de relations?' (Serres, 1994: 101). 'Choses' has been translated here as 'things' (as appears to be standard in Sheridan's translations of Foucault) in order to avoid confusion with 'objects' and to underscore the materiality of the statement.

pronounce Aboriginal words, and phones aren't great for cycling. It is this indeterminancy that is of interest here – the topological fluidity between science and culture (Lury et al., 2012) – and its relationship with infinity and cartography across both conceptual and material planes.

There are multiple links between topological structures and cartographic rationality. Serres, for instance, draws on cartographic metaphors throughout his work, describing his inquiry into topological modes of thinking as a 'navigational map' (Serres and Latour, 1995: 105) and an atlas (Serres, 1994), and as well arguing that geometry has a relationality with visuality across space and time in both form and thought (Serres, 2011). This is clear in Leibniz's writings and work: Leibniz was an avid builder of models that experimented with topology, calculation and the basis of the universal characteristic (Serres, 2014). His models are often posited as antithetical to Cartesian order (cf. Deleuze, 1992a; Farinelli, 2009; Serres, 2014), a descent away from the tablature of grid into the topological – the smallest atom of the monad, the development of the binary code system, and the fluid, malleable realm of the baroque. Deleuze states that '[t]he definition of Baroque mathematics is born with Leibniz' (Deleuze, 1992a: 17). In contrast to the straight lines of the Cartesian grid, the mathematical space of Leibniz is that of folds. For Leibniz, all straight lines have curves intertwined: there is no precise surface or point in the Leibnizian space, '[i]nflection is the authentic atom, the elastic point' (Deleuze, 1992a: 14). Inflections do not have coordinates, or verticalities, egocentric directionalities, or progressive qualities. Inflection is the *event* of geometry, in transformative movement: it is ideal and it is virtual (Deleuze, 1992a).

Further, where Descartes links number and geometry to reflect the stable external system of the world, Leibniz dismisses the Cartesian dualism, and brings the notion of space and mind to the stability of matter (Elden, 2013b). Leibniz argues that while space and matter may not be equivocal, they are inseparable: 'there is no space where there is no matter' (Leibniz and Clarke, 2007: 40). The cartographic technologies of the Leibnizian do not fix on the distinction between mentality and physicality, but rather on their co-constitution, their simultaneous existence under a single ordering principle.

For Leibniz, the principle of substitution is that words which are the same can refer to phenomena which are the same: a = b, in any context (De Risi, 2007; Rescher, 2013). This means that while space can be 'an order of things existing at the same time' (Leibniz, 2007: 9), it remains an *order*, a system which is stable, predictable and therefore, classifiable and calculable: a *mathesis universalis* (Batchelor, 2004). Furthermore, rather than a universal geometry like Descartes, Leibniz sought a universal characteristic that was irreducible, an ordering phenomenon that could be found co-existing across all systems (Leibniz, 1991). Such a characteristic could be combined and recombined in order to build the structures that we consider to be the world. Leibniz's God (Baudrillard, 1993) was to be found at the limit of the smallest (not the largest) infinity, within this irreducible force, which he called the *monad*, and its representation, which he called the *characteristica universalis*. This led to the development of a proto-enigma calculating machine, which used a base 2 (0/1) counting system as its universal characteristic (Rescher, 2013), the same system from which much of contemporary computing runs.

Like Parisi, Serres recognizes limits of indeterminancy in the spatial applications of Leibniz's universality. He argues that the 'beginnings of politics' (Serres, 1982b: 44) arrives in the shift from the perfect and ordered systems of Leibniz and Descartes to the networked, ambivalent system of Hermes. This system, claims Serres, is comprised of 'stations and paths', '[p] oints and lines', 'beings and relations' (ibid.: 10), less interested in universal order than universal translatability:

> The second system is that of Hermes. He is a polytheist, is multi-centered, a chain of hourglasses, a network of such chains. The angels that pass, be they gods or demons, occupy the crossroads: knots of exchange, changes, cuts, bifurcations of decision, spindles, bundles, where the many come in one single hand. The beginnings of politics. [...] The system of Leibniz is a limit of this system. (Serres, 1982b: 44)

Beyond the binaries and even beyond the hybrid, the system of Hermes encompasses the Cartesian and the Leibnizian, the fixed and the fluid, the location and the relation. Hermes transcends conversations about the benefits and detriments of digital technologies on sociocultural and spatial processes, specifically in terms of cartographic reason (Serres and Latour, 1995). The network of Hermes is not fixated on form, but flow, or 'the formation and distribution of the lines, paths, and stations, their borders, edges, and forms' (Serres, 1982b: 11). Hermes is the communicator who gives angels messages to carry between stations. Such messages metamorphose through this network, encountering parasites that alter, add to or detract from them.

Foucault (1995, 2003) and Deleuze and Guattari (1987) describe two types of power: as confining (*potestas*) or empowering (*potentia*); or in Serres's (1982b: 44) more literary terms, *gods* and *demons*. The system of Hermes is a system of translation and exchange, allowing angels – both god and demons – to work relationally between fixities, bringing together the various threads of what can be argued is the contemporary iteration of cartographic reason. As digital systems produce territories, the expression of power shifts as communications are co-opted by other systems of knowledge/power (such as capital), or what Serres (1982b: 52) calls the 'parasites'.

Serres recognises a productive transformation between the system of Leibniz and the system of Hermes – between the clean rationalism of enlightenment desire and the messy politics of a globalised world – the transformation in which this book takes hold. Here, there may be openings for other possibilities of thinking with, through and against digitalities which make space for resistant, counter-hegemonic and non- or de-colonial knowledge practices. As Parisi writes:

> What is important here is not that culture has become doomed by the automated rules that transform its variety of expressions into data that can be classified, profiled, and consumed. Instead, the addition of random quantities to finite procedures turns automation into a computational adventure resulting in the determination of new cultural actualities. (Parisi, 2013: x)

What might these 'new cultural actualities' be? From the moment an anticipatory cartography was projected onto a postcolonial landscapes, the birth of politics arose through the parasites, messy in their acquisitions, in ways which still emerge and transform contrapuntally in contemporary mobile mapping, but have yet to be examined and assessed in their cartographic nuances. The notion of cartographic truth is based in discursive structures: What constitutes knowledge? What gives particular forms valence over others? Where is truth recorded and kept? This is a different realm of philosophy – less the rigid posts of coordinate geometry and grids cast over the world, than shifting topologies (of objects, of power, of everything) that are deeply relational. In spatial terms, this discursive transformation of cartographic reason has a very different fix-point than the zero point (0, 0) of the Cartesian cartographers who drew their eyes across the surface and the volumes of Sydney and Hong Kong. The fix-points in this topological world are any and every point, adjustable and relational binaries – digital monads (Leibniz and Loptson, 2012) – that build upon each other through the network of Hermes (Serres, 1982a, 1982b).

The openings in parasitic digital infrastructures strike at the heart of this question of indeterminancy and the possibility for other digitalities to emerge from *within* as well as beyond calculative and classificatory

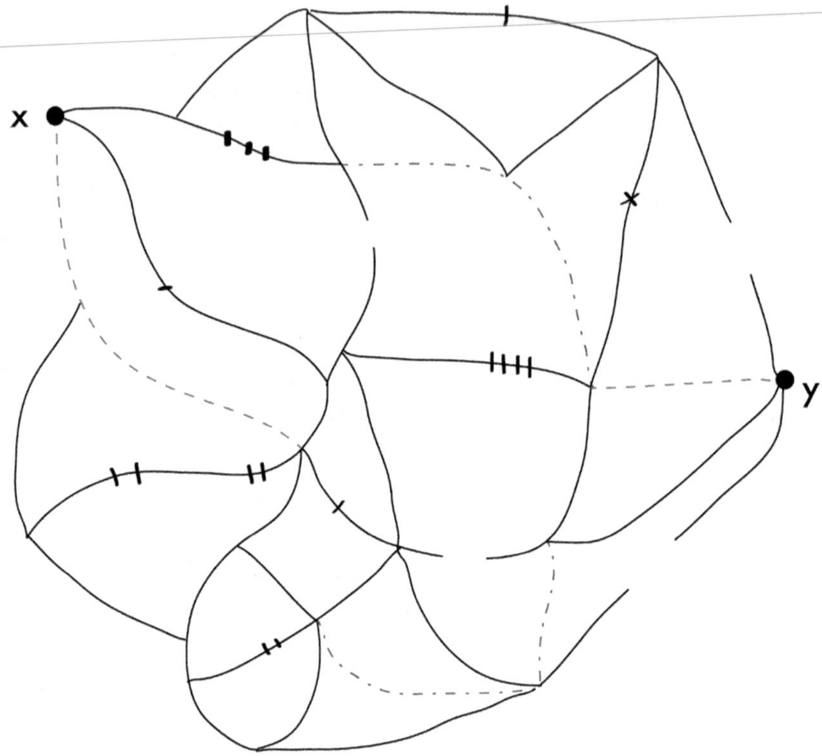


**Hermes**

Figure 9.2. *Hermes*. Visualisation showing the network of Hermes including bifurcations, parasites, obstacles, paths of angels (blue) and demons (red) between two points – x and y. Source: The author.

systems. As it stands, how these infinite quantities of data engage with and produce new possibilities through algorithms, Parisi (2013) describes as 'contagious', bound with immanent, imperfect and incomplete processes: 'Data production is an immanent process that unravels the gaps, blind spots, and incompatibilities within formal systems in their attempt to constantly invent new axioms and rules' (Parisi, 2013: xiv). Drawing on Guattari, she argues how metamodelling is a process where potentialities can occur beyond the rules or remit of the original model itself in *extraspace*. This *extraspace* is the products of potentialities, where metamodels can re-emerge with their own rules and logics, across both the conceptual and material. Most importantly, since space and matter are not total equivalencies – there still is, as Massey (2005) argued, openings for possibility.

The mathematics of infinity described by Cantor, and reaccounted into a digital realm by Parisi requires a mind-bending recognition of relationality and scale. But to circuit around the computational – just for a minute – and to resituate this conversation in the postcolonial urbanities that we have and will discuss, surely this is also a mirror to the lived realities of postcolonialism? The entirety of the world – as Borges wrote – is impossible to represent. For every infinity reached, yet another breaks off, or unfurls, or collapses inwards. The problem with postcolonial cartographies is precisely a fundamental incompleteness – both conceptually and materially – as entanglements of cartographers, planners and everyday people mistranslate between the desire for universalism and the reality of living in an 'other' space. In doing so, against the governmental and colonial logics of settlement, new and generative possibilities burst through the membranes, flood the present and leak into pasts and futures with persistent commonality. The *extraspace* was already determined in everyday resistances and misadventures, and metamodels are simply a way of saying 'the ways we live with' the ongoing dissonances and violences of colonial projects. It is well established that the brutalities of contemporary algorithmic surveillance were founded in 'statistical reason' and colonial regimes (Dubrovsky and Magnet, 2015). This can be especially seen in concerns surrounding algorithmic surveillance in the settler-colonial spaces, where, 'from the perspective of Indigenous peoples, the eye of the state has always been genocidal, because the problem is not primarily the surveillance strategies of the state, but the state itself' (ibid: 38).

This is not to say, however, that *other* digitalities are easily mapped against a priori structures of power. As Munster (2006) notes: 'as Olu Oguibe has argued, it will not do to bring predetermined conceptions of others' bodies to a discussion of the digital' (Munster, 2006: 152). This world of discourses, objects or monads or whatever post-human, peri-subject construction is described, is always, interminably and unavoidably basted in Western epistemes, ideologies and fallacies – in this case, arising out of the Age of Reason. Even the work of Foucault in its post-structural phantasmagoria falls prey to its own critique. In digital mapping, the tendency to lend authority to culture through scientific metaphors is perhaps misplaced in the heterogeneous worlds which are lived (Massey, 1991) and risks further undermining the subjugated knowledges and other behaviours that appear. These epistemes house these methodologies, and make it difficult to imagine outside of the self-imposed limits and values placed upon them. For instance, Serres's comments on Deleuze's expression of folding in the Baroque (Serres, 1994) is specifically contrasted against breaking: systems fold in upon themselves, yet are still constituted by the same conditions of possibility. But seeing breaks is important too: the destruction of both people and knowledge, irreversible decimation of landscapes and histories, centuries of subjugation and trauma are characterised not by the same entity folding in upon itself but two systems clashing, splintering, snapping, cutting and severing. There is violence and anger here, as violence as has been enacted by cartography (Neocleous, 2003), embedded in the practice of powers which cannot be epistemologically challenged without that, too, being colonised: 'The dynamics of power are rooted in difference' (Olsson, 1991b: 168), or perhaps better, 'inconsolable difference', which when consoled, becomes the same.

Cartographic digitalities also inherit cartographic rationalities and their bounding, territorial and geopolitical technologies (Pickles, 2004). Before we even consider computational architectures, we can see how, in Sydney, contagious architectures are already established the anarchaeologies described throughout the chapter. We could even argue that the cattle that wandered off and established the free herds of Western Sydney, the dialectics of Western and Aboriginal names, burial grounds which defy material transformation, in sand which *will not* stay on the beach or private spheres whose lights other people's lives out onto the street constitute contagious anarchitectures – potentialities prone not to the monumental of the artistic world, but bound up in the everyday and the mundane.

These examples appear not only because of the material-discursive impossibilities of mathematical infinities produced through *extraspace* but also because of what Gaskins (2016) calls a 'vernacular space', produced by techno-vernacular creativities. Techno-vernacular creativities are ad hoc and adaptive configurations where technologies are redeployed (even against their original designs) as resistances to established power. These are everyday creativities established through different combinations of people and technologies – though that may be extended to include materialities, animals, software, data, spaces and temporalities. The potentialities described here are political and not entirely bound up by mathematics and physical laws, as Parisi describes. Rather, they agitate at the internal and external limits of universal and rationalist totalities, constantly erupting and disrupting. Thus, we can consider these anarchitectures of contagion as a trajectory of rupturing spatial practices which find alternate and additional paths in digitalities: other spaces extend into other digitalities.

Our notions of experience are melting away into an ever-consumable present (Jameson, 1991), and the time it takes to identify, reason and reflect according to the Hegelian or Leibnizian methods, evaporates as soon as it is grasped.

> The *Monad*, of which we shall here speak, is nothing but a *simple* substance which enters into compounds; by '*simple*', is meant 'without parts'. [...] Now where there are no parts, there can be neither extension nor form [*figure*] nor divisibility. These Monads are the true atoms of nature and, in a word, the elements of things. (Leibniz and Loptson, 2012: 117, emphasis in the original)

Leibniz's monadology describes monads as irreducible, the lowest substrate of things, the 'true atoms of nature' (Leibniz and Loptson, 2012: 172). They create limits through the process of assembling and dissembling, and are the material and representational appearance of what Leibniz terms the 'infinity' of God, or soul (Leibniz and Loptson, 2012: 27). The link between the monadic and the digital in Leibnizian philosophy sits within the development of binary logic and arithmetic. The use of binary became particularly prescient with the development of electronic computing – where the on and off state of electronic switches could be precisely matched by the logic of binary – true = on/1, false = off/0. Thus, monadic forms of thought became central to computational technology and, contemporarily, still form the basis of most digital communication in its representational forms.

This is what I have come to call the 'monadic digital'. I am not arguing that Leibniz meant that binary code was a monad – there is little evidence to suggest that he did. Other philosophers, like Friedrich Nietzsche (1973) and Walter Benjamin (2003) have used the idea of the monad differently, emphasising the 'more than the sum of its parts' aspect of Leibniz's monadology, where the monad is desirous, chaotic, haunting and vibrant. Yet, as I argue throughout this section, the intersections between cartographic reason and subjugated knowledges, affects, interpretations and movements within mobile mapping, bring the tension between binary (as a rationalist and transcendental construct) and these more radiant readings of monadology to the fore. Therefore, rather than simply labelling 0 and 1 as monads – which is difficult considering how, as described above, digital, electronic computing blurs distinctions between experience, materiality and representation – I prefer to describe binary as monadic in both form and desire. Likewise, I term the systems of digital electronic representation as the 'monadic digitalities'.

While Leibniz's ideas are often counterposed to the Cartesian school of thought, there are also crucial commonalities between both, namely their basis in transcendence, universality and, to a lesser extent, order (Munster, 2006). The influence of Leibnizian philosophy becomes increasingly evident as mobile devices reshape space and time within urban environments, and as mobility between global and local becomes more compressed (Hjorth et al., 2012). The baroque saw the production of a geometric perspectivism – a trickster (Turnbull, 2000) – that did not offer the certitude of the Cartesian grid, but instead hid its structures under folds, billows, pleats and illusions: 'It is the privileged age of *trompe-l'oeil* painting, of the comic illusion, of the play that duplicates itself by representing another play, of the *qui pro quo*, of dreams and visions; it is the age of the deceiving senses' (Foucault, 2002b: 57).

Such illusions sneak dimensionality into flatness (in the case of the trompe l'oeil), creating systems of self-referentiality, using their own internal rules to produce transformative geometries that overcome space (Latour, 1987). Munster (2006) argues that the folds of digital media with bodies do not combine into a smooth surface, but produce dissonant gaps – 'interfolds'. Even within static representations, the bounds of geometry may become contradictory, in Escher-like lines and the folding of space and times. Binary code also operates in such a way, an ongoing symbolic exchange that orders the world under two digits (Baudrillard, 1993). Furthermore, the immense striation of levels of representation within digital, networked systems (and in particular, cartographic systems) continues to hold the spirit of the trompe l'oeil (Munster, 2013). The *mathesis universalis* of the Leibnizian universal characteristic results therefore in an illusion of dimensionality, against the force of homogeneity, in which 'Leibniz, eternally running after the untotalizable sum of ichnographies succeeded in closing his system with Universal Harmony' (Serres, 2008: 48).

Therefore, while the Cartesian workers of the technological *dispositif* fix a firm zero-point, the Leibnizian workers equally fix it on the subject, the viewer, the every-point (Bollnow, 2011). The senses are deceived, as new points emerge and disappear (Serres, 2008) and the *dispositif* becomes extended and elastic. As Conley, in the forward to Deleuze's *The Fold*, writes:

> A similar politics emerges from comparison of Descartes's and Leibniz's views on extension. For the former, the material world can be mapped out from the axis of the thinking subject, in rectilinear fashion, and can be divided into discrete units. [...] For the latter, neither the self nor the world can work so schematically. Everywhere the subject swirls in the midst of forces they exert [sic] stress that defines the individual body, its elasticity, and its bending motions in volumes that produce movement in and of extension. (Conley, 1992: xvii)

In the baroque, the illusion and universality come together in reason through the work of Descartes and Leibniz, with long-lasting consequences for a contemporary cartographic analysis. Counterpoising Cartesian and Leibnizian spaces has produced a particular dichotomy – where the representational qualities of the visual and the cartographic are considered to 'fix' fluidity and flows (Prytherch and Cidell, 2015: 20). I argue, however, that the foundation of cartographic reason is not based on the dichotomisation of fixity and fluidity, but rather on the rationalisation of both fixities and fluidities through cartographic reason, or what Pickles calls 'the technologies of the social body' (Pickles, 2004: 124). The stabilisation and *regulation* of relationality is entirely in keeping with the logics of cartographic reason, especially in postcolonial spaces – albeit along a fraternal trajectory of Leibnizian philosophy. Here, the order of binary becomes split from the tumultuous monad. Thus, as the cartographical image is applied to mathematical principles to solve more general problems of nature, society and culture (a = a, a ≠ b), during the Enlightenment, cartographic reason shifted from a reflective empirical description to become an ordering tool that transforms and stabilises nature according to the map, the territory and the state. This transformation foregrounds the continued abstraction of knowledge from materiality, the perception that the world – matter – is inherently ordered through stable systems which can be harnessed through representation and classification, and transformed into units of exchange (Kornwolf and Kornwolf, 2002).

Therefore, topology is not entirely free from the cartographic impulse. The impulse to produce choreographies of flows through fixities of form – the disassembling and reassembling of circulations – is central to the realisation of what Gregory (1994: 70) terms a 'cartographic anxiety' in the stability of Cartesian forms of rationalisation. This realisation of stability was important in the culmination of the system of Hermes, and proliferates throughout this book. Farinelli (2009: 120) measures the neo-Classical, Cartesian structures of 'the map, the territory and the state' in the sixteenth century against 'the globe, the network and the myth' in worldwide (globalised) digital communication. Yet, as I have argued, even where the systems of fixity and flow themselves may differ – from universal structures to universal characteristics – they share a founding discursive interoperability in the desire for stability in order and reason. These stable systems, in the case of Leibnizian globes, networks and myths, are what Farinelli calls a 'topological reason' (2009: 152). Topology is implicit in the mathematical scaling and modelling of space, based, like the coordinate system, between shape and number. The Cartesian technologies of the grid become interoperable through Leibnizian desires for universality: to find a common basis for all phenomena:

> Imperialism is not 'the art of transforming spheres into flat surfaces' (Sloterdijk, 1999: 909-911), of flattening the world, but rather *of translating an infinite series of maps that are incompatible into a single terrestrial sphere* (Galison, 2003: 77-152), according to the single major project of late modernity'[2] (Farinelli, 2009: 152, emphasis in the original)

The major project of late modernity which sought to conquer according to universal systems can be traced as far back as these early baroque ideas and the period of the Enlightenment (Harvey, 1989), whereby disobedient landscapes were wrenched, altered and reformed into unitary cartographic systems. On a discursive level, the *universal* in the Leibnizian *characteristica universalis*, together with its topological and inflective elasticities, can be considered a central part of cartographic reason. Furthermore, it is embedded in the functioning imperial ideologies of modernity that cohere and homogenise space into a single order. Here, I consider the formalisation of cartographic reason through the conceptual development of the 'ordered' social landscape, residing in a state between fixity of flow. I discuss how the cartographic technologies of elastic grids, choreographed flows, illusory borders and space-as-numbers, became materialised from an abstracted mathematical space into the experienced space of the postcolonial city.

What is important here is that we continue to think about mobile mapping practices as discursive practices – not to map the surface of emergence of the map itself, nor the phone, but to touch the undefinable surface through which cartographic reason emerges in mobile mapping, and make room for *other* digitalities to breathe. The world has also become more complicated – colonialism has created subjects that work within these binaries but live beyond them (Spivak, 1999). This means that, as Olsson argues, '[t]he crucial problem is, of course, that some facets of reality can be perfectly delimited, while others cannot' (Olsson, 1980: 20b), leaving 'fuzzy phenomena', which cannot be represented by the linguistic or semiotic tools that we have to hand, and when we try to, we engage in an epistemic violence.[3] Epistemic violence is central to postcolonial theory as well as theories of representation (Spivak, 1988). Orientalism (Said, 1978; Said, 2004) outlines precisely this point – that no matter how relational, radical or adaptable Western philosophies

2 Translated by author. 'L'imperialismo non è "l'arte di trasformare le sfere in superfici piane" [Sloterdijk 1999, pp. 909, 910, 911], di appiattire il mondo, ma piuttosto quella di tradure un'infinita serie di mappe tra loro incompatibili in un'unica sfere terrestre [Galison 2003, pp. 77-152], secondo l'unico grande progetto della matura modernità.'

3 It was, after all, to understand humans and history that Hegel created the dialectic (Hardt and Negri, 2004; Snow, 2001).

are, no matter how they hope to decentre themselves, their position or their humanism, the epistemologies of the world still operate on a spatiotemporal Cartesian grid that has its (0, 0) firmly fixed on Europe – one that has not changed significantly in digital coordinate systems. This, too, is a criticism of Foucault's work – and this book: although Said found the work of Foucault liberating and drew enthusiastically from it, he also argued that in the end that both the man and his oeuvre were resoundingly European, able but not necessarily willing to use the tools created to build a political purpose against the epistemological and disciplinary colonialism of the West (Said, 2004). Foucault, himself, also recognised the inherent and irreconcilable contradiction of his archaeological thesis:

> But I have obstinately gone on. Not that I am either certain of victory or sure of my weapons. But because it seemed to me that, for the moment, the essential task was to free the history of thought from its subjection to transcendence. (Foucault, 2002a: 223)

Here, we can find some commonality with Foucault's purpose, to not search for truths promised by mobile mapping but rather to seek out the potential to re-empower the practice of mobile mapping as a way of knowing and of doing that is not transcendental but embedded as a 'chiasm of thought-and-action', the digital as *doing, emerging, speaking back* and *struggling*. These are the other digitalities, those which are disruptive, chaotic and contradictory.

In Foucault's later interviews and writings, an explicitly political purpose develops. He argues that discourse is not a surface manifestation of power, but a principal operator: discourse is a 'strategic field, where elements, tactics, arms do not cease passing from one camp to another, swapping between adversaries and returned against those who use the same' (Foucault, 2001b: 123). This is a particularly important consideration in mobile mapping practices. What other kinds of digitalities are being obscured in a practice where the near and far appear at once, where discourses that have a spatiotemporal distance, like cartographic reason, converge into the everyday in a way which transcends the distinction between the epistemic and the ontic? This question is concerned with the subjugated knowledges which have been repressed or ignored over the course of the world's history in favour of various forms of rationality and scientific thinking, most apparent in recent developments in computation, media and technology:

> Both the specialised domain of scholarship and the disqualified knowledge of people have contained the memory of combats, the very memory

> that had until then been confined to the margins. [...] We have both a meticulous rediscovery of struggles and the raw memory of fights. (Foucault, 2003: 8)

This includes acknowledgements of struggles, epistemic violence, subjugated knowledges and excluded behaviours: 'hauntings, ghosts and gaps, seething absences and muted presences' (Gordon, 2008: 20). This tangent into politics, space and representation is important, and perhaps the most important single point of this chapter. This is not really a book about postcolonialism. Yet, as digital technologies emerge in postcolonial cities,[4] such as Sydney and Hong Kong, the strategic field of discourse is not a tabula rasa, a smooth surface upon which new inscriptions are made and contemporary struggles are illuminated. Neither city is a surface upon which a unified theory of being or of experience can be drawn. Rather, we find them peppered with chasms and all kinds of dangers lurking hidden in the grass. It is an unresolved terrain, which has been irreversibly shaped by colonial processes to favour hegemonic discourses. This cannot be ignored. Cartographic reason sits upon the high ground in a nearly impenetrable fortress, so high, perhaps, that it cannot be seen and now exists only in memory or in moments where the cloud clears and the infinitude of the sky is revealed. It is upon this terrain that digital maps are opened. The inscriptions of powerful digitalities and othered digitalities join the multitude of others that have incidentally scarred and restored the landscape, layering over them, digging into them, widening and darkening faint lines, and in doing so become transformed – they have no original state, they merely join millions of others of their kind in this bitter battlefield where silent and not-so-silent wars still rage.

4 This argument is most easily made about postcolonial societies because the struggle is more evident, and debates are already occurring, albeit in a muted manner. However, strategic fields such as these exist across the world, even in the most privileged societies, as Foucault recognised in researching the institutionalization of the body and bio-politics. In the asylum and the prison, and in society more generally, subjugated knowledges concerning discourses of bodies, health, sexuality and deviance also characterised similar uneven terrains, topographies constructed to favour certain discourses over others.

# 10. Classifying the digital

## Daren/Names

> 'If I don't see this name, I will not know where it is. I can't find in the map, you know, even this location.'

It's the Lunar New Year in Hong Kong and so the wet market, while bright and busy, seems unusually calm. Some vendors are still out, selling vegetables, fish and meat – their small stalls and restaurants interspersed rather than overcrowded across the ground floor of old buildings and spilling out onto the cemented road and into the cooler winter breeze. Sellers and buyers mill about conversing, and a group of shop owners take a lunch break together, eating pork and rice on the steps of one of the nearby shops. In the middle of the steady flows of people, Daren stands unfazed, searching intently on Google Maps on his phone.

'It's difficult to …,' he starts, before breaking off to focus on the phone again.

We've just finished lunch at a small restaurant that sells barbequed suckling pig, and now we're ready to start a hunt for art and graffiti in Soho. Looking up at the restaurant, 'Dragon Restaurant', Daren squints across the road before looking down again and tapping cautiously on his phone screen. A man pushes past us wheeling a cart, piled with garbage bags and a large black dustbin. Near my feet, a small grey rat runs along the gutter, searching for scraps.

'I'm not sure what street this is ….' Daren continues, 'I'm not sure what kind of location I am in. The street.'

I am unhelpful. I say that we are on Gage Street, but Daren's display interface is in Cantonese, and we'd be going off the urban plan rather than any toponymic familiarity. Daren zooms in again on the phone. He shows me how, on the map, the location seems to be somewhere east of where we should be, pointing at a restaurant named 'Dragon Restaurant'. He doesn't have the GPS switched on his phone because the constant feeding of information drains the battery. Furthermore, despite generally good

Wilmott, C., *Mobile Mapping. Space, Cartography and the Digital.*
Taylor & Francis Group, 2020
DOI 10.5117/9789462984530_CH10

Figure 10.1. *Fragments – Daren, Ellen, Ravi and Vicki.* (Left) *Daren's walk* – Sunday, 2 February, Central-Soho, midday, sunny; (centre-left) *Ellen's walk* – Monday, 3 February, Choi Hung-LOHAS Park, morning, sunny; (centre-right) *Ravi's walk* – Friday, 7 February, Tsim Sha Tsui, afternoon, sunny; (right) *Vicki's walk* – Saturday, 8 February. Central-The Peak, morning, overcast.

cell tower coverage all over the island, the tall buildings make the locating function imprecise and more confusing than helpful. GPS signals do not travel well through reinforced concrete, steel structures or thick walls and so blockages occur in densely populated urban areas like Hong Kong (Chao et al., 2001). Because the GPS signal does not work (like it does in Sydney), Daren has to manually work between the Google place names database and the landscape around him to discover where he is. Since the streets in Hong Kong are long and complicated – often moving through several neighbourhoods or suburbs, entering the street name is usually not precise enough to determine our location.

Looking up again, he takes a few steps forward towards the crossroads ahead. As we move, a Lexus pushes between the small food stalls and our position, and we are forced onto the narrow footpath momentarily. After it has gone on, we break out back onto the road and Daren points to a road sign that notes that we are on the crossroads with Graham Street.

'Now I can see that,' he laughs. 'If I don't see this name, I will not know where it is. I can't find in the map, you know, even this location.'

Yet, it doesn't entirely make a difference because Graham Street, a small steep alleyway that runs from the flattened areas of reclaimed land down near Des Voeux Street up to Hollywood Road, does not have a crossroads for triangulation. He looks back at the Central-Mid-Levels escalator and walkway system that runs parallel to Graham Street. Yet, he cannot make the escalators, the wet market and Graham Street appear at the same time on the screen with a zoom resolution that preserves their cartographic toponymy.

Daren's cartographic acrobatics are compounded by language glitches in the hybridity of Hong Kong cultures. Hong Kong has always been a space of (at least) two language systems – English and Cantonese – which has its own discursive problems embedded into the urban landscape. For every place in Hong Kong, there are two names, with varying indexicality between them

Figure 10.2. *Google Maps*. Daren stands on Gage Street and tries to find our location on Google Maps using the Google Pinyin.

on both an orthographic (writing) and phonographic (speaking) level. There have been many attempts to work between language systems – modes of romanising Chinese phonographic sounds into Latin alphabets – yet even this has its own problems in both reinforcing certain modes of power in language, and also failing to grasp the complexity of language in its spatio-cultural contexts. In Hong Kong, for instance, some streets were named first in Cantonese, and the English merely picked up the Pinyin characters while maintaining the phonography (like Mee Lun Street). Others were named first in English and the Chinese characters are approximations of the phonetic sound of the English words, often used for streets named after people or places like Des Voeux, or Tench. Other places have two names that are translations of meaning, either first from Cantonese or English – for instance, Temple Street. Some are from literal mis-transpositions such as Rednaxela Terrace, which is supposedly the result of an orthographic error in writing Alexander (in English, left to write) in Chinese (right to left) (Yanne and Heller, 2009). Others have names that are completely different, drawing from different experiences of the space, like the flower market. Of course, this has led to a double toponymy throughout Hong Kong with disjointed and uneven cartographic manifestations and Google Maps has inherited this problem.

Even Daren, who speaks English well, still uses Google Maps in Chinese. Although over his shoulder I can see how google.hk shows a combination of both the Chinese and English place names, Daren still inputs his searches in traditional Chinese. It is erroneous to assume that because English was the main administrative language of Hong Kong until the handover in 1997 that the region is bilingual. The vast majority of local residents speak Cantonese, or Putonghua (Mandarin), or some combination of both. Yet, the transitions between written or calligraphic scripts to digitised character sets – that is, the shift from writing on paper and writing on a digital device – has been mainly framed by European orthographic structures and alphabetical writing systems (like Latin, Greek or Cyrillic) as a result of the influence of the US and Europe in the development of computing and the Internet. However, East Asian language systems, such as Cantonese (which is one of the official languages of Hong Kong) do not operate semantically in the same way as European languages. Where the alphabets found in European languages contain a limited set of characters and numerals which form massive numbers of combinations to produce a massive number of words, the phonetic and semiotic mapping between the two Chinese character sets – traditional and simplified – is far more complicated (Allen et al., 2015). Unicode reports that over 70% of the codes sets that they produce are occupied by Chinese, Japanese and Korean (CJK)[1] characters – characters that are essential for users who read and write in those languages. This generates difficulty for Daren as he searches for place names in Hong Kong. There are limited methods to input Chinese character sets since the relationship between Cantonese phonetic sounds and orthography is more complex.

Daren refocuses on my earlier suggestion. We are on Gage Street. This is 結志街 in traditional Chinese, *git3 ji3 gaai1* in Cantonese Yale or *Jiézhì Jiē* in Pinyin. There is no input on Daren's phone to draw the traditional Chinese characters, and so what he must do is type in an approximation of the phonetic sound, which brings up a list of characters from which he can then choose the correct one. Of course, neither Cantonese Yale nor Pinyin are really written languages – rather, they are systems of Romanisation from East Asian spoken languages to Latin alphabets, and like pseudo-code, acts as a shortcut for meaning between two language systems. Cantonese and Mandarin Pinyin are not the same because Cantonese has more tones, and Google has its own Pinyin, developed by Google China, which is slightly different to the Cantonese Pinyin recognised by the Hong Kong Board of Examinations. This means that it's not as easy to input the phonetic sounds, and for Daren, becomes a guessing game between the Unicode character set, Google's Pinyin Romanisation designed for Mandarin and not Cantonese, and the way in which words are pronounced. Trying a few different spellings,

1 Some writers, such as Lunde (2009), also refer to a CJKV system that includes Vietnamese writing systems.

Daren eventually chooses the one that he thinks is correct, and the map jumps to another location too quickly for us to process where it has gone. Daren frowns.

'Right, so, is it in the wrong location?' I ask.

'Yah, – where is it?' He scrolls across the screen trying to find where we are in relation to the marker. When he entered Gage Street (結志街) into the map, the marker shows up further along the road than Daren knows we are. Even though the city is relatively compact, each block is profoundly vital along the navigational tree: the irregular and vertical urban plan makes it easy to get lost.

Daren gives up on trying to triangulate the street names and turns back to his method of trying to find nearby places. But this means coordinating between the haphazard and incomplete list of places names in Google Maps, and the places that Daren spies around us that may appear on that database. But the liveliness of the wet market doesn't map easily onto a CMS database: places that are important for Daren, like the best barbeque pork place around here (where we had lunch), are not important for Google Maps. Far from the patois dining spaces with plastic chairs and tables – that maintain business off local reputation – Google Maps prioritises the institutional and touristed spaces in Central in their place name database. This makes it difficult for Daren to work discursively between the cartographic imagination – or how Google Maps sees Hong Kong – and how he, himself, sees Hong Kong: a rupture between represented and lived spaces.

'Now I'm following – that restaurant – you can see?' Daren indicates back towards another restaurant on the other side of the road. The glowing neon tubes stretching across its frontage indicate that Lai Fong Yuen is open, but the empty tables outside shows that it by no means full. Pursing his lips, he locates the small red point, somewhere else to the west, annotated by traditional Chinese script. This casts a question of the meaning of place in a digital age. Zook and Graham (2007) term the interaction between massive data sets like those of Google and the user-inputted tags that denote spaces as places as 'DigiPlace' – an abstracted negotiation of meaning between geographic data and people's everyday spatial practices. All the same, however, what we see here, now, with Daren as he searches desperately for a location that is important enough to be accurately located on the map is that this negotiation is embedded in specific discourses that create hierarchies of place. The opportunity for Daren to negotiate with Google is predicated on him accepting certain modes of thinking which privilege digital visibility – the speciality of the cafes and bars that use social media to establish themselves on the digital plane. Ultimately, on the digital plane and on the platform of Google Maps, it is the curators of the Google Hong Kong database who decide what place is, assign place tags to locations and work between place and coordinates. Daren's role in this is to suggest places that he may search for, but ultimately, becomes bound up in the authority of the map – an authority that is rapidly waning.

'Oh my god – it's so far away. You see, it's here,' he points to the restaurant, 'but the point shows over there,' he points to the small red dot on the phone map somewhere unrecognisable. Back in Sydney, Ben had this issue with Goma in Africa and GOMA in Brisbane on Apple Maps, which was solved by the way in which Google Maps ranks searches according to proximity. Daren is not so lucky. The places that he types in – popular and reputable restaurants, well known to locals – do not even appear on Google Maps. The street names are bereft of clarity in a toponymic quagmire, and even when the street names can be found, the drop pins appear in ambiguous and arbitrary places along long roads winding around Hong Kong's hills. The cartographic digital maps built from a staunchly Western idiom simply flounder with Daren's experiences of place and names in Hong Kong.

These miscalculations are not such a leap from the cartographic eye (Ryan, 1996), embellished in the roles of surveyors and explorers who expected to see European landscapes on foreign soon-to-be-colonial shores, and brought those landscapes forth where they did not previously exist. Judging by the toponymic layout, Google Maps expects to see a particular kind of city in Hong Kong: one that is institutional, flush with big brands and transnational corporations that mirror the market forces shaping its urban geography. This is obvious in the toponymic patina of the places which digital maps list: major restaurants that appear in tourist websites, points of interest gauged to an extrinsic gaze of visitors to Hong Kong. The wet market is only loosely listed while the nearby Park n Shop supermarket is prominent, even though on the landscape it is so buried under market stalls and the restaurant signs peppering the airspace of the street that the small staircase leading up to its entrance can't be seen from the street. It's invisibility on the landscape and hypervisibility on the map also confuses Daren as he negotiates between his digital map and the street.

What the map does not understand is that the first restaurant inputted by Daren, Dragon Restaurant, is a common name and since the digital map has not listed every single place in the vicinity named as such, it re-centres the map and the drop-pin location off somewhere else nearby. Barbeque Suckling Pig restaurant is also a common name. Toponymic practices in Hong Kong tend to name places in ways that are descriptive or pragmatic, or to bring luck or to sell wares. The neoliberal ethic of making business recognition unique through branding has not entirely permeated spaces of consumption in Hong Kong, in the same way that they might in London or New York. Furthermore, in ever more emerging systems of interoperability, it turns out that toponymies of place which privilege uniqueness and identifiability – through branding, for instance – are more sympathetic to digital cartographic systems. This is because they hold specific and distinct meanings through toponymy but maintain semantic consistency across all platforms: bespoke markers across multiple, 'universal' systems of categorisation. For instance, Park n Shop supports a more malleable Latin Romanisation that works better with Unicode while being uniquely identifiable as a brand of supermarkets, networked through name and logo, which have a number of coordinate locations. The interoperability of semantic discourses means that epistemological systems invisible to Daren in the street are underscored by tagged geo-data, networks of semantic tags that unify language, number and image.

The restaurant that Daren is following now, Lan Fong Yuen (蘭芳園), does appear on the map. But Daren is struggling to find the correct Pinyin for the characters, and so it seems that the restaurant has either moved to a different place name or that the original position is incorrect.

'It doesn't matter,' he sighs. 'I will look up the old – see here it is here,' he shows me the phone. 'It's the old – before, it was the police "governmentary", but now it's changed to a heritage that is not – it functions as an art gallery now for some exhibitions – shall we visit there?'

Like numbers, letters and characters are made of lines. And now, lines are no longer strokes on paper, but equations and/or pixels on screens: birds in eggs/eggs in bird. A place name is not just a place name: it is comprised of letters or characters, which are comprised of lines that have their own systems and logics, and which are then coded into character sets with specific alphanumeric markers. Toponymic communication in digital mapping has taken on new levels of complexity, where even the structure of the image is governed by numeric systems and binary logics which, importantly, are formed primarily with English in mind.

As we walk along Gage Street towards the police station, Daren points out where the old wet market used to be. This is one of the older districts of Hong Kong, one of the first areas developed on the island, and one of the first collapsing of multiple cultures into one another. Around us, in amongst the soaring glass skyscrapers, are smaller, more traditional buildings, four or five stories high and adorned with thin metal window panes with geometric patterns and triangular rooftops.

'Used to be buildings like this,' Daren says. 'See, four to five stories high. But now they want to renew this district because this land is really expensive, so they destroy those old buildings and build very, very high buildings.'

'What happens to the people who live in these old buildings?' I ask.

'They are over 50 years old. This kind of roof – the top – means that this building is really, really old.' He points to the roof of a nearby building.

'Are there many left?'

'It's the Soho style,' he replies. 'Bars, cafes – they mainly serve those who work in Central, especially foreigners.'

We turn up a sharp incline onto Graham Street and head up into Soho and the Mid-Levels. As we reach the top of the hill, we turn onto Hollywood Road.

'From this horizontal line here' – Daren waves his hand along the road – 'this is Soho ....'

'Does it reference New York or London?'

'Yes. Soho is a style – lots of middle-class people – during the week, from Monday to Friday, there are lots of people – they come after work and have a drink over there, over here.'

Western-style bars lie between Chinese-style restaurants and food stores. One shop that sells sugar cane drinks sits with its shutters down next to a bustling bar-restaurant filled with foreigners across from us. Daren points towards the shop's old Cantonese sign and green tiled frontage, describing how drinking the tea from there will make you better.

'It's Chinese medicine,' he says. 'You drink it when you're sick.'

Further along Hollywood Road, Daren points down a small alleyway.

'You see – um – small variations in this area.'

The graffiti is multilayered, colours built over colours, new tags drawn over newly painted murals drawn over old tags.

'Sometimes I come here to check some exhibitions here. Sometimes, I like to read the graffiti along this – how do you say it?'

'Laneway?'

'Yeah, laneway – or corridor.' It's an adept correction on Daren's part – the narrowness of the passageway is closer to a corridor than a laneway, and even the smallest nuance of meaning, especially in names and labels, structures how the Hong Kong landscape is comprehended. This nuance is often lost in the process of fixing or translating a name (Cheung, 2010) and has equally afflicted street signs and cartography. Much of the long-form graffiti also is in English, although many of the tags are in Cantonese (and some of the smaller pieces). It makes me wonder who makes the graffiti – are they students like Daren, well-versed in English, or ex-pats, or tourists, or someone else in a city in which the old traces of colonialism are dissolving into new forms of transnationalism and globalisation?

'There is lots of this kind of graffiti,' Daren says.

'What language do you find the graffiti is normally in?'

'Usually English – I don't know why. I don't know why they – sometimes the message is very political but they used to write in English. I don't know why.'

Daren thinks that the graffiti is largely done by locals – and it's possible that English is preferential itself for its lack of ambiguity, the complexity of translation surmounting the desire to get the political messages across. There is a larger political conflict between Chineseness and Englishness that has irrupted from the swift handover of Hong Kong Island to China, along with the decision not to renew the lease on Kowloon and the New Territories. This, to a degree, can be mapped onto how language is used – English is the language of the past, and Mandarin of the future, while Cantonese sits uneasily in-between fighting against a politics of disappearance (Abbas, 1997). Despite the specificity of the intercultural and postcolonial landscape in Hong Kong, public discourse still operates in the spirit of globalised hegemonies and cultural hybridities – on walls as well as on maps.

Daren's earlier frustrations with Google Maps tie to a more significant problem about the epistemological hegemonies inherent in digital systems, which are then transferred to digital maps. Prior to the development of the Internet, universal cartographic models existed – yet, limitations were beholden to typeset or colour schemes or the borders of the page. The monadological basis of binary systems (although in theory should be more than able to accommodate the language systems that offered Leibniz his inspiration) have been developed in line with Western-centric models of communication. That is to say, it is no longer a question of the silences and absences on maps that J.B. Harley described, but rather that these silences and absences can be found at the foundation of the digital model of communication itself. If a 1:1 map of the territory could indeed be achieved in a digital world, it would lack the fundamental tools to produce a true mimicry: even the spacing of the Latin alphabet fails to maintain a seamless integration with a Chinese character containing a radical. Take Unicode, for instance, whose UTF-8 format is prevalent within HTML coding. Within alphabet systems, Unicode considers each letter to be one or more units of graphic meaning – graphemes – turned into glyphs. Thus, the letter 'p' or 'ó' is made of a circle and a line. But the graphemes used for European language systems are not the same for Chinese.

| Unicode Latin Alphabet – A with diaeresis | | | | | | | | | | | | | | | |
|---|---|---|---|---|---|---|---|---|---|---|---|---|---|---|---|
| Character | A | + | ̈ | = | Ä | | | | | | | | | | |
| Binary | 01000001 | | 11000010 10101000 | | 11000010 10101000 | | | | | | | | | | |
| Unicode | U+0041 | | U+0308 | | U+00C4 | | | | | | | | | | |
| **Non-encoded, non-unified Unicode CJK (Unihan)** | | | | | | | | | | | | | | | |
| Character | ⿳ | + | ⿲ | + | 丂 | + | 彡 | + | 丂 | + | 彐 | + | 皿 | = | [illegible] |
| UTF-8 (Binary) | 11100010: 10111111: 10110011 | | 11100010: 10111111: 10110010 | | 11100100: 10111000: 10000010 | | 11100101: 10111101: 10100001 | | 11100100: 10111000: 10000010 | | 11100101: 10111101: 10010000 | | 11100111: 10011010: 10111111 | | |
| Unicode | U+2FF3 | | U+2FF2 | | U+4E02 | | U+5F61 | | U+4E02 | | U+5F50 | | U+76BF | | |

Figure 10.3. *Unicode.* Comparison of Unicode composition between Latin alphabet (Ä) and a non-encoded Unicode CJK character, showing binary digits and Unicode. The Latin alphabet character at the top is comprised of two elements, whereas the CJK character at the bottom involves five ideograms (consisting of multiple graphemes and glyphs) plus two ideograph character markers – U+2FF2 and U+2FF3 – that form the structure of the character. The difference in binary size is marked, along with the UTF composition of the character. This is without the possible substitution of similar ideograms with different stroke variations.

The Chinese writing system consists of different sets of strokes – upwards and downwards, with breaks and without. Of course, such a system with a colossal number of character sets defies even the earliest prototypes of automated typesetting, including the typewriter and the computer. To draw a character is to combine lines, with vast nuance and specificity. To stroke, radicals are added – small inscriptions which change the meaning of a word – resulting in minor differentiation in the number of lines according to different languages, and borrowing and sharing certain ideograms with or without meaning attached. Furthermore, even in Chinese, there is not 'one' coherent system: dialects are varied throughout the region, to the point where Cantonese operates on its own systems of writing and pronunciation with several specific characters (which form their own Unicode character set). In Mainland China, Simplified Chinese was developed by the People's Republic of China in an attempt to unify the multitudinous variations, but since Hong Kong has been part of the British overseas territories since 1848, traditional Chinese maintained a tenuous cultural dominance.

Although minor differentiations are simple enough to enact on a lonely wall in a corridor in Soho, the implications of inbuilt Anglophone hierarchies are expanded in digital platforms. Multiple suggestions have been made about how to solve this uneasy integration between Anglophone and East Asian languages – in code and in typeset – yet all have had their limitations based as much in the discursive as the semiotic. Big5,[2] for instance,

2 Named for the conglomerate of five companies based in Taiwan (including Acer) that developed it.

experimented with a one bit per character system, which made the Chinese typeset comparable in memory terms to Unicode. At the same time, Big5 had poor integration with other orthographic systems, including the Latin alphabet, and required add-ons to make it work, resulting in uneven spacing and encoding. Unicode developed UTF-16 from UTF-8 in an effort to find the systemic space to assign values to 70,000 characters in the CJK system. But then, in order to reduce the sheer volume of the data set, they set about developing a controversial initiative, Unihan, which sought to unify CJK character systems as much as possible. The theory was that the two Chinese character sets, and the Japanese and Korean sets, were historically interlinked, resulting in a number of shared characters between them – or characters that were similar enough to be recognised between languages. However, this completely ignored the cultural specificities of stroke, weighting and radicals, which meant that translation was not as simple as originally thought, or that the generalisation of character systems would be seen as a sign of cultural imperialism. This was especially problematic for Japanese and Korean users, for whom minor but crucial differentiations in the calligraphic nature of the characters were lost in the haste to develop a single unified system – differences which were as much cultural as they were semiotic. At the same time, there was little attempt to integrate the two Chinese systems because there was recognition that the simplified Chinese was not as easily integrated with the traditional Chinese used in Hong Kong. Despite this, there are still complaints in Hong Kong that Google uses the simplified characters for particular places – or even switches between the two when labelling the same length of road – when they should be using the traditional characters.

Despite efforts by developers to contain the relationships between characters, Pinyin and phonetic pronunciation, certain meanings are still lost. Turning us back, Daren looks down at another road that leads towards Upper Lascar Road, where the antiques markets are. Near us, are three old Buddhist statues perched on a step, enclosed by a small metal railing.

'Here – it's really interesting – I was sitting here and took a picture with the three – many years before.'

'Where'd they come from?'

'Huh?'

'The three? Where'd they come from?'

'I don't know,' he laughs, 'but you know – this street is also called Mo Lo Gai. *Mo lo gai* means that they sell the very old stuff – see over there. But it's a holiday – they're closed.'

Old stuff like statues begets old stuff like antiques, Daren evoking a spatial serendipity where things of a certain age collect together. This kind of fluid intuition – of drawing things together according to a situated position and rereading space according to purpose, or meaning, or metaphor – countermands the structuring of space by Google Maps, which privileges toponymy and fixed categorisation through tags or metadata, rather than fluid and improvised reinterpretation.

The street, Mo Lo Gai (嚤囉街), to which Daren is referring is a combination of Upper and Lower Lascar Row, the antique market. But Daren's translation is somewhat abstracted from conventional transliteration and gives an insight into the difficulties of heteroglossia cartographies predicated upon algorithmic deciphering rather than cultural empathy. Mo Lo (嚤囉) is not a word that exists in the Chinese dictionary – it is a controversial term to describe people of South Asian origin, a further abstraction from the word Lascar, which was used in English to describe Indian seafarers (Antiques Advisory Board, 2010). All the same, Mo Lo Gai is often translated as Cat Street – a nickname for the thieves who sold their wares in the district, and Mo Lo is also a term used to describe Muslims – evident in the naming of Mosque Street as Mo Lo Mui Gai (摩囉廟街) – or 'Mo Lo' Temple Street. According to some (Kadison, 2009), young Cantonese speakers don't regularly use this word, and so may not be aware of the triplicate meanings. For Daren, it merely means a street where antiques are sold, its contemporary manifestation, as he has encountered it. How can a map, especially given the complications of digital transcription between writing systems, capture this complex duplication of meaning across two languages. Even the street itself is split into two in English, but is not known colloquially in Chinese as two separate spaces – although in Google Maps and on the street signs, the split is maintained, and the translation is still awkward (Cheung, 2010).

The meanings of Mo Lo Gai fold together in this space, the profane and the pertinent, the metaphoric and the specific, across cultural and linguistic barriers in a manner that resonates with the heteroglossia of postcolonial societies. But for cartographic reason, a discourse that fosters the need for absolute generalisation and equivalencies, the complexity of meaning and translation leads to multiple transliterations between Hong Kong, the East and the West. There are more troubling suggestions that the Chinese written language itself is a barrier to technological modernisation (DeFrancis, 1984) – as if the epistemological systems of computing weren't predicated on a different set of linguistic structures, which is a problem of logic, not of the Chinese language. Thus, colonialism continues in Hong Kong, and in the digital mobile map, in dramatically expanded ways. This is a more subtle colonialism – somewhat distantiated from the police stations, expensive bars and lifestyle landscapes that Daren so enthusiastically pointed out – but no less potent or divisive.

We reach another street and another mural monument on a wall.

'Here – it's changed a lot – because this pattern it cover a lot – there are many kinds of different graffiti underneath. And see that – they painted it again.'

'What's that?' he asks, pointing to a sign. 'I don't know this plaque – lots of French restaurants and Italy restaurants down that street – very expensive. One dish, HK$400 to 500. They sell lifestyles.'

## Ellen/Identities

'We're so lucky, you know?'

We get on the Mass Transit Railway (MTR) green line at Choi Hung (彩虹) Station. The ticket barriers chirp as travellers swipe in and out of the system with their Octopus cards. Ellen taps her card lightly on the round sensor, before the gates eagerly part allowing her a few seconds to move through before closing tightly behind her. I follow with my card, pausing for only a fraction in the seamless transition between the public thoroughfare of the station, and the other bounded space for those using the system. On the platform, Choi Hung Station is brightly decorated in rainbow livery wrapped around the poles and tiled along the walls. In Cantonese, Choi Hung means 'rainbow', and the station named after the nearby Choi Hung housing estate ties together a cross-reference in toponymy between the livery of Choi Hung Station and the brightly coloured residential buildings. As we wait, Ellen checks the information board hanging from the roof for the next train. The Hong Kong MTR is extensive, carrying millions of passengers every day. It stretches out from along the north shore of Hong Kong Island out into the far reaches of the New Territories and up to Tai Wo and the Hong Kong-Shenzhen border crossing with China. It has 87 stations built with curious regularity in design and architecture across ten coloured lines (not including the light rail). Between the live railway tracks and us are tall glass walls with sliding doors at ordered intervals. The glass prevents us from falling on the platform, but not from seeing the abundant advertising covered in QR codes, selling everything from baby formula to skincare regimes.

'Every MTR station is not the same,' Ellen tells me. 'If you go on some direction – the red line – it's not the same. Some are white, and you need to find the things, you know.'

Each station in Hong Kong has been assigned own colours across the spectrum. Choi Hung is Ellen's favourite because it's bright – a beacon in an unfamiliar landscape that is vertical, busy and crowded.

'The first time I came here was the scariest time.'

'Getting to Central all on your own?'

'Yeah, I need to ask somebody, you know. But sometimes people – they can speak English sometimes, and you can ask where is this and know what line you need to follow.'

'Yeah?'

'Yeah.'

'You didn't think to look it up on a map?'

'No. No, because when I first came here my phone – I didn't know how to use Google before and I just saw when now – er – like, maybe my friends you know, you just see when you just see this constant' – Ellen swipes her hand across an imagined screen as if scrolling through a digital map – 'and you can read the Google Maps. But I think here – some people, they don't use Google Maps – you know – because of the train, you know where you go ….'

'Okay.'

'Yeah, and you just follow the line, and you need to ask only the exit where you exit – that's it.'

'What about once you get off the train?'

'Off the train, you just read, you know, the signs on the wall or something – where you see them.'

The wayfinding system in Hong Kong – at least when it is linked to the MTR – is proficient. It revolves around several systems of categorisation: colours for train lines and stations, alphabetical identifiers for the complex system of exits (that often serve as meeting points) and a mixture of simplified three-dimensional maps to show how to exit the station and top-down maps pointing out areas of interest, marked with photos as well as descriptions. It's a foreigner's wayfinding system, really, designed for mapping in practice in the most general and cross-cultural way possible. The integration of the MTR with the wayfinding systems, however, results in a lingering dependence on transit as a mode of navigation. As the train comes into the stop, the glass doors open in rhythm with the train doors, and we hop onto the train.

'See here,' Ellen shows me LOHAS Park on the map above the doors inside the carriage. 'It is the last station, and you need to interchange to the other side. This is an adventure!'

Ellen has a few days off over the Spring Festival and has been using them to explore Hong Kong parks. In a story strangely reminiscent of this, a few days ago, she and some friends voyaged along the MTR orange line to Tsing Yi (青衣) before getting a bus to Park Island (珀麗灣), a small island between the New Territories and Lantau Island. They hoped to find Noah's Ark, a themed resort, where they wanted to spend the day enjoying the park and the beach.

'There is a park there,' Ellen smiles. 'I wanted to see it. Noah's Ark is supposed to the in the middle of the sea – in the Bible right? But it's only half in the sea,' she bursts out laughing. 'Like, what is wrong with you people?'

The park had disappointed her, but she took it in good humour. Branching out from the island into the surrounding water, Noah's Ark is somewhere between a theme park and a resort. It is ark, perhaps, more in spirit than in strict adherence to the biblical imaginary. However, Ellen never entered the park. Once she and her friends had arrived to find a walled resort, full of tall apartment complexes rising from the ground up to the overhead freeways, they realised that what they understood to be a public park was not necessarily so. Confused, her friend went up to the ticket booth and asked how to get in.

'They said you need to prepare HK$155 for the entrance, and she said "Oh my god – it's too expensive," you know. And you know what we did? We – yesterday – we just stayed outside' – Ellen laughs again – 'and just took pictures of the entrance.'

'So you just went there, and you had a look through the ...?' Her laughter is contagious, and I join in, struggling for breath.

'Yeah, you know, some parks here, are like so expensive, you know, for the entrance. But there's nothing inside. But you can stay outside – you can take pictures. Because in the park, you can, some you know, some – there's lots of, they put something there – like a big shell and from the sea, some creatures – just for a picture you know?'

HK$155 is a significant amount of money to pay for a picture. Inside, Ellen believes, was nothing so special as to warrant that percentage of her pay cheque, and she has six brothers and six sisters who she says are depending on her to make ends meet. The pictures she posts on Facebook are primarily for her family and friends so they can see where she is and what she is doing – and so outside the resort is just as good as inside for this purpose.

Money makes invisible boundaries in the space of Hong Kong, an excluding and segmenting practice in which cartographic imaginaries are deeply complicit. The toponymic nominal 'park' does not conjure up the grand visions of public space and of the commons that arose out of the nineteenth-century imaginaries. Hong Kong operates in a space of hyper-capital, but cartography has failed to capture this shift in its consistent and unflinching coded representational systems. Frampton et al. (2012) describe Hong Kong as a city in which public and private blend together: streets turning into shopping centres, residential spaces becoming thoroughfares, lobbies routing people between one space and the next. This is the dreamworld – or dream city, perhaps – of late capitalism (cf. Jameson, 1991) in which these two distinct spheres merge seamlessly.

'Hong Kong is like that,' she clasps her fist in an expression of its compact size. 'No need to be worried when you're lost – even if it is already midnight. You can still go home because the train is 24 hours.'

However, borders remain: invisible on maps but resolute in space, as mobility is offered to those who can afford it, and results in a kind of cartographic treachery for those who cannot. In Hong Kong, the MTR map, and Google Maps reroutes Ellen regularly and sets her up for disappointments that she takes in good faith and good fun.

'Yeah, sometimes I use Google Maps, like maybe when I'm alone and I get so scary, I don't know where to go, maybe first time I get ... yeah, the first time I came here, my first day off, it's so scary. I didn't know, oh my god, which people speak English, you know, you're shy and sometimes like, "Oh, what am I doing?" I went to find some Filipinos walking and I went "Hi," and I do something like that – I was just so shy and just show your – whatever,' she lets out a long breath, 'I need to go to a place and I don't know anything and you see the map,' she points back to the MTR line map, 'and it's like, ugh, it's wrong.'

The MTR map on the train is different from the ones on the walls in the station. Taking the philosophy of the London Underground Map to another level, it has flattened out the region instead focusing on the relationships between lines and interchanges. Although the information is technically the same, the new mode of display completely skews any real sense of distance between lines or stations that may have been implied by the fuller map.

'And these ones are different to the bigger ones,' I supply.

Yeah, because the bigger ones are like' – Ellen pulls her hands apart to their full width – 'and it has the harbour and stuff. And these ones don't – which I find quite confusing.'

As the train pulls into Kwun Tong, I look out at the landscape filled with more wall-like buildings.

'So what's at LOHAS Park?'

'LOHAS Park is like – I Google it last day, and I just read something in there that – uh – they have a museum, like some IMAX there – I'm not sure, but I just read some nature things – yeah, maybe we can sit down there and,' she laughs again, 'I'm not sure, too.'

Another park on the map, another collusion between cartography and toponymy built by branding exercises and global development in the pretence of open and borderless leisure space. We have travelled a long way from Central Park with Nick in Sydney, to LOHAS Park with Ellen in Hong Kong.

She looks back up at the MTR map above the door and her eyes follow the green line back towards Kowloon.

'Here's the blue one – going to China.'

One of her friends lives along that blue line somewhere in the New Territories. But she doesn't catch the blue line very often. Ellen describes how they often travel together along the green line, where her friend gets off at Diamond Hill – the stop before Choi Hung – to then catch a bus up north because it is too expensive to take the MTR that far.

'We've got to use our mind also, you know, not just parading in the train, and go somewhere else, you know. Because it's too expensive here – the train. Imagine every time you go out every Sunday if you need to have HK$100 for the day – lunch, dinner, breakfast sometimes.'

The train pulls into Tiu Keng Leng Station, and Ellen looks up.

'We're here.'

We get off onto the platform and walk across to the other line. The signs are not clear, and although we are trying to go to LOHAS Park, which is the end of the line, neither of the next two trains departing from either platform are headed that way. Ellen purses her lips and turns to a nearby passenger who is calmly waiting with his family and asks him how to get to LOHAS Park. He looks at me strangely with my camera attached to my head, before answering that the train to LOHAS Park will be the third train that arrives, as the line splits into two – Po Lam in one direction, and LOHAS Park in another. Eventually, our train comes and we get on, waiting briefly for another three stops before alighting.

Once again on a platform, Ellen picks a set of ascending escalators at random, and as we rise the familiar soundtrack of the MTR ticket barriers grows near.

'It's a proper adventure,' I muse, trying to get a glimpse of what lies at the top of the escalators.

'It's stressful, you know,' Ellen replies.

The escalators quickly open up onto the station concourse. No time to register our next move as the crowd behind pushes us forward. Ellen grabs my arm.

'LOHAS Park is Exit C.'

With no time to find my bearings and with impending panic, I reach for my Octopus card. 'How did you know?'

'It was on the sign.'

'Which sign?'

'Um, I can't find it now. Maybe this one?'

She points to a drop-down sign ahead of us, as we pass through the ticket barriers. Suddenly mustered up by the crowd of people headed towards the exit, Ellen quickly steps out of line to assess how many stairs there are. Seeing at least three flights rising up onto the overhead walkways, she directs us back towards the escalators. There is a long tiled barrier between the escalator and the stairs, which extends at least 6 feet out from the start. This has the effect of funnelling pedestrians into the escalator system before they have even encountered it, and relegating those who have faltered to the stairs. Ellen and I are a little late to the escalator queue, last minute vagabonds who skip into the line after baulking at the number of stairs. Narrowly missing the tiled b/ordering device (cf. Van Houtum et al., 2005), we hustle in, bustling grumbling pedestrians who have been waiting patiently and see their hard-fought position being queue-jumped. Cartographically absent and materially emplaced, the barrier rises to the occasion of ordering not just space by segregating and bounding territories, but also by managing and regulating the flows between them. Up we flow on the escalators, pushed to the side by others running up alongside us, and then onto the LOHAS Park covered walkway system. Our view in the distance is blocked by hoardings running along either side of the walkway, and when, finally, we come to a fork, we find a small section of untraversed space in which we can pause.

Ellen never realises that LOHAS Park is not a park. Walking along a long stretch of overhead walkways made of mixtures of grey – concrete, steel, paint – hoardings block any sense of what may lay next in the path, protecting the ongoing construction of the site. Formerly named 'Dream City', LOHAS Park – LOHAS is an acronym for 'lifestyle of health and sustainability' – is now a labyrinthine site of dis/infected enclave development (cf. Davis, 2006). It is a new production, meticulously planned and eagerly sold, that is self-contained and self-sufficient, a lifestyle as much as a residence. Wall-like buildings, 70 or more stories high and replicates of each other, curve around like a windbreak on a lea, drinking up as much of the view of Victoria Harbour as commercially and spatially possible. Much of the same after much of the same, walking along the monotonous walkway, Ellen comes to a fork.

'So,' I say to Ellen, 'where are we going?'

'So, where are we going?' she replies looking left and right. 'Here or here?'

'I don't know,' I answer.

'Let's try here.'

We go right. Small wisps of greenery poke through the fence, hinting at some grass, some trees, mountains in the distance – a potential gathering of verdant objects that may amount a park where we can sit and converse.

'Whoa,' Ellen gasps, 'do you see that?'

'What is it?'

'It's a mountain like ....' She flattens her hand straight up, as if calling the towering mountain to a stop. It sits tight against the back of the LOHAS Park complex, nudging it out onto the reclaimed land that has been built into the bay and reshaped the shoreline. Right again. Through the fence, the sun bounces off the glass windows of one of the residential high-rises, and we get our first glimpse of its irreconcilable height.

'Do you see the buildings – it's like ....' Ellen holds her hand high again.

Homes stacked like mountains, it's a vast upward expansion from the four- or five-storey buildings in Central and Soho that Daren pointed out. Somewhere unseen, a children's song is recited in English by young voices following an older one: *heads, shoulders, knees and toes, knees and toes.*

Another fork and we come to a glass rotunda floating in the air. In the middle, a stairwell decorated with a big colourful elephant leads downward. It is enclosed with windows and a door firmly closed shut with a security pad resting by its lock. Birds suddenly can be heard, and the hoardings are replaced by a barrier of trees standing tall and curving around the outside of the walkway. Water flows at the level of our feet down a water feature separated from us by a pane of glass, as rivulets disappear off a sharp edge into an unknown abyss. Just beyond the horizon of the water feature, we can see a green space replete with hazy chairs and footpaths. One of the many sources of the birdsong stares at us from atop an access-controlled gate, before flying off into the garden below. Looking at this expanse of space, Ellen frowns, calculating how we can go about finding the entrance to this garden.

'Maybe we need to go downstairs,' she suggests, before hustling me off towards one of the residences attached to the walkway so that we can find a way down.

As we try to find a way down to the garden, a woman with her daughter accosts us outside La Prestige No. 2, one of the seven residences that are connected to this walkway. Ellen and I are reasonably noticeable in this neighbourhood –a Filipina and an Australian with a video camera wandering in amongst a residential landscape built for Hong Kong's burgeoning middle classes. Mostly aspirational, the rent in this area is high, and its amenities promise a foothold in an ever-more desperate race to not be caught at the bottom of the widening income gap that is occurring globally and especially palpable in amongst the wealth of the Hong Kong Special Administrative Region (SAR).

'Excuse me,' she says to me, 'can my daughter ask you a few questions? She has to interview a foreigner.' Her daughter blinks at me from behind thick lenses.

'Yeah, no worries at all.'

Stepping in between Ellen and me, she hustles her daughter closer and speaks in Cantonese. Ellen effectively pushed out of the conversational circle, and so she hangs by my side where I try to make room, as she listens to the conversation with interest.

'Go on,' the woman encourages her daughter, whose facial expression has not changed.

'Uh,' the daughter looks at her worksheet, 'what is your name?'

Laughing, I tell her, spelling it out carefully.

'And what is your nationality?'

I provide this information, too. Her mother translates into Cantonese, and points at the sheet. Providing me with a list of places in Hong Kong, her daughter asks me where I have been and what location is my favourite (Victoria Harbour). Sighing, she reads the sheet carefully again.

'Can you take a picture with me?'

'Yeah, sure.'

'Last question,' the woman assures me, 'Thank you so much. I'm afraid you're busy or ....'

'That's okay, 'I reply. 'I'm doing my own interview with her, so it's all good.' I point towards Ellen. 'She's also a foreigner.'

The woman faces Ellen, suddenly interested.

'So what is your nationality?' she asks.

'Filipina,' Ellen replies, smiling.

'Okay.' the woman's face shifts so she is facing completely towards me now. 'I take the photo with you.' She talks to her daughter in an instructive tone, as she navigates the phone's interface. Blocked out of the conversation, Ellen slips behind her.

'We go there. Here there is sunshine.'

Bustling me towards the fence, cutting off quite a few people exiting the residence, she lines her daughter and me up for a photo. Ellen tries to help suggest a suitable location, but the woman ignores her.

'Okay, smile,' the woman commands. 'One, two, three, go.'

Camera at the ready, I've smiled, and the imitation click of the phone's camera sounds before I know what has happened.

'Okay. Thank you so much,' the mother says, 'Fantastic.'

I smile back at her.

'Thank you very much,' I reply.

She pockets her phone and turns to her daughter.

'What do you say?'

Her daughter blinks again.

'Thank you.'

'Yeah, thank you.' Her mother nods in approval.

'My pleasure.'

As the mother and daughter turn to leave, moving out towards the walkway, presumably in search of more foreigners, Ellen narrows her eyes in determination and she calls out after them.

'How do we go to LOHAS Park,' she asks, 'Which direction?'

The daughter stops and points back towards the towers.

'Here is the LOHAS Park,' she says to Ellen.

The woman has turned around now and re-enters the conversation, pushing in between her daughter and Ellen to talk to me.

'Sorry, LOHAS Park, where are you go?' she asks.

'We need to go to the ground, wherever,' Ellen continues. I catch on – and smile generously at the woman.

'Is there a park?' I ask.

'Yeah, a park,' Ellen supplements, 'where we ....'

The woman cuts off Ellen and points eagerly towards the garden.

'Ah, ah ah – I am registered – I will let you in.' She takes out her purse, and walking alongside her daughter, she reaches into her bag.

'You have to have a key,' she says to me, 'because, no, no, only resident can go.'

'Oh, okay.'

She steps between Ellen and me, forcing Ellen backwards behind me again.

'I will swipe you in.'

'Oh, thank you,' I say.

Ellen and I look at each other over her shoulder, and Ellen laughs.

'There are a lot of people. Do you live here? You not live here?' The woman asks me.

'No, I live in Central,' I reply.

'Oh, Central, I see, I see.'

'Yeah, we came out to see the park, so ....'

'Oh, I see.'

We near the gate now, and this time around it looks more formidable and unyielding. Tall glass panels on either side prevent people from jumping over the fence, and the metal gate – up to Ellen's head height – is shouldered on each side by tall metal poles.

'You go like this,' the woman says swiping the touchpad. 'Here we go.'

Ellen and I rush through the gate, scarcely able to believe that we got in.

'Thank you,' we both say at once.

'Have a nice day,' the woman replies. 'If you need to exit press this button there.' There is a small metal button on our side of the fence, nestled on a nearby railing out of reach of the barriers to prevent anyone using it for entry rather than exit.

'Okay,' Ellen says, 'thank you.'

'Fantastic,' I add, 'thank you very much. Have a good day.'

In unison, Ellen and I raise our hands up to wave.

'Goodbye.'

Four kinds of borders are described by Van Houtum et al. (2005): doors and windows, shade and light. Such borders shift and change in time and space – doors require keys and windows are not made for bodies but for air, light and objects to pass through. Shade and light change as the earth turns, creating new structures and new spatialities. Cartographic reason specialises in drawing borders, delimiting one area from the next, a graphic act that severs space into dialectics: here and there, inside and outside, included and excluded (Pickles, 2004). Cartographic reason also specialises in fixing borders, even where they may not be fixed and in searching for limits and placing flags there (Olsson, 1991a). Foucault (2001d) describes transgressive space at those limits, wherein the *action* of transgression is contained within the line that is crossed. But for Ellen, transgression is not in the passage through the gate. For Ellen, transgression is everywhere and nowhere, just as borders are everywhere and nowhere. This is the myth of cartographic reason. Borders are the livelihood of the nation-state, giving power to new forms of biometric control over who can go where and how (Amoore, 2006). The transnational movement of capital and labour – the kind that brought Ellen to Hong Kong to work as a domestic helper for a wage below that of the minimum set for locals – has shifted how those borders appear and where they can be found. The borderlands are no longer limited to the margins, to other spaces and the abject and forgotten – they can be found wherever power, culture and identity meet (Anzaldúa, 1987). In the globalised space of class and of movement as equally as the compact city of Hong Kong, borders can be found across space and *in space* as imagined and material fixities that represent power geometries. Not all borders look the same. Invisible lines dart across maps and through spaces as the cartographical logics that border and boundary turn their hand to ubiquitous and situated segregation. In Hong Kong, cartographies lie by design that started before place names were etched in paper, and before digital doors were built to keep people in and out.

The borders that Ellen encounters – in the MTR, at Noah's Ark and now at the entry to the garden in LOHAS Park – started well before she stumbled upon them. They started with the cost of the MTR system and the lie of the map, they started with the promise of open space where there is only closed space, and they started with the performativities that even in those open spaces, draw me in and exclude her and push her to the side. Before the words 'LOHAS Park' were printed on the MTR map, or coded into Google Maps it was already a space filled with borders. Money buys registration buys entry into the park. And before these borders were built into the landscape and linked to digital access systems, these spaces were already imagined with borders to protect residents from threats to the lifestyle of health and sustainability, to keep dreamt people within the dream city. Cartographical reason assists these dreams: of accessed and planned spaces, of lines drawn on paper and space and bringing into reality the misnomers that give the illusion of fluidity between public and private. Money equals mobility in much of Hong Kong. No one dreams that Ellen moves and the world that she, and hundreds of thousands of other domestic workers, inhabit on holidays and on Sundays completely change what the map means. Hong Kong becomes a new place, and private space and movement space is at least temporarily reclaimed. But today, in this bespoke edge of Hong Kong, this was a minor intervention facilitated by global hegemonies that made me someone worth interviewing, and Ellen someone to forget while she is detoured by borders, by boundaries and by bodies. But she does not see these borders as such. As she said earlier about Noah's Ark – beyond them, there is nothing. This is the wonder of the border – they obscure what lies beyond (and lie about what is obscured beyond).

We move away from the gate along an open-air walkway that leads to some stairs and to the park below. We can see the other side of the glass rotunda, covered in plants and greenery. Rocks peek out above the fence, artfully laid and masterfully placed to augment the flows of the garden. The panorama has opened out before us, now unfettered by fences and hoardings, and we can see across the harbour and out towards the smoggy skyline of Hong Kong Island. Behind it, houses dot upwards to Victoria Peak – the first power geometry in Hong Kong that separated those with money and those without.

Ellen bursts out laughing, doubling over as she walks along the path.

'See,' she giggles, 'we're so lucky, you know?'

## Ravi/Numbers

'I could visualise a map that was only numbers.'

Chungking Mansions sit at 36-44 Nathan Road in Tsim Sha Tsui (TST) on the Kowloon Peninsula. Nestled behind what was once Blackhead Hill, one of the two hilly outcrops that pierced Victoria Harbour, as reclamations have extended the urban landscape into the water, the Chungking Mansions once formed the nexus of a busy retail district. Built in 1961, the mansions largely accommodated Chinese residents moving into the peninsula before it became a first point of call for newcomers from South Asia and Africa, what Gordon Mathews (2011) has called the heart of 'low-end globalisation'.

As we walk down Nathan Road, Ravi explains how he is in Hong Kong for a visa extension, and staying in the Chungking Mansions. When I ask him how he first discovered the mansions, he tells me that he was referred to stay there by a travel agency.

'Hotels are too damn expensive,' he says. 'This is a little bit budget place – you have your own mind, and you sleep on an ordinary bed.'

Ravi registers his business in Hong Kong so that he can trade with China. Hong Kong is the Berlin Key (cf. Latour, 2000) between economies in the Eastern and Western hemispheres – if you know how to use it properly. Even though Hong Kong has been given special administrative status, maintaining its free port without import or export taxes, it is a gateway.

'But at the end of the day it's still China,' Ravi says. 'Put your office in Hong Kong. If you look on the map, it's still China.'

Walking out of the mansions, I am approached by several touters selling tailoring work.

'Tailor, madam?' they call as Ravi, and I walk past them. Ravi laughs and tells me that that doesn't usually happen. Chungking Mansions, with its narrow corridors lined with shops selling African gold, tailoring and Indian street food is low-key and, as Ravi describes, 'ordinary' compared to the high-rise wealth and international gaze of the rest of Hong Kong. At the same time, it serves as a meeting place for cultures, for encounters of a different modality. As Jayaram notes, 'If Hong Kong as a whole has long been an entrepôt between China and the rest of the world, Chungking Mansions has functioned as a mini-entrepôt' (2011: 94). Chungking was Ravi's first experience in Hong Kong as a potential businessman rather than a tourist.

'Frankly speaking, new place, definitely. But when I entered Chungking for the first time, I was directed by my friend to go to the station and just choose any exit. And then ask someone for Chungking. No need to use your head. Chungking Mansions, everybody knows this place. Once you reach outside of Chungking Mansions you will see many people standing there offering watches, hotels, guest houses, things like that. And you just look and choose one of them, see which one suits you.'

'Okay, okay.'

'So, that's how I did it for the first time.'

Without maps, Chungking stands out in the imagination – bolder and more multi-textured than cartography can express. Take any exit, ask any person on the street – cartographic specificity was also unnecessary in Ravi's first navigations to Chungking, which must have come as a relief given the complications of using maps in China.

'It's too funny! I've had a very bad experience with Google Maps,' he laughs. 'I've had too many good experiences, though, but one was the worst.'

'Okay?'

'I had to go to this very big, known supermarket in Guangzhou – the address says building number 351 Guan To Ta Dao Chung.'

I smile, 'okay ...?

'I search it on the Google Map, it showed me the place, I used direction, I said 'I want to go by bus', it showed me, okay, where do I catch the bus from,' he pauses and pulls out his phone. 'I got the bus, the direction was like this – we stop for a second, huh?' Ushering me onto a street corner, Ravi directs my gaze towards his screen centred on Guangzhou.

'Let's say, this road hey? The bus goes from here, the bus turns here, and I have to go this side. There was a stop at this corner.'

'Yeah?'

'I go down, I started walking this way.'

'Right, okay.'

'It showed walk about 200 m so I start to walk. But the place was not familiar – I have been there by taxi – but the way the bus took was different.

'Right?'

'Okay, so like crazy I walked, and then I started asking people – I know a little bit of Chinese so, where is this, this, this, this, and then I came to know I was actually walking the opposite way!'

We laugh, and Ravi continues.

'On the other side the bus was turning on the proper direction I want to go, I could have taken the bus well four more stops – and then? And then walk for about 100 m, and relax. I could have reached. So I ended up on total wrong place, total walking distance was about 600 or 700 m. I was too tired. I had to take a taxi and reach. This was the funniest experience I had using

Google Maps. And actually, Chinese maps, one of the maps called Baidu Maps, it's quite accurate, for China, as compared to Google Maps.'

'Interesting.'

'But I don't blame Google 100% for this because China has, has, has, it's somehow closed the doors for Google in many places.'

'So you tend to use Google Maps rather than Baidu Maps?'

'Because Baidu Maps, originally it's Chinese, I need to get used to typing Chinese.'

'Right.'

'It's not in English – or, what I have to do is, first get the full address in Chinese, or, in English, type translate, then paste it in a Baidu Map and then get the location. It's a bloody tedious job.'

'And even more tedious when you're standing on the street?'

I laugh as I remember the look of intense concentration on Daren's face, which is now mirrored by Ravi's mimicry. One way to get around guessing the Pinyin that digital mapping platforms use is through a translation program. There a direct link between the English Romanisation and the Chinese characters can be made without the need for a Pinyin riddle. But on a small screen, translating between languages, copying and pasting between applications (particularly if you're in a hurry) is a complicated and pernickety task.

'Exactly, that's why I don't tend to use Baidu Maps. I still use Google Maps at the end of the day. It's more user-friendly, if you want to make your own places, you can tag your own places.'

These features are useful for the frequent traveller. Ravi has to leave China every few months while he waits for his new business to open. After that, he can get a full visa with a registered business in China. Hong Kong is merely a tool in the cogs that provide access to China. And a relief by some senses, because it is also more than a stopover free port designed to move trade and people in and out.

'I can even go to Macao if I want. But Macao has no other meaning except if you want to go and gamble.'

We walk through Kowloon near East Tsim Sha Tsui Station, surrounded by large hotels laying flat against wide boulevards and public parks. It's a different atmosphere to TST – as if the original shoreline can be mapped in the shift in the streets. The mansions are surrounded by narrow streets wound like a skein – and here, the open space and wide streets take full advantage of the reclaimed land. Side by side, two spaces compressed and contorted differently under the clash between the local and the global. Under us, a tunnel burrows between TST and East TST, taking advantage of the flow of people between here and there, the near and the far, the high-end and low-end internationalism that supports the global economy in its neo-colonial and neo-imperial form. New colonialisms upon old, underwritten by discourses that have transformed if not ruptured, Ravi steers us towards a coastline both false and real, where the water and the sky reflect mise en abyme.

'In Hong Kong,' he gestures out towards the harbour, 'I don't worry about getting lost because most people, they can speak a little English and they can direct you to the metro station, you know, the MTR, and if you can find the metro station you can find a map or something. A huge display, okay, you can take this line or this line and reach where you want.'

'So would you say then that your experience of Hong Kong is very much defined by the metro system?'

'Exactly. But not by the bus. I don't know about the bus. Frankly speaking, if not metro, then I'll be worried about it. Then definitely, it's a compulsion to use a map. You find your way out, your way in. Whatever.'

A city built from the outside in, where the coastlines in the early maps of the British, Portuguese and Spanish were surveyed along the shore in fathoms and currents, and longitudes and latitudes now finds itself defined equally by an interior system of mass transit designed to bring people between China and Hong Kong. The south side of the island, where some of the older colonial residences can be found, has no such system – even though the MTR stretches into the far reaches of the New Territories. Ravi compares his experience in China, and with the Chungking Mansions with trying to find a small beach with a friend, somewhere between Stanley and Repulse Bay.

'I searched before I came, because it was pre-decided. We're going to go to this temple and go to this beach. So I searched on Google Maps, which bus number goes to this place, which metro goes to this bus, what are the best directions. After that, I noted down everything, because black and white is the best thing. Phone, no battery, power off, end of the story.'

A curious, but not unexpected caution of foresight.

'So you wrote it down by hand?'

'Yep. Also, I made a note on my phone, too.'

'Okay.'

'Just to be on the safer side,' he laughs.

'In duplicate?' Before us, an overhead pedestrian bridge rises over a motorway towards the harbour.

'Yeah, so we followed and we reached and it was perfect. In Hong Kong, I've never had any ...,' he trails off as we come to the motorway. 'Cross?'

He points towards the walkway, which now reveals a promenade that curves the foreshore, formed from the most recent of the reclamations. It is now a spectroscope to view the harbour, and the famous skyline of the north shore of Hong Kong Island covered in towers branded by international finance and trade. In the stepladder heights of the skyscrapers, a map can be traced of the transforming economies of Hong Kong, expressed in ambitious vertical architectures, by way of showing economic might.

Opened in 2003, Two International Finance Centre (2 IFC) is a tower that rises above the horizon, piercing out into the harbour and the sky. Slightly smaller in Admiralty, the Bank of China Tower, which opened in 1990 and was designed by I.M. Pei, stands proudly enveloped by tessellating triangles. And smaller still, between them sits the Hongkong and Shanghai Banking Corporation (HSBC) Building opened in 1985. Designed by Norman Foster as a modular and portable skyscraper, in its time it was once the most expensive building in the world but is now dwarfed by its new successors standing on either side. The skyline of a city unites branding with image, capital with spectacle (Grodach, 2009; Kaika, 2010).

'It's unusual when such a good application fails you. It's usual that it works ... but for a second that they don't work – you start blabbering about it.'

Underneath our feet, L'Avenue des Stars, Hong Kong's answer to the Hollywood Walk of Fame, is embossed into the pavement. It features the stars of Hong Kong cinema, including Jackie Chan and Bruce Lee. The cogs of colonialism are not only in banks but also in culture. Watching a busload of tourists from the mainland gather around each star set into the pavement, lining up patiently to take each have a photo taken with the handprints of their favourite actors, hair blowing across their faces, and the harbour twinkling in the background, Ravi and I chat about the sun and the coast and the wind and how one might go about navigating without a map. Ravi tells me how he can always tell where north is, because of the sun.

'Air can change directions in a second,' he clicks his fingers abruptly.

'Why do you think you find the sun?' I ask.

'It's more easier,' he replies, 'it's like, even if you don't remember the whole map, the whole geographical map of the city or the country or the state or whatever, then you just say, you can find the sun. Simple.'

I tell him about Nick, who found his way through the sun, and Cliff, who could locate east via the coast.

'Coasts,' Ravi states seriously, 'they don't have buildings too much. They have clear skies as compared to the cities, to the mountains, you could have had all the senses, but you got only one.'

'And what about stars?'

'Stars? That's in the night.'

For Ravi, these modes of navigation – sensory, intuitive, embodied – interact with the contemporary use of digital mobile mapping platforms (like Google Maps), folding around one another without melding, supplementing each other's failings. As he noted before – it's not until it fails that he even notices that it's working.

'It depends on the situation. Like, in an unknown city – definitely no paper maps. First, wastage of paper. Second, c'mon, it's too tedious to open a map, it's windy, the map's going this way and that way. So, I prefer the applications to the paper maps. But let them be more developed than what they are now. Especially with transport.'

Maps are deployed to move about. We have passed L'Avenue des Stars now, and are rounding the tip of the peninsula. This area was once a sandy bay but was leased from China to Britain in 1898 to accommodate the expanding population crowded by the mountainous terrain of Hong Kong Island. As that happened, the shoreline was expanded and reshaped, the bay that waxes and wanes with the tides filled into a fixed walled foreshore, resolute against space and time. Near us, a bus takes off at a set of traffic lights, and Ravi continues his criticism.

'Metro stations, they don't move. Buses, they are on the street. You need to be more specific about which bus stand to go to.' Ravi is realistic about the relationship between spatial fixity and cartographic knowledges. Fixed spaces, fixed routes, predictable flows aid in cartographic accuracy – nay, ensure it – and where space dissolves into heterogeneity and terminal openness, the authority of the map recedes. He describes how, in Hong Kong, no one uses street numbers any more, except old taxi drivers. Everyone else uses landmarks. But, he says, landmarks change while street numbers stay the same no matter what is built upon the land.

In front of us, a clock tower stands near the Hong Kong Arts Centre, without reference to its purpose, an anachronism in the contemporary luxury shopping centres all glass and steel. Ravi points to it, before indicating back towards Hung Hom.

'Below is the fast train to Guangzhou.'

The train runs between Hung Hom and Guangzhou East, a route that Ravi regularly catches during his visa applications. This route is a ghost of the Kowloon-Canton railway that ran between the two same cities and had its terminus below the clock tower here. Built shortly after the lease, its development had been long delayed by way of protecting powerful British shipping interests in the Pearl River Delta, travelling between Chinese Guangzhou (Canton), British Hong Kong and Portuguese Macao. This clock tower formed an apex of this triangle between three cities held by three competing powers, edged around the delta itself. New railways may be built, new cities like Shenzhen, Zhongshan and Zhuhai and Dongguan are urbanised, and new modes of travel by air and by car are developed, but still the triangular power geometry of the delta continues to be reinforced commercially and socially through loopholes in regulation and laws, idiosyncratic ghosts of a colonial past.

Ravi describes how – for him – there is a difference between people in Hong Kong and Guangzhou.

'The people in Hong Kong are fast,' he says, as we nearly get bowled over walking up the luxury shopping area near the China Ferry Terminal. 'You see, it's a free port – so matter what, it tends to be developed. You can move money in, and you can move money out. The whole city is a duty-free shop.'

We see now, where the nexus has shifted to Canton Road, a few parallel streets to the west. A new street adjacent decorated with multistorey designer stores like Louis Vuitton and Hermes, Canton Road connects the China Ferry Terminal with the foreshore and the new International Commerce Centre, the tallest building in Hong Kong. Watching the long lines of tourists snaking out of the stores, buying up handbags, we get approached again.

'Tailor, madam?' If Hong Kong is an East-West sandwich, then India is a 'big, big sandwich', Ravi laughs. And this accounts for Chungking Mansions and the large South Asian presence that is dotted all over the island in toponymy, buildings, people and culture. But the economic development between the regions was different, Ravi suggests, due to the lingering presence of Britain in Hong Kong well beyond the date of Indian independence.

'[Hong Kong] was ruled by the Britishers until the 90s. You see, the majority of development in Hong Kong is being done when the British were still here.'

'Why was it different do you think, with Hong Kong and India?' I ask.

'They left India earlier. Only one difference – free port – India wouldn't have been a free port. Apart from that, the same,' Ravi pauses. 'Even though they left India, they were still here,' he points to Haiphong Road, and the mosque on the corner of Nathan Road near the park, 'developing the place. Indians were welcome because Britishers were here. And they found it more comfortable because they already know who are Britishers, how they behave, what they want, what they don't want. So, they just got part of the system. They just became a huge part of the Hong Kong system. Immediately.'

I'm not an economist or an expert in Indian history, but I am a little sceptical of the frictionless enthusiasm in Ravi's account. At the same time, what we can agree on is that traces of this presence can be found everywhere – including being structured and hybridised into the economies of Hong

Kong. Furthermore, this begets familiarities (of oppression or opportunity) across different scales, spaces and times within the same empire, whether it is Hong Kong and India, or Hong Kong and Sydney.

Geometries of power, power geometries, geometric power and powerful geometrics – the first lines that segment Hong Kong were drawn on maps and on charts between the centre and the periphery, between points on the periphery, firming up edges and borders to manage the flow of goods and people in the global empires of the nineteenth and twentieth centuries. But maps have become stultified by their hubris, he explains, too busy fixating on the creating what I call Leibnizian universalities rather than their major purpose of navigation.

'They show you the inside structure of the mall, of library, of White House. C'mon we can have a tour of the inside of a house.'

He chortles. Instead of looking to the past, Ravi looks to the future. He is less interested in the histories eroding in space than securing and stabilising the future – fixing invisible Cartesian seawalls all over the region.

'But we can't afford to lose our destination,' he continues. 'Do you understand my point?'

'Yes, I do.'

'Let's say, for example, you planned a trip, okay, you want to go to the beach in the evening. I need five hours for that, before that I need to have my dinner or supper or anything, okay? Before that, I have free time: I can go to The Peak, this temple, or the market. Okay, so now you use the map – you want to navigate. But let's say you want to go to Market A and it sends you to Market B, but you've already seen that! You lose time. You lose time – that means that you lost the opportunity to B from A. Why? Because of the streets, the addresses ....'

Time, according to Ravi, equals opportunity – and lost time due to maps failing is lost opportunities. But it is not entirely the fault of Google Maps, a sentiment that he has repeated. He blames the landscape as much as the map, for not complying fully to the discourses of cartographic reason and the convenient and automatic interoperability that it offers with commercial markets, transport logics and digital platforms. He has a proposition for the future of mapping, one which echoes the logics of alphanumeric structures that combines both Cartesian geometries and Leibnizian universalism, to reshape the world and place invisible markers unmoved by the transformability of space.

'So, rather than showing which mall is there, or showing the structure of the mall, they could pinpoint where it is from numbers. When you were explaining it to me in the restaurant – I actually got so deep into it that I could visualise a map that was only numbers. Only numbers! A map that always gets you to the exact pinpointed location. Like I said there, number 154. What is this? Number 154 is Chungking Mansions, Nathan Road. Done, end of the story. Whether it is Chungking Mansions or they destroyed and made a whole new thing. You don't need to care about it.'

## Vicki/Lines

'It doesn't show its incline. You know, the green areas are mountains.'

Vicki and I meet two storeys high, just past the Central Market, somewhere near a Holly Brown coffee shop on the Central-Mid-Levels escalator and walkway system. I know this because this is the landmark that I've been given: 'Holly Brown on Queen's Road, Central – near the escalators and the market.' Precisely what defines this point as a good meeting space is not obvious on a map. As I follow Google Maps, it appears unobtrusive and ambiguous. However, when I arrive, the characteristics of the space become clearer than their expression on the map. This point is transitional for both the terrain of the escalator system and the island landscape itself. At this point on Queen's Road, the flat foreshore and the covered overhead walkways transform dually into a steep mountainous landscape whose sudden change in incline is mapped by the contours of the escalator system, as it shifts between automated and paved walkways. After we find each other, Vicki directs us straight onto the escalators. We're walking to Victoria Peak – the highest point on Hong Kong Island – a weekly form of exercise that she undertakes to maintain her fitness. In a city with a lack of flat land, hill-climbing and hiking are popular outdoor exercises and Hong Kong has preserved ample nature parks and reserves to foster this kind of activity. But first, we need to find the start of Old Peak Road, the paved path we will take up to the mountain. This means trailing up the escalators towards the Botanic Gardens, and following the contours until we reach its start point. As we stand motionless on the escalators, the city passing us by on our upwards journey, Vicki shows me a route that traces around spurs and valleys alike, in such a convoluted manner that I give up understanding and relent to becoming utterly subservient to her navigational skills.

When I tell Vicki that I can't understand the map (with a caveat that I am ill with tonsillitis from the pollution so we'd better not get stuck halfway up the mountain), she laughs.

'Signs are often not that accurate,' she says. 'Sometimes it's hard to tell what street you are on. So even for locals to get off you need to look up.'

She points to one of the signs hanging from the roof of the walkway. It has several arrows pointing downwards towards sets of stairs that descend back to street level, with notations about which streets you will encounter if you follow them. To get down, you need to look up – a sentiment that is distinctly (and perhaps uniquely) Hong Kongese. Hong Kong occupies multiple levels. As noted earlier, Frampton et al. (2012) argued that there is no ground plane. This is not entirely true; the ground plane as a site for markets and cars, for everyday encounters as well, still maintains a crucial role in Hong Kong. Yet, it is arguably because the ground plane is so mountainous that the multilevel structures between escalators and stairs, underpasses and overhead walkways, and shopping centres that rise to dizzying heights. Buildings are constructed up the hill in a sophisticated style of terracing that has sometimes been prone to landslides. As these buildings were built higher, we find that the escalator system, for instance, moves between the fourth floor of one building, and the third of the next, as the ground elevation rises, but the walkway parallels sea level. In some regard, the ground plane contributes to its own ambiguity. Ahead of us, we suddenly hit street-level in Soho, and cross a road before continuing up, a brief meeting between two separate planes. Vicki points to the bars and restaurants that Daren spoke about during our conversation a few days earlier.

'It used to be more residential area here, as well,' she explains, 'but, um, in the last decade actually there were museums, art collectors come here, start new business and transform.' The entire area has changed dramatically in the past 50 years, alongside a rapid rise in population and the globalisation of Asian markets not just in trade, but also in manufacturing and industry. We turn a corner and see a small machine with a touchpad sitting to the side. Vicki takes out her Octopus card and lightly touches it as we walk past, impressively maintaining her rhythm as it beeps while we move out of earshot.

'It allows me to have a HK$2 reduction on my return back [home]'

Behind us, more beeps sound as others touch on, headed either up or down between Central and the Mid-Levels.

'These "cat" stations are usually far from the MTR exits.'

As we move upwards into Soho, Vicki points out how the buildings themselves work. The lower levels, from approximately our eye height to the ground (wherever that may be) are for restaurants and boutiques, while the upper levels are more residential. She points us off the walkways around the beginning of where the Mid-Levels start, at one terraced street that snakes around the hills. A school sits to our left, blending in with the mix of residential and commercial zonings melded together.

'I went to this primary school, and two decades ago there was not this kind of restaurant.'

The restaurant in question is an American-style steakhouse, prohibitively priced because of the rarity of beef and high importation costs. There is little farming land in Hong Kong for beef production, again due to the steep terrain. Like Daren, Vicki describes how the buildings have changed since she was small, due to the influx of wealthy tourists and expatriates who make the Island their home. All the same, she assures me earnestly, we're not lost.

'I know the way because I've been here several times before.'

Having lived her whole life in Hong Kong, and given that it is a relatively small region, I wonder if she ever needs a map. She does. She likes to see and to check her route even though mainly she just relies on her own experiences of the landscape.

'Sometimes I look it up before and sometimes I use GPS ... and some of it is experience.'

She navigates point to point, she explains, picturing the closest point in her head, and then going from there. She looks for landmarks that she knows, small waypoints in the upward landscape between which she can navigate. These waypoints help because they form an apex on the incline, and give a more accurate sense of relative distance along the unexpected pedestrian hypotenuses – true distances that are invisible on flattened maps like the one she has on her phone.

The layering of levels in Hong Kong is revealed to be complicated. This part of the city, which is less tithed to the ground plane intersects at various points in order to facilitate movement between the levels. In doing so, it warps the cartographic mode of understanding distance – the length between two points.

Yet, it's a strange transformation – the landscape itself, as can be seen in the earliest Chinese and even British maps and images of the island, emphasises the mountainous terrain that rises immediately out of the foreshore. This terrain was uneven and jagged, allowing little room for the geometric urban planning popularised by the square structure of Beijing, or the triangular patterns of Hausmann's Paris. Collinson's early maps included a ground level perspective showing the shape of the mountains, and annotating them with names and approximate height. Soon after the production of Collinson's maps, surveying parties were sent out across the island to measure how high the hills were, and to produce topographical maps with contour lines to get a sense of how island was formed. These maps in plan view, from an abstracted eye above tracing imagined perspectives, were redolent of a different kind of verticality. Scholars interested in vertical territories often argue that maps flatten the landscape, and so ignore the politics of elevation (Graham and Hewitt, 2012; Harris, 2015; Shelton et al., 2010; Weizman, 2002). However, looking around at the urban landscape of Hong Kong – the steepness of footpath and walkway inclines juxtaposed to the relative levelling required to build skyscrapers – it is arguable that, if anything, the map does not flatten verticality and instead generalises the rate of incline along contour lines. Between two points, contours suggest a consistent and predictable line, a geometrically driven hypotenuse, an inference about what lies in-between.

But what lies between the contour lines is an uneasy ally. To the casual surveyor, the space between two contour lines can be flattened and dug into the hillside to make way for residential high-rises – like those that Vicki was mournful to find where we left the escalators. But the space between contour lines is also heterogeneous and unpredictable – to assume regularity between these points, and then to draw that onto paper, into code, and eventually, into the landscape merely reinforces the same cartographic impulses and retraces the same cartographic imaginations albeit on a vertical rather than horizontal plane. Upwards, might as well be northwards, for the importance that height plays in the vertical landscape.

'North is the Mid-Levels,' Vicki states vigorously. 'If we go to The Peak, we will have to go all the way north.'

She points towards Victoria Peak rising out of the city and defying the flattened spatial imagination. In actuality, The Peak is almost directly due south from where we are. Vicki understandably conflates 'importance' – in this case, verticality – with 'northness' reminiscent of the discursive framework that Black argues is typical of the Euro-centrism of the cartographic imagination (Black, 1997). Like parks for Ellen, north for Vicki is relative – cardinal directions that are more relevant to a subjective reading of landscape and map than strict adherence to the cartographic lines drawn across the world. The contours on the map suggest nothing about the compass, yet the contours on the landscape rearrange it all the same.

'So,' Vicki continues, 'we go all the way up. So, we go Old Peak Road.'

'Is there a "new peak road"?' I joke.

Vicki laughs, 'I guess it's the tram.'

'So we are going to The Peak.'

And so, we head south towards the Mid-Levels, through the Botanic Gardens and up into more residential areas. As we approach the beginning of the Old Peak Road, I am suddenly light-headed, and my decision not to heed my doctor's advice and stay in bed is becoming a regret of epic proportions.

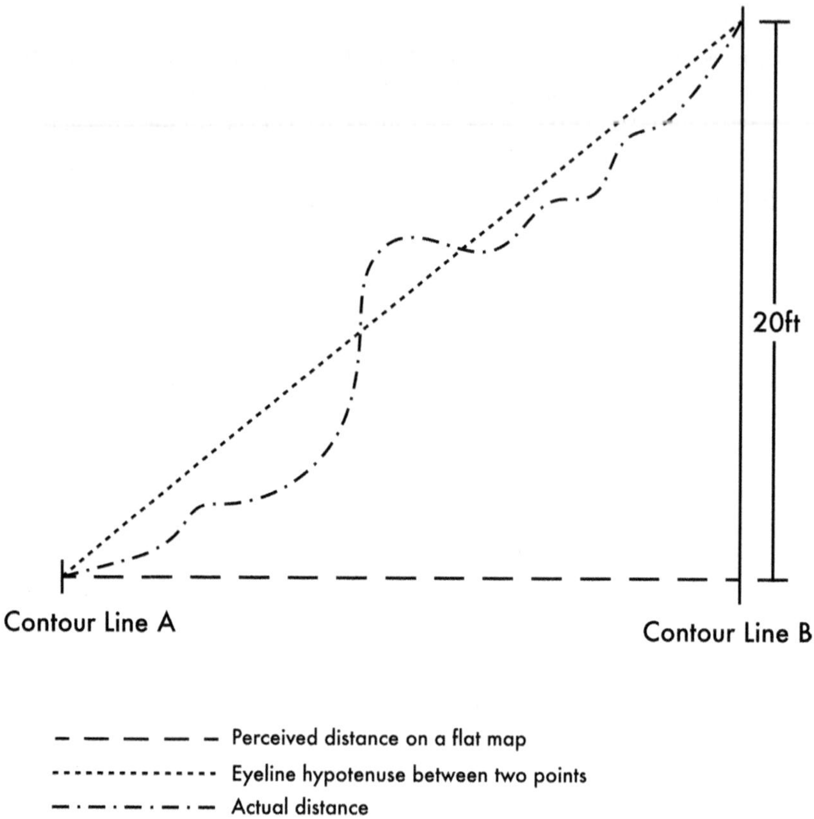


Figure 10.4. *Generalisations.* Contours only measure at certain intervals, and so average and regulate the incline of the slope, even where it might be uneven and inconsistent.

I must have looked slightly grey, because Vicki suddenly turns to me, as the road grows unconscionably steep.

'Even though it's steep, it's very well paved. It's well paved because this road is kind of an old route to The Peak before the train or ....'

The Peak was attractive to colonial residents due to the cool winds that offered some relief from the summer humidity, which still can be traced in amongst the large colonial villas that pepper the hillside like white blocks in the green terrain. Many had servants who would carry them up and down the hill in sedan chairs, and so the quality and accessibility of the road only had to accommodate this possibility rather than making it generally accessible. But now, there is barely enough room for cars to pass and the steepness of the curves makes me wonder how residents descend from here down to Central.

People don't like to walk, Vicki tells me, but prefer to catch the bus. These are also expensive apartments, so many residents own cars or take taxis and leave the walking to those who can't afford to do otherwise. The higher up towards The Peak and the higher up the number of floors, the more expensive the apartment. Verticality has its premium, too.

Finally, we are out of the urban area, and we move into the nature park up in The Peak. Before us, a long concrete road rises up and curves, its destination obscured by the thick tree canopy and rocky outcrops. We pause briefly at a pagoda for some water, before setting off again on the second leg of the journey.

'This is the hiking trail,' Vicki nods towards the path ahead. 'This road takes us up to shopping mall – 30 minutes.'

About 100 m into the trail we pass a small moss-covered stone that marks the boundary of the City of Victoria. First called Queenstown in 1841, Victoria is the name of the capital of Hong Kong Island under British rule, called so by the British to honour Queen Victoria. Victoria isn't marked on our map, nor on many others. This lone boundary stone is a remnant of that landscape, lying dormant against the hillside. In, *Atlas: Tales of an Imaginary City* (2012), Dung writes about the legendary city of Victoria, as (re)encountered 5000 years in the future by archaeologists. He describes how the Chinese had a different idea of the layout than the plans published in 1903 outlining the six boundary markers of Victoria. Instead, nine *yuens*, or neighbourhoods – Central, Sheung Wan, Sai Wan, Wan Chai, for instance – lie throughout the city and have now subsumed the city of Victoria since the handover in 1997. There is a meaningful entanglement here – with our own archaeology of mobile mapping – as we accidentally bump into a future already lived, seeing the archaeology of the past already eroding, and how lost spaces once so cartographically resolute now linger somewhere in space.

As I tumble on by the boundary stone (red in the face and short of breath), I pause again and turn back to the city below. I question why at this place, why at this point, was the boundary drawn on the map and marked here in space. This is a boundary for a city that no longer exists in name – and what was contained within and beyond the transgressive line that once segregated this space (and arguably still does) is not clear. Old documents that planned the city list four *wans*, or districts, bounded by six stones and this particular contour as the southernmost point where Old Peak Road meets Tregayer Road. At this height, perhaps, the hills become more cliffy and steep, unable to be reformed into ordered city spaces.

As we move deeper into the mountain, banyan trees clutch at the rock face with long roots and birds cawing in the trees. Vicki tells me that there is a danger here. She only walks on well-paved paths because she's afraid of heights – a liability in such a high-rise city – and she always thinks she's going to fall. She is also scared of snakes – although no one has ever been bitten – and of falling rocks. The cliffs along the paved paths are carefully monitored with each face being assigned an identification number that tracks its condition – another alphanumeric system that reasserts potential danger, while at the same time assuaging through the technologies of categorisation and calculation. What this cartography of cliff faces would look like on a screen interface, I can only imagine, numbers dotted over flat surfaces, glimpses of verticality on an otherwise horizontal imaginary.

Drawing on these thoughts, I ask Vicki how she knows where the well-paved paths are. She shows me on her phone an app that the Hong Kong government has released to encourage outdoor activities. This app says what kind of path the walking route is and whether it is paved or not. In addition, she says as she points to the screen, the maps show the contours, so she can tell how steep the hiking trail is, and judge how difficult and how long the walk will be. The app jumps to Old Peak Road, where we have paused on a corner and says that it should take about 30 minutes.

'I don't think it's too optimistic. It's feasible. Because it's not too long,' she points up out of the canopy to a white futuristic building perched on a saddle between two mountains, 'It's just steep.'

The building is The Peak Tram stop, a small shopping centre with a 360-degree viewing platform on top. It's difficult to gauge from this angle, but its position seems to indicate that it would be possible to see both sides of Hong Kong Island, from Central and Admiralty below us to Repulse Bay and Stanley on the other side.

'The Peak,' Vicki says, 'is one of the steepest trails.'

I am not surprised. At a consistent incline of 40 degrees, my knees and my calves are feeling the burn and the pressure in my ears – made worse by illness – is throbbing. Vicki, on the other hand, bounds up the hill.

'Hong Kong is more vertical than Beijing or Seoul,' she waits for me at the next corner, 'and lots of Japanese and Korean tourists come to Hong Kong for the hiking trails. Lots of nature.'

It's a lovely spot – below us we can see almost the full scope of the city stretching out into Victoria Harbour. On the other side, the Kowloon Peninsula dwarfed by the new ICC that makes the IFC and Bank of China towers look rather small in comparison. The Star Ferry runs between the two, a slight blur cutting a white stripe through the water. It is a dialectic vantage point from the one that Ravi and I walked by earlier, looking up at the buildings and The Peak from sea level. The contours are different from the sea to the mountain than the mountain to the sea. The transition is illuminating – the cartographic eye positions itself, first from the sea looking inwards staring up at the intimidating mountains, and then from the highest point looking down. As it does, the top-down, Apollonian eye transforms from awe to survey, in the conquest of colonisation as it shifts from calculation to control.

San Dai means the top of the mountain in Cantonese, Vicki tells me. In this toponymic version, Victoria Peak is just the peak, and even then not quite a pinnacle. This explanation appears diminutive against the grandeur of the British imperial vision and refreshingly pragmatic – based in landscapes if not imaginaries, in mapping rather than cartographic reason. The top of the mountain looms above us, and, along the road, we stumble upon a small shrine adorned with burnt-out incense sticks and glittering golden traditional Chinese characters.

'What is this?' I ask Vicki.

'This is Kun Yi,' she replies, 'for people who believe in the gods.'

Kun Yi, a practice of worshipping goddesses and gods, of ancestors, is a tradition of southern China. Not hailing from Beijing, from Shanghai, or London, Kun Yi originates in the vestiges of the Hakka tribes who once inhabited this area before the British.

'The air here is much better,' she continues.

I'm not sure what this means, since the pollution from Shenzhen and Guangzhou reaches here equally well. But perhaps it settles in the valleys, and the air is undoubtedly cooler even in the industrial haze. I ask her how much longer we have to go. I feel bad because I am slowing her down, although I suspect only the most sprightly person could keep with her upbeat pace. All the same, the pollution is irritating my throat, and I have developed a problematic wheeze.

Vicki looks at me curiously and then pulls out her phone.

'I don't think maps work. I'll try.'

Staring intently at her screen, she pulls up the Google Maps application and swivels it around with her thumb. Coming to rest on a large green figure, decorated with haphazard white squiggles and centred in the middle of the island, she shows it to me.

'The Peak is here,' she says, pointing to a nondescript patch within the green mass. She looks back up at the Peak Galleries, before squinting at the map again. 'It doesn't show its incline. You know, the green areas is mountains.'

The 'green areas' fail spectacularly at conveying the mountainous verticality of The Peak district. In its homogenising practices, cartography has implanted a certain flatness of space – yet all the while regulating how any verticality might be understood. It seems absurd that the map wouldn't show incline, given that this is the governing feature of the terrain. Even

Figure 10.5. *Regimentations.* As Vicki uses the hiking app, on the right a small green plaque can be seen. This plaque registers and numbers this slope as part of the Hong Kong slope-management scheme to prevent erosion and landslides. Each slope has a unique identifier.

the contours that would be expected on a topographic map are given up in this version to privilege roads and buildings.

'So we are getting closer.'

The map shows us zigzagging along the green area – currently moving away from The Peak – in a manner redolent of stupidity. In fact, the whole map conveys very little information at all that aids us in determining the distance, steepness and time. This is not quite like the situation with Nick, where one should be able to 'feel' the hills and make sure that you remain on the same path. It is impossible not to feel the hill here – as it stands over you – and you become subservient to the ambling zigzags and the memory of someone who knows the way. There is no scope here for claiming your own navigational territory, and so the map rather than assisting reinforces your impotence.

As we climb, Vicki shows me another app on her phone, this time a hiking maps app released by the Hong Kong SAR government. One of the earliest projects undertaken by the region post-1997 was to commence a cartographic project to survey and document the SAR – spatial knowledge is belongs to empires, rather than spaces, and so the British government retreated with much of this information and data. These maps form the basis for a number of trails ranked by length, incline and difficulty throughout Hong Kong's country parks – designed to get Hong Kongers moving and enjoying the natural landscape. The maps Vicki shows me do contain the topographic information – and The Peak appears as a bubble of compact, almost colliding lines, drawn smoothly across the screen.

# 11. Stabilising the Digital

## Taylor/Memories

> 'I try not to rely on the map so much. Just, sometimes, I think that it can guide you to the wrong way ....'

From highs to lows, the area in north-east Kowloon is characterised by a vast flatness in the ground plane of the landscape: a complete dichotomy to the hills encountered by Vicki a few days earlier. In this landscape, mid-rise residential buildings soar up from the ground like sticks in a field, their lower levels visually supported by a complex network of above and below ground freeways and motorways. There is no MTR here – having caught a bus from Nathan Road in TST, right outside the Chunking Mansions, this landscape is disorienting away from the familiar structure of the transit system. Taylor has decided to take me on a hike, to a small fishing village east of here, situated on a thinner section of the harbour called Lei Yue Mun. The peninsula upon which it stands forms the westernmost point of Junk Bay, subject to the reclamations that support the new LOHAS Park development where Ellen and I visited. As we walk out from the windbreak of the building and onto the lea of parks and schools and construction sites, the air grows cold from wind chill and the humidity drops.

'You're so lucky today,' Taylor says to me, laughing with sarcasm. 'Today, it is very cold.'

I laugh with him, and thinking of the long walks in the sun that I undertook in Sydney, I remind him that it could be worse – it could be very hot. He nods in agreement, before indicating ahead with his nose.

'So, we go back to ...,' he pauses. 'It's called the village with the wall.'

This is a literal translation of the name of the fishing village – presumably named because of the concrete typhoon shelter that reaches out into the small port, protecting the boats from storms. This name is at once pragmatic and poetic. It is deeply embedded in the memory of the landscape, lingering regardless of the transformation of urban terrains.

---

Wilmott, C., *Mobile Mapping. Space, Cartography and the Digital.*
Taylor & Francis Group, 2020
DOI 10.5117/9789462984530_CH11

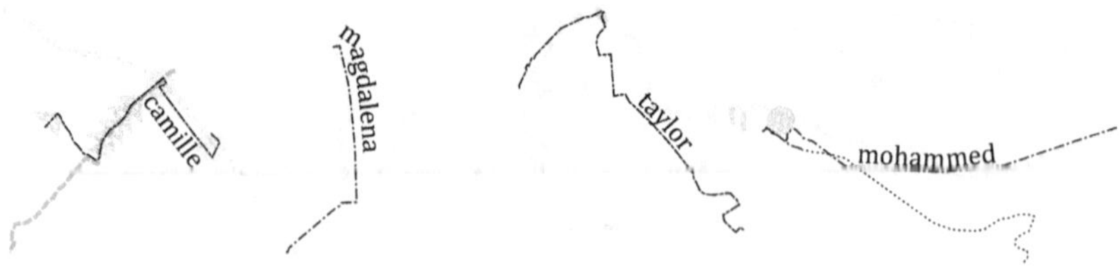


Figure 11.1. *Fragments – Taylor, Camille, Madgalena and Mohammed.* (Left) *Taylor's walk* – Tuesday, 11 February, To Kwa Wan-Yau Tong, afternoon, overcast; (centre left) *Camille's walk* – Thursday, 13 February, Central-Soho, evening, overcast; (centre right) *Magdalena's walk* – Friday, 14 February, Central Ferry Pier-Mong Kok, morning, sunny; (right) *Mohammed's walk* – Saturday, 15 February, Causeway Bay-Admiralty-The Peak, morning, overcast.

'So it's that kind of place,' Taylor continues, 'and then, uh, I just have a vague direction.' He points eastwards, into the greying sky. Our view blocked by freeways and hoardings, the ambiguity of his navigation is reflected in the ambiguity of our viewpoint. This flat land, surrounded by ghostly mountains that melt into the vanishing point under the haze of the pollution and the winter, affords only ambiguity from a heads-up view. He looks at me and laughs.

'I don't care actually about which exact streets I'm going to have to go, I just have the vague direction.'

'Okay,' I pull my woollen scarf around my shoulders as we wait to cross at some pedestrian lights. Behind us, the tall buildings of Kowloon Tong, before us, a small playground, with green plants sprouting out of red-tiled garden beds.

'Because, um, I think it was the main skill when we are, when we were having our cycling trip, we don't know which street we are going to have.'

The cycling trip in mention was a journey that Taylor and some friends took through Europe not long prior. Rather than taking trains or buses, they cycled through Germany, the Netherlands, Belgium and France with their kit packed into panniers. This journey seems to have been influential on Taylor's mobility practices – rather than being bound to the MTR system, he now avidly cycles throughout Hong Kong – which he claims is faster, cheaper and more straightforward than public transport. Hong Kong does not have the same political will towards cycling infrastructure as Sydney – the bicycle lanes that Nick and I chased throughout Chippendale are absent here, and I have seen no plans to build separated cycle ways or other facilities to encourage cycling as a quotidian, rather than recreational, activity.

On the one hand, the same ambivalence that Nick felt towards maps is echoed in Taylor's sentiment. Taylor, too, maps in his mind the curves and inclines of the landscape. On the other hand, however, Hong Kong is a dense city, with many tightly packed streets and an elaborate urban plan. I ask Taylor if not knowing where he is going, having a vague idea and letting it unfold before him as he goes, makes him feel more vulnerable than comfortable. The facial expression he returns to me – eyes directly towards mine, eyebrows raised, and a small smile – dismisses this concern out of hand.

'I don't want to concentrate on the detail that may not be meaningful,' he replies. 'I don't want to use my brain so much to find which exact street to go, yeah to go ....'

As the lights change, we cross, and Taylor takes in a breath.

'I try not to rely on the map so much. Just, sometimes, I think that it can guide you to the wrong way and not detailed enough for you to read,' we turn past a barrier and into the park, 'and then you basically interpret the meaning of the map and then you may get to the wrong place.'

Taylor has, in his mind, a fix-point – a destination. This is not a point that he can see in ocular terms, but a cognitive map (Kitchin and Freundschuh, 2000) that rests within his mind. The map provides too much detail – offering a panacea to spatial navigation – while failing to personalise and trace the future journey. In a city as busy as Hong Kong, rather than focusing on the toponymic detail of street names or being mislead and detoured by all the extraneous information that is housed within the map interface, Taylor simply prefers to follow his geographic intuition – an inner compass that assists him in determining which way to go. Taylor's mode of voyage is a journey in classical terms – the map gives way to mapping, as it is embodied and traced through and into the spaces in which he walks and cycles, a spatiotemporal act based upon a mode of personal instinct, trust and discovery.

'So, let me see,' Taylor looks around and seeing only the park and tall hoardings, he chuckles, 'how can we get ...? Actually, ah, there is something right there.'

He points towards a large construction site sitting between us and Kowloon Bay, where the Kai Tak Airport once lay. Beyond, Victoria Harbour and the tall peaks of Hong Kong Island emerge in a haze – the horizon just above the top of the hoardings.

'But,' Taylor looks around again, 'ah, there is the sea. And then, so, we have to ...' – he makes a curving motion with his left hand towards the right side as if corralling the wind to pass him by – '... go this way.'

'Go around the sea ...?'

'Go around the sea.'

As Taylor gestures the route to me, at the end of a park sits a small rectangular boulder on a granite pedestal.

'So, I think it is one of the historical monuments in Hong Kong – yah – this is Sung Wong Toi.'

On the stone, three characters no more than a foot high are carved in and painted in red to stand out against the dappled marl: 臺王宋, *Song Wang Tai*,[1] 'Hall of the King of the Sung'.[2]

'This?' I ask. He nods.

'This is, uh, you know a little bit about Chinese history?'

'A little bit.'

'Uh, there was a dynasty called Song.'

'I know there was an emperor who died somewhere around the Pearl River Delta.'

'Yeah, here,' he says emphatically. 'That was here. It has his name.'

A tablet in the garden reminds us that this boulder once sat protruding from the top of a hill, Sacred Hill (聖山), which rose above the coast not too far from here. At the top of this hill, curved around a massive boulder on its peak was a terrace, inscribed with the story of the Song loyalists whose last days were spent in Kowloon Bay. The dynasty of the Southern Song ended in 1276 after the capture of the city of Lin'an (now called Hangzhou). Resistance remained in the form of Song loyalists, but they were disorganised and militarily uncoordinated, retreating south to Guangdong, and then, finally Kowloon Bay. It was a foggy day that the loyalists chose for a decisive battle, at Yashan in the delta of the Pearl River in 1279. The weather played against them, and unwilling to submit to Mongol (Yuan) rule, as the Song surrendered thousands of loyalists threw themselves into the sea and drowned. With them, the Song councillor and leader, Liu Xifu. He had been tasked with protecting the last emperor, the infant Zhao Bing, and is said to have jumped overboard still holding the child in his arms. The inscriptions, including those on the rock at the end of the park, are believed to have been made later (Bard, 1988), sometime during the Yuan dynasty (1271-1368) (ARUP/MTR Corporation, 2011).

This story held great appeal for Chinese immigrants arriving in Hong Kong. In the early twentieth century, the terrace became a site of ritual

1 There are a number of different Pinyin translations of the phrase 'Sung Wong Toi'. This Romanisation is taken from an 1899 Hong Kong gazette (Hong Kong Gazette, 1899) detailing the history of the site. Hon Tze-Ki (2011) uses the pinyin 'Song Wang Tai' in his article documenting the transformation of the site into a place of cultural memory, in line with the vernacular usage of the spelling *Song* rather than *Sung*. *Sung Wong Toi* however remains the translation written on the nearby streets, the park sign and the Google Map.

2 There are also a number of translations of 'Song Wang Tai' into English – this is a direct quote from the Hong Kong Gazette (1899) – but it is also known as the Song King's Terrace.

Figure 11.2. *Topologies*. Sung Wong Toi playground with the carved boulder at the end.

and ceremony, a 'saga of resistance and martyrdom' and a 'focal point of poetic and artistic imagination for the high moral ideas of the Southern Song loyalists' (Hon, 2011: 136). After it was destroyed by the Japanese during the Second World War, the terrace was rebuilt in 1959 as a monument, what Hon (2011) argues is a *lieu de mémoire*. Drawing from Nora, memory, in Hon's account, is juxtaposed to history to underscore the 'hidden, subterranean and competing memories that exist in human society. These memories – sometimes highly idiosyncratic, sometimes unabashedly personal, and sometimes decidedly colourful and mournful – reveal the plurality of lives and social groups that are not easily coalesced in a uniform and singular nationalist history' (Hon 2011: 138). In this reading, Sacred Hill, and Song Wang Tai are not so much 'places', but rather, have transformed into cultural texts – places that travel, transform and are the cumulative result of a temporality based in place. Yet, it is also possible to say that such sites are also journeys, not because place is always in-becoming (cf. Casey, 1993), but because space is always open. The archaeology of Song Wang Tai rests in space, not text, from a boulder on a hill to a monument in a park, it is re-spatialised and reinterpreted: its discourses are deeply spatialised. As McFarlane suggests:

> The journeys told here take their bearings from the distant past, but also from the debris and phenomena of the living present, for this is often a double insistence of old landscapes: that they be read in the *then* but felt in the *now*. (McFarlane, 2012: 33)

To consider Song Wang Tai in such terms is to conceive of it a dual journey: the end point of the travels of the Song loyalists, recorded *in situ*, in stone, at a site where they once stood. It is also the beginning of another – that of storytelling, the retelling and reinterpretation of that journey – a spatio-cultural journey that is indeed heterogeneous and open.

As Taylor and I leave the Sung Wong Toi playground, we are met by a long promenade of tall white hoardings, ushering us on to the east, obscuring from our line of sight what lies just beyond. From the tops of the hoardings, the necks of cranes reach out into the sky, immobile and silent, in mimicry of the skyscrapers afar.

'So, this area should be the old airport of Hong Kong,' Taylor tells me.

'Here?'

'Yeah, this.' He points towards the hoardings. I cannot see any sign of an airport in the construction site. However, where it is obscured from view, it sticks out in the cartographic imagination. This was not the airport on Lantau Island where I landed in January. But still, my mind retains planimetric images of two long oblong shorelines breaching Kowloon Bay. These harsh geometric shapes fill in the bay and stand in contrast against the minor revisions of the shoreline in TST, where Ravi and I explored.

'Does the runway still exist?' I ask.

'Yeah, still exists. Maybe I'll show you,' Taylor pulls out his phone and opens Google Maps. Using his thumb and forefinger, he centres it on our current location.

'So, I think we are some, somewhere like there,' he traces the map with his fingers, 'there is the runway.'

He scrolls across the page.'

Yah, this one,' before tapping it and pinching the area in order to zoom out, 'Yeah. We are here. The runway.'

This is the site of the old Kai Tak Airport, infamous for its short runway, short turn during the landing sequence and proximity to residential buildings. It was built in 1925 to accommodate air traffic and underwent a number of extensions (to both the runway and the terminal area) and the addition of a new runway before its closure in 1998, and the opening of the Chep Lap Kok Airport on Lantau. The original platform of the airport was land reclaimed by two businessmen and then taken over the by government after the collapse of their venture. A slipway was built for seaplanes in 1928, and an aeroplane hangar and control tower in 1935. Then, in 1941, Hong Kong fell under Japanese occupation – and remained so for the rest of the Second World War. During this time, Hong Kong was a strategic base for the Japanese armed forces (demonstrated through their meticulous cartographies of the region). It is at this point that three spaces, Sung Wong Toi, Kai Tak Airport and the Kowloon Walled City, become interlinked through the restructuring and redistribution of space – as a resource, rather than a site of memory, of habitation, or of affect. The Japanese expanded Kai Tak, flattening Sung Wong Toi and demolishing an outer wall of the infamous Chinese walled city, purportedly for resources, but also to make way for further developments. In this period, relatively brief in comparison to the longevity of the site, Sacred Hill ceased to be a hill, and Sung Wong Toi was no longer a terrace. Even the walled city had lost one of its walls.

Yet, one of the blocks remained intact – that which Taylor and I saw earlier – and in 1945 the government built a small garden around it: 'a silent witness to Hong Kong's distant past and its early ties to imperial China' (Kwan and Kwan, 2008: 3), a ghost haunting the modernist future of air travel. By its close, Kai Tak was the third busiest airport in the world, in line with Hong Kong's economic role as a free port and trading hub in Asia. But capacity – the popular discourse of need and expansion – isn't the reason that Taylor gives for the relocation of the airport to Chep Lap Kok. Instead, he describes how the planes came so close to residential areas, close enough, he jokes, that you could see from the plane into the windows of the apartments on either side of the runway. There was a 'big noise', he says. This must have been incredible due to the proximity of the jets to the apartment blocks as the noise of millions of journeys roaring past, aurally intersecting with the everyday lives of people, Hong Kongers, in their kitchens and on their roofs, making their own everyday noises.

It's difficult to imagine how this airport once operated within the landscape – it is eerily quiet, and the hoardings eliminate any sense of distance or spatial relations between the vista before us, and what we saw on Taylor's map.

'It's amazing,' I say, indicating towards the airport, 'because you can see on the map but you can't ....'

'You can't!' Taylor jumps impressively high, attempting to see over the hoardings while I laugh.

'And so what are they doing with this now?'

'Uh,' he looks around. On one of the hoardings is an information panel – a combination of written and visual material outlaying the plans for the construction and development around us.

'So we can look at this card here. So, the ....' He pauses. In a strange repetition, of imagery, of imagination, the oblong shape of Song Wang Tai appears here, too.

'... the Song?' I supplement.

'The Song, yeah.'

The image appears embedded in a pastiche of other imagery. It is less a cartographic representation than an atmospheric visualisation (Rose et al., 2014), an image of the city (Lynch 1960) rather than a plan of it.

'And what's this park at the back here?' I query 'This building here?'

'I don't know,' Taylor hesitates. 'I think that this picture means that they want to mix the – uh – development part of Hong Kong and the historical part of Hong Kong together.'

I laugh.

'Right, okay.'

'Yeah, in here,' he points towards the image, and then gestures towards the construction sites all around us. 'So, it says that the development of, ah, the Shatin to Central link.'

'Yeah, okay.' The construction is for a new MTR line, running between the ever-growing commuter town of Shatin, in the north-east of the New Territories, and Central, on Hong Kong Island. In addition to this, the airport will be transformed into a new passenger cruise ship terminal, to accommodate influxes of Chinese passengers arriving by boat from Guangdong and Shanghai.

This landscape is almost entirely transformed now, the landscape that the Song overwritten by new stories and new etchings: 'The Sacred Hill is long gone; what remains is a piece of inscribed rock that tells the story of the loyalty of the Southern Song' (Hon 2011: 136).

Such etchings are more than text – they are embodied in the traces of paths that are made and mapped. A new set of journeys then, that tour through this space, by train and by boat, paths intersecting with one another. Gathering here, at this place, generations of journeys intertwine – stories that defy the fixed temporality of the map. Not quite palimpsests – such happenings do not just rewrite one another leaving faint traces of the lines that were traced before. Rather, they cohabitate, side by side, bubbling up and receding, silent in presence and vocal in absence. Sacred Hill defies the nature of cartographic reason because it no longer exists. Indeed, traces of it can be found in the names of roads and playgrounds, but it is not the lingering toponymy that gives it the power of mythology. As Taylor said: 'It has his name.' It is the story of the endpoint of a journey that links this place with the start of many others, like the journey undertaken by Taylor and me here, now, and in the future, past the Choi Hung Estate, half-completed freeways and on to the fishing village. Massey (2005) emphasises the role of 'flows' in time-spaces embedded the irreversibility of Bergson's time and the temporality of human experience. Flows intertwine travel through the world as they intersect with other journeys – and other stories – that gather, circling, in space. A haunting whirlpool of pasts and futures combine in this pocket of reclaimed waterfront – hills that cannot be resurrected and boulders that cannot be restored.

Time and space are not so separate in Cantonese or Mandarin. *Last* and *above* share no differentiation, and neither do *next* and *below*. Space-times/time-spaces are more complex and intertwined than the irreversible time of Bergson, or, conversely, the reversible time of Einstein and others. The countdown clock erected in Tiananmen Square, set for 30 June 1997, the date at which Hong Kong would be handed over to China, proposed a different view of time (Ren, 2010), one which in which repetition and regimentation become neo-liberal tools of the state, a Chinese imperial vision retraced across a vast distance. Cartographic reason measures space, but it can also take the chronological vision, the parcelling of space into fillable, productive segments (cf. Debord, 2010) and disperse it between near and far. Cartographic reason melds the past and the future together in space by way of a haphazard conquest, the loss of any cognitive map in an endless barrage of presentness (Jameson, 1991) that suggests the future is already built in the now, our journeys already laid out before us according to the discourses that structure our knowledge.

Staring at the strange pastiche of images on the information panel, and the brief description to the left, Taylor sniffs.

'So that's what I said,' he seems satisfied. 'They say we will have MTR here many years ago – later – many years later.'

## Camille/Mobilities

'... the GPS system in Hong Kong is hectic, you know.'

'It's loading,' Camille murmurs as she taps the grey screen on her smartphone. 'It's slow.' After a long moment (or two) that suspends our conversation in waiting, the screen flashes brightly, and orange and yellow lines start to form, pixelated, across the screen, cut through by a tentative blue line spanning the width of the app.

'Aberdeen Street,' she continues. 'I have sort of an idea of where Aberdeen Street is.' The screen becomes stuck in unreadable pixelation, and Camille pinches out the screen in an attempt to see the blue line in its entirety. 'Hurry up, hurry up.'

'Do you have good reception here?' I ask. *Here* is somewhere in the dark, multilevel labyrinth of Central Station (中環) on the island. Backed against a wall to avoid colliding with the hectic pedestrians pushing past, escalators block my view in two directions, and to our right, the bright eggshell light of *outside* makes it impossible to gauge how near the next building is.

'Mmm,' Camille replies. 'My connection is slow. Okay, there we are.' Her screen has suddenly come into focus, the zoom level of the map adjusting to the appropriate level of detail, large clusters of pixels sharpening into approximations of curves.

'Okay, we're in Central somewhere ... Exit A,' she pauses again and looks around. Hong Kong MTR stations often have a taxonomic system where each possible exit is labelled with a letter. Given the complexity of the MTR stations and the blurring between public and private spaces, it provides clarity to the skein of pathways structured in volumetric space, routing travellers out of the MTR according to their destination. They also offer a convenient meeting place – to meet at Central Station is not adequately specific, and if Camille had given me that instruction, we would never have found each other. Instead, Camille directed me to meet her at Exit C, at the bottom of some escalators leading up to a footbridge, and from there we walked into another building, and into this passageway, now somewhere near Exit A on Queen's Road. Staring at Camille's map, the relationship between the points is entirely unclear. I carefully followed the information panels on the station concourse to reach Exit C. These maps were presented in a multidimensional format – not the flat planimetric views used by the Google Maps on Camille's screen, but a volumetric depiction based on multiple levels (or planes) not dissimilar to the maps drawn in the Hong Kong guide *Cities without Ground* (Frampton et al., 2012). Between each level, escalators going up and down and spindling arms stretching out, appropriately lettered, for each exit.

Camille looks up from her phone and squints at the luminescent barrage between us and Queen's Road.

'So that's there,' she nods her head towards the light, 'And then we walk up some escalators.'

She falls silent again, looking at the screen, all the while scrolling and pinching the map interface.

'That's a tunnel.... The escalator goes all the way up here to Soho,' she points to the screen, 'and then we go west.' Suddenly, she raises her head abruptly and looks me in the eye. 'Okay!' She says emphatically.

'Okay!' I echo.

'Ya.'

She turns and starts walking out towards the light.

'Lead the way,' I smile as I follow her. 'Is that Exit A?'

'Yes'

Queen's Road is bright and busy – narrow footpaths teeming with pedestrians. The tactics of touring and detouring (De Certeau, 1984) happen in tandem, a negotiation ill-prepared and off the cuff as Camille moves smoothly between other pedestrians, and my shoulder gets bumped while I struggle to keep pace. Cracks and crevices in the pavement, signposts and poorly parked cars tumble into the comparative slowness of elderly residents, people walking while reading phones, and those struggling along with prams create arrhythmic patterns. De Certeau (1984) blames discourse for teaching people which way to go – establishing rhetorics of walking and turning as a mode of spatial organisation. At the same time, he describes how 'the long poem of walking' (De Certeau, 1984: 101) is manipulative: '[i]t creates shadows and ambiguities', reshaping spatial organisations, and 'selects and fragments the space traversed' (ibid.). As we stutter on, I see: those who move fast and slow, those who give way and those who do not – space is organised in the mode of movement, the thrum of objects in space, and spaces in objects. The distance between here on the street and the darkened thoroughfare, before, is not in length, not something that can be measured by the kilometres on the map, nor calculated into time spent journeying. The distance is found between two sets of pedestrian rhetorics, felt and embodied, the synchronicity of Camille's pirouettes compared to my ugly footsteps, movement against stillness. Discourse is elastic, at least if we accept that it orders as it draws lines, structures as it bounds spaces, and freezes as cartographic imaginations are cast in stone. Even in flux, in topological Leibnizian modes, cartographic reason is stretched but never broken, over the ethno-spatial assemblages that erode urban landscapes as soon as they are formed. This is the illusion of movement, an expansive reach that is extended from a centre point that nary twitches. Yet, as it approaches the edge of its reach, surely such a discourse must find itself favouring immobility: it is difficult to be subsumed into the map when other bodies collide into you, smashing your focus with opposing rhetorics, fragmenting your attention and casting doubt on your memory.

Camille does not come to Central for any reason other than work – thus she is not too familiar with the path that we have been instructed to take. Central is different, she explains – and there is not much here.

'Except for luxury brands – if you're into shopping, come to Central. Or if you want to go to bars and stuff, then Central, yes,' she frowns, 'because it somehow has a stronger Western culture in there, in Central.'

'Okay.'

'So it pretty much, it still feels pretty British, as compared to now.'

'Is it because there are more expats here?'

She considers this question seriously. 'Probably.'

'And does it feel different out in Sha Tin and TST?'

'Uh huh.'

'And Kowloon? I mean, if it feels Western here, how is it different to other places?'

'Umm ....'

'Is it about people, or is it about the space or ...?'

'I think it's about the people, and also the shops around here, they're all – I don't know – most of the stuff is written in English. I mean, in the whole Hong Kong everything is written in English but, um, I don't know, it just feels different. It just seems different. I'd say in TST, as compared to Central, TST has a stronger sense of tourism.'

'Yeah?'

'And there are more tourists – mainlanders – from going to, um, TST. Whereas in Central there are more Westerners coming here.'

'Okay.'

'And um, Westerners love to stay in Central, too, when they're visiting. Yeah. And say Shatin, Shatin used to be a – a very fun place for locals, but, um, all these shopping centres got renovated so there's lots of gold and lots of, I don't know, pharmaceutical stuff, to, uh, facilitate tourism, so it has changed a lot.'

She stops suddenly and stares up the hill, grazing the height of a nearby skyscraper with her eyes. She speaks, moving only her lips.

'Keep going straight.'

'Keep going this way? Or ...?' I trail off while I wait for her to finish her silent calculations. Her eyes flick back to me.

'Or we can,' she chuckles.' Yeah, keep going straight.'

As our footsteps fall into a rhythm again, we take up our conversation from its temporary suspension. I ask Camille what relationship space – or the lack thereof – in Hong Kong might have with the different impressions she feels in different areas.

'I think it's also about how businesses build their brand. Because space is very expensive in Hong Kong, so if you have lots of space, that means that you're a very well-off company.'

Space, in Camille's interpretation, is deeply intertwined with real estate. Hong Kong is small: the space of the SAR has already been bounded and bought. Space, it seems, can be consumed, an ostentatious display of wealth and power. A warped spatiality, then, entirely dichotomous for the always-open and full-of-potential space that Massey describes. What happens when space becomes land formed as a resource through the geographical imagination (Gregory, 1994), terrain, etched into territory through the cartographic imagination and episteme, given power through the formation of the discourse of cartographic reason. Yet, the archaeological traces of this thinking are not so clear-cut: cultural practices meld together, shifting, adapting, blossoming, under the encouragement of the global market.

'Do these tend to be Western companies?' I query blindly, stupidly.

'Uh,' she squeezes in between two people coming the other way, as someone crashes into me. 'I think so. European companies, especially with fashion and stuff like that. But if it's gold, then it's Hong Kong – local – companies.'

Ahead, spanning high across the width of Queen's Road, a set of two concrete footbridges, parallel to each other and the ground. Camille points to the footbridges without stopping, until we are almost under them.

'We're gonna go up there.'

'Up here?'

'Yes.' She grins and nods her head.

'Okay.' It is not obvious how we get up there, and it must have shown in my expression.

'But we'll figure out how to get up there,' she adds before we burst out laughing.

'That's always fun.'

'That's always fun. But it shouldn't be hard because,' another round of laughter, 'I assume it's easier to find places in Central.'

To our right, the Hang Seng Bank glows green with fluorescent light, the Dow Jones price indexes flashing rapidly on a screen.

'This is a footbridge that should link to some escalators,' remarks Camille.

I drag my eyes back towards the footbridge.

'Should?'

'Should.'

'And you know this from memory? Or ...?'

'Partially from memory, because I knew how to get to the escalator that way,' she points back towards the hill where she so intently gazed earlier, 'but through the footbridge, I don't think I've done it.'

'Okay.'

'Yep.'

'So you also have an idea, kind of, roughly how far?' I frown, remembering my walk with Vicki.

'Roughly.' she affirms.

The Hang Seng Index blinks brightly against our surroundings overcast by the footbridge. The light brings water to my eyes, making me wince, while Camille continues unfettered. *22285.70 today, at 16:01, up 322.81.* Into the bank we go, as Camille ushers us inside.

'This way I guess,' and then she stops, 'into a bank?'

She looks up and around. A set of escalators goes up left and down right between a platform suspended halfway up into the empty space above. On the platform several bank workers sit, typing earnestly on their computers. Security to our right eyes us suspiciously, as Camille looks around and sighs.

'... And, it doesn't go any further up.'

'Right,' I raise my eyebrows, 'okay.'

We exit the bank and immediately encounter another set of escalators.

'Here we go,' Camille points to a sign just near the foot of the first: 'To Footbridge. Walkway.'

'This is the right level of "up"?'

'Yes,' She looks resolutely pleased, "Cos it only goes up one level there, instead of two levels.' We come to the end of the escalator, '... I think.'

Another set appears, continuing it's upward run facing the opposite direction. Camille glances ruefully back towards the bank.

'Is it also hard to tell what is a bank or a shop, and what is public space?' I ask.

'Ah – there has been an argument, earlier. You know Times Square in, um, Causeway Bay? They used to block all this open area, and then said it's part of the Times Square, so you're not allowed to stay here. You're not allowed to stand here or smoke here or do anything, because it's part of the shopping centre. But then, um, some architect, sort of, looked through the documents and said, "Hey, no, that's a public space."'

'Ah, okay.' Times Square shopping centre bleeds across levels. It draws directly from the underground Causeway Bay Station through a network of tunnels lines with luxury fashion stores, fans out into a massive forecourt adorned with a clock and large digital screens and rises upwards in a multilevel shopping centre with well-known restaurants.

'It's only that they've decorated it so that it looks like parts of the Times Square.'

'Right.

'And then, somehow use it – and then now, it's open area. Again. Looks like part of Times Square.'

The conversation about public space in Times Square is a discursive space in which cartographic reason, mobility and 'the image of the city' (Lynch, 1960) collide. Moving, as both Debord (2010) and De Certeau (1984) have argued, is structured in part by the shape of the city – lines on paper auguring streets and buildings, coloured streaks denoting main thoroughfares and roads, and facilitating certain modes of touring and navigating urban space. However, they both also argue that detouring, with all the strategies and tactics employed by pedestrians or travellers, can also be a mode of resistance to the hegemony of the urban plan. However, the cartographic shapes of the mobilities fostered by Times Square are multidimensional and multi-rhythmical, less underscored by the potency of the urban plan than in moderating speed, preventing stopping and controlling how, where and when people flow through the networks of the building. Boundaries in the cartographic imagination – lines that exist elsewhere in planning archives and on architectural documents – are instead installed into the material flows of the city through situated visual cues – as Camille noted, 'looks like parts of the Times Square'. This visual legibility is in the same spirit as the 'image of the city': a coherent, accessible and most importantly, readable visual system that aids navigation and wayfinding, and invokes (or even constructs) urban atmospheres, the *feel of a place*. Under this system of legibility, differential mobilities can be gathered together in space and homogenised under a bounding practice. Once homogenised, once space is transformed into something less open and with limited possibility, even mobility can be calculated and controlled: the fast pace of the commuting pedestrian transformed into the slower pace of the window shopper, and the even slower movements of the customer; the speed of the lifts rising 20 storeys high (or more), relaxed into the seated focus of the diner and the patient stillness of those who wait for, and in, the elevator.

Camille and I walk through the old market hall at the base of the escalators. On the outside wall sits a visual rendering of parkland in Hong Kong, replete with open green space. In the middle, a woman wanders between the leafy outcrops. At some point, an unknown orator, keen to have their voice heard, has stuck a speech bubble emanating from the small woman in the middle. 'Where has my dream city gone?' it reads, echoing the discussion that Camille and I have just broken off, and foregrounding a more extended debate about the role of private and public interests in Hong Kong. Mobility is tangled in this mess: Hong Kong is a city that values movement – of people, of transport, of goods and capital. It is, and it has been, a free trade port, a door to China and the East, a node in a colonial network, a super-dense hypermodern city, with massive trade movement in and out. These are descriptions that evoke the way in which mobility has *always* been key to the constitution of Hong Kong: in journeys, from Song emperors to British colonials across the empire to Chinese immigrants and now mainland tourists; in trade, from opium, to cargo, to people; in capital; from the HSBC to the Bank of China; and also displacement, from the early Hakka tribes to the Harbour itself.

Peculiar, but not unique, to this discussion, is the role of cartographic reason. Cartographic reason, like other discursive formations, traces itself into material landscapes from the geometric imagination to the lines on the map, to the terrain. Times Square has carved itself into public space regardless of the map: its bounding practices are not drawing lines by creating consumers. Times Square adopts the lines lingering from previous material interventions by planners and cartographers and rebrands them as consumer spaces, demarcated by new forms of visual coherence. Cartographic reason finds itself adept at adaption: new forms of colonisation by private space, new modes of calculation and control.

Inside the building, Camille points to a small art installation on our right-hand side. In contrast to the small shops closed for the New Year on our left, roller doors rolled right down, padlocks hanging off their clasps. To our right is a wooden platform with art hanging off the walls, and small palms and benches on which to sit.

'This is a fun place, because, uh, they sort of build this to show local art and stuff,' Camille says.

'What was here before?'

She indicates towards the shops on our left.

'Just like that.'

'Just like these shops?'

'It looks better – they tried to put some plants in there because there is a lack of plants in Hong Kong, there's no greens in Hong Kong.'

The light outside assaults us as we move outside the market building.

'Yay, another bridge, and then escalators,' Camille smirks, taking out her phone. 'Let me check how far up we have to go.'

We move from the footbridge to the first of the escalators. Ghosts of the walk that Vicki and I took resonate against the plastic moving arm rails, and I can almost hear our conversation echo against my memory.

'How far up?' I ask. Not how far, or how long, or even how far along we have to go – it is the decisive *up* in Camille's statement that intrigues. As in all the conversations I have had in Hong Kong, *up* is a distinct and persistent undertone. *Up* suggests a specific kind of mobility – a journey that ambles up contours, a path that moves from two-dimensional etchings to three-dimensional embodiments, and four-dimensional tracings. *Up* disrupts the planimetric view of mobility augured by the flat Cartesian coordinate system, by adding a third: $x$, $y$ and $z$. It decentres the omniscient viewpoint of (0, 0, 0) by developing relational gazes with relational cartographies: from up there to up here, down there to down here. Camille stares at her phone, and then arches her neck, looking past the confines of the escalator system to the street two storeys (or more) below.

'We are ...,' she says, searching and straining her eyes. 'That's Stanley Street and Stanley Street is ....' Back to the screen, a shorter focus, a flatter landscape. '...somewhere.' She finds it and shows me.

'Stanley Street.' I check the street name below. (A glimpse of Daren in the market catches the corner of my eye.)

'Okay.'

'So we're going up Stanley Street and then, from here ...,' she shows me on her phone, tracing her finger up the length of the line symbolising the escalator on the screen, as the background scrolls with her, 'and then we are going up Wellington Street then,' people rush to overtake us, racing up the escalator, as Camille squints at the screen trying to make out the label of the next street, 'then that street, and then Hollywood Road,' she zooms in on the screen again, 'and that's Hollywood Road, which we get off there and then walk that way,' she smudges the screen with her finger, 'and then walk up.'

The path mapped out before us along the screen, an illusion of the imaginary, left only for us to embody it. The transition from points, to lines, to flows and fluidities – from the topological to the material – translates discourse into experience, while also complicating it. As Serres takes pains to remind us: something is always lost in the process of translation. Paradoxes abound in the upward plane: not moving and yet moving by standing still on the escalators, looking down to see which street we pass while trying to discern how to go up, faster in stillness than in movement. Below us, the streets disappear into a near horizon, lost under the geometries of the escalator system.

'This is Wellington Street,' Camille points downwards. 'This is good. We're in the right direction.'

'In the right direction.' I join the smile in her voice, bewildered as to how we could go any other way.

'And these escalators are interesting cause, like, in this hour, it goes up. After office hours, it goes down, so that all these office people can go to the MTR station.'

The escalators, it seems, are not unidirectional. Mobility must be managed, accommodating the movement of people, and in a vertical space that is up and down, as well as left and right, to and fro.

'I don't know the exact times, but they do have times,' Camille offers further. As with Times Square, mobility becomes a site of categorisation,

Figure 11.3. *Choreographies.* Camille looks at her phone while travelling the Central-Mid-Levels escalator and walkway system. Since the GPS does not work, she triangulates her position with the street signs below as she moves past them.

calculation and control according to discourses and processes invisible in the fabric of the city.

'How do you know the times – is there a website? Or do you just know?'

'I have no idea,' Camille raises an eyebrow.

'It's one of those things where people in Hong Kong find out stuff without ever knowing how to find that,' I say, laughing, as Camille smirks.

'That.'

'Yep.'

'I think they should have signs somewhere, but I have no idea where. I've seen something, somewhere. But I can't recall. Yep.'

We walk from one escalator to the next, stilted by the sudden change in pace and the use of our legs rather than the mechanical mover whisking us along.

'You know what I find weird – you know from airports to wherever, you have all these escalators type of thing, but they aren't stairs – they're just flat,' she frowns, looking at the next set rising in front of us. 'Kind of like these ones. They're flat, too.'

I laugh, nodding at the escalators before us.

'They do at least go on a slope.'

'Yep, but those are just on flat land.'

On the next escalator, the streets move swiftly below us.

'Uhhh – okay. We just passed that street, and we're going ... this should be Hollywood Road and then we're going' – she makes a curving motion with her hand, like Taylors and Tanija's – 'that way .... We can only turn that way. And then get off the escalators – elevator – footbridge, keep walking straight and then left. At some point.'

She follows the route with her thumb, checking down again to see where we are.

'I notice you're not using the blue dot,' I say.

'I'm not using a ...?'

'You're not using the little blue dot that tells you where we are.'

''Cos I didn't open my GPS.'

''Cos other people have said that it's useless?'

'I find that.'

''Cos it's never exactly where you want it?'

'GPS, the GPS system in Hong Kong is hectic, you know, they have tried to make it better and better but they can't because we have too many buildings.' Camille affirms what Daren had said before, standing not too far away on Stanley Street.

'Yeah.'

'And they can't detect exact location.'

'So, we seldom use it here. It's getting better, but still, it's not totally 100% accurate.'

Off the escalators again.

'So, this is Hollywood Road.'

'Okay, going down.'

'Going down.'

As we descend back into the busy swarm of Hollywood Road, where pedestrians and trucks swerve through the road, we stop briefly outside the same teashop that Daren brought to my attention. The disparity between the moderated bi-directional flows of the escalators – standing still going up to the east, walking down the stairs to the west – and the hectic scatter of the divergent, oppositional, frictional asynchrony is marked, least by the ache in my legs. Motioning back towards the escalators, I laugh with Camille, telling her how I appreciate the lengths Hong Kong goes to in order to enable my laziness. She laughs out loud, attracting the brief attention of those passing by.

'Because we have to save up our energy for work. For overtime work.'

It's a grim view that mobility comes to resemble efficiency. In this resemblance, the vast networks of escalators, travelators, interlocking levels and public/private osmosis simply serve the mobility of higher up the food chain: labour, objects, capital.

Small restaurants and food stalls adorn the laneways that branch off the main road, gathering places hidden from the surveillance of the cartographic gaze. Camille tells me how she prefers to eat here, rather than the massive chain stores that can be seen dotted throughout Hong Kong.

'And because we have all these chain shops. The local community in Hong Kong is trying to support little shops, not the chain shops, so they don't die. Because it's very difficult to survive in Hong Kong – Aberdeen Street, phew.'

Our final destination arrives, situated high at the top of the hill. It is difficult to survive in Hong Kong – to know when to stop and hold against the barrage of flows and when to move, to catch the backwind of the crowd and use it to bolster you forward. The mobilities in Hong Kong are scalar – a fundamental point of geometries, an apex in geometries of power. Big to small, near to far, fast to a standstill, material to abstract – the movement between extremes map onto the cartographic limits of the dash and the line. How precisely this unfolds is yet to be determined, but the lines are drawn in the sand and are now reaching into the air and deep into the ground, and all that is left for us to trace them and see where they lead.

## Magdalena/Senses

'I need to walk the city through, you know, right?'

Magdalena and I meet on the northern shore of Hong Kong Island, at the Janus face of land and sea near the many ferry piers that stitch between the two sides. She greets me where I wait, underneath the shade of Central Pier dwarfed by the nearby International Finance Centre. A crisp winter breeze caresses my shoulders and paints white tips on the harbour waves that, in turn, glint under the sunlight sneaking through the smog. Behind me, a white wall is cut in two by a shadow (sun on one side, shade on the other). The shadow strikes through words written in black which say: '7 – Star Ferry Pier'. This is the pier to TST, on the other side of the Victoria Harbour. It is a popular trip, run via the iconic Star Ferry, and significantly cheaper than the MTR that travels along a very similar path between Central and TST.

Proposals for the removal/relocation of the piers on the Central side of Victoria Harbour have been met with fierce controversy (Ku, 2012; Ng et al., 2010). The Star Ferry Pier appears older than it is, partly due to the arrival and departure of the vintage ferries and the old-fashioned put-put-put sound they make as they surf across the water. Even from a distance, the small bottle-green ferries stand out against the waves, two storeys high and packed with travellers whose faces are pressed up against the interior glass. Mirroring the ferries, the pier consists of two storeys of round columns at even intervals, interspersed with fencing along the sides and connected by a contemporary staircase and long ramps in the same bottle green as the ferries themselves. We walk along the lower level of the pier, quickly and fluidly, with barely enough time to catch a glimpse of the posters and promotions pasted on the poles.

'For me, that was the only way to get to know Hong Kong when I came here. I need to walk the city through, you know, right? I once asked people directions, but once I know this is there ....' Magdalena waves her hands about; her black smartphone clutched tightly in her left fist.

'You're able to figure it out?'

'Yeah, absolutely.'

Instincts are at the forefront here, as the familiar beep of Octopus cards being registered on barcode machines signals our increasing proximity to the gates and the ferry terminal beyond. Already near the barriers, Magdalena whisks me towards them and the jetty beyond while laminated signs funnel us into gates according to our mode of payment. Magdalena does not miss a step as she flows through the Octopus card gate gracefully – perhaps she even speeds up – talking constantly and gesticulating enthusiastically.

A small black fan hangs from the ceiling of the pier, turned off and stationary in the winter chill, not blowing the faintest breeze across the information board that charts the history of the Star Ferry Pier. This pier is the fourth generation of piers built on the south side of Victoria Harbour. Each new pier has saddled a new shore, as the slow encroachment of the land into the sea has been mapped by new iterations of land reclamations. Before 1985, 33 sq. km of reclamations were carried out (Ning et al., 2010), with a total of 60 km by 1996, almost the same again (Survey and Mapping Office, 1996). The first Star Ferry Pier was built in 1890 to accommodate mobility between Kowloon and Hong Kong Island, primarily for local Chinese residents. It was located where Central Station now lies beneath the ground several hundred metres away. It is difficult to imagine the water lapping beneath my feet at the same spot where Camille and I stood and searched for our path up into Soho. Shorelines are not fixed – they are spaces of transition, a blurring between elements as sand is mixed in the wash of waves. Yet, the process of making maps is the process of etching out fixed lines, even where there were none before. Pickles (2004) describes how the drawing and reading of a line produce dialectical images: here/there, inside/outside, near/far. The fixity of the line between shore and sea is no different: the lines of cartographic reason are etched first into the imagination, and then into the landscape. And so, in Hong Kong, we see this space of elemental osmosis erased on the map and then reduced in material flexibility as walls of earth are built into and stabilised against the shifting fluidity of the sea. Cartographic reason does not merely structure how people move in Hong Kong, but it also structures how landscapes move (and, indeed, even moves landscapes itself).

The ferry has not yet arrived, and passengers gather around the clear barrier while they wait. Magdalena directs us right up to the gate. She wants to be one of the first to get on, and as the ferry pulls up beside us and docks, the last load of passengers begin to disembark. She watches impatiently as more people gather near us, the familiar push of a crowd worrying our backs. We hold our ground and Magdalena keeps talking animatedly.

'I was in love in Hong Kong before – you know, I used to live in Mainland China.'

'Yep.'

'So, I would visit to work for a few days, or just to visit friends here but ... so I was in love in Hong Kong. And I felt, "Wow, I really start to leave Mainland and get married to Hong Kong," but actually I think I've changed ....'

The gate opens and Magdalena bustles us down onto the ferry in a hurry. Stepping quickly over the gangway, she turns left and chooses a seat in the centre of the front section of the lower deck. Gradually the seats around us start to fill, and as I sit on a bench facing backwards towards her, I nudge her on back to our previous conversation.

'You've changed?'

'I've changed – so this place is no longer appealing to me, you know?'

Magdalena moved from Mainland China to study for a master's degree at the University of Hong Kong. Looking back out towards the water, she stares at the reclamations being made as part of the West Kowloon Cultural District, before casting her eyes back towards 2 IFC, which stands towering over the small ferry terminal.

'I think the city is really about money. And this is unbelievable.'

It does seem unbelievable, but then, as our conversation with Ravi revealed – Hong Kong has always been about money for some. Jacobs (1996) argues that the cities at the edge of empires were, in a way, the first global cities. These were cities that were not necessarily designed to stand on their own but, rather, were created in service to a vaster network of movement, trade and production, resources that eventually flowed from periphery to centre.

Like Sydney, Hong Kong was built looking outward, after it was surveyed looking inward; the first infrastructure introduced by new settler-colonials was dotted around the coastline while they built up the wealth and capability to move further into the centre. The shoreline acts as a kind of mediator between settlement and movement – a site of contestation. The second ferry pier constructed in 1912 was a grander affair. The previous terminal was a slightly ramshackle building comprised of a large triangle-roofed shed with the words 'Central Ferry Terminal' painted in large letters. It looked much like the first iteration of the Kai Chek Airport – slapdash and temporary, as if it couldn't quite believe that it was here to stay. This new terminal, however, had a massive arched glass window, and a strong awning to protect travellers in the rain. It was a typical design of the period and of colonial Hong Kong, light and airy and constructed to let the treasured crosswinds breeze through. It sat at the bottom of Ice House Street, not far north-east from Central Station, at the near-exact cusp between the flat foreshore and the rise of the mountain peaks.

This new pier was a space conceived by planners and cartographers, in the most Lefebvrian terms (Ng et al. 2010) – one in which the conflict and tensions of race and rights to the city conflicted against the potential for a lived space on the waterfront. Stationed along a wide and bright promenade, Queen's Road, the pier was at home amongst the austere banks and merchant houses typical of a port city and a trading post at the periphery of the British Empire. These neighbourly buildings where inherent to the way that the new pier was conceived – as part of an urban plan, as well as a statement about the role of the ferry in the new empire connecting East and West. Its design was also predicated upon the axiomatic and colonial assumption – as we have seen already in our mappings of Hong Kong – that there were two distinct societies in Hong Kong: British and Chinese (Ng et al. 2010). This has not entirely changed – Camille spoke sincerely of the difference between the Chinese and the expatriate sections of Hong Kong, and even now, as Magdalena explains that the island mostly has everything that she needs and it is only now after five months that she has begun to explore further afield.

Magdalena scrunches her nose.

'People can be so locked in this monochromatic world.'

It's a wonderful phrasing, and as the waves move but the ferry does not, it encourages me to consider in spatial terms, how shorelines, too, may act as locks. Shorelines are the masters of monochrome and on the page they are the incarnation – perhaps even the absolute simplification – of the Sassurean Bar (cf. Olsson, 1991b) that suggests that A = B. The first scientific maps made after the Convention of Chuenpi in 1841 by Captain Sir Edward Belcher were naval maps – this, as we saw with Cliff in Botany Bay – is reasonably usual in colonial maps as most colonies were approached by the sea. Belcher's maps showed considerable scientific detail of the interior of the island but were, however, fixated on the shoreline, on what Empson

(1992) calls 'the shape of Hong Kong'. Shape, in this case, is a planimetric view, which outlines the edginess of an island, a roving geometry, the closing of a single line to make a figure. The shape of the island is the shoreline built through careful surveys and triangulations – but, until air travel, is rather imagined. Early Chinese maps of the Pearl River Delta, too, inscribed the shape of the island – yet, as noted earlier in this book, the grids of the Chinese probably had more influence from the gridded writing systems than any mathematical faith towards Aristotelian logic. Even the viewpoint that Vicki and I had, staring down at the island from the saddle that leads up to Victoria Peak, did not have that perfect flat perspective, without vanishing points or horizons, which typifies Belcher's planimetric etchings. So, we can say something happened when the first lines of the shore of Hong Kong Island and Kowloon[3] were inscribed according to the logics of longitude and latitude.[4] Yet, despite geometric precision, the line between shore and sea is an imagined line – a barrier that represents an incursion from outside. This is then reflected in the strange duality of society recast into the space between Chinese and British residents. Furthermore, once the power of the line begins to surpass the power of the shore, the point at which the map has become the territory, with careful surveys, that line can then be moved – one hundred feet, or two hundred, or three hundred or more.

The shoreline in Hong Kong, in its every iteration, is a question of the process of colonisation. Since the time when the Ice House Road ferry pier was built, new shadows have risen along this shoreline, far further out into the harbour and far taller than anything imagined at the beginning of the twentieth century. Shorelines fix imaginations – creating boundaries and differences – yet shorelines are not fixed in the imagination. This is the role cartographies play in shaping the world – and in Hong Kong, cartographies are often about cartographic reason and parcelling the landscape into single unit commodities that can be bought and sold. Passengers shuffle on the ferry and stare out at the harbour around them. A high-pitched whistle is made, and then the ferry is released from the dock. It rocks against the side of the pier, making the Magdalena slide softly in her seat. Unlike the MTR which is dotted with digital screens, being on the ferry is a wondrously analogue adventure.

3 Belcher refers to Kowloon as 'Cowloon', but it has been changed here for consistency.

4 An earlier map by Alexander Dalrymple produced in 1780 also shows the entire outline of the island, however, interestingly, no longitude is noted. For more information on this, see Hall Empson's excellent *Mapping Hong Kong* (1992).

'There are moments when I walk through Victoria Road .... I don't know if you've ever been there?'

I shake my head, bewildered at the sudden change in topic.

'So, it's next to Kennedy Town, and, like, I go from Kennedy Town to the south, through – ah – along the Sand Bay. Then you look,' she smiles and holds up her smartphone. 'I'll show you pictures in a second – you're just so grateful that you have this chance of being here because it's so stunningly beautiful.'

Later in 1957, another Star Ferry Pier was built in a modernist style, designed by local architect Hung Yip Chan. The pier stood tall with two wharves striking out on other side and a tall monolithic clock tower in the middle. It was further out to the north-east again, this time near the bottom of where Edinburgh Street and it came to be known as Edinburgh Street Ferry Pier. There is an emphasis, in the urban plan, on flat land where wide streets and freeways can be built to accommodate and direct the flow of the urban population. Despite the leasing of Kowloon across the water, Hong Kong had flat land short in supply.

Another whistle and the ferry engines switch from a hum to a roar. Slowly, it takes off from the pier, and I am overcome by a strange feeling of vulnerability as we are cast off from the steadfast shore. Boats were a way of life when I was growing up, but I never quite managed the uneasy sense of the aqueous uncertainty that moves between the boat and the seabed. To see a surface that is not firm, and to not be able to see what lies beneath is a dizzying feeling – at odds with the comfort of the map. Comprehending the bathymetric meaning of the small numbers dotted along the coastlines of Belcher's maps is difficult. How can such numbers be interpreted into the rivulets and trenches shaped by the harbour currents? Under this unsteady green ferry lies an element that defies cartographic reason, and still puts up one of the fiercest challenges to the shifts that are enforced into its domain. The pollution and sedimentary disturbance of reclamation practices cause temporary pollution, lasting long enough to fundamentally alter the way that the seabed functions, but short enough that the upheaval of silt does not make it onto the map. The life of the bottom of the sea is disbanded for the purposes of those who live above it.

Pondering this, I ask Magdalena why she is not headed to Mong Kok using the MTR. It is quicker and easier – although perhaps not as scenic. As the words tumble out of my mouth, Magdalena's facial expression becomes increasingly earnest and she shakes her head vigorously.

'Whatever the experience is, I want to go through it.' She makes a surfing motion with her hand – the same kind that others have used to describe a path they see in their head.

To go through an experience, for Magdalena, is not to go under it – to channel beneath the surface sitting in a purpose-built capsule, the monotony only broken up by the colourful livery of the MTR stations. For Magdalena, to go through an experience is exertive and embodied, performative and most importantly *active*.

'I have a hard relationship with Hong Kong, but I'm not giving up,' she exclaims, 'I want to *be* in the city. I want to feel it, you know.'

I do know – it's similar to Daren's ethos of wanting to see what's happening on the ground, and Nick's sentiment of feeling his way through. This emotion is challenging to express – yet in its incalculability, its inability to be reasoned, there is a kind of resistance to the monitored, ordered, managed and controlled environments enacted (once in naval charts and now in mobile phones) by those who favour cartographic reason. The bathymetry of Belcher does not capture the lurching sensation of the ferry – its depths focus on a more stable metric. Neither does the pale blue of the map on the smartphone (severed by a blue navigational line) control or make constant the speed at which the ferry slowly rises and quickly sinks. Yet, when you have only spent five months in a city you must have a way of finding your destination – feeling is important, crucial even, but Hong Kong is a city that is fast, and like Camille and I found, wrong turns are easy to make. Magdalena smiles when I inquire further as to how she gets actually around and takes a breath before responding.

'I usually have my destination, okay, I go *somewhere*.' Her emphasis is on the final word, *somewhere*. Like Ravi, Magdalena is a person who has destinations – but it is the path that interests her, not necessarily the final result.

'I know where is it – well, um, now I'm pretty much familiar with the city. But, in the beginning, I would just Google – Google Map – the place. I would look at the map,' she traces an invisible map like it was on an upward screen or information board, 'and I have the map here,' she holds up her phone, 'on my smartphone but somehow it's more complicated from my point of view to use this one – though I've learned to use this one, too. So anyway, once I reach my destination, and I still have time, I just walk around randomly, you know? I just look around – okay, you know – follow my instincts, or follow the light.'

To 'follow the light', another strange tendency without a proper vocabulary. As Magdalena says this, the light shines off the water and hits the glass windows and the metal seats of the ferry. Again, it's easy to see what she means. The feel of a place – much as Ben described it back in Sydney – has much to do with light, from cool green parks to bright open spaces. As Ravi noted, the light of a place also has to do with the sun and the water, and Nick, the shadow it casts from the hills. The light is a navigational tool – and in Hong Kong, it strikes me that Victoria Harbour retains a peculiar prismatic light that bounces between water, glass and steel. Even at night, when the light show on the harbour is reflected back into the sea, light has an integral part to play in comprehending the sense of a place. The maps that Magdalena looks at on Google Maps have a different light, directed through screens and circuits, in a material-virtual choreography (Cubitt et al., 2015). The history of digital and media geographies – from computing, digital media, screen studies, new media, sensors and smart cities – starts with the development of manufactured light, developed in tandem in the nineteenth century with industry and urbanism. The gas lamp, the daguerreotype, the magic lantern, the electric lamp, the absorption of light into film, and its projection through film onto screens or paper, the illuminations, the use of light for telegraphy, radio signals, switches, lidar, remote sensing, facial recognition, touchscreens: light – as Cubitt et al. (2015) have argued – is essential to digital technology. Edensor (2015) describes the world as being in a state of 'ubiquitous illumination', spurred on by the surveillent apparatus of the modern city. Darkness, on the other hand, is home to seedy, resistant, Indigenous or deviant practices, decried by the bourgeoisie. The spectacle of illumination is a modern spectacle – bound in narratives of technological progress, affective or auratic media, and capitalist consumption. From the gas lamp, to the neon tube, the projection, the LED, the LCP, the plasma screen, the touch screen: different forms of light have interrupted the darkness, and recast stranger and stranger shadows into the world.

A grinding noise captures Magdalena's attention, and we realise that the ferry has embarked at TST and we hadn't noticed. Quickly, Magdalena rises to her feet and sweeps past the passengers waiting patiently for the gangway to be lowered. As is does, she hurries me off quickly and sets off on foot again at top speed. It was an incredibly short journey across the harbour – eight minutes to be specific. One hundred years ago, just shortly after the pier at the end of Ice House Road was built, this journey would have taken nearly twice as long. However, decades of reclamations, particularly since the Second World War, have made their impact on more than just the shape of Hong Kong. This whole area near Kowloon is a site of reclamation – and with every set of proposed reclamations comes new sites of controversy for those wishing to preserve Hong Kong's environmental and cultural heritage.

Magdalena is encountering Hong Kong at the point where it is one of the world's most global cities, with financial, commercial and logistical

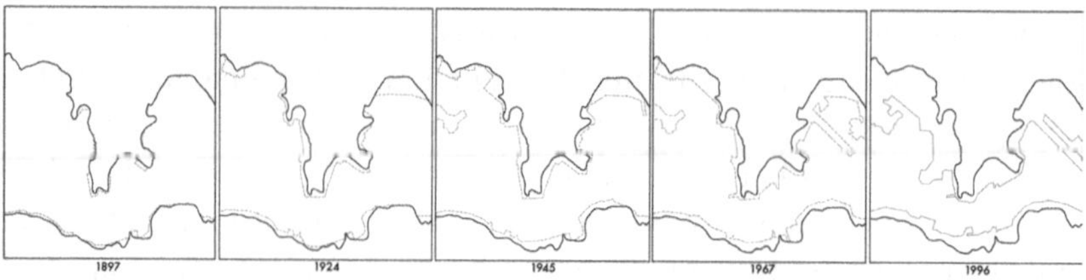


Figure 11.4. *Stabilisations.* This figure depicts progressive land reclamation in Hong Kong from 1841 to 1996. Source: Data from the Hong Kong SAR Survey and Mapping Office.

trade pouring in and out every day. These landscapes, along the northern shore of Hong Kong Island and Nathan Road, have undergone significant transformation – not least the billowing reclamations into the harbour that render our ferry journey five minutes shorter than it was in 1900. It must feel strange for those who have lived decades in Hong Kong and take this journey often that their walking time is gradually lengthened across the reclaimed ground and their time sitting on the ferry is ever more shortened.

As we step out from the pier, a small man wearing an orange robe is playing Hare Krishna. Magdalena points him out to me without stopping.

'That guy is always here.'

He's a familiar face for me too – or at least a familiar sound. The music he plays travels up the audio tunnels created by the landscape around TST, and every time I have found myself at the cultural centre or chasing something down along the shores of the Kowloon Peninsula, I can often hear wafts of his music.

'Do you go to Mong Kok very often?' I ask Magdalena curiously.

'No,' she replies, 'it's a new discovery, actually.'

Prior to the handover, Abbas (1997) described Hong Kong not as a culture, but as an economy. Post-1997, Chu (2013: 3) describes Hong Kong as 'caught in a paradox' between culture and economy. Its status of a global city, an East-West entrepôt, becomes increasingly tenuous:

> When China surpasses Hong Kong in terms of capitalism, Hong Kong culture can no longer retain its special role between China and the world – at that point, China has become the world. Hong Kong's singular, ambiguous but prolific existence has changed. And the loss of 'in-betweenness' fuzzes the edges, shifts the foci and alters the shape of its cultural identity. (Chu, 2013: 3)

A liminal boundary that appears less porous on the map than it is on the landscape, the harbour is also a fuzzy edge. Before the leasing of the Kowloon

Peninsula, it was a space of cross-cultural encounter, a liquid boundary between China and Britain. Then, the boundary was moved to the northern edge of the Kowloon Peninsula, cemented into a street named Boundary Road. Foreshore reclamations have changed its shape, and now it has become a place of spectacular lightshows as millions stare out across it every year. Spaces of action are equally fuzzy: it becomes more urgent to shape out what Hong Kong means as old knowledge disintegrates into fast experience that hides the cynicism towards non-conformity (Hui and Lau, 2015).

Spaces that do not change become liminal – one, two, three times removed from their origins. Even Magdalena's experience in mainland China has not fully prepared her for the vertiginous barrage of the busyness of Hong Kong that Ravi so embraced. In Hong Kong, pasts become present in palimpsestic form (Huyssen, 2003). Never entirely erased, colonial residues become integrated into the global gaze and consumption of urbanity that now characterises Victoria Harbour.

'I think ...,' she starts, 'I kind of have a feeling in Hong Kong that everything is fake, you know, that – maybe it's the amount, the number of people living here. Again, it's my first big city, like really big city experience. So, prices for food – you know, for a bowl of noodles, in Mainland you pay 6 yuan. Here, 20! You feel – I know the rent and everything, but *this* bowl of noodles should be cheaper. And you know this. And it's – I think – my guess is that the more people live in the one place, you know, this number creates different layers, you know, that distance us from what is basic – from what is really needed, you know?'

'Yeah?'

'I feel far away from my basic needs here, you know? Well, I can experience them every day, but people are distracted here.'

Magdalena is dancing around a more complicated issue here – emanating from her experiences of Hong Kong's complex and rapid spatiality. It is difficult to explain it on paper – the speed of change, of development and of the refiguring of the landscapes is not only, as Abbas (1997) suggests, a culture of disappearance, but a celebration of it (Botz-Bornstein, 2012). In Hong Kong, after 1997 and the economic crash of 1998, cultures folded inwards whilst looking outwards. Erni (2001) describes this as a turn towards China in the wake of Hong Kong's instability and China's strong economic growth. The rate of growth and decay in Hong Kong is mercurial, as money flows in and out of its financial centres and the rest of 'everything' rushes to keep up and to make change (Ortmann, 2015). In this space, Magdalena has chosen an anachronistic way of negotiating this speed. Her desire to walk, but not necessarily to slow down, mirrors the remnants of a colonial past that embody the landscape and the flows around her. She uses cynicism against itself, persisting in being liminal where Chu (2013) says that liminality might disintegrate. This is the privilege of the outsider. But it can appear within, too. The clock tower and the Star Ferry Terminal (both anachronisms in the shift towards hypermodern landscapes and rapid mass-transit) become steadfast. Palimpsests, they adapt to change, and maintain their historical roles from an older modernity: telling the time and moving people across the harbour.

Now, as we walk down Nathan Road, the scale of these restructures becomes clearer as the out-of-reach high-capital space of the harbour is replaced by the tangible retail space of the street. Neon signs crowd out into the empty space of the road, tumbling over one another to claim any advertising space that is left. The 'mansions' of the 1950s, the remnants of the first wave of post-war immigration, sit side by side with towering glass skyscrapers that have restaurants on the 26$^{th}$ floor. People are, as she said earlier, 'locked in a monochromatic world'. So, Madgalena walks everywhere, lives in paradoxes, and maps intuitively.

On the ferry, Magdalena told me that she might look up somewhere on Google Maps to get a general idea of where it is, but usually once she arrives, she prefers to 'walk around', follow her instincts and 'get a sense of the place'. One way is to embed herself into the landscape on her own terms, by discovering at her own pace. Passing by the Survey and Mapping Office on Nathan Road, she tells me about a recent walk she took through one of the vast protected country parks that constitutes the majority of the region. She walks often, seeking the solitude of the New Territories.

'I had a very interesting, a very beautiful experience, actually, two weeks ago. I went to hike – to Lantau – and suddenly, we were in the, uh, sylvan area, you know, the forest, and I heard birds, and … I cried. I thought, "Oh, my god," birds. I was so deeply moved by this …' – she squints at the overcrowded signs of Nathan Road – '… natural experience, right, I would never think in my life – past life – that the birds singing would touch me so deeply because it was so normal thing to hear, so, yeah.'

She pauses as I laugh.

'In Kunming, I was living in a neighbourhood with a lot of trees and everything. And my parents, they have a villa with, you know, a huge garden – every evening you would hear birds. And suddenly I found myself, wow, *birds*, long time no hear …,' a small smile flickers, 'and then I talked to some of my classmates and some of my friends, and yeah – I'm not the only one who has had this experience with birds.'

Liminal phenomena persist in small, shared experiences, in poignancy and self-deprecation. The fluctuating and disintegrating forces of Hong

Kong are not totalising, and cartographic reason cannot entirely erase terrains into a tabula rasa. The palimpsestic landscape still lingers, by definition, never fully erased. Sacred hills might become small monuments, but they still bear names of the complex entrepôt that this region has always been. Away from this hypervisibility, invisible ghosts also exist, borne through special memories based in the persistence of people. Little birds, little basics, Magdalena finds her own persistence in paths and peace. She also borrows others, like the Star Ferry, which continues because of a strong political campaign that argued these small green boats were integral to the identity of Hong Kong. Yet, there are others, like the clock tower, which she misses altogether – this is the remnant of someone who is not part of this story, but whose actions intersect with ours, a glance in the periphery of our memory. These things tell a different story to a culture of disappearance, and perforate the grids and topologies of cartographic reason.

## Mohammed/Volumes

> 'The cool thing about Google, they have like a 3D map, you know.'

Mohammed has a twofold plan, which he explained to me over a breakfast of gado-gado. Now, entering the Causeway Bay Station, the plan seems a little vague.

'So, we're going to go to Admiralty and then we're catching a bus?'

'Yeah, we're going to catch a bus from there.'

'Okay ….'

'Yeah, going to Admiralty, because I – I just want to see some building in Admiralty.

'See what in Admiralty?'

'Some building, they have like, architecture, there's a lot of architecture and building, and you know I want to see the building.' Mohammed studied architecture at university and now divides his time between working in architecture and travelling extensively throughout Asia.

'Yeah?'

'… because there are a lot of building,' I laugh as I finally understand what he is trying to say, perhaps a little unkindly, but he joins in, 'because, you know, this is my first time in Hong Kong, so I not ….'

'You want to see the skyscrapers?'

'Yeah!'

Once a naval dockyard built across land and sea, Admiralty is deep into the artificial foreshore, sitting between Central and Wan Chai. The flat land established by reclamations is well-suited for the tall skyscrapers needed to maximise commercial space in Hong Kong, and so, every round of reclamations that established the Edinburgh Place Ferry Pier in 1957 has seen an extension of skyscraper geographies (Graham, 2014) into the harbour. Planning in Hong Kong is also not an integrated process. It is split between three different branches of town planning, building development and land lease control (Cartier, 1999).

The result now is a poorly bounded space – housing mostly banks, office towers, shopping centres and the new central government office – utilitarian, hypermodern and bleeding into the surrounding neighbourhoods like shards of glass shattered on a floor. Skyscrapers, and other tall structures maintain a dual embodiment. On one hand, there is a practical element in finding new ways to accommodate the inflating populations of global cities in both work and living. Airspace has been described as 'dead space' in low-rise landscapes, especially in architectural terms, and for cities like Hong Kong which are bereft of even terrain, the skyscraper poses a solution to a growing problem. Furthermore, the politics of aerogeographies (Adey, 2010), has been largely attributed to the planimetric view of the map, and its reflection in the cartographic imagination: 'Geo-politics is a flat discourse. It largely ignores the vertical dimension and tends to look across rather than to cut through the landscape. This was the cartographic imagination inherited from the military and political spatialities of the modern state' (Weizman, 2002).

However, on the other hand, the skyscraper, like other forms of architecture, maintains a symbolic order – it reasserts colonial power and generates a 'placeless' territory ruled by global capital (Abbas, 1997). Geopolitical power is not just a matter not of 'cutting through' but also of 'looking up' – looking being a core domain of cartographic reason. Yet, this power remains contested (Law, 2002). For this purpose, dichotomising looking across against cutting through landscapes is dangerous: as we have seen throughout this book, the cartographic imagination is both capable of looking across (surveying) and cutting through (rationalising). Rather, looking up (and looking across) engages a second mode of embodiment taken on by skyscrapers as metaphorical: a symbol of power, of progress and of relationality (McNeill, 2005). Cartographic discourse, like cartographic reason, is hinged, to a degree, on looking: for what is a point or a line if it is not seen? We saw this with the complex imagined perspectives of Tanija searching for her route to the Harbour Bridge in Sydney, with Vicki imagining contour lines around the shape of The Peak, and with Camille counting imagined streets between the map and the landscape. Cutting is a mode of abstraction, an imagination of the jagged depth of holes in landscapes (like the Argyle Cut) made by archaeologists or geologists. Unlike cuts, skyscrapers are not intended to be cut through: they are intended to be looked up at, generally from below, their height and their potency inscribed by the relationality of the viewer being small, and the skyscraper being tall, an inverse of the theory of the vanishing point. A skyscraper is thoroughly deictic – it starts with the story of a finger and an eye.

I have an intuition about the building Mohammed wants to see. The nearest MTR station to my residence is Admiralty, and so I traverse through this terrain often. Several times, as I have been wandering between home and Admiralty Station, I have been accosted by (primarily young) tourists sporting expensive cameras with large fish-eye lenses asking me the direction of the Bank of China Tower. It is the tallest building in the area, and at night has an impressive visual display of geometric lights, illuminating the triangular structure of its support beams. Standing on the opposite side of Victoria Harbour in Kowloon with Ravi, the Bank of China Tower loomed above the HSBC Building and the Lippo Centre, and now, as Mohammed sets a wild pace, and given his background in architecture, I suspect this is becoming a theme.

'Is it the Bank of China building that you want to …?'

'Yeah, yeah!' He cuts in immediately.

'Yeah,' I smile, 'I thought so.'

Chinese architect I. M. Pei accepted the commission for the Bank of China Tower in 1982, and it was completed seven years later in 1989. It is a 368-metre-tall tower of 72 storeys – the tallest in the SAR when it was completed.[5] It was received by 'geomancers as influencing Hong Kong's transition from British to Chinese rule' (McNeill 2005: 45), and it is difficult to tell whether post-1989 Pei would have accepted the commission giving his increasingly critical stance towards China (Wiseman, 2001). Despite this, it maintains a robust symbolic role in navigating Hong Kong's place on a global landscape: one foot in China, one foot in the West, both feet together, in sync, in the landscape. The attention this role has gained now attracts all manner of visitors who determinedly make their way through a volumetric landscape incised with multilevel freeways and underpasses to see and photograph it.

5 It has now been supplanted by Central Plaza, 2 IFC and, more recently, the International Commerce Centre on the West Kowloon Cultural District.

Having only arrived late last night, seeing the Bank of China Tower is the first point of order for Mohammed, and then, it seems, we will head up by bus to The Peak. He hasn't yet bought an Octopus card and so, turning away from the electronic barriers, we walk towards one of the ticket machines lined up against the wall. Next to us, a large metal plate embossed with raised lines detailing the plan of the building, and small Braille descriptions blast out a repetitive, high-pitched and saccharinely happy tune. The sound cuts through the bass-tone hum of domestic helpers hurrying to their Sunday lunches, and the beeps of the Octopus card readers – like the Pied Piper calling us in with his piccolo flute. Metal grating on metal against this sound, Mohammed inserts coins in time, one by one, into the 'single journey ticket-issuing machine'. This is a machine that I have never used. Accepting the money and spitting out the change, it issues a small orange ticket that Mohammed takes and inserts into the ticket barrier. I tap on ahead and move quickly through the gate, unprepared for the different rhythms between MTR cards and tickets. As I rush ahead, I end up having to go back and wait while Mohammed tries another machine, waits for the magnetic stripe on the ticket to be read, go through the revolving metal bar and collect it on the other side. When we arrive at Admiralty, the choreography continues. Mohammed gets stuck again exiting through the barrier. A grimace crosses Mohammed's face as he tries to move through the barrier and ends up with a bar of metal smashing against his torso. He tries again. The machine refuses to read his ticket and he takes it out and walks impatiently over the station officer who swipes him through.

On the station concourse in is an information panel, *Admiralty Station Street Map*, in the same style as the one at Central Station. On the cartographic representation, flattened roadways are interspersed with three-dimensional illustrations of fifteen or so of the tall buildings that can be found in Admiralty, among them, the Lippo Centre and the Bank of China Tower. The HSBC Building I know, from memory, is just off the edge of the map towards Central, and so, at least in this visual rendition, it is completely absent. On each side of the map, a heading is formed for each exit attached to a list of local landmarks that can best be reached by taking this route. Where these lists note skyscrapers, they are accompanied by a photograph of the exterior of the building, taken from below, highlighting defining characteristics and incidentally performing a visual expression of high modernism.

'B, eh?' Mohammed asks, pointing at the map.

'B,' I affirm.

'This way.'

We exit the MTR at the Lippo Centre on Queensway and Mohammed takes out his phone. Staring at it, he taps and swipes before looking up at me.

'The cool thing about Google, they have like a 3D map, you know?'

'Yeah,' I nod twice.

'In Hong Kong only, either – yeah, in Singapore they do have it but only the buildings don't really look like the building.'

The three-dimensionality that Mohammed is describing is in form, rather than in specificity. Like the information panel, Google Maps has placed three-dimensional volumetric figures upon the flat surface of the map. However, divergently, Google Maps maintains the top-down planimetric view using shadow to indicate height and depth, rather than switching between a top-down, and bird's-eye viewpoint. Given the flat screen of Mohammed's phone, this has the effect of taking a notion of vertical space into volumetric space (Shelton et al., 2010) and then, counterintuitively, compressing it into a single flattened image. The detail of the buildings – colour, material, texture – are not represented here. On the map, the Bank of China Tower is a square comprised of what appears to be a square pyramid on a cube. The Lippo Centre is depicted with two octagonal prisms, and the HSBC Building designed by Sir Norman Foster, is a ghostly shape that resembles the MTR exit symbol turned 90 degrees clockwise and given breadth. Compared to the vantage point enjoyed by Ravi and I on the TST foreshore, or even watching it get smaller as I sailed away in the Star Ferry with Magdalena, it is a feat of topological interpretation to take the iconic image of a building and imagine what it would look like from the top down.

Scrunching his nose and frowning at where the Bank of China should be, Mohammed seems disappointed at the result of his mental gymnastics, and uncertain that the little blue dot is in the right location.

'Yeah, this is not right,' he says.

It's not in the right location, and he struggles to recognise the Bank of China Tower by way of comparison. One of the key discourses of Pei's design, based in local interpretations of *fengshui*, was that the building 'rose like a knife blade and its reflective facade, angular edges and triangular forms projected malevolent forces, some aimed directly at the British Governor's residence' (Cartier, 1999: 193). This mode of interpretation pivots upon an axis from the ground to the sky – looking up or across at the skyscraper, in situ with the hills behind where the governor's house sits. Even so, other interpretations, comparing the tower to bamboo or as a high-rise symbol of modernity, or an ode to Hong Kong's future in China, still are based in discourses of verticality predicated upon looking at it from a perspective that is lived. Even from The Peak, the building rises high, the inclined cut of its roof sliding back towards the island an important defining feature. The shading on the Google Maps barely gives any indication of this, and the monumentality of the design, as well as its metaphoric symbolism and the relationality of geopolitics, re-established in the visual relationality between ground and sky, is wholly lost. The Lippo Centre partially blocks our view of the Bank of China Tower, and so turning back to his phone, he searches for the name. The marker lands and not recognising the three-dimensional shape of the building, Mohammed frowns again.

'So it's here,' he says. 'But see the building is like there ....' Holding the phone, he starts walking before stopping again. 'Yeah, it's true. The dot is not like in the dot, right?' The blue dot is not in the right location jerking around the screen. The Bank of China is to our near direct west. Mohammed looks up and points north-east.

'Over there.'

Taking a few steps, he stops again holding his phone up high. A full minute goes by where he stares at his phone before he points south-east towards the Bank of China and mouths silently, 'but it's over there.'

I can't help myself and burst out laughing – suddenly the scores of confused tourists make sense in the GPS quagmire, and the reasoning of Daren, Vicki, Taylor and Camille in turning their location services off makes perfect sense.

'Can you not figure out which way ...?'

Mohammed cuts me off.

'Yeah – this way.' He points eastwards. I blink at him, and he bursts out laughing, too. 'Because I see this park.' He shows me on the map.

'Admiralty Gardens,' I read aloud as he points towards a retaining wall holding a small green space, 'is there, okay ....'

'It's quite a tall building, isn't it?'

'We go that way right?'

'Yep.'

'Then I'm good.' He chuckles.

And then, curiously, eyes on the map before we reach the gardens he makes an impulsive and inexplicable left turn. We head east underneath the Lippo Centre and towards the taxi rank replete with scarlet Hong Kong Island taxis, and a construction site ahead with bright saffron tractors.

Suddenly, Mohammed stops and shakes his head.

'Naaaaaaahhhhh.'

He turns 180 degrees and points back towards the direction we just came.

'That way.' He laughs.

As we retrace our steps, I ask him at what point he realised that we were going the wrong way. Was it because we were headed into a construction zone?

He laughs again.

'No,' he says, 'it's just because I see the Google Map, the arrow show here,' he gestures behind us, 'but it should be heading,' he points ahead of us, 'here.'

'So the Google Map was pointing in exactly the wrong direction?'

'Yeah.'

We head out onto Queensway, and the tower emerges from behind the Lippo Centre.

'The building is there,' he exclaims, and motions to me to cross the road.

'The bad thing,' he says, 'is when you use GPS you drain the battery, you know?'

'It does, yeah.'

'I hope, after this, they have the technology to reduce the power consumption for the GPS.'

Above us, the twin glass buildings of the Lippo Centre stand. Known first as the Bond Centre until 1988 (after it was purchased by Australian businessman Alan Bond, before the demolition of his financial empire), it was designed by American architect Paul Rudolph, a contemporary of both Pei and Foster. This was not typical of Rudolph's work. His love of brutalism is not reflected in the glass façade and it was unusual for him to cover up the floor lines in his work, which gave his towers a sense of scale. Furthermore, in other works he extended happily across the horizontal plane, a luxury not afforded in Hong Kong (Bruegmann, 2010). Yet, the peculiarity of the Lippo Centre rests in its context in Hong Kong: already surrounded by functional brick and concrete skyscrapers, the design of the two towers was to draw in and reflect the deep colours of the sky and harbour so that it would stand out against the hundreds of other concrete towers dotting the hills. Knowing that these buildings would be standing next to Pei's design of the Bank of China Tower, and Foster's of the HSBC Building, Rudolph designed these buildings so that they would be visually paradoxical:

> It seems clear that he wanted the Bond towers to simultaneously function as background structures, forming part of the street wall along Queensway (the major artery that connects the Central business district with the emerging Wanchai business district to the east), and as foreground buildings, serving as objects of interest on the skyline as seen from the bay. Indeed, they are at once monument and urban infill. (Bruegmann, 2010: para 6)

Again, we can see how vertical landscapes occupy two perspectives: to look up and to look across. And looked at they were, and interpreted in their own way.

It is barely a coincidence that the Lippo Centre sits where the foreshore of Hong Kong Island once ran, in the exact place that, in 1866, the crew of the HMS *Rifleman* drove a copper bolt into the wall of the naval dockyard. The *Rifleman* was a survey vessel, tasked with carrying out cartographic surveys across the island, which, in the situation of Hong Kong, was based on a landscape more vertical than horizontal. In Sydney, they established a fix-point by way of the Principal Roads marker in Circular Quay, but the crew of the HMS *Rifleman* were short of a vertical fix-point. The tides plagued them and they were too far from the standards established in England for them to be useful. So, somewhat arbitrarily, they took a copper bolt, not more than four inches long, and hammered it into the side of Storehouse No. 12. The bolt, later known as 'The *Rifleman*'s Bolt', set the mean sea level in Hong Kong – a fixed point in the vertical cartographic imagination from which calculations could be made. In doing so, this small bolt became an agent of cartographic reason, stabilising the sea against the land. Of course, the sea continued to do whatever it wanted, and the sea level datum was changed twice between then and now: first through the Principal Datum, established from tidal observations (against which many tall buildings in Hong Kong are measured) and, second, through the Chart Datum, four feet lower again (Survey and Mapping Office, 1996). This has created a haphazard urban experience, where the measurement of verticality does not quite measure up to its imagination.

This imagination has as much emphasis on looking as on measuring: to survey (from the French, *surveiller*, to look, to survey and also to surveil). Power is implicit in this translation – and the limits of representation for cartographic reason are not bound to flat planes or horizontal surfaces. Key to the expression of such reason is relationality: the small against the tall, the far against the near. The Lippo Centre is a reminder of this potential, nestled humbly near two giants of the architectural world. Ahead, Mohammed points out that Cotton Tree Road, a raised arterial route that leads up to the Mid-Levels, is impairing our view of the Bank of China Tower.

'I just want to take some picture,' he says.

'So where do you want to go? Up?'

'Yeah, up.'

He directs us around a corner and up some stairs to see if we can't find a better view. The stairs move in an anti-clockwise direction, and we emerge

Figure 11.5. *Reflections*. The view as Mohammed and I emerge onto the footpath of the raised motorway, Cotton Tree Drive. The Bank of China Tower sits in the foreground on the middle-right with intersecting triangular lines, and the modular HSBC Building can be made out in the background of the far right. The Lippo Centre above where we stand can be seen reflected in the glass panels of the Bank of China Tower.

on a terrace of the Lippo Centre that leads to Cotton Tree Road. Mohammed takes out his phone and raises it, taking a photo as cars and buses race past us on the road.

'Wow,' he turns to me and smiles, 'before this, I just saw this in a book, you know.

'Even though it's 80s design, it's really good.'

'Yeah.'

'It looks modern even though now it's like 26 years old.'

He kneels down on the footpath to get a good shot, one that encapsulates the sheer height of the building. Then, getting up, it's over in a flash.

'Maybe we can try to take the bus from here.'

The awe – the consumption of the visual spectacle has been and gone, underwritten in a new era of digital media that focuses on the reproducibility, rather than the experience of the monumental image. He searches on his phone for the location of the bus stop, the Lippo Centre lingering in the backdrop.

'Let's have a look,' I nod.

We walk down a set of stairs on the other side of the Queensway, decorated with pale blue and green railings. Halfway down, he stops again.

'Nooo,' he moans, 'they ask us to take a tram here, like.' He shows me the phone.

'No,' I respond, 'that takes us to the Peak Tram. Google Maps has suggested that we walk and then take the Peak Tram up to The Peak. But Mohammed wants the view of the island from the bus. He's heard that, on the saddle between two mountains, you can almost see both sides of the island at once. Google Maps does not work, and Mohammed cannot remember what bus to take.

'My host last night told me there is a bus from Admiralty to the top.'

Google Maps is not assisting him, so he switches to search to try to figure out the bus number so he can find where it stops. He begins to get increasingly frustrated.

'So, it's bus number 15, right?'

'Bus number 15?' I parrot.

'I think so.'

'So, where does it go from?'

He reads from a page he has found.

'Use Admiralty Exit C1. The bus stop is there.'

'So, we go back to Admiralty then? What site is this?'

'This is Trip Advisor.'

'Ah, okay.'

'So,' he points behind towards the Lippo Centre again, 'we go back there. So, it's bus number 15.' He walks and reads at the same time, slowly up the stairs and a little fast on the flat footpath.

'Bus number 15' he repeats again.

'It's strange Google Maps keeps trying to make you go on the tram.' The Peak Tram is a private company – popular amongst tourists who can afford the comparatively high transport fee, or residents of The Peak, who get special discounts.

'Yeah, it's trying to make us go the fastest way.'

Later, once we reach the bus stop, he takes the opportunity while we wait to take some more photographs of the Bank of China Tower. I.M. Pei, he tells me, is his favourite architect. Then, his eyes fall on the HSBC Building that, until now, has been all but forgotten.

'And the guy who designed the Hong Kong Shanghai Bank over there, the HSBC, is not Chinese – Norman Foster.'

The building sits obliquely, falling into its surroundings. The HSBC is a god in the pantheon of colonial Hong Kong finance. Now a London-based British company, it opened in 1865 in Hong Kong and, like the ferry piers, has occupied a number of different sites. This one, designed and built between 1978 and 1985, is a modular design with a strong exoskeleton allowing light through. The components were manufactured entirely in the United

Kingdom and were shipped to Hong Kong, where they were assembled on site. Mohammed knows a bit about this building, too, although it holds his interest less. Next to the high modernity of the Bank of China Tower, and the upward reaching ambition of 2 IFC and now the ICC, the HSBC Building seems elderly, and a little small. Raising his camera, and taking a picture, Mohammed turns back to me.

'They say that the building, the Hong Kong and Shanghai Bank, they can assemble the building back ....' I squint at him, as he tries again.

'They can take the building away, put it somewhere else, assemble the building somewhere, because, uh, they think that China, I mean that China going to take back Hong Kong, they will assemble the building back, put it somewhere else,' he traces its exoskeleton with his finger, 'that's why they rigged it, the design like, you can assemble it, it looks like Lego.'

# Part 5

## Mobile Mapping

# 12. Conclusion: Endings and Beginnings

*Twelve months after my walk with Mohammed, I was sitting on a tram which ran along Queensway as it stopped briefly outside the HSBC Building. Facing backwards at the rear of the tram, the Lippo Centre was in view through the open window, and I looked at it, remembering our conversation and Mohammed's love of tall skyscrapers that did not show up properly on 3D maps. In this space and time, however, the Lippo Centre towers appeared somehow different, and an old woman noticed me staring and prodded me to get my attention.*

*'These buildings,' she said pointing towards them. 'They are called the Koala Buildings.'*

*'Koala?' I must have looked surprised because she grabbed my chin and pointed my face towards them again.*

*'Look, like the Australian animals. Koalas.'*

*It only took a second or so and I saw them in a curious convergence between the two cities, large glass koalas climbing up the trunk of the building.*

By way of another moment, in *Ghostly Matters*, Avery Gordon (2008) describes a list she asked a class to make of the reasons that Toni Morrison gives in *The Bluest Eye* for why dreams may die. The list the class made was expansive and seemingly arbitrary: from systems of power and supremacist violence to emotions like hatred and disappointment; from the meteorological to *lost teeth* and *furniture without memories*. Of this list, Gordon writes:

> This turns out not to be a random list at all, but a way of conceptualizing the complicated workings of race, class and gender, the names we give to the ensemble of social relations that create inequalities, situated interpretive codes, particular kinds of subjects, and the possible and impossible themselves. (Gordon, 2008: 4)

The koalas climbing up the Lippo Centre may, too, fall into this description. The struggle is not in holding the answer in the palm of the hand, the struggle is in the searching and knowing that there is no answer (no single answer)

---

Wilmott, C., *Mobile Mapping. Space, Cartography and the Digital.*
Taylor & Francis Group, 2020
DOI 10.5117/9789462984530_CH12

Figure 12.1. *The Lippo Centre*. Photo taken from the back of a tram outside the HSBC Building at 1 Queen's Road, Central.

which alone can comprehend the impossible intertwining of knowledge, experience and being as they become mediated through technologies, bodies and spaces. Like a bird in an egg and an egg in a bird, the circular logic of discourse, not least of cartographic reason, appears to have no beginning and no end. Yet, somewhere in the designs of fix-points, equals signs, universal characteristics and intersecting lines, there are experiences, tactics and hauntings which bubble and surface, warping and disrupting the quest for an absolute geometry that displaces the openness of space. Like the koalas, the moments that led Gordon to a project of hauntings were that 'ghostly things kept cropping up and messing up other tasks [she] was trying to accomplish' (Gordon, 2008: 8). 'Messing up' is also a good phrase to describe the gradual emergence of this book: what was at first an account of neat lines and clear boundaries, of total systems and infinite calculability, an account of cartographic reason expressed through imaginations and impulses became messed up by the everyday business of living by the people with whom I walked and those that appeared unexpectedly on trams, in archives, in landscapes.

The question that Gordon asked her class is as equally profound as the answers they gave: by starting from dreams we can begin to understand their disappearance and the negative space that their absence casts. This is a complicated, haunted surface, in which the expectations of consistency and clarity towards academic research are laid aside to reveal fragile complexity and deep anguish: those other things for which there are not necessarily words, and not necessarily theories or tools. If we were to ask a similar question here of the stories woven together throughout this volume, we, too, would find an account of scattered objects and moments, violences and emotions, spaces without times, and times without spaces. We could ask *Why do dreams die?*, or we instead could ask *How can space be open?*, or *Why are lines drawn?* and *Why do points pierce the surfaces of our experiences?*, or indeed, *What is mobile mapping?* The answer may well be the same.

The opening chapters of this book offered some idea of what may appear in our search: *coordinate (fix) points*, *intersecting lines* and *invisible grids drawn all over the globe*; *copper bolts*, *clocks* and *sextants*; *binary codes*, *hexagrams* and *all things described in numbers*. Yet, as the trajectory changed (or even started again from a different angle) deep into the *lived* spaces that we produce, it became clear that these things, this list of ideas and objects, only centre the world as far as we let them. As we wandered through Sydney and Hong Kong, stories breathed life into experience, unveiling the chaos, openness and potentiality of space that already exists against the cartographic and digital desire for systems of fixity and order – we only have to search. There is evidence that we are not trapped in the embryonic sac of discourse, within which the twins of Leibniz and Descartes share DNA. If we start within this space of discourse, we become bound to stretch, and to lash out and to try to pierce the membrane and hope that what waits on the other side is not an eternal empty darkness, but maybe hope, maybe potential, maybe openness. In this divergent search in the corners of experience, waypoints do not help, nor do maps, or compasses, hourglasses or sextants, algorithms or codes.

We need different models beyond texts and contexts of understanding the everyday relations brought forth by cartographic reason, and so we can turn, as we have here, towards the spatial and the social. However, in this search and throughout these stories, something always appeared in the corner of the eye, disappearing at any attempt to focus upon it. This absent presence, arguably, is a kind of haunting, wherein ghosts cast shadows:

> If haunting describes how that which appears to be not there is often a seething presence, acting on and often meddling with taken-for-granted realities, the ghost is just the sign or the empirical evidence if you like, that tells you a haunting is taking place. (Gordon 2008: 8)

Instead, as we attempt to understand what happens in space, between cartographic reason and everyday life, we can look to something else: absences in the map (Harley, 1988a) and poetic presences in space (Bachelard, 1994), haunted memories (Huyssen, 2003) and the ghost in the machine (Ryle, 2009). Gordon describes the ghost as a social figure: a person, or a metaphor, or inscribed deep into storytelling. Haunting is a sociological construction, brought about by and through people.

Given the experiences in these stories, we must ask if a ghost can also be a spatial figure, not just apparent in the sociological imagination but an apparition in the spatial imagination? To this end, Gordon continues onwards with her description of how haunting may appear through ghosts:

> The ghost or the apparition is one form by which something lost, or barely visible, or seemingly no there to our supposedly well-trained eyes makes itself known or apparent to us, in its own way, of course. The way of the ghost is haunting, and haunting is a very particular way of knowing what has happened or is happening. Being haunted draw us affectively, sometimes against our will and always a bit magically, into the structure of feeling of a reality we come to experience, not as cold knowledge but as a transformative recognition. (Gordon, 2008: 8)

This what we have learnt by starting from space first, from outside and the other, from openness and possibility, is that the convergence of the rationalists is only a speck in the multiple, heterogeneous spaces produced by bodies, landscapes, memories, stories and maps into which we are drawn willingly or otherwise. Bodies move, and spaces shift, landscapes surprise and failure is imminent: difficult, terrible seething absences and silenced presences sit, dispersed, waiting, haunting. These stories have unearthed other answers to the questions of dreams, lines and mobile mapping. Unauthorised readings of argot spaces are enacted through *hidden stairs, the Koala Buildings, sand dunes, forked roads, colourful flags, bike paths* and *impromptu translations*. Pasts are passed across space from one person to another with only sound waves as witnesses, whispers of *clandestine marriages, graffiti walls, visa waiting times, the feeling of the landscape, four-breakfast cats, storm fronts, getting in* and *sacred spaces*. Remnants of palimpsest histories linger in *boundary stones, names carved in boulders, abandoned brick kilns, Tank Streams, stolen rocks*, and *monumental landings*. Reminders of past incursions and the colonial present appear, too, *old ferries* dock at *new piers*, *bank towers* become *market indexes*, *public spaces* are transformed by *electronic gates* and *market stalls* grow to *shopping centres*.

Or, we could also go the other way: *from space to mapping, and mapping to space*.

*Part 2: Space/Sydney* was in search of spaces: finite moments in infinite complexity, the paradoxical and obtrusive. We searched for the spatial practices in mobile mapping, brought forth through heterogeneity, possibility and morphologies always in occurrence. We exercised in the backstreets with Marianna as she evokes the transformative potential of everyday space by wandering through the same landscapes week after week. We spun around and through Martin Place to Moore Park with Kyja, unsettling new spaces with old spaces (and old spaces with new spaces). We looked through cliffs and found a hidden route to the Harbour Bridge with Tanija, and troubled the representation of spirituality in art, map and landscape architecture with Sarah. With Nick, we felt the shape of the roads and the hills, drove north with Shaun and his GPS, and Cliff told us a story of misreading spaces between maps and landscapes. Ben imagined his way through space, getting more lost with maps than without and, finally, Cassie reimagined maps altogether, peering into people's lives (and her own) and finding her own way.

What then of cartography and code? *Part 3: Cartography/Cities* tried to make some sense of the philosophical, historical and geographical trajectories of cartographic reason from lines to numbers. It discussed how lines have come to permeate the cartographic imagination, but that not all lines are equal, or even – and that even reason becomes unreasonable. Then, we discussed how numbers increasingly have become implicated in the representational structures of the world, renegotiating materialities and visualities. We saw, too, how the intertwining Enlightenment philosophies of Descartes and Leibniz have reconverged in new territories, with different implications and interpretations in a digital world.

In *Part 4: Digital/Hong Kong* we turned these thoughts back to the intricacies of everyday digital mappings – not just of cartographic reason but the minute rationalities of drawing lines, writing names and representing manifold landscapes on flat surfaces in a digital age. We started with Daren at Gage Street wet market, as he struggled to map the names of the landscape onto the names of the cartography. We then explored spatial bordering practices and their intersection with data, culture and economies with Ellen, and next, how economies transcend and/or reify cartographic lines with Ravi. After Ravi was Vicki, as we traced the contours of Soho and The Peak district on our way up to Victoria Peak, and the intersections between mapping, cartographic reason and the experience of journeying with Taylor. Mobility was central to mapping with Camille, as we travelled along the escalator system looking up, and looking down, tracing the porous boundaries of public and private space, and moving shorelines with Magdalena and the diminishing length of the trip across Victoria Harbour on the Star Ferry. Finally, with Mohammed, we saw mapping move from points to lines, to two-dimensional figures to volumetric and vertical interpretations of space, the transition from modern to hypermodern to postmodern cartographies (cf. Mitchell, 2008).

What does it mean to engage with maps and mappings in the geo-coded world? asks Pickles (2004) in the conclusion of *A History of Spaces*:

> Map after map, layer after layer, identity after identity, combing and recombining, crashing and compounding, erasing and reconfiguring [...] sedimentations, striations, inscriptions, projections, gorings, scalings [...] markings on the multi-subject that is walking through the garden to check the mail. Codings and recodings producing subject and world along axes of difference, as dwelling, access, flow, consumer, owner, borrower, neighbour; indemnities and codings that multiply subjectivities in interesting and always unexpected overdetermined ways. We are, in this sense, over-coded as multiply coded shifting, decentered identities. That is, we are rhizomatic. (Pickles, 2004: 180)

Perhaps we are overcoded and overdetermined, subjugated by cartographic eyes and impulses, anxieties and logics, and by association, the geographic, terminologies, imaginaries and categories of the world. To shift in this circular logic, again like an egg-in-bird-in-egg, is to be caught up in the tangled identities cast upon our lives and our stories by cartographic reason. Pickles turns to critical cartographies for the future – cartographies that reimagine and remap the boundaries and lines of identity/difference, inclusion/exclusion, knowledge/power, cartographies that shatter logic in digital experiments and bring forth the tenacious ambiguity of difference à la Farinelli and Olsson.

Yet, perhaps there is a different answer to the critical tensions within cartography and cartographic media, which lies entirely outside the discourses inherent to the tradition. Throughout these stories, the Janus-faced agents of representational hope and obliteration (constellations of the cartographic and the otherwise-dispersed) arrived in different 'here-and-nows' (Massey, 2003), intertwining with the flows of bodies and memories. These moments of appearance shifted from *little blue dots* to *sticky notes*, *kilometres per hour* to *blue-green snakes*, *sporting fields* to *disobedient landscapes*, *ambivalent Pinyin* to *asking people where to go* and from *Cartesian fixity* to *Leibnizian mobilities* to *something else again, something different, something silent, something ... some thing.*

The genealogical project taken on by Foucault towards the end of his life traced the 'insurrection' of 'subjugated knowledges' (Foucault, 2003). What precisely constitutes a subjugated knowledges is a collection of descriptions, knowledges that are: 'naïve', 'insufficiently elaborated', 'below the required level of erudition', 'noncommonsensical' and 'local'; and knowledges that 'have, in a way, been left to lie fallow, or even kept in the margins' (ibid.: 7-8). The genealogy of subjugated knowledge is 'a meticulous rediscovery of struggles and the raw memory of fights' (ibid.: 8): it is visceral and at times, brutal, but also, usually, epistemological. This is a very particular description in its own ambiguity, yet one that is perhaps too distant for the threads of sadness, attention, anger, intuition, treachery, feeling and hopefulness that wound around and through the everyday moments of encounter with cartographic reason discussed in this book. All the same, it is a good starting point, because it opens up without seeking to close, and because it allows us to underscore that the shudders of subjugated knowledges (and whatever else they may be) have a far reach, even to those clasped in the inextricable grasp of discourse. Furthermore, like Massey and Gordon, Foucault's description emphasises that even beyond the limits of representation, these moments speak – in a way.

Most importantly, however, Foucault's work on subjugated knowledge turns us towards a word of caution that Foucault stresses at the very beginning of his lectures at the Collège de France:

> [O]nce we have excavated our genealogical fragments, once we begin to exploit them and put in circulation these elements of knowledge that we have been trying to dig out of the sand, isn't there a danger that they will be recoded, recolonized by these unitary discourse, which having first disqualified them and having then ignored them when they reappeared, may now be ready to re-annex them an include them in their own discourses and their own power-knowledge effects? (Foucault, 2003: 11)

In other words, aren't we afraid that, now we have identified an intensity of occurrences that perhaps exist anterior to the rules of lines and points, they may collide and eventually be dissolved into the scripture of cartographic reason? Are we not afraid that by discussing these things in their specificity, by assigning them names and giving them a status, a relationality, a place in academic and geographic lexicons that we, too, re-inscribe the same brutalities of representation and order that caused them to surface in the first instance? This is a real and paradoxical concern – one which is central to how we conclude here in both spirit and in practice – and one that pivots at the question of 'subjugation' itself.

One difficulty is that we have little vocabulary with which to comprehend what mapping means in the age of mobile media, especially compared to what it has always meant. Certainly tactility, hapticity and embodiment – the swipes and the taps and the twirls and the awkward fixation of putting a finger on the screen – can be catalogued with ever-increasing detail. We can create new words to capture the minutiae of processes of moving through cartographic space or cartographically moving through space. We can name each of those bubbling feelings – of space, of loss, of the way, of 'y'know', of hope, of heaviness, of 'not-right' or 'odd', of disquiet, of 'secrets', 'swamps', 'birds', and having 'his name', of luck and of change. Or we could let it go – and accept that by creating such a taxonomy of the othered and the haunting, the absent and the hyper-visible tension that permeates a space we are bringing it into the fold under the terms that have already been set by the finger and the eye, by lines of power whose territory reaches all the way up to the limits of language (Olsson, 2007; Olsson, 1980; Olsson, 1991b). And so I will refer to these things here as simply *things*, although at times they might be different, because this word allows for some understanding while promoting enough vagueness and ambiguity to slip from the desire of calculation and control. Why should we bring these precious stories, these examples of a 'delicate empiricism' which have been carefully and gently placed in our care and curatorship, into another fold, without permission and use them to create new systems of interoperability, of equivalencies and of generalisation?

These stories have taught me that we must give up on the project of toponymies and taxonomies of experience. We must learn to resist the cartographic impulse to categorise, calculate and control. Rather, we must tell stories, in which the multifaceted refractions of these experiences can be viewed through a prism that has no limitations on difference and less likelihood of repetitions. As equally as there is a space and a role for these desires, we must also recognise that by entrapping ourselves in the nets that they cast, we miss the occasions in which the epistemes of rationality and the discourses of cartographic reason amount to violence against the lived realities that are dwelled.

The encounters in these stories are what they are. At times this has required a mode of interpretation – but this interpretation is my own and where possible I have tried to trace the trajectories of cartographic reason and space where they seem to appear. I do not and cannot pretend to understand and elucidate the complexity of spaces inhabited by each of the people who so generously gave me their time. Nor can I hope to understand their intentions by way of their words and their actions. Gordon's assertion that 'life is complicated' is not too far away from Massey's that the modernist project of generalizable theory sits uneasily against the multivalent and simultaneous 'ongoing stories of the world', and to assume an authority on the everyday lives of people based upon a collection of stories and a constellation of events, moments and encounters is completely counterposed to the purpose of this work. Authenticity is lost the moment it appears, a flash in the pan, which cannot be resurrected or reconstructed. The stories as they are told in this book are but one reading, a collection of cumulative experiences during a short journey through two cities. Through ghosts and haunting, it is possible to avoid 'de-contextualised relativism' or 'free-pluralism' (Gordon, 2008); it is possible to say something meaningful without saying something that re-enacts the violence of boundaries (Pickles, 2004).

If anything, stories like these are merely magnifications of themes felt in moments of mobile mapping – but fall far from the promise of cohered and holistic descriptive clarity. The objective of total description, or any attempt to capture and to cast into stone, or ink, or pixels, or algorithms the completeness of experiences as they occur and are remembered – really to map all the dust as it settles and before it is blown up again – is an exercise in futility, an impossible exactitude in science. This is a deep description but it is not complete, nor does it desire to be: by no means is the ambition of these stories to create a 1:1 map of a territory, already imagined with a cartographic eye, or to draw all things under a single binary system.

Until this point, we have shied away from the discussion of modernism and post-modernism that seems to be required of a piece of writing such as this. In casting distinctions between grand narratives and small stories, we should talk about these long-form theoretical fields that span the globe, tendrils of thinking that can be lumped together, haphazardly, as unified bodies of thought. Before this book, the discussions over universality/difference unfurl (Butler et al., 2011; Serres, 2011), and no doubt they will continue on after. Yet, I rather view this as a distraction from the point: have we ever been (post)modern (cf. Latour, 1993)? Having been embroiled in the stories here, in their unambiguous diversity, and the subsequent attempts to make sense of what they may mean, then/now/together/alone, in the debates about space and experience and the defining philosophies of our age, I tend to side with Gordon and Massey against the demand to position yourself and your writing on this particular battleground. Subtly, both scholars argue that neither the modernist positivities nor a postmodern critique of representation solves the very present problems of capitalism, domination and neo-liberal desire. Postmodernism applied too enthusiastically as something new, or something continuing (Jameson, 1991) becomes something of an accidental hypocrite. Drawing on Bauman, Gordon critiques the 'antighost' project of postmodernist desire to represent, to capture and to express *all* 'that resembles modernity's positivities more than it concedes' (2008: 13); drawing on Laclau, Massey (2005) laments the assertion that a crisis of representation necessarily equates to a crisis of spatiality, and by association, the assertion that the only way we can understand space is through the limitations, the closure and the stasis of representation. For the moment, in understanding the bridge between cartographic reason and mobile mapping we are limited in what we can do and what we can say – we become bound by the limits of representation, and pushing them further and farther only tells us more of the systems about which we already know.

And so it is impossible to be sure. Gordon suggests, however, that she *is* sure of one thing: '*it's not that ghosts don't exist*' (Gordon, 2008: 13). We can take this promise to make a possibility that space holds potential in spite of systems of representation, and that somewhere all the collisions, misunderstandings, tactics and strategies, missteps, detours and multiplicities offer us the briefest glimpse at what may exist outside the chiasm-of-thought-and-action of cartographic reason. Chasing total certainty down the rabbit hole of lines and points is, as Olsson (2007) adeptly states, abysmal. Chiasms become chasms, and we remain stuck.

By starting from the outside (and the other) the allure of epistemological reason might be decentred. This is why we have started from space, waded through cartography and ended with code – to give space a chance, in the way that Massey (2005) means. There reaches a point where we need to stop waiting for openness and potential to make itself known and reconsider the role that we have in shaping possibility – most especially in cartography. But this does not mean surrendering to models of generalizability and interoperability: this does not mean capitulating to the terms of cartographic reason. What these stories have unveiled is that the heterogeneity, the resolute complexity and eternal chaos of space has an inherent value and vitality in how we shape and are shaped by the world. They are surface inscriptions of deeper actions and embodiments, bubbles on the water, the top few layers of an archaeological dig into what mobile mapping means, and what it can do.

When we cease to look at texts and start to look at processes, experiences, ontologies and discourses, the geo-codes, binary systems and algorithms that calculate space in new and automated ways are not emphatically different from the triangulations, geometries and rationalities that came before. It is a mistake to assume that it is a taken-for-granted reality that the authority of cartographic reason rests upon a particular mathematical or scientific method (Feyerabend, 2010). Rather, this authority is predicated upon a persistent and unyielding insistence for a uniformity of spatial experience. This is expressed in the desire for totalising spatial epistemologies and results in a strange ontological transformation as they come to associate their own being-in-space with the signs and symbols of cartographic reason by way of little blue dots, street addresses, pass-cards and geographic data.

By placing space first, these stories inadvertently became a political project counter to the 'dead and the fixed' interpretation of space by Foucault (Massey, 2005). They also became a political project to open up different ways of understanding mapping and maps by way of experience and understanding, performance, embodiment, memory and affect. Understanding space in this way, by carefully warding away the limitations of a Cartesian-Leibnizian rationality, there are also opportunities to rewrite history, away from the rusty, dusty archives of colonial mapping projects. By arguing space away from the 'dead and the fixed' (Foucault, 1984) into the lively, open and transformation, Massey also opens up time away from the General History critiqued by Foucault (Foucault, 2002a; Foucault, 2002b). The unities of one space, common places and single histories become a veritable mosaic of multiplicities, interrelations and coevalness (Massey, 2005). I thought at the beginning of this project that structuring the work this way would take on a descriptive axiom – that it would be possible to merely describe what we see and go from there. But I was fooling myself – the project was political from the start as I wilfully and desperately searched for a way of comprehending the role of the mobile map beyond the technological determinism and constructivism of the interface. It is impossible to move beyond this entirely – the words and the gestures that we use are bound up in the histories of science and technologies, from code and algorithms, coordinates, hard drives to disks, to screens and buttons. Yet, these stories reveal that in the intercoding of discourse, representation and experience, knowledge is not subjugated, as Foucault suggests. There is agency to be found, to produce our own representations and give power to the everyday embodiments, emotions and affects – transformative recognitions – without subjugating them to words, lines and numbers. In blossoming flowers, and hidden staircases, and family myths, manifold translations and staying outside (and sometimes going inside) the gates, ghosts appear in a realm beyond the conventions of epistemology and discourse as they are understood by Foucault. And so space it is then, 'which is neither a container for always-already constituted identities not a completed closure of holism' (Massey, 2005: 12). Space is our opportunity to understand without categorising, to suggest rather than conclude, to see rather than catalogue, to feel rather than describe. This incompleteness and ambiguity of space is central to the possibility – not of a redemptive politics – but of hope: 'This is a space of loose ends and missing links. For the future to be open, space must be open too' (Massey, 2005: 12).

This leads to my final remark: that while haunting may take on 'the lost subjects of history', the seething and the lingering fragments of the lived brutalities of colonialism and capitalism, not all ghosts are filled with trauma and sadness. Indeed, the process of uncovering hauntings, of pointing to the occluded and excluded knowledges and experiences, may equally erupt as a process of joy as despair. Ellen's determination to find happiness in being locked out of Noah's Ark (and likewise getting into the garden at LOHAS Park), for instance, is not diminished by the violence of private spaces. Similarly, Sarah's experiences of loss in Hyde Park, and Shaun's outburst at the erasure of names and people are too easily read as the sadness of 'native informants', rather than stories about radical desires to undermine or undo the power of cartographic reason. These are not resistances in the sense of counter-mapping (cf. Dalton and Mason-Deese, 2012) or critical cartography (cf. Crampton and Krygier, 2006; Krygier and Wood, 2009): they are not maps against cartographic reason or the unbearable surveillance of the cartographic eye. Ambitions like this are difficult in cities like Hong Kong and Sydney because they risk basing epistemological authority in colonial discourse that is always, irreparably, hegemonic. It is important to note that in cartography, haunting does not always irrupt in the ways that we expect. There is joy, too, in getting lost. Although cartographic reason casts shadows of doubt on everyday navigations and intuitions, hesitations in remembering the way and uncertainty in recognising street names and landmarks, the expression of getting and being lost, of finding new things, and the way out again, emerged as a theme again and again: from Marianna, at first point, finding a permaculture garden to the end where Mohammed laughs at impenetrability of the Google 3D map, and his own navigational ambivalence.

As we shift towards digital technologies, this has become a more urgent, and perhaps more serious project, as new modes of surveillance enter into the public and private domains. Much has been written of the brutal intersection of cartographic reason and spatial power, tracing its tendrils of erasure and conquest. To understand these geometries of power at a global and urban scale is an important project, which may help up comprehend what it means to be mediated, to know space, and, indeed, to experience it. But on the other side of the scale, in the everyday and the habitual, these abstract systems of power become lived realities. To live cartographic reason is quite another thing entirely, and for this reason, it is equally important to open up a discussion about what it means to be in a space shaped by cartographic eyes, imaginations and impulses, about the roles that maps do and don't play in our lives. This implicitly involves tracing the everyday vernacular practices that are developed impromptu, spontaneously and surprisingly to live with these powerful discourses.

There is a futurity through the ghosts that inhabit space – through the lively presence of absence – as equally as we can imagine a future filled with the cartographic media, maps and landscapes produced through the logics of cartographic reason. This is a more difficult task because it starts with the unknown – a map that erases itself rather than carves out its own shape – until it eventually becomes a space of possibility. The actions of the here-now become embedded into spaces that fold in and open up: the beyond-the-limits of representation, the more-than-representational, the not-quite-representational lingers and shifts and irrupts. Furthermore, by understanding cartographic media through a lens of mobile mapping rather than by focusing on cartography or media there opens up more possibility to understand the vast and deep array of practices that defy, revolt and undermine the potent discourses that have been so exhaustively critiqued by geographers and media theorists alike.

This space is of humility, as we encounter the important and influential other *things* that exist outside but shape our lives, even if we don't and can't find names for them. To discuss without naming, to encounter without capturing, to evoke without closing: this is a project for next time. And it must be a project pinned on possibility and hope – the sheer determination to encounter out not only the networks of power but also the modes of resistance on their own terms: 'It seems to me, it is quite reasonable to take some delight in the possibilities it opens up' (Massey, 2005: 14).

# References


Abbas A (1997) *Hong Kong: Culture and the Politics of Disappearance.* Hong Kong: Hong Kong University Press.

Abrahamsson C (2008) Topoi/graphein. PhD thesis, Uppsala University.

Adey P (2010) *Aerial Life.* London: Wiley.

Aiton E, Shimao E (1980) Gorai Kinzō's Study of Leibniz and the *I Ching* Hexagrams. *Annals of Science* 38: 71-92.

Akkerman A (2001) Urban Planning in the Founding of Cartesian Thought. *Philosophy and Geography* 4: 141-167.

Allen J et al. (2015) *The Unicode Standard: Version 8 – Core Specification.* Mountain View, CA: Unicode Consortium.

Amoore L (2006) Biometric Borders: Governing Mobilites in the War on Terror. *Political Geography* 25: 336-351.

Anderson B (1991) *Imagined Communities.* London: Verso.

Anderson B (2015) *Encountering Affect.* Surrey, UK: Ashgate.

Anderson J (2004) Talking whilst Walking: A Geographical Archaeology of Knowledge. *Area* 36: 254-261.

Andrews JH (2002) Introduction: Meaning, Knowledge and Power in the Map Philosophy of J.B. Harley. In: Harley JB, Laxton P (eds) *The New Nature of Maps: Essays in the History of Cartography.* Baltimore, MD: Johns Hopkins University Press, pp. 1-32.

Antiques Advisory Board (2010) Jamia Mosque, No. 30 Shelley Street, Central HK. Office of Antiquities and Monuments, Government of Hong Kong.

Anzaldúa G (1987) *Borderlands: The New Mestiza.* San Francisco, CA: Aunt Lute Books.

ARUP/MTR Corporation (2011) Cultural Heritage Impact: Study for Tai Wai to Hung Hom Section. Environment and Planning Department, Government of Hong Kong.

Ash J (2015) *The Interface Envelope: Gaming, Technology, Power.* New York: Bloomsbury.

Ashton P (1995) *The Accidental City: Planning Sydney since 1788.* Sydney: Hale and Iremonger.

Augé M (1995) *Non-places: Introduction to an Anthropology of Supermodernity.* London: Verso.

Ausiello G., Petreschi R (2013) *The Power of Algorithms: Inspiration and Examples in Everyday Life.* London: Springer.

Austroads (2003) *Towards a Nationally Consistent Approach to Route Identity.* Government Publication AP-R224-03. 23 June. CanPrint Communications. https://www.onlinepublications.austroads.com.au/items/AP-R224-03 [last accessed 2 January 2018].

Bachelard G (1994) *The Poetics of Space*. Boston: Beacon Press.

Banivanua-Mar T, Edmonds P (2010) *Making Settler Colonial Space: Perspectives on Race, Place and Identity*. London: Palgrave

Banks M (1990) The Seductive Veracity of Ethnographic Film. *Visual Anthropology Review* 6(1): 16-21.

Barad K (2007) *Meeting the Universe Halfway: Quantum Physics and the Entanglement of Matter and Meaning*. Durham, NC: Duke University Press.

Bard S (1988) *In Search of the Past: A Guide to the Antiquities of Hong Kong*. Hong Kong: The Urban Council.

Batchelor R (2004) Binary as Transcultural Technology: Leibniz, Mathesis Universalis, and the Yi-Jing. In: Glimp D, Warren M (eds) *Arts of Calculation: Quantifying Thought in Early Modern Europe*. Basingstoke: Palgrave Macmillan, pp. 229-252.

Baudrillard J (1993) *Symbolic Exchange and Death*. Trans. Grant I. London: Sage.

Baudrillard J (1994) *Simulacra and Simulation*. Ann Arbor: University of Michigan Press.

Belyea B (1992) Images of Power: Derrida/Foucault/Harley. *Cartographica: The International Journal for Geographic Information and Geovisualization* 29: 1-9.

Benjamin W (2003) On the Concept of History. Trans. Jephcott E. In: Eiland H, Jennings MW (eds) *Walter Benjamin: Selected Writings, Volume 4: 1938-1940*. Cambridge, MA: Belknap Press of Harvard University Press, pp. 389-400.

Bennett J, Beudel S (2015) *Curating Sydney: Imagining the City's Future*. Sydney: UNSW Press.

Berlant L, Povinelli E (2014) Holding up the World, Part III: In the Event of Precarity ... A Conversation. *e-flux* 58.

Biggs M (1999) Putting the State on the Map: Cartography, Territory, and European State Formation. *Comparative Studies in Society and History* 41: 374-405.

Black J (1997) *Maps and Politics*. Chicago: University of Chicago Press.

Bollnow O (2011) *Human Space*. London: Hyphen Press.

Booth D (2002) The Dark Side of Surf Lifesaving. *Journal of Sport History* 29: 7-13.

Borges JL (1998) On Exactitude in Science. In: *Jorge Luis Borges: Collected Fictions*. London: Penguin Books, p. 325.

Botz-Bornstein T (2012) A Tale of Two Cities: Hong Kong and Dubai – Celebration of Disappearance and the Pretension of Becoming. *Transcience* 3(2): 1-16.

Boyd D, Crawford K (2012) Critical Questions for Big Data. *Information, Communication & Society* 15: 662-679.

Boyde M (2013) Cultural Myths and Open Secrets: The Cattle Industries in Australia. *Southerly: A Review of Australian Literature* 73(2): 256-273.

Braun B (2000) Producing Vertical Territory: Geology and Governmentality in Late Victorian Canada. *Cultural Geographies* 7(1): 7-46.

Brawley S (1995) *Vigilant and Victorious: A Community History of the Collaroy Surf Life Saving Club, 1911-1995*. Collaroy, Australia: Collaroy Surf Life Saving Club.

Brennan-Horley C et al. (2010) GIS, Ethnography and Cultural Research: Putting Maps Back into Ethnographic Mapping. *The Information Society* 26(2): 92-103.

Brown KM, Dilley R, Marshall K (2008) Using a Head-Mounted Video Camera to Understand Social Worlds and Experiences. *Sociological Research Online* 13. http://www.socresonline.org.uk/13/16/11.html [last accessed 2 January 2018].

Bruegmann R (2010) The Architect as Urbanist. *Places Journal*, February. https://placesjournal.org/article/the-architect-as-urbanist-part-1/ [last accessed 2 January 2018].

Butler J, Laclau E, Žižek S (2011) *Contingency, Hegemony and Universality: Contemporary Dialogues on the Left*. London: Verso.

Callon M, Latour B (1981) Unscrewing the Big Leviathan: How Actors Macro-Structure Reality and How Sociologies Help Them Do So. In: Knorr-Cetina K, Cicourel A (eds) *Advances in Social Theory and Methodology*. London: Routledge, pp. 277-303.

Carlton M (2012) Margaret, a Commonsense Class Act. *Sydney Morning Herald*, 24 March.

Carroll JM (2007) *A Concise History of Hong Kong*. Lanham, MD: Rowman & Littlefield.

Carter P (2009) *Dark Writing: Geography, Performance, Design*. Honolulu: University of Hawai'i Press.

Cartier C (1999) The State, Property Development and Symbolic Landscape in High-rise Hong Kong. *Landscape Research* 24: 185-208.

Casey E (1993) *Getting Back into Place: Toward a Renewed Understanding of the Place-world*. Bloomington: Indiana University Press.

Castells M (1994) *Technopoles of the World: The Making of 21st Century Industrial Complexes*. New York: Routledge.

Ceruzzi P (2012) *Computing: A Concise History*. Cambridge, MA: MIT Press.

Chabert J-L (2012) *A History of Algorithms: From the Pebble to the Microchip*. London: Springer.

Chabot S (2002) Transnational Diffusion and the African-American Reinvention of the Gandhian Repertoire. In: Smith J, Johnston H (eds) *Globalization and Resistance: Transnational Dimensions of Social Movements*. Lanham, MD: Rowman & Littlefield, pp. 96-112.

Chao J et al. (2001) An Experimental Investigation into the Performance of GPS-Based Vehicle Positioning in Very Dense Urban Areas. *Journal of Geospatial Engineering* 3: 59-66.

Chatwin B (1998) *The Songlines*. London: Vintage Classic.

Chen T (2017) The Postrepresentational Cartographies of Global Asia. *Verge: Studies in Global Asias* 3: vi-xiv.

Cheung S (2010) Translation of Short Texts: A Case Study of Street Names in Hong Kong. MA thesis, University of Queensland.

Chu CL (2012) Speculative Modern: Urban Forms and the Politics of Property in Colonial Hong Kong. PhD dissertation, University of California, Berkeley.

Chu Y-W (2013) *Lost in Transition: Hong Kong Culture in the Age of China*. New York: State University of New York Press.

City of Sydney (2011) *Sydney Cycleways*. http://www.sydneycycleways.net/.

Clancy R (2011) *Maps That Shaped Australia*. Bathurst, NSW: Land and Property Information.

Clifford J (1997) *Routes: Travel and Translation in the Late Twentieth Century*. Cambridge, MA: Harvard University Press.

Clifford J, Marcus GE (1986) *Writing Culture: The Poetics and Politics of Ethnography*. Berkeley: University of California Press.

Coleman S, Collins P (2011) An Uncomfortable Discipline?: 'Dislocating Anthropology' as Process of Practice. In: Coleman S, Collins P (eds) *Dislocating Anthropology? Bases of Longing and Belonging in the Analysis of Contemporary Societies*. Newcastle upon Tyne: Cambridge Scholars Publishing, pp. 1-18.

Conley T (1992) Translator's Foreword. In: Deleuze G (ed.) *The Fold*. Minneapolis: University of Minnesota Press, pp. ix-xx.

Connor S (2004) Topologies: Michel Serres and the Shapes of Thought. *Anglistik* 15: 105-117.

Cook J (1770) A Journal of the Proceedings of His Majesty's Bark *Endeavour* on a Voyage around the World, by Lieutenant James Cook, Commander, Commencing 25 May 1768-23 October 1770. In: State Library of NSW Textual Records.

Cooper B (2013) *Mapping Manhattan: A Love (and Sometimes Hate) Story in 75 Maps*. New York: Harry N. Abrams.

Cosgrove D (1999) *Mappings*. London: Reaktion.

Cosgrove D (2003) *Apollo's Eye: A Cartographic Genealogy of the Earth in the Western Imagination*. Baltimore, MD: Johns Hopkins University Press.

Cosgrove D, Daniels S (1988) *The Iconography of Landscape: Essays on the Symbolic Representation, Design and Use of Past Environments*. Cambridge: Cambridge University Press.

Cover J, Hartz G (1994) Are Leibnizian Monads Spatial? *History of Philosophy Quarterly* 11: 295-316.

Crampton J (2001) Maps as Social Constructions: Power, Communication and Visualization. *Progress in Human Geography* 25: 235-254.

Crampton J (2002) Thinking Philosophically in Cartography: Toward a Critical Politics of Mapping. *Cartographic Perspectives* 41: 4-23.

Crampton J (2003) Cartographic Rationality and the Politics of Geosurveillance and Security. *Cartography and Geographic Information Science* 30: 135-148.

Crampton J (2009) Cartography: Performative, Participatory, Political. *Progress in Human Geography* 33: 840-848.

Crampton J (2011a) Cartographic Calculations of Territory. *Progress in Human Geography* 35: 92-103.
Crampton J (2011b) *Mapping: A Critical Introduction to Cartography and GIS*. Chichester: Wiley Blackwell.
Crampton J, Elden S (2007) *Space, Knowledge and Power: Foucault and Geography*. Aldershot: Ashgate.
Crampton J, Krygier J (2006) An Introduction to Critical Cartography. *ACME: An International E-Journal for Critical Geographies* 4: 11-33.
Cubitt S, Palmer D, Tkcaz N (2015) Introduction: Materiality and Invisibility. In: Cubitt S, Palmer D, Tkcaz N (eds) *Digital Light*. London: Open Humanities Press, pp. 7-20.
Dalton C, Mason-Deese L (2012). Counter (Mapping) Actions: Mapping as Militant Research. *ACME: An International E-Journal for Critical Geographies* 11: 439-466.
Davis M (2006) Fear and Money in Dubai. *New Left Review* 41: 47-68.
Debord G (2010) *Society of the Spectacle*. Detroit: Black and Red.
De Certeau M (1984) *The Practice of Everyday Life*. Berkeley: University of California Press.
DeFrancis J (1984) *The Chinese Language: Fact and Fantasy*. Honolulu: University of Hawai'i Press.
Del Casino V, Hanna S (2005) Beyond the 'Binaries': A Methodological Intervention for Interrogating Maps as Representational Practices. *ACME: An International E-Journal for Critical Cartographies* 4: 34-56.
Deleuze G (1992a) *The Fold: Leibniz and the Baroque*. Minneapolis: University of Minnesota Press.
Deleuze G (1992b) Postscript on the Societies of Control. *October* 59: 3-7.
Deleuze G (1995) *Negotiations*. New York: Columbia University Press.
Deleuze G, Guattari F (1987) *A Thousand Plateaus: Capitalism and Schizophrenia*. Trans. Massumi B. Minneapolis: University of Minnesota Press.
Deleuze G, Hand S (1988) *Foucault*. Minneapolis: University of Minnesota Press.
Deller J (2012) *Sacrilege*. London: Glasgow International Festival of Visual Art/Mayor of London/Arts Council England.
Denzin, N (1989) *The Research Act*. 3rd ed. Englewood Cliffs, NJ: Prentice Hall.
De Risi V (2007) *Geometry and Monadology: Leibniz's Analysis Situs and the Philosophy of Space*. Basel: Birkhäuser.
De Souza e Silva A (2006) From Cyber to Hybrid: Mobile Technologies as Interfaces of Hybrid Spaces. *Space and Culture* 9: 261-278.
De Souza e Silva A, Sutko D (2009) *Digital Cityscapes: Merging Digital and Urban Playspaces*. New York: Peter Lang.
Dittmer J (2014) Geopolitical Assemblages and Complexity. *Progress in Human Geography* 38(3): 385-401.

Dodge M, Kitchin R, Perkins CR (2009a) *Rethinking Maps: New Frontiers in Cartographic Theory*. Abingdon: Routledge.

Dodge M, Perkins C, Kitchin R (2009b) Mapping Modes, Methods and Moments: a Manifesto for Map Studies. In: Dodge M, Kitchin R, Perkins C (eds) *Rethinking Maps: New Frontiers in Cartographic Theory*. London: Routledge, pp. 220-243.

Dreyfus H, Rabinow P (1983) *Michel Foucault: Beyond Structuralism and Hermeneutics*. Chicago: University of Chicago Press.

Dubrovsky R, Magnet S (2015) *Feminist Surveillance Studies*. Durham: Duke University Press.

Dung K-C (2012) *Atlas: Tales of an Imaginary City*. New York: Columbia University Press.

Eades G (2015) *Maps and Memes: Redrawing Culture, Place and Identity in Indigenous Communities*. Toronto: McGill-Queens University Press.

Eco U (1986) Architecture and Memory. *VIA Architecture and Literature: Journal of the Graduate School of Fine Arts University of Pennsylvania* 8: 88-94.

Edensor T (2015) Introduction to Geographies of Darkness. *Cultural Geographies* 22(4): 559-565.

Edney M (1997) *Mapping an Empire: The Geographical Construction of British India, 1765-1843*. Chicago: University of Chicago Press.

Elden S (2005) Missing the Point: Globalization, Deterritorialization and the Space of the World. *Transactions of the Institute of British Geographers* 30: 8-19.

Elden S (2006) *Speaking against Number: Heidegger, Language and the Politics of Calculation*. Edinburgh: Edinburgh University Press.

Elden S (2013a) *The Birth of Territory*. Chicago: University of Chicago Press.

Elden S (2013b) Leibniz and Geography: Geologist, Paleontologist, Biologist, Historian, Political Theorist and Geopolitician. *Geographica Helvetica* 68(2): 81-93.

Empson H (1992) *Mapping Hong Kong: A Historical Atlas*. [Hong Kong]: Government Information Services.

Erni JN (2001) Like a Postcolonial Culture: Hong Kong Re-Imagined. *Cultural Studies* 15(3-4): 389-418.

Evangelidis B (2018) Space and Time as Relations: The Theoretical Approach of Leibniz. *Philosophies* 3: 1-15.

Evans L (2015) *Locative Social Media: Place in the Digital Age*. London: Palgrave Macmillan.

Farinelli F (1992) *I segni del mondo. Immagine cartografica e discorso geografico in età moderna*. Firenze: La Nuova Italia.

Farinelli F (1994) Squaring the Circle, or The Nature of Political Identity. In: Farinelli F, Olsson G, Reichert D (eds) *Limits of Representation*. Munch: Accedo, pp. 11-28.

Farinelli F (1998) Did Anaximander Ever Say (or Write) Any Words about the Nature of Cartographical Reason. *Philosophy and Geography* 1: 135-144.

Farinelli F (2009) *La crisi della ragione cartografica*. Torino: Einaudi.
Farinelli F, Olsson G, Reichert D (eds) (1994) *Limits of Representation*. Munich: Accedo.
Farman J (2012) *Mobile Interface Theory: Embodied Space and Locative Media*. London: Taylor & Francis.
Featherstone M (2004) Automobilities: An Introduction. *Theory, Culture & Society* 21: 1-24.
Feyerabend P (2010) *Against Method*. London: Verso.
Flannery T (2000) The Birth of Sydney. Sydney: Text Publishing.
Foucault M (1976) Orientations. In: Wade S (ed.) *Chez Foucault*. Los Angeles: Circabook, pp. 1-3.
Foucault M (1980) Eye of Power. In: Gordon C (ed.) *Power/Knowledge: Selected Interviews and Other Writings, 1972-1977*. New York: Pantheon, pp. 146-165.
Foucault M (1984) Des espaces autres. *Architecture/Mouvement/Continuité* 5 (October), pp. 46-49.
Foucault M (1985) An Interview with Michel Foucault. *History of the Present* 2-3: 14.
Foucault M (1986) Of Other Spaces. Trans. Miskowiec J. *Diacritics* 16(1): 22-27.
Foucault M (1995) *Discipline and Punish: The Birth of the Prison*. New York: Vintage Books.
Foucault M (1998) *Aesthetics, Method and Epistemology*. New York: New Press.
Foucault M (2001a) Entretien avec Michel Foucault [1980]. In: Defert D, Ewald F, Lagrange J (eds) *Dits et écrits II. 1976-1988*. Paris: Gallimard, pp. 860-914.
Foucault M (2001b) Le discours ne doit pas être pris comme ... In: Defert D, Ewald F, Lagrange J (eds) *Dits et écrits II. 1976-1988*. Paris: Gallimard, pp. 123-124.
Foucault M (2001c) Nietzsche, Freud, Marx. In: Defert D, Ewald F, Lagrange J (eds) *Dits et écrits I. 1954-1975*. Paris: Quatro Gallimard, pp. 592-607.
Foucault M (2001d) Preface á la trangression. In: Defert D, Ewald F, Lagrange J (eds) *Dits et écrits I. 1954-1975*. Paris: Gallimard, pp. 261-266.
Foucault M (2001e) Prisons et asiles dans le mécanisme du pouvoir. In: Defert D, Ewald F, Lagrange J (eds) *Dits et écrits 1. 1954-1975*. Paris: Gallimard, pp. 1389-1393.
Foucault M (2001f) Sur l'archéologie des sciences. Réponse au cercle d'épistémologie. In: Defert D, Ewald F, Lagrange J (eds) *Dits et écrits 1. 1954-1975*. France: Gallimard, pp. 724-759.
Foucault M (2001g) Theatrum Philosophicum. In: Defert D, Ewald F, Lagrange J (eds) *Dits et écrits 1. 1954-1975*. Paris: Gallimard, pp. 943-967
Foucault M (2002a) *The Archaeology of Knowledge*. London: Routledge.
Foucault M (2002b) *The Order of Things*. London: Routledge.
Foucault M (2003) 'Society Must Be Defended': Lectures at the Collège de France, 1975-76. In: Bertani M, Fontana A (eds). New York: Picador.
Frampton A, Solomon JD, Wong C (2012) *Cities without Ground: A Hong Kong Guidebook*. San Rafael, CA: ORO Editions.

Galloway A (2004) *Protocol: How Control Exists after Decentralization*. Cambridge, MA: MIT Press.

Galloway A, Ward M (2006) Locative Media as Socialising and Spatializing Practice: Learning from Archaeology. *Leonardo Electronic Almanac* 14.

Gamson WA (1991) Commitment and Agency in Social Movements. *Sociological Forum* 6: 27-50.

Garbutt R (2015) A Stutter in the Landscape. Research Seminar, The Centre for Human Rights Education and the Department of Communication and Cultural Studies, Curtin University of Technology. https://echo.ilecture.curtin.edu.au:8443/ess/echo/presentation/2ede7708-3a38-4f90-852e-e74c017de1ad [last accessed 2 January 2018].

Gaskins N (2016) Afrofuturism on Web 3.0: Vernacular Cartography and Augmented Space. In Anderson R, Jones C (eds) *Afrofuturism 2.0 The Rise of Astro-Blackness*. London: Lexington Books, pp. 27-44.

Gehl J et al. (2007) Public Spaces, Public Life: Sydney. Gehl Architects. https://issuu.com/gehlarchitects/docs/issuu_516_sydney_pspl2007.

Genoni P (2012) The Sydney Harbour Bridge: From Modernity to Post-modernity in Australian Fiction. *Journal of the Association for the Study of Australian Literature* 12(1).

Gerlach J (2010) Vernacular Mapping, and the Ethics of What Comes Next. *Cartographica: The International Journal for Geographic Information and Geovisualization* 45(3): 165-168.

Gerlach J (2014) Lines, Contours and Legends: Coordinates for Vernacular Mapping. *Progress in Human Geography* 38(1): 22-39.

Gibson C (2006) Sydney's Creative Economy: Social and Spatial Challenges. In: Freestone R, Randolph B, Butler-Bowden C (eds) *Talking about Sydney: Population, Communication and Culture in Contemporary Sydney*. Sydney, Australia: UNSW Press, pp. 185-197.

Giddens A (1990) *The Consequences of Modernity*. Stanford, CA: Stanford University Press.

Glasze G, Perkins C (2015) Social and Political Dimension of the OpenStreetMap Project: Towards a Critical Geographical Research Agenda. In: Arnsanjani JJ et al. (eds) *OpenStreetMap in GIScience*. Heidelberg: Springer Verlag, pp. 143-166.

Goodchild M (2007) Citizens as Sensors: The World of Volunteered Geography. *GeoJournal* 69: 211-221.

Goodchild M (2009) Neogeography and the Nature of Geographic Expertise. *Journal of Location-Based Services* 3: 82-96.

Gordon A (2008) *Ghostly Matters: Haunting and the Sociological Imagination*. Minneapolis: University of Minnesota Press.

Graham S (2014) Super-tall and Ultra-deep: The Cultural Politics of the Elevator. *Theory, Culture & Society* 31(7-8): 239-269.

Graham S, Hewitt L (2012) Getting off the Ground: On the Geopolitics of Urban Verticality. *Progress in Human Geography* 37: 72-92.

Gregory D (1994) *Geographical Imaginations*. Cambridge, MA: Blackwell.

Grodach C (2009) Urban Branding: An Analysis of City Homepage Imagery. *Journal of Architectural and Planning Research* 26: 181-197.

Haklay M (2013) Citizen Science and Volunteered Geographic Information: Overview and Typology of Participation. In: Sui D, Elwood S, Goodchild M (eds) *Crowdsourcing Geographic Knowledge: Volunteered Geographic Information (VGI) in Theory and Practice*. Amsterdam: Springer, pp. 105-122.

Hall S (2001) Constituting an Archive. *Third Text* 15: 89-92.

Haraway D (1988) Situated Knowledges: The Science Question in Feminism and the Privilege of Partial Perspective. *Feminist Studies* 14(3): 575-599.

Haraway D (1991) *Simians, Cyborgs and Women: The Reinvention of Nature*. New York: Routledge.

Haraway DJ (2016) *Staying with the Trouble: Making Kin in the Chthulucene*. Durham, NC: Duke University Press.

Hardt M, Negri A (2004) *Multitude: War and Democracy in an Age of Empire*. New York: Penguin.

Harley JB (1988a) Maps, Knowledge and Power. In: Cosgrove DE, Daniels S (eds) *The Iconography of the Landscape: Essays on the Symbolic Representation, Design, and Use of Past Environments*. Cambridge: Cambridge University Press, pp. 277-307.

Harley JB (1988b) Silences and Secrecy: The Hidden Agenda of Cartography in Early Modern Europe. *Imago Mundi* 40: 57-76.

Harley JB (1992) Deconstructing the Map. In: Barnes TJ, Duncan JS (eds) *Writing Worlds: Discourse, Text, and Metaphor in the Representation of Landscape*. London: Routledge, pp. 231-247.

Harley JB (2001) *The New Nature of Maps: Essays in the History of Cartography*. Baltimore, MD: Johns Hopkins University Press.

Harris A (2015) Vertical Urbanisms: Opening up Geographies of the Three-Dimensional City. *Progress in Human Geography* 39(5): 601-620.

Hartz GA, Cover JA (1988) Space and Time in the Leibnizian Metaphysic. *Noûs* 22(4): 493-519.

Harvey D (1989) *The Condition of Postmodernity: An Enquiry Into the Origins of Cultural Change*. Oxford: Blackwell.

Harvey D (2000a) Cosmopolitanism and the Banality of Geographical Evils. In: Comaroff J, Comaroff J (eds) *Millennial Capitalism and the Culture of Neoliberalism*. Durham, NC: Duke University Press, pp. 271-310.

Harvey D (2000b) *Spaces of Hope*. Berkeley: University of California Press.

Harzinski K (2010) *From Here to There: A Curious Collection from the Hand Drawn Map Association*. New York: Princeton Architectural Press.

Healy C (1997) *From the Ruins of Colonialism: History as Social Memory*. Cambridge: Cambridge University Press.

Hjorth L, Burgess J, Richardson I (eds) (2012) *Studying Mobile Media: Cultural Technologies, Mobile Communication and the iPhone*. New York: Routledge.

Hjorth L, Khoo O (2015) Intimate Entanglements: New Media in Asia. In: Hjorth L, Khoo O (eds) *Routledge Handbook of New Media in Asia*. London: Routledge, pp. 1-15.

Hobson EW (1913) *'Squaring the Circle': A History of the Problem*. Cambridge: Cambridge University Press.

Hon T-K (2011) A Rock, a Text, and a Tablet: Making of the Song Emperor's Terrace as a Lieu de Mémoire. In: Matten M (ed.) *Places of Memory in Modern China: History, Politics, and Identity*. Leiden: Brill, pp. 133-165.

Hong Kong Gazette (1899) Sung Wong Toi Reservation Ordinance 1899. *Historical Laws of Hong Kong Online*. https://oelawhk.lib.hku.hk/items/show/89. Accessed 22nd January 2018.

Hoskins I (2009) *Sydney Harbour: A History*. Sydney: UNSW Press.

Hostetler L (2001) *Qing Colonial Enterprise: Ethnography and Cartography in Early Modern China*. Chicago: University of Chicago Press.

Hughes R (2003) *The Fatal Shore: A History of the Transportation of the Convicts to Australia, 1787-1868*. London: Vintage.

Huhtamo E, Parikka J (eds) (2011) *Media Archaeology: Approaches, Applications and Implications*. Berkeley: University of California Press.

Hui PK, Lau KC (2015) 'Living in Truth' vs Realpolitik: Limitations and Potentials of the Umbrella Movement. *Inter-Asia Cultural Studies* 16(3): 348-366.

Huxley M (2006) Spatial Rationalities: Order, Environment, Evolution and Government. *Social & Cultural Geography* 7(5): 771-787.

Huyssen A (2003) *Present Pasts: Urban Palimpsests and the Politics of Memory*. Stanford, CA: Stanford University Press.

Jacobs J (1962) *The Death and Life of Great American Cities*. London: Jonathan Cape.

Jacobs JM (1996) *Edge of Empire: Postcolonialism and the City*. London: Routledge.

Jakubowicz A, Ho C (eds) (2012) *'For Those Who've Come Across the Seas ...': Australian Multicultural Theory, Policy and Practice*. Melbourne: Anthem Press.

James D (2013) Signposted by Song: Cultural Routes of the Australian Desert. *Historic Environment* 25: 30-42.

Jameson F (1991) *Postmodernism, or, the Cultural Logic of Late Capitalism*. Durham, NC: Duke University Press.

Jayaram N (2011) Review of Gordan Mathews, *Ghetto at the Centre of the World: Chungking Mansions, Hong Kong*. *China Perspectives* 2: 93-94.

Joseph, GG (2011) *The Crest of the Peacock: Non-European Roots of Mathematics (Third Edition)*. Princeton: Princeton University Press.

Kadison D (2009) Can a Street Name Be Biased? Some Think So. *South China Morning Post*, 4 October.

Kaika M (2010) Architecture and Crisis: Re-inventing the Icon, Re-imag(in)ing London and Re-branding the City. *Transactions of the Institute of British Geographers* 35: 453-474.

Kamiyama K (dir.) (2005) *SA: Time of the Machines – MACHINES DÉSIRANTES*. Season 1, episode 15, of *Ghost in the Shell: Stand Alone Complex* [television series]. Japan: Production I.G., Inc., 20 February.

Kane C (2014) *Chromatic Algorithms: Synthetic Color, Computer Art, and Aesthetics after Code*. Chicago: University of Chicago Press.

Karskens G (1999) *Inside the Rocks: The Archaeology of a Neighbourhood*. Sydney: Hale and Iremonger.

Karskens G (2009) *The Colony: A History of Early Sydney*. Sydney: Allen and Unwin.

Katz J (2001) *How Emotions Work*. Chicago: University of Chicago Press.

Kirsch G, Rohan L (2008) *Beyond the Archives: Research as a Lived Process*. Carbondale: Southern Illinois University Press.

Kitchin R, Freundschuh S (eds) (2000) *Cognitive Mapping: Past, Present and Future*. London: Routledge.

Kitchin R, Perkins C, Dodge M (2009) Thinking about Maps. In: Dodge M, Kitchin R, Perkins C (eds) *Rethinking Maps: New Frontiers in Cartographic Theory*. London: Routledge, pp. 1-25.

Kitchin R, Perng S-Y (eds) (2016) *Code and the City*. London: Routledge.

Kluitenberg E (2011) On the Archaeology of Imaginary Media. In: Huhtamo E, Parikka J (eds) *Media Archaeology: Approaches, Applications and Implications*. Berkeley: University of California Press, pp. 48-69.

Knott J (2000) The 'Conquering Car': Technology, Symbolism and the Motorisation of Australia before World War II. *Australian Historical Studies* 31: 1-26.

Kornwolf JD, Kornwolf GW (2002) *Architecture and Town Planning in Colonial North America*, 3 vols. Baltimore, MD: Johns Hopkins University Press.

Krygier J, Wood D (2009) Ce N'est Pas le Monde (This Is Not the World). In: Kitchin R, Dodge M, Perkins C (eds) *Rethinking Maps: New Frontiers for Critical Cartography*. London: Routledge, pp. 189-219.

Ku AS-M (2012) Remaking Places and Fashioning and Opposition Discourse: Struggle over the Star Ferry Pier and the Queen's Pier in Hong Kong. *Environment and Planning D: Society and Space* 30: 5-22.

Kwan S, Kwan N (2008) *The Dragon and the Crown: Hong Kong Memoirs.* Hong Kong: Hong Kong University Press.

Laita L (1980) Boolean Algebra and Its Extra-Logical Sources: The Testimony of Mary Everest Boole. *History and Philosophy of Logic* 1: 37-60.

Lammes S (2017) Digital Mapping Interfaces: From Immutable Mobiles to Mutable Images. *New Media & Society* 19(7): 1019-1033.

Lang JT (1956) *I Remember.* Sydney: Invincible Press.

Latour B (1987) Opening One Eye While Closing the Other … A Note on Some Religious Paintings. *Sociological Review* 35 (Supplement S1): 15-38.

Latour B (1986) Visualisation and Cognition: Thinking with Eyes and Hands. In: Kuklick H (ed.) *Knowledge and Society: Studies in the Sociology of Culture Past and Present* Greenwich, CT: Jai Press, pp. 1-40.

Latour B (1993) *We Have Never Been Modern.* Cambridge, MA: Harvard University Press.

Latour B (1998) Ein Ding ist ein Thing – A (Philosophical) Platform for a Left (European) Party. *Concepts and Transformation* 3(1/2): 97-112.

Latour B (2000) The Berlin Key or How to Do Words with Things. In: Graves-Brown P (ed.) *Matter, Materiality and Modern Culture.* London: Routledge, pp. 10-21.

Latour B (2013) *An Inquiry into the Modes of Existence.* Cambridge, MA: Harvard University Press.

Latour B, Woolgar S (1979) *Laboratory Life.* Princeton: Princeton University Press.

Laurier E et al. (2008) Driving and Passengering: Notes on the Ordinary Organization of Car Travel. *Mobilities* 3: 1-23.

Law L (2002) Defying Disappearance: Cosmopolitan Public Spaces in Hong Kong. *Urban Studies* 39: 1625-1645.

Law J, Lin WY (2010) Cultivating Disconcertment. *Sociological Review* 58(2): 135-153.

Leibniz GW (1697) Binärcode. Brief an Rudolph August, Herzog zu Braunschweig und Lüneburg, sog. Neujahrsbrief, 12. Januar 1697, Briefseite, GWLB: LBR II 15, Bl. 19v. Leibniz Central. http://dokumente.leibnizcentral.de/index.php?id=54 [last accessed 7 November 2019].

Leibniz GW (1705) Leibniz-Handschriften zur Mathematik, 1705, LH 35, 4, 20. http://digitale-sammlungen.gwlb.de/resolve?id=00068017 [last accessed 7 November 2019].

Leibniz GW (1991) *Discourse on Metaphysics and Other Essays.* Trans. Garber D, Ariew R. Indianapolis: Hackett.

Leibniz GW, Bouvet J (n.d.) Leibniz-Bouvet Correspondence. Trans. and annotations Berkowitz A, Cook DJ. https://leibniz-bouvet.swarthmore.edu/letters/letter-i-4-november-1701-bouvet-to-leibniz/ [last accessed 7 November 2019].

Leibniz GW, Clarke S (2007) Exchange of Papers between Leibniz and Clarke. Ed. Bennett J. http://www.earlymoderntexts.com/assets/pdfs/leibniz1715_1.pdf [last accessed 2 January 2018].

Leibniz GW, Loptson P (2012) *Discourse on Metaphysics and Other Writings*. Trans. Latta R, Montgomery G. London: Broadview Editions.
Leszczynski A (2009a) Poststructuralism and GIS: Is There a 'Disconnect'? *Environment and Planning D: Society and Space* 27: 581-602.
Leszczynski A (2009b) Rematerializing GIScience. *Environment and Planning D: Society and Space* 27: 609-615.
Leszczynski A (2015) Spatial Mediation. *Progress in Human Geography* 39(6): 729-751.
Leszczynski A, Crampton J (2016) Introduction: Spatial Big Data and Everyday Life. *Big Data and Society* 3(2): 1-6.
Lévy J (2012) A Cartographic Turn? *EspacesTemps.net*, 27 February. http://www.espacestemps.net/articles/a-cartographic-turn/ [last accessed 2 January 2018].
Lorimer H (2005) Cultural Geography: The Busyness of Being 'More-Than-Representational'. *Progress in Human Geography* 29: 83-94.
Lorimer H (2009) Caught in the Nick of Time: Archives and Fieldwork. In: DeLyser D et al. (eds) *The Sage Handbook of Qualitative Research in Human Geography*. London: Sage, pp. 248-273.
Lunde K (2009) *CJKV Information Processing*, 2nd ed. Sebastopol, CA: O'Reilly Media.
Lury C, Parisi L, Terranova T (2012) Introduction: The Becoming Topological of Culture. *Theory, Culture & Society* 29: 3-35.
Lynch K (1960) *The Image of the City*. Cambridge, MA: MIT Press.
Maclehose J (1977) *Picture of Sydney and Strangers' Guide in New South Wales for 1839*. Sydney: John Ferguson in Association with the Royal Australian Historical Society.
Manning E (2015) Against Method. In: Vannini P (ed.) *Non-Representational Methodologies: Re-Envisioning Research*. London: Routledge, pp. 52-71.
Marvin C (1990) *When Old Technologies Were New: Thinking about Electric Communication in the Late Nineteenth Century*. New York: Oxford University Press.
Massey D (1991) A Global Sense of Place. *Marxism Today* 38: 24-29.
Massey D (1993) Power-Geometry and a Progressive Sense of Place. In: Bird J et al. (eds) *Mapping the Futures: Local Cultures, Global Change*. London: Routledge, pp. 59-69.
Massey D (2003) Some Times of Space. In: May S (ed.) *Olafur Eliasson: The Weather Project – Exhibition Catalogue*. London: Tate Publishing, pp. 107-118.
Massey D (2005) *For Space*. London: Sage.
Massumi B (2002) *Parables for the Virtual*. Durham, NC: Duke University Press.
Mathews G (2011) *Ghetto at the Centre of the World: Chungking Mansions, Hong Kong*. Chicago: University of Chicago Press.
Mattern S (2017) *Code, Clay, Data and Dirt: Five Thousand Years of Urban Media*. Minneapolis: University of Minnesota Press.

McFarlane C (2010) The Comparative City: Knowledge, Learning, Urbanism. *International Journal of Urban and Regional Research* 34(4): 725-742.

McFarlane C (2016) The Geographies of Urban Density: Topology, Politics and the City. *Progress in Human Geography* 40(5): 629-648.

McFarlane R (2012) *The Old Ways: A Journey on Foot*. London: Penguin.

McNeill D (2005) Skyscraper Geography. *Progress in Human Geography* 29: 41-55.

Merriman P (2007) *Driving Spaces*. Oxford: Wiley Blackwell.

Mitchell P (2008) *Cartographic Strategies of Postmodernity: The Figure of the Map in Contemporary Theory and Fiction*. New York: Routledge.

Monmonier M (1996) *How to Lie with Maps*. Chicago: University of Chicago Press.

Munster A (2006) *Materialising New Media: Embodiment and Information Aesthetics*. Hanover, NH: Dartmouth University Press.

Munster A (2013) *An Aesthesia of Networks: Conjunctive Experience in Art and Technology*. Cambridge, MA: MIT Press.

Neocleous M (2003) *Imagining the State*. Maidenhead: Open University Press

Nespor J (2000) Anonymity and Place in Qualitative Inquiry. *Qualitative Inquiry* 6(4): 546-569.

Nietzsche FW (1973) *The Will to Power*. Trans. Kaufmann W, Hollingdale R. New York: Vintage.

Ng MK, Tang WS, Leung D (2010) Spatial Practice, Conceived Space and Lived Space: Hong Kong's 'Piers Saga' through the Lefebvrian Lens. *Planning Perspectives* 25(4): 411-431.

Ning ACT et al. (2010) *Towards a Sustainable Reclamation for Hong Kong*. Hong Kong: HKIE Environmental Division, Hong Kong Highways Department.

Nissim R (2011) *Land Administration and Practice in Hong Kong*, 3rd ed. Hong Kong: Hong Kong University Press.

Nitecki A (2008) Making Connections. In: Kirsch G, Rohan L (eds) *Beyond the Archives: Research as a Lived Process*. Carbondale: Southern Illinois University Press, pp. 37-46.

NSW Government Office of Environment and Heritage (2008) *Macquarie Place Precinct*. State Heritage Inventory/Heritage Office 5053111, S90/05437, H04/00091/8 (ICONS). http://www.environment.nsw.gov.au/heritageapp/ViewHeritageItemDetails.aspx?ID=5053111 [last accessed 2 January 2018]

NSW Government Transport, Roads and Maritime Services (2013) *Alpha Numeric Route Numbers – A New Road Numbering System*. http://www.rms.nsw.gov.au/roads/using-roads/alpha-numeric/index.html [last accessed 2 January 2018].

Northern Territory Government (2016) Place Names Register Extract: Uluru/Ayers Rock. http://www.ntlis.nt.gov.au/placenames/view.jsp?id=10532 [last accessed 2 January 2018].

Nugent M (2005) *Botany Bay: Where Histories Meet*. Sydney, NSW: Allen and Unwin.

Olsson G (1979) Social Science and Human Action or On Hitting Your Head on the Ceiling of Language. In: Gale S, Olsson G (eds) *Philosophy in Geography*. Dordrecht: Holland: D. Reidel Publishing Company, pp. 287-307.

Olsson G (1980) *Birds in Egg/Eggs in Bird*. London: Pion.

Olsson G (1988) The Eye and the Index Finger: Bodily Means to Cultural Meaning. In: Golledge RG, Couclelis H, Gould P (eds) *A Ground for Common Search*. Santa Barbara, CA: Santa Barbara Geographical Press.

Olsson G (1991a) Invisible Maps: A Prospectus. *Geografiska Annaler: Series B, Human Geography* 73: 85-91.

Olsson G (1991b) *Lines of Power/Limits of Language*. Minneapolis: University of Minnesota Press.

Olsson G (1993) Chiasm of Thought-and-Action. *Environment and Planning D: Society and Space* 11: 279-294.

Olsson G (2007) *Abysmal: A Critique of Cartographic Reason*. Chicago: University of Chicago Press.

Olsson G (2010) Mapping the Forbidden. *Fennia: International Journal of Geography* 188: 3-10.

Ortmann, S (2015) The Umbrella Movement and Hong Kong's Protracted Democratization Process. *Asian Affairs* 46(1): 32-50.

Parikka J (2013) *What Is Media Archaeology?* Oxford: Wiley.

Parikka J (2015) *A Geology of Media*. Minneapolis: University of Minnesota Press.

Parisi, L (2013) *Contagious Architecture: Computation, Aesthetics and Space*. Cambridge, MA: MIT Press.

Park R (1974) *A Companion Guide to Sydney*. Sydney: Collins.

Patrikeeff F (1989) *The Mouldering Pearl: Hong Kong at the Crossroads*. London: Octopus Publishing.

Peckhaus V (2009) Leibniz's Influence on 19$^{th}$ Century Logic. In: Zalta E (ed.) *The Stanford Encyclopedia of Philosophy* [Fall 2009 edition]. Stanford: Stanford University. https://plato.stanford.edu/archives/spr2014/entries/leibniz-logic-influence/ [last accessed 2 January 2018].

Pegg RA (2014) *Cartographic Traditions in East Asian Maps*. Honolulu: University of Hawai'i Press.

Perkins F (2004) *Leibniz and China: A Commerce of Light*. Cambridge: Cambridge University Press.

Perkins R (2008) They Have Come to Stay. In: Perkins R (ed.) *First Australians*. Sydney, Australia: Sydney Broadcasting Service (SBS).

Peters JD (2015) *The Marvelous Clouds: Toward a Philosophy of Elemental Media*. Chicago: University of Chicago Press.

Philo C (1992) Foucault's Geography. *Environment and Planning D: Society and Space* 10: 137-161.

Pickles J (2000) Cartography, Digital Transitions and Questions of History. *Cartographic Perspectives* 37: 4-18.

Pickles J (2004) *A History of Spaces: Cartographic Reason, Mapping, and the Geo-Coded World*. New York: Routledge.

Picon A, Ponte A (2003) *Architecture and the Sciences: Exchanging Metaphors*. New York: Princeton Architectural Press.

Pinder D (2007) Cartographies Unbound. *Cultural Geographies* 14(3): 453-462.

Povinelli E (2002) *The Cunning of Recognition: Indigenous Alterities and the Making of Australian Multiculturalism*. Durham, NC: Duke University Press.

Pratt M (1992) *Imperial Eyes*. London: Routledge.

Prytherch D, Cidell J (2015) Introduction: Transportation, Mobilities, and Rethinking Urban Geographies of Flow. In: Cidell J, Prytherch, D (eds) *Transport, Mobility, and the Production of Urban Space*. London: Routledge, pp. 19-44.

Rankin W (2016) *After the Map: Cartography, Navigation and the Transformation of Territory in the Twentieth Century*. Chicago: University of Chicago Press.

Reichert D (1998) Weisen der Welterzeugung: Zur Möglichkeit einer Geographie aus der Welt [Ways of worldmaking: Towards the possibility of a geography from the world]. *Geographica Helvetica* 3: 112-118.

Ren H (2010) *Neoliberalism and Culture in China and Hong Kong: The Countdown of Time*. London: Routledge.

Rescher N (2013) *On Leibniz*. Pittsburgh: University of Pittsburgh Press.

Resina JR, Ingenschay D (2003) *After-Images of the City*. Ithaca, NY: Cornell University Press.

Richardson I (2005) FCJ-032 Mobile Technosoma: Some Phenomenological Reflections on Itinerant Media Devices. *The Fibreculture Journal* 6. http://six.fibreculturejournal.org/fcj-032-mobile-technosoma-some-phenomenological-reflections-on-itinerant-media-devices/ [last accessed: 7 November 2019].

Rose G, Degen M, Melhuish C (2014) Networks, Interfaces and Computer Generated Images: Learning from Digital Visualisations of Urban Redevelopment Projects. *Environment and Planning D: Society and Space* 32: 386-403.

Rose-Redwood R (2006) Governmentality, Geography, and the Geo-Coded World. *Progress in Human Geography* 30(4): 469-486.

Rose-Redwood R (2012a) Introduction: Governmentality, House Numbering, and the Spatial History of the Modern City. *Urban History* 39(4): 607-613.

Rose-Redwood R (2012b) 'A Regular State of Beautiful Confusion': Governing by Numbers and the Contradictions of Calculable Space in New York City. *Urban History* 39(4): 624-638.

Rose-Redwood R (2012c) With Numbers in Place: Security, Territory, and the Production of Calculable Space. *Annals of the Association of American Geographers* 102(2): 295-319.

Rose-Redwood R, Tantner A (2012) Introduction: Governmentality, House Numbering, and the Spatial History of the Modern City. *Urban History* 39(4): 607-613.
Rossi A (1984) *The Architecture of the City.* Cambridge, MA: MIT Press.
Rossiter N (2003) Processual Media Theory. *symplokē* 11: 104-131.
Ryan S (1996) *The Cartographic Eye: How Explorers Saw Australia.* Cambridge: Cambridge University Press.
Ryle G (2009) *The Concept of Mind.* London: Routledge.
Rynasiewicz R (1996) Absolute versus Relational Space-Time: An Outmoded Debate. *Journal of Philosophy* 93: 279-306.
Sadler S (1999) *The Situationist City.* Cambridge, MA: MIT Press.
Said EW (1978) *Orientalism.* New York: Pantheon.
Said EW (1990) Yeats and Decolonization. In: Eagleton T, Jameson F, Said EW (eds) *Nationalism, Colonialism and Literature.* Minneapolis: University of Minnesota Press, pp. 68-90.
Said EW (1993) *Culture and Imperialism.* London: Vintage Books.
Said EW (1997) *Beginnings: Intention and Method.* London: Granta Books.
Said EW (2004) *Orientalism* and After. Interview with Anne Beezer and Peter Osbourne. In: Viswanathan V (ed.) *Power, Politics and Culture: Interviews with Edward W. Said.* London: Bloomsbury, pp. 208-232.
Sassen S (2001) *Global City: New York, London, Tokyo.* Princeton: Princeton University Press.
Saukko, P (2003) *Doing Research in Cultural Studies: An Introduction to Classical and New Methodological Approaches.* London: Sage.
Schlunke K (2008) Captain Cook Chased a Chook. *Cultural Studies Review* 16: 43-54.
Schlunke K (2013) One Colonial Thing: Material Remembering and the Bark Shield of Botany Bay. *Continuum: Journal of Media and Cultural Studies* 27: 18-29.
Schuurman N (2000) Trouble in the Heartland: GIS and Its Critics in the 1990s. *Progress in Human Geography* 24: 569-590.
Schuurman N (2009) The New Brave New World: Geography, GIS, and the Emergence of Ubiquitous Mapping and Data. *Environment and Planning D: Society and Space* 27(4): 571-580.
Serres M (1982a) *Hermes: Science, Literature, Philosophy.* Trans. Anderson M. Baltimore, MD: Johns Hopkins University Press.
Serres M (1982b) *The Parasite.* Trans. Schehr I. Baltimore, MD: Johns Hopkins University Press.
Serres M (1994) *Atlas,* Paris: Editions Juilliard.
Serres M (2008) *The Five Senses: A Philosophy of Mingled Bodies.* Trans. Sankey M, Cowley P. London: Continuum.
Serres M (2011) *Les origines de la géométrie: tiers livre des fondations.* Paris: Flammarion.

Serres M (2014) *Le système de Leibniz et ses modèles mathématiques*. Paris: PUF Presses Universitaires de France.
Serres M (2017) *The Origins of Geometry*. Trans. Burks R. London: Bloomsbury.
Serres M, Latour B (1995) *Conversations on Science, Culture and Time*. Ann Arbor: The University of Michigan Press.
Sheller M, Urry J (2000) The City and the Car. *International Journal of Urban and Regional Research* 24: 737-757.
Sheller M, Urry J (2006) The New Mobilities Paradigm. *Environment and Planning A: Economy and Space* 38(2): 207-226.
Shelton B, Karakiewicz J, Kvan T (2010) *The Making of Hong Kong: From Vertical to Volumetric*. London: Taylor & Francis.
Shields R (2013) *Spatial Questions: Cultural Topologies and Social Spatialisation*. London: Sage.
Snow D (2001). Collective Identity and Expressive Forms. In: Smelser N, Baltes P (eds) *The International Encyclopedia of the Social and Behavioral Sciences*, 26 vols. Oxford: Elsevier, I, pp. 2212-2219
Sobel D (1998) *Longitude*. London: Fourth Estate.
Söderström O (1996) Paper Cities: Visual Thinking in Urban Planning. *Cultural Geographies* 3: 249-281.
Soja EW (1989) *Postmodern Geographies: The Reassertion of Space in Critical Social Theory*. London: Verso.
Soja EW (1996) *Thirdspace: Journeys to Los Angeles and Other Real-and-Imagined Places*. Cambridge, MA: Blackwell.
Soja EW (2000) *Postmetropolis: Critical Studies of Cities and Regions*. Cambridge, MA: Blackwell
Sparke M (1998) The Map that Roared and an Original Atlas: Canada, Cartography, and the Narration of Nation. *Annals of the Association of American Geographers* 88(3): 463-495.
Spearritt P (2000) *Sydney's Century: A History*. Sydney: UNSW Press.
Spinney JE (2003) Mobile Positioning and LBS Applications. *Geography* 88: 256-265.
Spivak GC (1988) Can the Subaltern Speak? In: Nelson C, Grossberg L (eds) *Marxism and the Interpretation of Culture*. Urbana: University of Illinois Press, pp. 271-314.
Spivak GC (1990) Poststructuralism, Marginality, Postcoloniality and Value. In: Collier P, Geyer-Ryan H (eds) *Literary Theory Today*. Ithaca, NY: Cornell University Press, pp. 198-211.
Spivak GC (1999) *Critique of Postcolonial Reason*. Cambridge, MA: Harvard University Press.
Stewart K (1996) *A Space on the Side of the Road: Cultural Poetics in an 'Other' America*. Princeton: Princeton University Press.
Stewart K (2007) *Ordinary Affects*. Durham, NC: Duke University Press.

Stiegler B (1998) *Technics and Time, 1: The Fault of Epimetheus*. Stanford, CA: Stanford: Stanford University Press.

Stoler AL (2002) Colonial Archives and the Arts of Governance. *Archival Science* 2(1): 87-109.

Stone L (1949) Elizabethan Overseas Trade. *Economic History Review* 2: 30-58.

Sui D, Goodchild M (2011) The Convergence of GIS and Social Media: Challenges for GIScience. *International Journal of Geographical Information Science* 25: 1737-1748.

Survey and Mapping Office (1996) *Reclamation and Development in Hong Kong. AR/9/RD.* 4th ed. Hong Kong: Hong Kong Government.

Syme P (1821) *Werner's Nomenclature of Colours, with Additions, Arranged so as to Render It Useful to the Arts and Sciences*. Edinburgh: William Blackwood. https://archive.org/details/gri_c00033125012743312 [last accessed 2 January 2018].

Sydney Gazette (1810) Plan of the New and Old Names of Streets, in the Town of Sydney, with Explanation and References. *Sydney Gazette and New South Wales Advertiser*, 6 October.

Sydney Morning Herald (1913) Sydney's Dangerous Traffic. *Sydney Morning Herald*, Tuesday 3rd June, p. 8.

Sydney Morning Herald (1924) The New Road Era. *Sydney Morning Herald*, Friday 11 April, p. 15.

Tench W (1789) *A Narrative of the Expedition to Botany Bay: With an Account of New South Wales, Its Productions, Inhabitants, &c.: to Which is Subjoined a List of the Civil and Military Establishments at Port Jackson*. London: J. Debrett.

Tench W (1793) *A Complete Account of the Settlement at Port Jackson in New South-Wales, Including an Accurate Description of the Situation of the Colony; of the Natives and of Its Natural Productions*. London: J. Sewell Cornhill.

Thalis P, Cantrill P (2013) *Public Sydney: Drawing the City*. Sydney: The Historic Houses Trust of NSW and the NSW Mint.

Thielmann T (2010) Locative Media and Mediated Localities: An Introduction to Media Geography. *Aether: The Journal of Media Geography* 5: 1-17.

Thrift N (2004a) Driving in the City. *Theory, Culture, and Society* 21: 41-59.

Thrift N (2004b) Movement-Space: The Changing Domain of Thinking Resulting from the Development of New Kinds of Spatial Awareness. *Economy and Society* 33(4): 582-604.

Turnbull D (2000) *Masons, Tricksters and Cartographers: Comparative Studies in the Sociology of Scientific and Indigenous Knowledge*. Amsterdam: Harwood Academic Publishers.

Urry J (2004) The System of Automobility. *Theory, Culture & Society* 21: 25-39.

Van Houtum H, Kramsch O, Zierhofer W (2005) *B/ordering Space*. Aldershot: Ashgate.

Verhoeff N (2012) *Mobile Screens: The Visual Regime of Navigation*. Amsterdam: Amsterdam University Press.

Visker R (1995) *Michel Foucault: Genealogy as Critique*. London: Verso.

Wade S (1978) *Chez Foucault*. Los Angeles: Circabook.

Warf B, Sui D (2010) From GIS to Neogeography: Ontological Implications and Theories of Truth. *Annals of GIS* 16: 197-209.

Warringah Council (2015) *Aboriginal Warringah*. http://www.warringah.nsw.gov.au/environment/about-warringah/aboriginal-heritage [last accessed 1 September 2016].

Weizman E (2002) The Politics of Verticality. *Open Democracy*, 23 April. https://www.opendemocracy.net/ecology-politicsverticality/article_801.jsp [last accessed 7 November 2019].

Wilhelm H (1967) *The I Ching or Book of Changes*. Princeton: Princeton University Press.

Williams M, May T (1996) *Introduction to the Philosophy of Social Research*. London: University College London Press.

Wilmott C (2016) Small Moments in Spatial Big Data: Calculability, Authority and Interoperability in Everyday Mobile Mapping. *Big Data and Society* 3: 1-16.

Wilmott C (2017) In-between Maps and Media: Movement. *Journal of Television and New Media* 18(4): 320-335.

Wilson M (2017) *New Lines: Critical GIS and the Trouble of the Map*. Minneapolis: University of Minnesota Press.

Wiseman C (2001) *The Architecture of I.M. Pei*. London: Thames & Hudson.

Wood D, Fels J (1992) *The Power of Maps*. New York: Guilford Press.

Yanne A, Heller G (2009) *Signs of a Colonial Era*. Hong Kong: Hong Kong University Press.

Zielinski S (2006) *Deep Time of the Media: Toward an Archaeology of Hearing and Seeing by Technical Means*. Cambridge, MA: MIT Press.

Zook M, Graham M (2007) Mapping DigiPlace: Geocoded Internet Data and the Representation of Place. *Environment and Planning B: Planning and Design* 34: 466-482.

Zukin S (2010) *Naked City: The Death and Life of Authentic Urban Places*. New York: Oxford University Press.

Zylinska J (2009) *Bioethics in the Age of New Media*. Cambridge, MA: MIT Press.

# Index

For Product Safety Concerns and Information please contact our EU representative GPSR@taylorandfrancis.com Taylor & Francis Verlag GmbH, Kaufingerstraße 24, 80331 München, Germany

**Batch number: 10725973**

Printed by Printforce, the Netherlands